International organizations funding directory

International organizations funding directory

First Edition 2004

Europa Publications
Taylor & Francis Group

LONDON AND NEW YORK

© **Europa Publications Limited 2004**
11 New Fetter Lane, London EC4P 4EE, United Kingdom
(A member of the Taylor & Francis Group)

ISBN: 1 85743 247 9

Development Editor: Cathy Hartley
Contributor: Karina Holly
Proof-reading: Simon Chapman

Typeset in New Century Schoolbook 9/10½.

Typeset by Unwin Brothers Limited, The Gresham Press, Old Woking, Surrey; printed and bound in Great Britain by Antony Rowe Ltd, Chippenham, Wiltshire

Contents

Indexes

Abbreviations

ACP	African, Caribbean and Pacific (countries)	GNP	Gross National Product
AIDS	Acquired immunodeficiency syndrome	HIV	Human immuno-deficiency virus
Al.	Aleja (Alley, Avenue)	Hon.	Honorable; honorary
Apdo	Apartado (Post Box)	ICT	Information and communications technology
Approx.	Approximately		
ASEAN	Association of South East Asian Nations	i.e.	id est (that is to say)
Asscn	Association	IT	Information technology
Ave	Avenue		
		Ltd	Limited
BC	British Columbia		
Bldg	Building	m.	million
Blvd	Boulevard	Man.	Manager; management
BP	Boîte Postale (Post Box)	MD	Maryland
		MEP	Member of the European Parliament
CA	California		
CBO	Capacity-Building Organization	MFI	Micro-finance Institution
CIS	Commonwealth of Independent States	NATO	North Atlantic Treaty Organization
cnr	corner	NGDO	Non-Governmental Development Organi-zation
c/o	care of		
Co.	Company		
CSO	Civil Society Organization	NGO	Non-Governmental Organization
Cttee	Committee	NIS	Newly Independent States (of the former USSR)
DC	District of Columbia		
Devt	Development	No.	Number
DF	Distrito Federal	NW	North-West
DG	Directorate-General	NY	New York
EC	European Community/ Communities	OECD	Organisation for Economic Co-operation and Development
ECOSOC	Economic and Social Council (of the United Nations)		
		ON	Ontario
EU	European Union	Pl.	Place
Gen.	General	POB	Post Office Box
GmbH	Gesellschaft mit beschränkter Haftung (Limited Liability Company)	QC	Québec
		q.v.	quod vide (see)
		qq.v.	quae vide (see—plural)

Rd	Road	UNDP	United Nations Development Programme
Sec.	Secretary		
SME	Small and Medium-Sized Enterprise	UNESCO	United Nations Educational, Scientific and Cultural Organization
Sq.	Square		
St	Street; Saint		
Str.	Strasse; strada (street)	UNICEF	United Nations Children's Fund
UK	United Kingdom	US	United States
UN	United Nations	USA	United States of America

Introduction

'The United Nations once dealt only with Governments. By now we know that peace and prosperity cannot be achieved without partnerships involving Governments, international organizations, the business community and civil society. In today's world, we depend on each other.'

− Kofi Annan, United Nations Secretary-General

The *International Organizations Funding Directory: Grants and Projects Involving Non-Governmental Organizations* is the first international book of its kind. One might ask why, considering the thousands of millions of dollars and euros distributed by international organizations to communities either directly through, or in partnership with, non-governmental organizations (NGOs), it has remained a relatively unresearched area for funding opportunities. The complexity of the subject, compounded by the diversity of the organizations from which funds and opportunities for partnerships are available, appears to have previously proved too difficult to compile into a workable directory. In addition, the attitudes of the international community itself towards civil society have changed dramatically in recent years, reflecting the recognition, as expanded above by Kofi Annan, that in the 21st century NGOs play an intrinsic role in societal development. The timing of this publication reflects the change of policy direction by the world's major multinational and international institutions and the new opportunities available to NGOs and civil society organizations.

That said, the compilation of this directory was no easy task. Thorough research into the activities, and several thousand policies and programmes, of intergovernmental organizations, multinational institutions, development banks and similar organizations uncovered many funding opportunities, but also revealed the diverse and often confusing approaches taken by these organizations towards societal development and consequently to civil society itself.

One piece of research, carried out as a work in progress by Kate Barron, a graduate student of Development Studies at the School of Oriental and African Studies of the University of London, and published in the June 2003 edition of *Alliance* magazine (www.allavida.org/alliance), identifies the difficulties of determining how NGOs interact with multilateral organizations: 'We have found it difficult to decipher the structure, goals and terminology of various organizations with respect to NGOs and civil society'. Not least, as Barron points out, because of the difficulty in ascertaining the types of activity undertaken: 'Definitions of what constitutes "participation" between civil society and multilateral organizations vary greatly'. Intergovernmental and international organizations are in no way homogeneous in their approaches to working in partnership with civil society and NGOs. Some fund through specially constructed foundations, others establish funding programmes with various other international organizations, as well as with NGOs, companies and other sources of either funding or expertise, while others operate independently.

This Directory is therefore unique in its grouping together of the whole range of activities, grants and projects relevant to NGOs and civil society. In some instances there may be an open call for funding proposals, in others the emphasis is on dialogue and partnership, whilst in yet others, NGOs are called on for their support in implementing specific components of a development programme, primarily at grassroots or community level.

While there is a degree of information already available on international funding sources, primarily from the agencies themselves, this is not always in the most obvious places. For example, it can be difficult to ascertain exactly which department or section of an international organization is actually responsible for a funding programme. In addition, the obvious sources of information may prove to be the most difficult to decipher. For example, the immense *Official Journal* of the European Union (EU) (http://publications.eu.int/general/en/oj_en.htm), published every working day in all 11 official languages of the EU and containing details of the EU budget and calls for expressions of interest for EU programmes and projects, is undoubtedly useful, but not comprehensive, as it does not provide contact information or list dates for calls for proposals. Therefore, it can only really usefully be used as a starting point for research. Likewise, the UN's Non-Governmental Liaison Service publishes *Go Between*, a bi-monthly publication providing details to NGOs and other interested parties on the institutions, policies and activities of the UN system, but partly due to its periodical nature and necessary brevity, it presents only a snapshot of activities relevant to NGOs, and no overall source of information on UN funding and partnerships with NGOs exists. Moreover, while guides may exist for NGOs looking to specific international organizations for funding, for example the EU, outside Europe there is precious little information available.

The Major Donor Organizations
The main donor organizations, in Europe and internationally, with an emphasis on socio-economic development, particularly in the developing world, are the EU and the UN. The basic criterion for inclusion in this Directory has been that organizations must be multinational or intergovernmental, with a remit extending beyond one single country or territory. This means that national governmental funding organizations, including, for example, the US Agency for International Development (USAID) and the UK government's Department for International Development (DfID), both of which have sizeable budgets for funding development initiatives supported by NGOs, are not included. Likewise, European Community funding programmes and other international initiatives targeting individual countries are generally excluded, with the exception of significant programmes aimed at strengthening peace and socio-economic development in specific territories, for example the Palestinian Autonomous Areas.

At the heart of the system of international organizations and multinational co-operation for development both locally, nationally, regionally and internationally, is the UN. However, because of its labyrinthine structure—only matched by that of the EU—it is hardly surprising if it is daunting to the NGO researcher. For example, under the remit of the UN's Economic and Social Council and the General Assembly fall the programmes and funds of the UN, including among them the well-known United Nations Development Programme (UNDP), the United Nations Development Fund for Women (UNIFEM) and the United Nations Children's Fund (UNICEF), as well as a diverse range of other UN entities including the United Nations Research Institute for Social Development (UNRISD), the United Nations Office for Project Services (UNOPS), the Joint United Nations Programme on HIV/AIDS (UNAIDS) and the Office of the United Nations High Commissioner for Human Rights (UNHCHR). Other specialized units within the UN system, including the International Labour Organization (ILO), the International Bank for Reconstruction and Development (IBRD, the World Bank), the World Health Organization (WHO), the United Nations Educational, Scientific and Cultural Organization (UNESCO), the International Fund for Agricultural Development (IFAD), and the Food and Agricultural Organization of the United Nations (FAO) also come under the remit of the Economic and Social Council, while the Department of Economic and Social Affairs, the Office on Drugs and Crime (UNODC) and the Office for the Co-ordination of Humanitarian Affairs (OCHA) come under the direct remit of the UN Secretariat. Each of these units operate their own programmes, in all cases involving NGOs, but there lacks a consistent line of approach. In addition, many UN-funded programmes are supported by specialized voluntary trust funds, established by agencies of the UN to channel funds into certain areas of priority concern, for example the Voluntary Trust Fund on Contemporary Forms of Slavery and the Trust Fund in Support of Actions to Eliminate Violence Against Women. The responsibilities of sections of the EU are similarly difficult to unravel. For example, programmes concerned with disability are the responsibility of Directorate-General Information Society, rather than, as one might assume, under the responsibility of Directorate-General Employment and Social Affairs.

Apart from the EU and the UN, including the IBRD's development and funding initiatives, other sizeable regional funders are the Asian Development Bank (ADB), South Asian Association for Regional Co-operation (SAARC), Organization of the Petroleum Exporting Countries (OPEC), Pan American Health Organization (PAHO), the Organization of American States (OAS), the Association of South East Asian Nations (ASEAN), the Commonwealth, and a whole sub-level of intergovernmental organizations set up under the patronage of the major organizations and institutions. In addition, a number of development banks are listed, aside from the IBRD, which exist primarily to promote economic, financial and technical co-operation and the acceleration of economic growth within their region, but collaborate with NGOs in pursuit of their aims. These include the Inter-American Development Bank (IDB), the Islamic Development Bank (IDB), the Arab Bank for Economic Development in Africa (BADEA, part of OPEC), the Black Sea Trade and Development Bank (BSTDB), the Asian Development Bank (ADB) and the European Bank for Reconstruction and Development (EBRD).

Implementation of Funding Programmes
In many cases, despite the policy and funding originating from a multinational or intergovernmental source, it is the implementing agency which acts as the key source for the provision of information. In certain cases the implementing agency is an international NGO, for example the WWF (World Wide Fund for Nature) or the International Youth Foundation, or a research institute. There are also numerous examples of collaboration both between UN organizations and with non-UN international and intergovernmental organizations, with often no clear lead partner, adding further confusion for the NGO looking to enter into partnership.

Importance of Policy
An important principle for successful involvement with many of the institutions listed in this Directory is not to restrict any approach just to requests for funding. NGOs need to get involved with policy as well. The main role of all the

organizations listed here—with the exception of a few specialist foundations established by multinational organizations precisely for the purpose of making grants to NGOs, for example to support educational study or to promote cultural activities, including the ACP Cultural Foundation and the ASEAN Foundation— is to guide the socio-economic development of a region, or to improve the life chances of children under the age of five, or to promote agricultural sustainability, combat desertification, support education for all, any of a number of programmes primarily based on development policy and extending opportunity. Invariably NGOs fit into the overall execution of policy, but increasingly as partners, rather than beneficiaries simply channelling funds to communities, as the traditional role has been for NGOs *vis-à-vis* their relationship with private foundations and corporations.

Just as the European Commission has roles other than merely to support NGOs, the UN was established to promote international co-operation and achieve peace and security. Thus, for an NGO to receive funding from the EU, it must further EU policy objectives and support transnational co-operation. In the case of the UN, an NGO must be able to demonstrate how its activities fit into one of the policy units of the UN system, which may not be straightforward. However, there are some key principles underpinning the UN's approach to dealing with civil society and other organizations, which can be used as an overall guide to seeking involvement with the UN. These include the Millennium Development Goals (MDGs), the Resolution 55/2 UN Millennium Declaration in which the member states of the UN pledged to meet the MDGs by 2015. However, the UN cannot meet these Goals alone, and hence the MDGs aim to give greater opportunity to the private sector, NGOs, and civil society in general, to contribute to their realization, which aim specifically to:

1. Eradicate extreme poverty and hunger;
2. Achieve universal primary education;
3. Promote gender equality and empower women;
4. Reduce child mortality;
5. Improve maternal health;
6. Combat HIV/AIDS, malaria and other diseases;
7. Ensure environmental sustainability; and
8. Develop a global partnership for development.

Other important UN policy initiatives include the Convention on the Elimination of All Forms of Discrimination Against Women (CEDAW), adopted in 1979 by the UN General Assembly, which should also be borne in mind by NGOs formulating programmes for UN funding. Some UN programmes specifically support the implementation of CEDAW, for example the Women's Human Rights programme of the UNIFEM Arab States Regional Office (UNIFEM ASRO) and the APGEN (promoting gender equality in the Asia Pacific) programme of UNDP's Regional Bureau for Asia and the Pacific (RBAP). There are also many other examples of Conventions and Declarations which form the bedrock for action for the UN institutions and all other international organizations, and which should form the basis of an NGO's research, before an initial approach is formulated.

We have sought to include in this Directory only organizations where clear funding opportunities for NGOs exist. However, in recognition of the importance of the new role of NGOs within the international system as policy shapers and not just executors, there are also opportunities listed for NGOs holding consultative status with various international organizations. In certain cases, for example the UN Industrial Development Organization (UNIDO), this is the sole route into NGO relations with international organizations, while other organizations, including the ADB, have established specialized NGO Centres or Units to address their relations with NGOs.

So, how should NGOs use this book? As is probably clear by now, they should not view it as a simple guide to funding opportunities, and should not exclude international organizations not listed, as their non-inclusion does not necessarily indicate their lack of contact with NGOs; it might just be less evident. For some programmes there may be a simple procedure to follow to apply for funding, but, with the vast majority, there are a diverse number of elements for the development of co-operation which must be carefully researched before an initial approach for funding is made. Not least, the need for international co-operation: just as the numerous international organizations listed here are increasingly looking to build transnational partnerships between themselves, so the NGO which is to tap successfully into the funding available is required to build its own international partnerships, thereby demonstrating its own commitment to Kofi Annan's vision of a world where peace and prosperity is achieved through partnerships, and not just individual actions.

Karina Holly
Editor of *Philanthropy in Europe*, a magazine appearing every two months informing on fundraising and philanthropy across Europe.
March 2004

African Capacity Building Foundation (ACBF)

An independent, capacity-building institution established in 1991 through the collaboration of the African Development Bank, the International Bank for Reconstruction and Development (IBRD—World Bank), the United Nations Development Programme (UNDP), African governments and bilateral donors; created in response to the severity of Africa's capacity problem and the challenge to invest in people and institutions in sub-Saharan Africa.

Activities: Aims to strengthen the core public sector in African countries and its interface with the private sector and civil society, and to support regional initiatives in the area of specialized training, policy analysis, applied policy research, negotiation and policy advocacy, through grants principally for core projects and programmes, as well as providing seed funding for the emergence of suitable institutional frameworks for country-level co-ordination of capacity-building activities. Current priorities are: economic policy analysis and management; financial management and accountability; strengthening of national statistics; public administration and management; strengthening of policy analysis capacity of national parliaments; and professionalization of the voices of the private sector and civil society.

Geographical Area of Activity: Sub-Saharan Africa.

Restrictions: No support for individuals, funding physical infrastructure such as buildings or endowments, nor for undergraduate scholarships or grants for purely personal needs. Support for graduate and postgraduate fellowships is generally provided through grants to universities and other beneficiary organizations, which are responsible for the selection of recipients.

How to Apply: Following a call for proposals initiated by the Foundation or letter requesting financial support from the Foundation, the Foundation's programme staff may ask the grant-seeker to submit a formal proposal, for which there are guide-lines indicating elements that should be included in the proposal.

Address: 7th Floor, Southampton Life Centre, 77 Jason Moyo/Second St, POB 1562, Harare, Zimbabwe.

Telephone: (4) 790398; *Fax:* (4) 702915; *Internet:* www.acbf-pact.org; *e-mail:* root@ acbf-pact.org.

Partnership for Capacity Building in Africa (PACT)

Established by the World Bank's Public Sector Reform and Capacity Building Units and implemented by the African Capacity Building Foundation (ACBF), to address the problem of inadequate capacity for development in sub-Saharan Africa.

Activities: Aims to improve the capacity for development in sub-Saharan Africa through making grants to African NGOs, governments and private-sector

1

organizations in public–private–civil society partnerships, for projects working to improve the public sector and its interface with the private sector and civil society, promoting good governance and sustainable development.

Geographical Area of Activity: Sub-Saharan Africa.

How to Apply: Apply directly to the African Capacity Building Foundation (q.v.).

Address: 7th Floor, Southampton Life Centre, 77 Jason Moyo/Second St, POB 1562, Harare, Zimbabwe.

Telephone: (4) 790398; *Fax:* (4) 702915; *Internet:* www.acbf-pact.org; *e-mail:* root@acbf-pact.org.

African Development Foundation

Established in 1984 by US Congress to promote broad-based, sustainable development in sub-Saharan Africa.

Activities: Provides funding to grassroots NGO projects over a broad range of sectors in sub-Saharan African countries, including Benin, Botswana, Cape Verde, Ghana, Guinea, Nigeria, Mali, Namibia, Niger, Senegal, Tanzania, Uganda, and Zimbabwe, with the aim of responding to African initiatives, fostering active participation and ownership, and strengthening African capacity to alleviate poverty and promote growth at the grassroots level. Following a strategic review of its policies, the Foundation focuses on fulfilling a number of key objectives, including: promotion of micro- and small enterprise development to generate income and employment; improving community-based natural resource management (NRM) for sustainable rural development; increasing participation of African grassroots enterprises and producer groups in trade and investment relationships with the USA and within Africa; strengthening civil society and local governance; and encouraging African governments to expand grassroots participation in policy-making and resource allocation processes.

Geographical Area of Activity: Sub-Saharan Africa, including Benin, Botswana, Cape Verde, Ghana, Guinea, Nigeria, Mali, Namibia, Niger, Senegal, Tanzania, Uganda and Zimbabwe.

How to Apply: Grants are made directly to grassroots community organizations and NGOs.

Publications: Issue Briefs.

Contact: Board of Directors Nathaniel Fields (Pres.); Ernest G. Green (Chair.); Willie Grace Campbell (Vice-Chair.); Claude Allen.

Address: 1400 Eye St, NW, 10th Floor, Washington, DC 20005-2248, USA.

Telephone: (202) 673-3916; *Fax:* (202) 673-3810; *Internet:* www.adf.gov; *e-mail:* info@adf.gov.

Agence Française de Développement (AfD)

FONDS FRANÇAIS POUR L'ENVIRONNEMENT MONDIAL (FFEM)

The Agence Française de Développement, France's principal executing agency for project aid, operates in more than 60 countries of Africa, Asia, the Pacific, the Caribbean, the Indian Ocean, Mediterranean and South-Eastern Europe, and in French overseas departments and territories, through a network of 45 local agencies around the world. The FFEM is a bilateral fund created in 1994, financed from the official budget, but additional to France's official development aid.

Activities: Grants are made to private- and public-sector projects in the fields of: strengthening productive investment; improving access to basic education, health and drinking water; and promoting urban development and local development in rural areas, with an overall emphasis on conservation of the environment, combating poverty and the reduction of gender inequalities.

Geographical Area of Activity: Africa, Asia, the Pacific, the Caribbean, Indian Ocean states, Mediterranean and South-Eastern Europe and French overseas departments and territories.

How to Apply: An application for funding in support of a project is submitted by its local promoters to the AfD office in the field, which is responsible for the project identification stage. Following a feasibility study the decision is taken, with support from the operational staff at AfD headquarters, whether to proceed with the next stage, an appraisal of the proposition's technical, economic, organizational and financial viability. It is at this point that the financial package is worked out with the client.

Financial Information: Total budget approx. 440,000,000 French francs (1999–2002).

Address: 5 rue Roland Barthes, 75598 Paris Cedex 12, France.

Telephone: 1-53-44-31-31; *Fax:* 1-44-87-99-39; *Internet:* www.afd.fr/groupe/ffem_1 .cfm.

Asian Development Bank (ADB)

NGO CENTRE

Relations with NGOs

The Bank co-ordinates its activities with NGOs based on its Framework for NGO co-operation, published in May 2003, with the aim of promoting transparency of information and project co-operation. Its NGO Centre, which was established in 2001, aims to: gain first-hand knowledge of and experience with NGOs; engage NGOs in a continuing dialogue; and improve the Bank's institutional capacity to interact proactively with NGOs.

Activities: The Bank's NGO Centre actively seeks the input of NGOs for the provision of specific expertise, policy development and technical advice through participation in regional conferences and seminars, primarily within the fields of agriculture and rural development, social infrastructure, urban development, water supply and sanitation, health and population, education and human resources development, small-scale industry and credit, and environmental protection.

Geographical Area of Activity: Asia.

Contact: Contact Robert J. Dobias.

Address: POB 789, 0980 Manila, Philippines.

Telephone: (2) 632-6783; *Fax:* (2) 636-2220; *Internet:* www.adb.org/ngos/default .asp; *e-mail:* ngocoordinator@adb.org.

POVERTY REDUCTION

Asian Development Bank (ADB)–Department for International Development Technical Assistance Co-operation Fund for India

Established in June 2001 by the ADB, to help the Bank in its work to reduce poverty in India.

Activities: In an effort to reduce poverty in India, the Fund makes grants to: participatory poverty assessments and other poverty-focused surveys; appraisal studies for sector lending; studies examining the issues of developing an enabling environment for poverty reduction; poverty-focused monitoring, evaluation, and impact assessment work; poverty-focused conferences, workshops, and mutual learning events; and the recruitment of consultants to support ADB's role and capacity to address poverty issues.

Geographical Area of Activity: India.

Financial Information: Total funds £20,000,000; funded by the Department for International Development of the UK government.

Contact: Country Dir T. L. De Jonghe; Deputy Country Dir Sudipto Mundle; Head, Infrastructure Akanda Albab; Head, Project Admin Patrick Lizot; Senior Project Implementation Officer Alex K. Jorgensen; Senior Finance and Admin Officer T. Abraham Cherukuzhy.

Address: 4 San Martin Marg, Chanakyapuri, New Delhi 110 021; POB 5331, Chanakyapuri H.P.O., New Delhi 110 021, India.

Telephone: (11) 24107200; *Fax:* (11) 26870955; *Internet:* www.adbindia.org; *e-mail:* adbinrm@adb.org.

Co-operation Fund in Support of the Formulation and Implementation of National Poverty Reduction

Established by the Netherlands government and administered by the Asian Development Bank (ADB).

Activities: The Fund helps ADB's developing member countries formulate, prioritize, implement, monitor, and reformulate national poverty-reduction strategies, through technical assistance grants, for collaborative work with stakeholders in the developing member countries and research support; regional training and capacity-building activities; and piloting of participation activities for poverty reduction and governance.

Geographical Area of Activity: ADB member countries: Afghanistan, Azerbaijan, Bangladesh, Bhutan, Cambodia, People's Republic of China, Cook Islands, Fiji, Hong Kong, India, Indonesia, Kazakhstan, Kiribati, Republic of Korea, Kyrgyzstan, Laos, Malaysia, Maldives, Republic of the Marshall Islands, Micronesia, Federated States of Mongolia, Myanmar, Nauru, Nepal, Pakistan, Papua New Guinea, Philippines, Samoa, Singapore, Solomon Islands, Sri Lanka, Taiwan, Tajikistan, Thailand, Timor Leste, Tonga, Turkmenistan, Tuvalu, Uzbekistan, Vanuatu and Vietnam. Current focus on Cambodia, Indonesia, Pakistan, the People's Republic of China, Uzbekistan and Vietnam.

How to Apply: Proposals should focus strongly on national poverty reduction strategy formulation; show evidence of country ownership, and the inclusiveness of the proposed approach; promote sound collaboration with other donors; not substitute for activities that would otherwise be financed by ADB (additionality factor); and support systemic poverty reduction.

Financial Information: Initial contribution from the Netherlands government of approx. US $6,000,000.

Contact: Dir Poverty Reduction and Social Development Division Brahm Prakash.

Address: POB 789, 0980 Manila, Philippines.

Internet: www.adb.org/nprs/default.asp; *e-mail:* bprakash@adb.org.

Japan Fund for Poverty Reduction

An untied grant facility established by the Japanese government and the Asian Development Bank (ADB) in May 2000, to assist ADB clients to effectively tackle the poverty and social consequences that resulted from the 1997–99 global economic and financial crises.

Activities: The Fund aims to initiate and support innovative programmes that have high potential for improving the affected countries' situations; provide relatively rapid, demonstrable benefits through initiatives that have positive prospects of developing into sustainable activities over the long term; and assists programmes designed and implemented by local populations and civil society organizations (CSOs). CSOs can partner with the Fund in two ways: in collaboration with the ADB task team currently managing existing ADB financed projects in conceptualizing and designing the proposed grant, or through executing Fund grants through recipient central or local government institutions.

Geographical Area of Activity: ADB member countries: Afghanistan, Azerbaijan, Bangladesh, Bhutan, Cambodia, People's Republic of China, Cook Islands, Fiji, Hong Kong, India, Indonesia, Kazakhstan, Kiribati, Republic of Korea, Kyrgyzstan, Laos, Malaysia, Maldives, Marshall Islands, Federated States of Micronesia, Mongolia, Myanmar, Nauru, Nepal, Pakistan, Papua New Guinea, Philippines, Samoa, Singapore, Solomon Islands, Sri Lanka, Taiwan, Tajikistan, Thailand, Tonga, Turkmenistan, Tuvalu, Uzbekistan, Vanuatu and Vietnam.

How to Apply: Civil society groups are advised to establish contacts with the country teams directly or through the NGO liaison officers/civil society specialists in ADB field offices.

Financial Information: Total funds US $90,000,000.

Publications: Annual Report.

Address: POB 789, 0980 Manila, Philippines.

Internet: www.adb.org/jfpr/default.asp.

Poverty Reduction Co-operation Fund (PRF)

Established in July 2002, the Fund is a grant facility of the Department for International Development (DFID) of the UK government.

Activities: The Fund aims to help the Asian Development Bank (ADB) reduce structural poverty in its developing member countries, through supporting technical assistance and small-scale pilot investment projects with systemic poverty-reduction impacts that serve as good examples for broader ADB investments and refocus its operations to be more poverty-relevant, including technical assistance for capacity and institution building. Specifically, support is provided for the provision of advisory inputs; thematic and sector work; monitoring, evaluation, and impact assessment; public conferences, workshops, and other events; innovative activities such as micro- and pilot projects, with clearly demonstrable results; national experts based in resident missions of ADB, working on poverty analysis, and poverty-related gender issues; stakeholder participation, and governance issues; outreach and communication; and administrative costs of fund management.

Geographical Area of Activity: Less-developed member countries, excluding India.

Restrictions: No funding for permanent staffing costs (e.g. salaries and training), nor work that is not country-based (albeit cross-border activities can be supported if they have a measurable impact on a country's poverty situation).

How to Apply: To be eligible proposals must have a strong poverty-reduction focus; support the relevant ADB Country Strategy and Programme and the policies of the government; be designed to support shared poverty-reduction objectives in the existing and pipeline activities of other funding agencies, enhance effectiveness, avoid duplication, and accelerate learning; not substitute for activities that would otherwise be financed by ADB (additionality factors); maximize local expertise and civil society participation; and support systemic poverty reduction. The final date for approval by ADB of PRF-financed activities is 31 March 2006.

Financial Information: Total funds US $58,000,000; funded by the DFID of the UK government.

Contact: Dir Poverty Reduction and Social Development Division Brahm Prakash; co-ordinator Armin Bauer.

Address: POB 789, 0980 Manila, Philippines.

Internet: www.adb.org/PRF/default.asp; *e-mail:* abauer@adb.org.

Asian Productivity Organization (APO)

An intergovernmental regional organization established by Convention in 1961 to increase productivity in the countries of Asia and the Pacific.

Activities: Programmes cover industry, service and agriculture sectors, with a specific focus on socio-economic development, the development of NGOs, green productivity, integrated community development, and agricultural marketing and institutions. Organizes seminars, study meetings and training workshops, funds and provides technical training and expertise, funds rural development projects and research studies, and awards fellowships.

Geographical Area of Activity: Bangladesh, People's Republic of China, Fiji, Hong Kong, India, Indonesia, Iran, Japan, Republic of Korea, Laos, Malaysia, Mongolia, Nepal, Pakistan, Philippines, Singapore, Sri Lanka, Thailand and Vietnam.

How to Apply: To participate in an APO programme, contact must be made with the relevant National Productivity Organization (NPO); applications must be processed and submitted through the concerned NPO to the APO Secretariat.

Contact: Sec.-Gen. Takashi Tajima.

Address: 1-2-10 Hirakawacho, Chiyoda-ku, Tokyo 102-0093, Japan.

Telephone: (3) 5226-3920; *Fax:* (3) 5226-3950; *Internet:* www.apo-tokyo.org; *e-mail:* apo@apo-tokyo.org.

Association of South East Asian Nations (ASEAN)

NGO Affiliation

ASEAN offers affiliation to NGOs, in order to draw NGOs into the mainstream of ASEAN activities so that they are kept informed of major policies, directives and decisions of ASEAN and are given the opportunity and the privilege of participating in ASEAN activities, and to ensure interaction and a fruitful relationship between the existing ASEAN bodies and the NGOs.

Activities: An ASEAN-affiliated NGO enjoys the following privileges: it may use the name ASEAN and display the official ASEAN emblem in correspondence and communications and its official meetings; it may submit written statements or recommendations and views on policy matters or on significant events or regional or international concerns, to the ASEAN Standing Committee through the ASEAN Secretariat; it may submit its own project proposals for Third Party funding to be channelled through the ASEAN Secretariat to the Standing Committee for approval; it may initiate programmes of activities for presentation to its link body for appropriate action; at the discretion of the Chairman of the link body, it may through its representative attend meetings of the link body for consultation on matters and issues of direct concern to the NGO; for purposes of doing research for its projects, it may be allowed access to ASEAN documents on a selective basis in consultation with the ASEAN Secretariat and/or its link body; subject to rules and regulations, it may be allowed the use of the facilities of the ASEAN Secretariat for its official meetings and other official activities in Jakarta; and it is supported to become self-reliant in terms of its material requirements.

Geographical Area of Activity: South-East Asia.

How to Apply: The ASEAN Secretariat shall receive and process applications for affiliation. If the Secretary-General considers them in conformity with the guide-lines, he shall refer them to the ASEAN National Secretariats with the recommendation, which shall respond within two months. If the responses are in the affirmative or in the absence of expressed objection within four months after receipt, the applications shall be submitted to the ASEAN Standing Committee for consideration. Application for affiliation shall include information regarding the nature and purpose of the applicant NGO, its constitution and by-laws, its membership, its function, activities, and projects.

Address: 70A Jalan Sisingamangaraja, Jakarta 12110, Indonesia.

Telephone: (21) 726 2991; *Fax:* (21) 739 8234; *Internet:* www.aseansec.org/6069 .htm; *e-mail:* ratih@aseansec.org.

ASEAN CENTRE FOR ENERGY (ACE)

ASEAN Energy Facility Programme

Established by the ASEAN Centre for Energy to fund energy and environmental projects in ASEAN countries.

Activities: The Programme's priorities are: stimulating regional energy projects and initiatives proposed by the energy industry, either public or private, from the European Union (EU) and ASEAN, and contributing to the implementation of ASEAN's Plan of Action for Energy Co-operation 1999–2004; stimulating projects, which have a regional ASEAN dimension and which also clearly have European added value, including featuring the diversity of the European experience in terms of institutional or technological options; and stimulating projects with measurable impacts, for example in terms of energy produced or saved, pollution avoided, business induced and intra-ASEAN co-operation. In 2003 priority was given to demonstration projects and PV (photovoltaic)/solar, wind energy and mini/micro-hydro projects within the renewable energy subsector. Applicants must be non-profit organizations from the public or the private sector of the EU member states or from ASEAN countries, or in the case of private/commercial organizations, declare the project implementation on a non-profit basis.

Geographical Area of Activity: EU member states and ASEAN countries: Brunei, Cambodia, Indonesia, Laos, Malaysia, Philippines, Singapore, Thailand and Vietnam.

How to Apply: Application forms available on the website.

Financial Information: Global budget €5,500,000; grants range from €20,000 to €500,000, up to 50% of the project's total costs.

Address: ACE Bldg, 6th Floor, Jalan H. R. Rasuna Said, Block X-2, Kav. 07-08, Kuningan, Jakarta 12950, Indonesia.

Internet: www.aseansec.org; *e-mail:* info@aseanenergy.org.

ASEAN FOUNDATION

Formally established during the ASEAN Commemorative Summit in Kuala Lumpur on 15 December 1997; aims to support projects which uplift the social condition of the peoples in the ASEAN member states.

Activities: Operates by organizing and supporting activities carried out by NGOs, that promote education, training, health and culture, as well as providing fellowships and supporting exchanges of ASEAN young people and students, and promoting collaborative work among academics, professionals and scientists. Also implements projects assigned by ASEAN Leaders of Ministers, collaborates with the relevant ASEAN bodies, initiates its own flagship projects as well as organizing projects in partnership with ASEAN governments and the private sector.

Geographical Area of Activity: South-East Asia: ASEAN member countries.

Financial Information: Funded by the Indonesian government and the other ASEAN member countries.

Address: 70A Jalan Sisingamangaraja, POB 2072, Jakarta 12110, Indonesia.
Telephone: (21) 726 2991; *Fax:* (21) 739 8234; *Internet:* www.aseansec.org; *e-mail:* public@aseansec.org.

ASIA–EUROPE FOUNDATION (ASEF)

Established in 1997 by the members of the Asia–Europe Meeting (ASEM) in order to promote better mutual understanding between the peoples of Asia and Europe, through greater intellectual, cultural and people-to-people exchanges between the two regions.

Activities: Activities include conventions, symposia, seminars, public lectures, youth camps, art competitions, performances, exhibitions, and other events. Focuses on three areas: intellectual exchanges; people-to-people exchanges; and cultural exchanges.

Geographical Area of Activity: ASEM/ASEF member countries: Austria, Belgium, Brunei, People's Republic of China, Denmark, Finland, France, Germany, Greece, Indonesia, Ireland, Italy, Japan, Republic of Korea, Luxembourg, Malaysia, Netherlands, Philippines, Portugal, Singapore, Spain, Sweden, Thailand, UK, Vietnam, and the European Commission.

Financial Information: Funded by contributions from member governments.

Contact: Exec. Dir Delfin Colome; Deputy Exec. Dir Kim Sung-Chul.

Address: 1 Nassim Hill, Singapore 258466, Singapore.

Telephone: 6874-9700; *Fax:* 6872-1206; *Internet:* www.asef.org; *e-mail:* info@asef.org.

Cultural Exchange Programme

The Programme aims to add value to cultural exchange initiatives between Asia and Europe, within three major focus areas: youth in arts exchange; networks among professionals; and dialogue on cultural policy.

Activities: Within the field of cultural dialogue and heritage the Programme aims to: encourage dialogue and discussions on cultural policy and management as a way to foster co-operation between cultural organizations and professionals from Europe and Asia; co-organize conferences and workshops which give shape to the Asia–Europe Museums Network (ASEMUS) for the common aim of sharing cultural heritage; answer experts' needs and initiate workshops focused on Asia–Europe tangible and intangible cultural heritage. In the area of cultural industries, the Programme co-organizes professional workshops which answer the needs of professionals in the fields of TV programmes, music and publishing; facilitates the sharing of experiences, techniques and information; and works towards future co-productions/co-publications. In the area of artistic creativity supports performing and visual arts activities, which aim to support Asia–Europe creations; develop encounters for future artistic co-operation and career opportunities; and promote works on a common project for Asian and European young artists.

Geographical Area of Activity: Asia–Europe Meeting/Asia–Europe Foundation member countries: Austria, Belgium, Brunei, People's Republic of China,

Denmark, Finland, France, Germany, Greece, Indonesia, Ireland, Italy, Japan, Republic of Korea, Luxembourg, Malaysia, Netherlands, Philippines, Portugal, Singapore, Spain, Sweden, Thailand, UK, Vietnam, and the European Commission.

How to Apply: See website for details.

Contact: Dir, Cultural Exchange Chulamanee Chartsuwan.

Address: 1 Nassim Hill, Singapore 258466, Singapore.

Telephone: 6838-4715; *Fax:* 6732-4371; *Internet:* www.asef.org; *e-mail:* info@asef .org.

Intellectual Exchange Programme

The Programme aims to contribute to policy and academic debates as well as strategic thinking on themes of current and future inter-regional importance between Asia and Europe.

Activities: Sub-programme areas are: international relations, concerning debate and discourse on regional issues; governance, including bridging the gap between government and civil society; education, science and technology; and cultures and civilizations. Organized activities include seminars and workshops on gender and human rights issues. Proposals are accepted from government ministries, research institutions, think-tanks, NGOs, the business sector, universities, cultural organizations, and the media.

Geographical Area of Activity: Asia–Europe Meeting/Asia–Europe Foundation member countries: Austria, Belgium, Brunei, People's Republic of China, Denmark, Finland, France, Germany, Greece, Indonesia, Ireland, Italy, Japan, Republic of Korea, Luxembourg, Malaysia, Netherlands, Philippines, Portugal, Singapore, Spain, Sweden, Thailand, UK, Vietnam, and the European Commission.

How to Apply: Details available on the website.

Address: 1 Nassim Hill, Singapore 258466, Singapore.

Telephone: 6838-4715; *Fax:* 6732-4371; *Internet:* www.asef.org; *e-mail:* info@asef .org.

People-to-People Exchange: Asia–Europe Foundation (ASEF) Youth Connections Grants

Part of the Foundation's People-to-People Exchange initiative, launched in June 2003 and scheduled to run until May 2005.

Activities: A grant programme open to youth and youth-oriented organizations in the Asia–Europe Meeting (ASEM) member countries: Austria, Belgium, Brunei, People's Republic of China, Denmark, Finland, France, Germany, Greece, Indonesia, Ireland, Italy, Japan, Korea, Luxembourg, Malaysia, Netherlands, Philippines, Portugal, Singapore, Spain, Sweden, Thailand, UK, Vietnam, and the European Commission, for projects promoting contact and co-operation between young people of Asia and Europe. Funded activities include youth forums, seminars or symposia, youth roundtables, youth camps, youth work camps, youth volunteer activities, exchange programmes (involving exchange of office-holders or staff of youth organizations), training programmes and courses.

Geographical Area of Activity: ASEM/ASEF member countries: Austria, Belgium, Brunei, People's Republic of China, Denmark, Finland, France, Germany, Greece, Indonesia, Ireland, Italy, Japan, Korea, Luxembourg, Malaysia, Netherlands, Philippines, Portugal, Singapore, Spain, Sweden, Thailand, UK, Vietnam, and the European Commission.

How to Apply: Application forms are available on the website.

Financial Information: Maximum grant available approx. €10,500.

Contact: Dir, People-to-People Exchange Zainal Arif Mantaha; Project Exec. Catherine Pabalan.

Address: 1 Nassim Hill, Singapore 258466, Singapore.

Telephone: 6838-4715; *Fax:* 6732-4371; *Internet:* www.asef.org; *e-mail:* cathy@asef.org.

People-to-People Programme (P2P)

The Programme aims to enable individuals from Asia and Europe to learn about the other region through activities that foster personal relationships, including activities that provide participants from one region with opportunities to live, study and work in the other, and form the foundation of a solid network for further co-operation between the two regions in the future.

Activities: Projects and activities come under three broad categories: Educational Exchanges and Cross-Cultural Learning, including the Asia–Europe Classroom (AEC), the Asia–Europe Foundation (ASEF) University Programme and the Asia–Europe Meeting (ASEM) Educational Hub–Education and Research Network (AEH–EARN) which provide opportunities for multi-level educational exchanges between Asia and Europe; Youth Co-operation, including the Asia–Europe Youth Forum, the Asia–Europe Youth Camps, the Asia–Europe Young Volunteer Exchange programme and ASEF Youth Connections Grants (q.v.), which are designed to stimulate long-lasting interests in and commitment to the other region at early stages of the careers of the younger generation in the two regions; and the Asia–Europe Nexus, which aims to bring the broader public into the ASEM engagement process, through support for activities that are targeted at promoting personal contacts between leaders of a broad range of sectors in Asia and Europe, including civil society, legislators/parliamentarians, journalists and entrepreneurs. Projects in this area include the Asia–Europe Young Leaders Symposium, the Asia–Europe Young Parliamentarians Meeting, the Asia–Europe Young Entrepreneurs Forum and the Asia–Europe Journalists Exchange.

Geographical Area of Activity: ASEM/ASEF member countries: Austria, Belgium, Brunei, People's Republic of China, Denmark, Finland, France, Germany, Greece, Indonesia, Ireland, Italy, Japan, Korea, Luxembourg, Malaysia, Netherlands, Philippines, Portugal, Singapore, Spain, Sweden, Thailand, UK, Vietnam, and the European Commission.

How to Apply: See website for details.

Contact: Dir, Cultural Exchange Chulamanee Chartsuwan.

Address: 1 Nassim Hill, Singapore 258466, Singapore.

Telephone: 6838-4715; *Fax:* 6732-4371; *Internet:* www.asef.org; *e-mail:* info@asef.org.

DEPARTMENT OF ENVIRONMENT AND NATURAL RESOURCES

ASEAN Regional Center for Biodiversity Conservation (ARCBC): Research Grants

A programme run by the ARCBC, which was set up to serve as the central focus for networking and institutional linkage between ASEAN member countries and between ASEAN and European Union (EU) partner organizations, to promote the capacity of ASEAN to promote biodiversity conservation. The EU provides the programme resources and ASEAN provides technical support and a location for the Center.

Activities: Promotes applied research in the field of biodiversity conservation, through the provision of grants for research which aims to provide solutions to issues on biodiversity conservation throughout ASEAN; improve standards of research in terms of methodology and skills; promote collaboration among ASEAN institutions and between ASEAN and the EU; provide direct benefits for poverty alleviation and gender and development; and prepare and package research results in a form that is accessible to non-scientists. Applications are accepted from individual scientists, technicians and researchers, institutions, government agencies and NGOs from participating ASEAN countries. Grants have previously been awarded within the themes of valuing biodiversity, ecological restoration, and taxonomy and systematics. Also maintains an office in Quezon City.

Geographical Area of Activity: ASEAN countries.

Financial Information: Co-funded by ASEAN and the EU; total research awards €2,274,022 (2001).

Contact: ASEAN Co-Dir Gregorio Texon; EU Co-Dir Dr John MacKinnon.

Address: POB 35015, Los Banos, Laguna 4031, Philippines.

Telephone: (49) 536-1659; *Fax:* (49) 536-2865; *Internet:* www.arcbc.org.ph; *e-mail:* research@arcbc.org.ph.

Baltic Marine Environment Protection Commission—Helsinki Commission (HELCOM)

The Baltic Sea Joint Comprehensive Environmental Action Programme (JCP)

Established in 1992 by the signatories of the Helsinki Convention, to support preventive and curative measures in the Baltic drainage basin to restore the ecological balance of the Baltic Sea by reducing pollution loads.

Activities: Operates within six areas: policies, laws and regulations; institutional strengthening and human resource development; investment activities addressing point and non-point source pollution; management programmes for coastal lagoons and wetlands; applied research; and public awareness and environmental education.

Geographical Area of Activity: Baltic countries.

Financial Information: Total programme budget approx. €18,000,000,000.

Contact: Sec. Claus Hagebro; Asst Leena Heikkila.

Address: Katajanokanlaituri 6B, 00160 Helsinki, Finland.

Telephone: (9) 62202223; *Internet:* www.helcom.fi/helcom/groupstaskforce /helcompitf.html; *e-mail:* helcom@helcom.fi.

Baltic Sea Secretariat for Youth Affairs

The Secretariat was established in 2002 by the Baltic Sea states to promote the active participation of young people in the development of democratic and pluralistic civil societies in the states of the Baltic Sea region.

Activities: Aims to promote the involvement of young people in the Baltic Sea States through strengthening Baltic Sea co-operation in the youth field, increasing youth mobility and youth exchange in the region, promoting the participation of young people in policy structures in the Baltic Sea area, promoting youth issues as a cross-sectoral topic, including disadvantaged young people in the activities of youth organizations and structures, and co-operating with other regional youth structures in the Barents, Nordic or Mediterranean regions. Activities include co-ordinating different forms of co-operation activities between youth policy structures, governmental and non-governmental youth organizations, and funding youth projects. Other initiatives include the establishment of the the Barents Regional Youth Forum and the Baltic Sea Youth Forum.

Geographical Area of Activity: Baltic Sea states.

Contact: Contact Sandra Weidemann.

Address: Holtenauer Str. 99, 24105 Kiel, Germany.

Telephone: (431) 8009847; *Fax:* (431) 8009841; *Internet:* www.balticsea-youth.org; *e-mail:* info@balticsea-youth.org.

17

Black Sea Trade and Development Bank (BSTDB)

Special Funds

Through its Special Funds programme BSTDB aims to play a catalytic role in the greater Black Sea region for both public- and private-sector operations consistent with its dual mandate, principally in filling key niches which promote regional economic activity, but which are not adequately covered by other institutions.

Activities: The Funds are used to support activities and pilot studies by governments, international organizations, private banks and enterprises in the priority areas of feasibility and environment studies, regional research studies, and financial reporting.

Geographical Area of Activity: Black Sea region.

Contact: Pres. Mustafa Gurtin.

Address: 1 Komninon St, 54624 Thessaloniki, Greece.

Telephone: (2) 310290400; *Fax:* (2) 310221796; *Internet:* www.bstdb.org; *e-mail:* info@bstdb.org.

Building and Social Housing Foundation

World Habitat Awards

Established in 1985 by the Building and Social Housing Foundation as part of its contribution to the UN International Year of Shelter for the Homeless.

Activities: The annual awards are made to human settlements projects that provide practical and innovative solutions to current housing needs and problems, in both developed and developing countries and which are capable of replication. Eligible organizations are: individuals, organizations or governments which have an innovative and practical solution to housing problems and needs from any country of the world, existing projects or those designed specifically for the competition, and previous entrants who can re-submit an application in subsequent years providing that the project has been further developed in the intervening time period.

Geographical Area of Activity: International.

How to Apply: Two-stage entry of preliminary and final submissions: preliminary submissions comprise a concise summary of all aspects of the project; from these preliminary submissions, 12 projects are selected by an Assessment Committee to go forward to the Final Submission stage of the competition. The final submissions are assessed by a panel of international judges and, where necessary, project visits are carried out.

Address: Memorial Square, Coalville LE67 3TU, UK.

Fax: (1530) 510332; *e-mail:* wha@bshf.org.

Caribbean Community and Common Market (CARICOM)

Regional Research Agenda for Development Through Culture, Youth and Sport

A programme of CARICOM, which was established by the Treaty of Chaguaramas signed on 4 July 1973; as of February 2002, the successor entity is the Caribbean Community, including the CARICOM Single Market and Economy (CSME).

Activities: Aims to guide research to inform the development of sustainable integrated community-based programmes which utilize culture and sport to promote individual health and social well-being. The programme also aims to inform associated policy, advocacy and evaluation processes; and foster the development of indigenous models, methodologies and materials.

Geographical Area of Activity: Caribbean countries.

Address: Bank of Guyana Bldg, POB 10827, Georgetown, Guyana.

Internet: www.caricom.org; *e-mail:* carisec2@caricom.org.

Caribbean Conservation Association (CCA)

Founded in 1967, CCA's membership comprises 20 regional governments, 86 Caribbean-based NGOs, 17 non-Caribbean institutions, as well as individual, sponsoring and student members.

Activities: The Association's activities span five major programme areas: the formulation and promotion of environmental policies and strategies; information collection and dissemination services; promotion of public awareness through environmental education activities; research about, support for, and implementation of natural resource management; and projects to foster sustainable development assistance for cultural patrimony programmes. Initiatives include the Caribbean Regional Environmental Programme (CREP), which aims to strengthen regional co-operation and build greater awareness of environmental issues in the Caribbean forum of African, Caribbean and Pacific states, through a combined programme of sustainable livelihood interventions, awareness-building initiatives, capacity building, and direct conservation or environmental remediation interventions; the Non-Whaling Programme, which seeks to raise awareness and promote non-whaling activities as a means of developing sustainable livelihoods in the Caribbean; and the Coastal and Marine Management Programme (CaMMP), which develops and implements projects and activities to facilitate the responsible management of coastal and marine resources in the wider Caribbean.

Geographical Area of Activity: Caribbean.

Contact: Exec. Dir Dr Joth Singh.

Address: Chelford, The Garrison, St Michael, Barbados.

Telephone: (246) 426-5373; *Fax:* (246) 429-8483; *Internet:* www.ccanet.net.

Caribbean Council

CARIBBEAN COUNCIL FOR EUROPE

The Caribbean Council for Europe is an autonomous body within the West India Committee of the Caribbean Council.

Activities: Provides information to and advocates on behalf of companies and associations affected by changes in European Union, World Trade Organization or US policy. Also organizes conferences, seminars and initiatives designed to bring together government, private-sector, and NGO stakeholders to discuss and develop specific policy and economic development initiatives to support the effective economic transition process in the Caribbean.

Geographical Area of Activity: Caribbean countries.

Contact: Chair. Yesu Persaud; Exec. Dir David Jessop.

Address: Suite 18, Westminster Palace Gardens, 1–7 Artillery Row, London, SW1P 1RR, UK.

Telephone: (20) 7799-1521; *Internet:* www.caritag.com/europe/index.html; *e-mail:* david.jessop@caribbean-council.com.

CARIBBEAN FOUNDATION

Established by the Caribbean Council.

Activities: The Foundation aims to promote European Union (EU)–Caribbean relations through distribution of scholarships and bursaries to Caribbean students wishing to study in the EU, and for students from the EU wishing to study in the Caribbean.

Address: Suite 18, Westminster Palace Gardens, 1–7 Artillery Row, London, SW1P 1RR, UK.

Internet: www.caritag.com/foundation/index.html.

Caribbean Food Corporation (CFC)

Established by Caribbean Community and Common Market (CARICOM) member states in 1976, with headquarters in Trinidad; began operations 1979 as the implementing agency for the region's food and nutrition strategy and as a regional agri-business investment and development organization within the Caribbean Community.

Activities: CFC works with the public and private sectors through promoting and financing viable agri-business enterprises in CARICOM member states, to facilitate regional food self-sufficiency, reduce food imports and generate/save foreign exchange. Also arranges and finances technical, managerial and marketing services; provides agency services for regional agriculture projects; and establishes joint ventures or owned subsidiaries.

Geographical Area of Activity: Caribbean countries.

Contact: Man. Dir E. C. Clyde Parris; Man., Admin. and Finance A. L. Phillips.

Address: 30 Queen's Park West, PO Bag 264B, Port of Spain, Trinidad and Tobago.

Telephone: 622-5827; *Fax:* 622-4430.

Central American Commission for Environment and Development (CACED—Comisión Centroamericana para el Ambiente y Desarrollo)

Founded in 1989; members include the governments of Belize, Costa Rica, El Salvador, Guatemala, Honduras, Nicaragua and Panama.

Activities: Aims to establish regional mechanisms for co-operation among governmental, non-governmental, and international organizations to promote the wise use of natural resources, control of pollution, and the establishment of ecological balance in the region. Member organizations include the Central American Council on Forests and Protected Areas.

Geographical Area of Activity: Central America.

Address: Plaza Madre Tierra, Edificio 11, Segunda Planta, Blvd Orden de Malta Sur, Santa Elena, Antiguo Cuscatlan, La Libertad, El Salvador.

Internet: www.ccad.ws.

Centre on Integrated Rural Development for Asia and the Pacific (CIRDAP)

A regional, intergovernmental and autonomous institution established in July 1979 by the countries of the Asia and the Pacific region, on the initiative of the Food and Agriculture Organization of the UN, with the support of several other UN bodies and donor countries and agencies; promotes rural development initiatives in Afghanistan, Bangladesh, India, Indonesia, Laos, Malaysia, Myanmar, Nepal, Pakistan, Philippines, Sri Lanka, Thailand and Vietnam.

Activities: The Centre's underlying focus is on the structural transformation of rural society and the economy to ensure a life without deprivation for the rural poor and making their development process self-sustaining. Active in four thematic areas: agrarian development; institutional/infrastructure development; resource development, including human resources; and employment, with the following operational programmes: Macro Policy Issues in Poverty Alleviation; Participatory Approaches to Employment Generation, Credit, Provision of Infrastructure and Local Resource Mobilization; Gender Issues in Development; and Environmental Concerns, including Disaster Management for Sustainable Rural Development. Operates micro-credit schemes, provides technical capacity-building support, promotes collaborative projects, supports pilot projects, and carries out training, in conjunction with NGOs and national and regional organizations.

Geographical Area of Activity: Member countries: Afghanistan, Bangladesh, India, Indonesia, Laos, Malaysia, Myanmar, Nepal, Pakistan, Philippines, Sri Lanka, Thailand and Vietnam.

Contact: Dir-Gen. Dr Mya Maung.

Address: Chameli House, 17 Topkhana Rd, GPO Box 2883, Dhaka 1000, Bangladesh.

Telephone: (2) 956-3384; *Internet:* www.cirdap.org.sg.

CILSS—Comité Permanent Inter Etats de Lutte Contre la Sécheresse au Sahel (Permanent Inter-State Committee on Drought Control in the Sahel)

Sahel Foundation

The Foundation was created in 1994 by a convention signed by the Comité Permanent Inter Etats de Lutte Contre la Sécheresse au Sahel (CILSS) member states: Burkina Faso, Cape Verde, Chad, Gambia, Guinea-Bissau, Mali, Mauritania, Niger, and Senegal.

Activities: Aims to support the work of CILSS, by funding research into food security and the fight against the effects of drought in the Sahel region, with the target of developing a new ecological equilibrium Also aims to act in cases of emergency in times of flood or famine.

Geographical Area of Activity: Burkina Faso, Cape Verde, Chad, Gambia, Guinea-Bissau, Mali, Mauritania, Niger and Senegal.

Financial Information: The Foundation aimed to have assets of US $30,000,000.

Address: Executive Secretariat, 03 BP 7049, Ouagadougou 03, Burkina Faso.

Telephone: 37-41-25; *Fax:* 37-41-32; *Internet:* www.cilssnet.org; *e-mail:* cilss@fasonet.bf.

Programme on Food Security

The Comité Permanent Inter Etats de Lutte Contre la Sécheresse au Sahel (CILSS) was formed in September 1973; it is an intergovernmental organization composed of nine Sahelian countries: Burkina Faso, Cape-Verde, Chad, Gambia, Guinea-Bissau, Mali, Mauritania, Niger and Senegal.

Activities: The current mandate of CILSS is to invest in research on food security and in the struggle against the effects of drought and desertification in order to achieve a new ecological equilibrium in the Sahel region. The programme supports sustainable agricultural development, the prevention of food crises, and the promotion of small and medium-sized agro-industrial businesses. Research is carried out in co-operation with partner organizations.

Geographical Area of Activity: Burkina Faso, Cape Verde, Chad, Gambia, Guinea-Bissau, Mali, Mauritania, Niger and Senegal.

Address: Executive Secretariat, 03 BP 7049, Ouagadougou 03, Burkina Faso.
Telephone: 37-41-25; *Fax:* 37-41-32; *Internet:* www.cilssnet.org; *e-mail:* cilss@
fasonet.bf.

Colombo Plan for Co-operative Economic and Social Development in Asia and the Pacific

A regional co-operation organization launched in 1951 as a co-operative venture in economic and social development by seven Commonwealth countries. It now has 24 member countries.

Activities: Promotes development through South–South partnerships among its developing member countries in Asia and the Pacific, by providing a forum for discussion, at regional level, of developmental needs. Also encourages member countries to participate as donors and recipients of technical co-operation, and executes programmes to advance development in member countries. Operates four programmes: Public Administration, providing training in all sectors of public administrations in the context of market-oriented development; South–South co-operation, which utilizes the successful technology experience of some developing countries with training to transfer these skills to other developing countries, in the fields of fisheries management, productivity improvement, small enterprises, poverty alleviation, human resource development in industry and agriculture, investment and trade promotion and technology, and environmental issues in agriculture and tourism; Drug Advisory programme, which works with governments, international bodies and NGOs in the region to deliver more effective anti-narcotics programmes; and the Colombo Plan Staff College for Technician Education, which trains management and technical staff from member countries.

Geographical Area of Activity: Asia and the Pacific.

Contact: Dir Dr Hak-Su Kim; Sec. T. J. Arifeen.

Address: 12 Melbourne Ave, POB 596, Colombo 4, Sri Lanka.

Telephone: (1) 581813; *Fax:* (1) 581754.

The Commonwealth

A voluntary association of 54 sovereign states, which work together to achieve the international goals of facilitating the advancement of democracy, human rights and sustainable development.

Activities: Active in a range of fields, both directly and through affiliated organizations, including democracy, education, gender, globalization, health, human rights, legal co-operation, science and technology, small states, strategic planning and evaluation, sustainable development, environment, and youth empowerment. Operates its own programmes, working in collaboration with NGOs, governments, and international organizations.

Geographical Area of Activity: Commonwealth member states: Antigua and Barbuda, Australia, Bahamas, Bangladesh, Barbados, Belize, Botswana, Brunei, Cameroon, Canada, Cyprus, Dominica, Fiji, Gambia, Ghana, Grenada, Guyana, India, Jamaica, Kenya, Kiribati, Lesotho, Malawi, Malaysia, Maldives, Malta, Mauritius, Mozambique, Namibia, Nauru, New Zealand, Nigeria, Pakistan, Papua New Guinea, St Kitts and Nevis, St Lucia, St Vincent and the Grenadines, Samoa, Seychelles, Sierra Leone, Singapore, Solomon Islands, South Africa, Sri Lanka, Swaziland, Tanzania, Tonga, Trinidad and Tobago, Tuvalu, Uganda, UK, Vanuatu, Zambia and Zimbabwe.

Financial Information: Funded by member governments, the Commonwealth Fund for Technical Co-operation, the Commonwealth Youth Programme, and the Commonwealth Science Council (qq.v.); total budget £11,436,070 (2002–03).

Contact: Sec.-Gen. Donald C. McKinnon.

Address: Commonwealth Secretariat, Marlborough House, Pall Mall, London, SW1Y 5HX, UK.

Internet: www.thecommonwealth.org.

COMMONWEALTH ASSOCIATION FOR MENTAL HANDICAP AND DEVELOPMENTAL DISABILITIES

Founded in 1983 to link professionals across the Commonwealth who are active in the field of mental disability.

Activities: Operates training programmes in conjunction with the World Health Organization (q.v.), on early childhood psycho-social development, as well as running programmes on prevention of childhood blindness, prevention of epilepsy, and prevention of brain damage through head injury.

Geographical Area of Activity: Commonwealth countries.

Publications: Newsletter.

Contact: Pres. Prof. M. S. Akbar; Sec.-Gen. Dr V. R. Pandurangi; Programme Co-ordinator Dr Ganesh Supramaniam.
Address: 36A Oberton Place, Sheffield S11 8XL, UK.
Telephone: (114) 268-2695; *Fax:* (114) 267-8883.

COMMONWEALTH COUNTRIES LEAGUE (CCL)

Founded in 1925 to secure equality of liberties, status and opportunities between men and women and to promote understanding throughout the Commonwealth.

Activities: Aims to promote the education of women throughout the Commonwealth, and their advancement, through sponsorship of poor Commonwealth girls of high academic ability to enable them to complete their secondary education in their own countries. Also fundraises through the annual Commonwealth Fair, organized and run by women from the Commonwealth High Commissions, affiliated organizations and CCL members; operates a programme of talks and social functions; supports the Sadd-Brown Library, held with the Fawcett Library at the London Guildhall University, which contains a wide-ranging collection of books about women in the Commonwealth.

Geographical Area of Activity: Commonwealth countries.

Restrictions: No grants for primary or tertiary education.

Publications: Newsletter (three times a year); Annual Report; Information Brochure.

Contact: Pres. Lady Ramphal; Chair. Marian Kermanshahchi; Hon. Sec. Floi Stewart-Murray.

Address: 96 High St, Hampton Wick, Kingston-upon-Thames KT1 4DQ, UK.

Telephone: (20) 8943-3001; *Fax:* (20) 8458-0763.

COMMONWEALTH FORESTRY ASSOCIATION (CFA)

Established in 1921 as the Empire Forestry Association; its mission is to promote good management, use and conservation of forests and forest lands.

Activities: Collaborates with national, international and NGOs in the management of joint events on topics of global and Commonwealth interest. The Association finances the Queen's Award for Forestry, which recognizes outstanding contributions to forestry by an individual.

Geographical Area of Activity: Commonwealth countries.

Publications: Commonwealth Forestry Review (quarterly); Members' Handbook.

Contact: Pres. Duke of Buccleuch and Queensberry; Chair. Peter J. Wood.

Address: Oxford Forestry Institute, South Parks Rd, Oxford OX1 3RB, UK.

Telephone: (1865) 275072; *Fax:* (1865) 275074; *Internet:* www.cfa-international.org.

COMMONWEALTH FOUNDATION

An inter-governmental organization originally founded in 1965 to support the work of the non-governmental sector within the Commonwealth, in particular the strengthening of civil society, sustainable development and poverty eradication, and to facilitate pan-Commonwealth and inter-country connections between people, their associations and communities at all levels.

Activities: The Foundation supports programmes in four areas: Civil Society, including developing citizen input into making society better; Professional Exchange, supporting the work of over 30 Commonwealth Professional Associations; Arts and Culture including the Commonwealth Writers Prize; and the annual Commonwealth Understanding Fellowship Scheme. *Ad-hoc* responsive grants are also available in these four areas. Priority is given to projects incorporating the following values: respect for diversity and human dignity and opposition to all forms of discrimination; adherence to democracy, the rule of law, good governance, freedom of expression and the protection of human rights; the elimination of poverty and the promotion of people-centred development and progressive removal of the wide disparities in living standards among Commonwealth member countries; and international peace and security, the rule of international law and opposition to terrorism. Also hosts an on-line discussion forum.

Geographical Area of Activity: Countries of the Commonwealth.

How to Apply: Details on applying for grants are available on the website.

Financial Information: Funds are provided by Commonwealth governments.

Publications: Common Path (quarterly); application information and information brochures.

Contact: Chair. Graça Machel; Dir Colin Ball; Deputy Dir Rudo Chitiga.

Address: Marlborough House, Pall Mall, London SW1Y 5HY, UK.

Telephone: (20) 7930-3783; *Fax:* (20) 7839-8157; *Internet:* www.commonwealthfoundation.com; *e-mail:* geninfo@commonwealth.int.

COMMONWEALTH FUND FOR TECHNICAL CO-OPERATION (CFTC)

Established by Commonwealth Heads of Government in 1971 and administered by the Commonwealth Secretariat in London, the CFTC is the principal means by which the Commonwealth promotes economic and social development and the alleviation of poverty in member countries.

Activities: The Fund operates on the principle of mutual assistance, with member governments contributing funds on a voluntary basis and obtaining technical assistance as needed. It is largely demand-driven and responds to requests from governments and regional organizations for technical assistance, including in-house and external consultants to advise on a range of areas; including export, enterprise and agricultural development, economic and legal issues, and assistance in implementing programmes of training, capacity building and public-sector reform.

Geographical Area of Activity: Commonwealth countries.

How to Apply: Requests for assistance must come from Commonwealth governments, or from regional organizations with a substantial Commonwealth membership, and be channelled through the designated CFTC point of contact, who is normally in the Planning, Finance or Establishment Ministry. Requests should include: a concise statement of the problems faced, and of the type of assistance sought; a description of the project, its background, objectives and terms of reference; details of the organization responsible for the project and of counterpart staff; job description and title of post to be filled, if appropriate; and qualifications and experience required of an adviser, consultant or trainer; and when assistance is needed and for how long.

Financial Information: Total budget £22,220,000 (2002–03).

Address: c/o Deputy Sec.-Gen. Devt Co-operation, Commonwealth Secretariat, Marlborough House, Pall Mall, London, SW1Y 5HX, UK.

Telephone: (20) 7747-6520; *Fax:* (20) 7930-0827; *Internet:* www.thecommonwealth .org/whoweare/cftc/cftc.html; *e-mail:* cftc@commonwealth.int.

COMMONWEALTH GAMES FEDERATION

The Federation links the national Commonwealth Games Associations to promote the four-yearly Commonwealth Games, establish rules and regulations for their conduct and encourage amateur sport throughout the Commonwealth. The first Games, held at Hamilton in Canada in 1930, were called the British Empire Games. In 1954 the title was changed to the British Empire and Commonwealth Games, in 1966 to the British Commonwealth Games and, in 1978, to the Commonwealth Games.

Activities: The Federation promotes the Commonwealth Games, held every four years, as well as encouraging the holding of various Commonwealth championships and the development of sport throughout the Commonwealth. Also supports the Commonwealth Heads of Government Meetings Committee for Co-operation through Sport in its efforts to strengthen the Commonwealth Games and the Games Federation, encourages governments to use sport as a means of social and educational development, and assists educational initiatives through sports development and physical education.

Geographical Area of Activity: Commonwealth countries.

Contact: Pres. Prince Edward; Chair. Michael S. Fennell; Hon. Sec. David M. Dixon.

Address: Walkon House, 3–10 Melton St, London NW1 2E8, UK.

Telephone: (20) 7383-5596; *Fax:* (20) 7383-5506; *Internet:* www.commonwealthgames.com.

COMMONWEALTH HUMAN ECOLOGY COUNCIL (CHEC)

Established in 1969, CHEC encourages and promotes an understanding of human ecological principles and their application in Commonwealth countries and beyond. It has chapters in over 20 Commonwealth countries, and a membership of over 500 organizations and individuals.

Activities: CHEC aims to inject human ecology into every level of development, bringing together governments, experts and community members in common action to increase the opportunities for people to live in harmony, in a lasting fashion, with their natural, social and cultural environment. Develops educational initiatives, including founding ecology courses at universities and other educational institutions, and funds and acts as a technical facilitator and long-term partner with other organizations, contributing to the implementation of self-help programmes.

Geographical Area of Activity: Commonwealth countries.

Publications: CHEC Journal; CHEC Points (newsletter); *COSTIE* and other publications.

Contact: Acting Chair. Dr D. W. Hall; Exec. Vice-Chair. Zena Daysh.

Address: Church House, Bayswater, London W2 5LS, UK.

Telephone: (20) 7792-5934; *Fax:* (20) 7792-5948; *Internet:* www.tcol.co.uk/comorg /CHEC.htm; *e-mail:* checq@breathe.net.

COMMONWEALTH HUMAN RIGHTS INITIATIVE (CHRI)

Founded in 1987 to raise the significance of human rights for the Commonwealth and, as far as possible, to improve the human rights situation of citizens in Commonwealth countries.

Activities: Promotes human rights in Commonwealth countries through organizing workshops and projects, covering a range of fields, including prisons and policing in South Asia, the right to information; tribal and indigenous rights; and refugee rights in Africa. Also carries out research and leads human rights fact-finding missions.

Geographical Area of Activity: Commonwealth countries.

Publications: Put Our World to Rights; Act Right Now; Rights Do Matter; Restoring Childhood; The Right to a Culture of Tolerance.

Contact: Chair., Advisory Commission Dr Kamal Hossain; Chair., Exec. Cttee Soli J Sorabjee; Chair., Trustee Cttee Richard Bourne; Dir Maja Daruwala.

Address: K-92, Hauz Khas Enclave, New Delhi 110 016, India.

Telephone: (11) 6864678; *Fax:* (11) 6864688; *e-mail:* chriall@nda.vsnl.net.in.

33

THE COMMONWEALTH JEWISH COUNCIL

Founded in 1982; aims to provide links between Commonwealth Jewish communities, and with Commonwealth governments. Membership includes the Jewish communities of 36 Commonwealth countries.

Activities: Operates through providing funding for a variety of social, educational, religious and other communal projects. Also holds meetings and consultations with governments and community leaders, a conference, held every two years, and exhibitions; creates regional links between communities; strengthens religious life, including assistance with the provision of religious and educational facilities, leadership and relief of poverty; provides support for the restoration of synagogues and cemeteries, finances educational and travel scholarships; and makes annual awards for services to Commonwealth and Jewish communities.

Geographical Area of Activity: Commonwealth countries.

Publications: Newsletter (two a year); *Jewish Communities of the Commonwealth.*

Contact: Pres. Lord Janner; Chair. Jeff Durkin.

Address: BCM Box 6871, London WC1N 3XX, UK.

Telephone: (20) 7222-2120; *Fax:* (20) 7222-1781.

THE COMMONWEALTH OF LEARNING (COL)

COL helps extend, improve and link distance education facilities in the Commonwealth. It was established as an intergovernmental organization.

Activities: Aims to act as a catalyst in developing collaborative initiatives between organizations, with projects including: STAMP 2000+, providing in-service skills training to teachers in Southern Africa; the Canada Caribbean Distance Education Scholarship Programme; and an educational research programme carried out in collaboration with the International Research Foundation for Open Learning. Also acts as a capacity builder, using methodologies of open, distance and technology-mediated learning to the benefit of a wide range of socio-economic priorities; offers a number of information and resource databases; organizes conferences and special events; and offers consultancy and professional services to organizations.

Geographical Area of Activity: Commonwealth countries.

Contact: Chair., Board of Governors Lewis Perinbam; Pres. and Chief Exec. Prof. Gajaraj Dhanarajan.

Address: 1285 West Broadway, Suite 600, Vancouver, BC V6H 3K8, Canada.

Telephone: (604) 775-8200; *Fax:* (604) 775-8210; *Internet:* www.col.org; *e-mail:* info@col.org.

COMMONWEALTH NETWORK OF INFORMATION TECHNOLOGY FOR DEVELOPMENT (COMNET–IT)

A network organization whose mission is to foster the building and enhancing of institutional and human networks through the mediation of computer communication networks.

Activities: The organization facilitates the brokering and funding of information technology-related projects, develops Internet-based services and engages in capability building through policy and training workshops.

Geographical Area of Activity: Commonwealth countries.

Financial Information: Funders include the government of Malta, Malta Information Technology and Training Services Ltd, and the Commonwealth Secretariat.

Contact: Exec. Dir Henry D. Alamango.

Address: Gattard House, National Rd, Blata l-Bajda HMR 02, Malta.

Telephone: 25992902; *Fax:* 21234746; *Internet:* www.comnet-it.org; *e-mail:* comnetadm@gov.mt.

COMMONWEALTH PARTNERSHIP FOR TECHNOLOGY MANAGEMENT LIMITED (CPTM)

Established in 1995 by the Commonwealth Heads of Government, CPTM is an independent government/private-sector partnership created to provide advisory services to Commonwealth countries, institutions, and organizations on technology management as a tool for macroeconomic development.

Activities: Operates as a networking organization utilizing the expertise and skills of its members who offer their services voluntarily. Carries out two major initiatives: the Country Task Programme whereby CPTM annually develops a portfolio of projects to be implemented in Commonwealth Countries; and, secondly, the National, Regional, and International Smart Partnership Dialogue Programme, which brings together government leaders, public-sector, civil society organizations and labour organizations in an informal interactive environment to facilitate trust and a co-operative approach to the management of the macroeconomic environment throughout the Commonwealth and beyond.

Geographical Area of Activity: Commonwealth countries.

Publications: Annual Report.

Contact: Chief Exec. Dr Mihaela Y. Smith.

Address: 14 Queen Anne's Gate, London SW1H 9AA, UK.

Telephone: (20) 7222-3773; *Fax:* (20) 7930-1543; *Internet:* www.cptm.org; *e-mail:* smartpartnership@cptm.org.

COMMONWEALTH SCIENCE COUNCIL

An intergovernmental organization with membership open to all of the member countries; seeks to pool the scientific and technological resources within the Commonwealth to help improve the economic, environmental, social and cultural development of the Commonwealth as a whole. At present there are 36 members, represented at Council meetings by senior scientists or science executives.

Activities: Facilitates the application of science and technology for sustainable development through the networking of knowledge using modern information technologies. Initiatives include: the Commonwealth Knowledge Network, enabling the sharing of knowledge and resources in such areas as energy, biological diversity and genetic resources, and water and mineral resources; and innovation and technology foresighting, enabling countries to develop national systems of innovation and assisting member countries in implementing the Rio Conventions on the environment.

Geographical Area of Activity: Commonwealth countries.

Financial Information: Total budget £912,005 (2002–03).

Address: Marlborough House, Pall Mall, London SW1Y 5HX, UK.

Internet: www.comsci.org.

COMMONWEALTH SERVICE ABROAD PROGRAMME (CSAP)

Launched by the Commonwealth Secretariat and run in conjunction with the Commonwealth Fund for Technical Co-operation (CFTC, q.v.), as a volunteer-based programme to meet the needs of member governments.

Activities: The Programme aims to assist in the design, development and implementation of people-centred, mass impact projects utilizing the expertise of high achieving and young professional volunteers, in response to specific requests from member countries for assistance. Since March 2001 the Programme has supported over 80 projects in the fields of poverty reduction, enterprise development, application of new information and communications technologies, and environment and heritage preservation.

Geographical Area of Activity: Commonwealth countries.

Address: Commonwealth Secretariat, Marlborough House, Pall Mall, London, SW1Y 5HX, UK.

Telephone: (20) 7747-6520; *Fax:* (20) 7930-0827; *Internet:* www.thecommonwealth .org/whoweare/cftc/cftc.html; *e-mail:* cftc@commonwealth.int.

COMMONWEALTH SOCIETY FOR THE DEAF—SOUND SEEKERS

A registered UK charity, which supports deaf people, particularly children, in developing countries of the Commonwealth.

Activities: Promotes the health, education and general welfare of the deaf in developing Commonwealth countries, by encouraging and assisting in the development of educational facilities, the training of teachers of the deaf, and the provision of support for parents of deaf children; organizing visits by volunteer specialists to developing countries; providing audiological equipment and organizing the training of audiological maintenance technicians; conducting research into the causes and prevention of deafness; and initiating projects to help Commonwealth countries to develop and sustain their own programmes.

Geographical Area of Activity: Less-developed countries of the Commonwealth, including Bangladesh, Barbados, Belize, Botswana, Ethiopia, Fiji, Ghana, Guyana, India, Jamaica, Kenya, Lesotho, Malta, Namibia, Nigeria, Papua New Guinea, Seychelles, Sierra Leone, South Africa, St Lucia, Swaziland, Tanzania, Tonga, Trinidad and Tobago, Uganda, Zambia and Zimbabwe.

Financial Information: Total income £403,915, expenditure £325,569 (2002).

Publications: Annual Report.

Contact: Board of Directors: Chair. Ivan Tucker; Vice-Chair. Navnit Shah; Chief Exec. David Baker.

Address: 34 Buckingham Palace Rd, London SW1W 0RE, UK.

Telephone: (20) 7233-5700; *Fax:* (20) 7233-5800; *Internet:* www.sound-seekers.org .uk; *e-mail:* sound.seekers@btinternet.com.

COMMONWEALTH YOUTH EXCHANGE COUNCIL (CYEC)

Founded in 1970, CYEC aims to promote contact between groups of young people aged 16–25 in the United Kingdom and other Commonwealth countries through two-way educational exchange visits.

Activities: Activities include: providing information, advice and networking support for the planning and preparation of exchanges; grants to British youth organizations for outgoing and incoming visits; training courses and seminars for youth workers, teachers and young people; youth forums and special projects to develop Commonwealth youth exchange.

Geographical Area of Activity: Commonwealth countries.

Publications: Annual Report; Newsletter.

Contact: Chair. Trevor R. Hall; Dir Vic Craggs.

Address: 7 Lion Yard, Tremadoc Rd, Clapham, London SW4 7NQ, UK.

Telephone: (20) 7498-6151; *Fax:* (20) 7720-5403; *Internet:* www.cyec.org.uk; *e-mail:* mail@cyec.demon.co.uk.

GENDER AND YOUTH AFFAIRS DIVISION

Commonwealth Youth Programme

Run by the youth department of the Commonwealth Secretariat; the Programme works for a world where young women and men (aged between 15 and 29) can reach their full potential, use their creativity and skills as productive members of their societies and take control of their own lives.

Activities: Promotes youth development through its Mainstreaming Youth programme, including funding initiatives promoting youth participation and leadership that facilitate the role of young people in the political process, as voters, members of political organizations, heads of lobbying groups, and candidates for election; economic enfranchisement, helping young people achieve their own career aspirations, with support provided through the Commonwealth Youth Credit Initiative (CYCI); Human Resource Development, providing young people with the opportunity to invest in themselves, through education and work programmes; and youth empowerment in the field of health, particularly HIV and AIDS, through funding education and social change initiatives. Also maintains regional offices in Australia, Guyana, India and Zambia.

Geographical Area of Activity: Commonwealth countries.

Financial Information: Total budget £2,308,500 (2002–03).

Publications: Strategy papers and reports.

Address: Gender and Youth Affairs Division, Commonwealth Secretariat, Marlborough House, Pall Mall, London SW1Y 5HX, UK.

Telephone: (20) 7747-6462; *Fax:* (20) 7930-1647; *Internet:* www.thecommonwealth .org/cyp; *e-mail:* cyp@commonwealth.int.

ORGANIZATION OF COMMONWEALTH ASSOCIATIONS (OCA)

Established as Commonwealth Professional Associations in 1983; represents the collective views and activities of many Commonwealth NGOs, mainly the Commonwealth professional associations.

Activities: Promotes development in Commonwealth countries by assisting member organizations in those countries; also offers technical assistance through the exchange of information, and co-operates with the Commonwealth Foundation (q.v.), Commonwealth Liaison Units and other international organizations.

Geographical Area of Activity: Commonwealth countries.

How to Apply: Any pan-Commonwealth NGO is entitled to be a member, provided it is recognized as such by the Commonwealth Foundation and a majority of the members of the OCA approve.

Contact: Chair. Marianne Haslegrave; Sec. John Havard.

Address: c/o Commonwealth Medical Asscn, BMA House, Tavistock Square, London WC1H 9JP, UK.

Telephone: (20) 7383-6095; *Fax:* (20) 7383-6195; *e-mail:* 72242.3544@compuserve .com.

THE ROYAL OVER-SEAS LEAGUE

Founded in 1910 by Sir Evelyn Wrench to promote friendship and understanding; it is a self-funding, non-profit-making organization that operates under a Royal Charter, and is pledged to work for the service of others, the good of the Commonwealth, and humanity in general. There are reciprocal clubs, branches or chapters in over 70 countries, and a sister clubhouse in Edinburgh. The League aims to support the ideals of the Commonwealth, encourage young Commonwealth artists and musicians, encourage Commonwealth friendship and support welfare work.

Activities: The League has over 22,000 members world-wide. It encourages the arts, in particular among the young people of the Commonwealth, through staging an Annual Music Competition, an Annual Open Exhibition and a Literary Lecture programme. Also commissions works of art and musical compositions, and awards scholarships to artists and musicians for travel and study overseas. In 1995 the League initiated joint welfare projects including travelling eye camps in Sri Lanka, and projects in Namibia which support school bursaries and resource materials for bushmen and farm children. The League also offers clubhouse, conference and private dining facilities in London and Edinburgh.

Geographical Area of Activity: Commonwealth countries.

Publications: Annual Report; Branch Newsletters; *Overseas* (quarterly magazine).

Contact: Patron Her Majesty The Queen; Vice-Patron HRH Princess Alexandra; Grand Pres. Lord Grey of Naunton; Chair., Central Council Sir Geoffrey Ellerton; Deputy Chair. Roger Lilley; Hon. Treas. G. R. Prentice; Dir-Gen. Robert Newell.

Address: Over-Seas House, Park Place, St James's St, London SW1A 1LR, UK.

Telephone: (20) 7408-0214; *Fax:* (20) 7499-6738; *Internet:* www.rosl.org.uk; *e-mail:* info@rosl.org.uk.

SIGHT SAVERS INTERNATIONAL—ROYAL COMMONWEALTH SOCIETY FOR THE BLIND

Founded in 1950 by Sir John Wilson to prevent and cure blindness and promote the welfare, education and employment of blind people in developing countries.

Activities: Operates in over 25 developing countries in the field of blindness prevention and cure. Works in co-operation with the World Health Organization (WHO, q.v.) and major international NGOs. Projects are designed and delivered with the assistance of local and regional organizations and national agencies in order to bring services to the maximum number of people. Support is given to local organizations and governments to teach basic eye care skills and hygiene to adults and children. Funding is also provided for eye screening camps, operations, treatments, education, surgical training, and rehabilitation programmes. Also a member of Vision 2020, a WHO initiative which aims to eliminate avoidable blindness by 2020.

Geographical Area of Activity: Less-developed countries, including Bangladesh, Gambia, India, Malawi, Mali, Nigeria, Pakistan, Tanzania and Uganda.

Financial Information: Total expenditure £10,880,000 (2001).

Publications: Annual report and accounts; *Sight Savers News; Try to See it My Way;* and a variety of leaflets describing the Society's work.

Contact: Trustees: The Society is governed by a council of 18 members; Pres. HRH Princess Alexandra; Chair. Sir John Coles; Exec. Dir Richard Porter.

Address: Grosvenor Hall, Bolnore Rd, Haywards Health RH16 4BX, UK.

Telephone: (1444) 446600; *Fax:* (1444) 446688; *Internet:* www.sightsavers.org; *e-mail:* generalinformation@sightsavers.org.

SMALL STATES SECTION

Economic Affairs Division

A department of the Commonwealth Secretariat.

Activities: The Section carries out training programmes for health workers and develops training materials according to need. Programme delivery is carried out in partnership with international health organizations, pan-Commonwealth organizations and other NGOs.

Geographical Area of Activity: Commonwealth countries.

Contact: Deputy Dir Dr Elilawony J. Kisanga.

Address: Marlborough House, Pall Mall, London SW1Y 5HX, UK.

Telephone: (20) 7747-6128; *Fax:* (20) 7747-6235; *Internet:* www.commonwealthsmallstates.org; *e-mail:* e.kisanga@commonwealth.int.

SOCIAL TRANSFORMATION PROGRAMMES DIVISION (STPD)

Education Section

Strives to achieve the target of providing every person with an access to basic education and meeting the Millennium Development Goals; now merged with the Gender and Health Sections (qq.v.) to form the Social Transformation Programmes Division (STPD). The education programme is guided by the decisions made in Commonwealth Heads of Government Meetings (CHOGM) and Commonwealth Education Ministers Conferences.

Activities: The main aims of the education programme are to: enrol all children in primary school and achieve completion of primary schooling; encourage girls to attend school, empower women and eliminate gender inequality in primary and secondary schooling; improve enrolment and retention; support non-formal education programmes; promote education in post-conflict societies; ensure access to high quality education; and promote multiculturalism and an awareness of heritage among young people. Activities include providing policy advice, sharing best practice, funding capacity-building programmes, and awarding scholarships and fellowships for overseas study.

Geographical Area of Activity: Commonwealth countries.

Address: Marlborough House, Pall Mall, London SW1Y 5HX, UK.

Telephone: (20) 7747-6460; *Fax:* (20) 7930-1647; *Internet:* www.thecommonwealth .org/stpd/index.html; *e-mail:* info@commonwealth.int.

Gender Section

Formerly part of the Commonwealth Secretariat's Gender and Youth Affairs Division (GYAD); now merged with the Health and Education Sections (qq.v.) to form the Social Transformation Programmes Division (STPD).

Activities: Addresses the following priority areas based on the Harare principles: gender mainstreaming; human rights and HIV/AIDS; engendering macro-economic politics; political empowerment and peace building; and creation of a

Knowledge Network. Organizes conferences and symposia, lobbies governments and collaborates with civil society and international organizations to achieve its goals.

Geographical Area of Activity: Commonwealth countries.

Contact: M. Roberts.

Address: Marlborough House, Pall Mall, London SW1Y 5HX, UK.

Telephone: (20) 7747-6460; *Fax:* (20) 7930-1647; *Internet:* www.thecommonwealth .org/gender/index.html; *e-mail:* gad@commonwealth.int.

Health Section

Commonwealth health priorities are established by Commonwealth Heads of Government and Ministers of Health; the Section has merged with the Gender and Education Sections (qq.v.) to form the Social Transformation Programmes Division (STPD).

Activities: The Health Section focuses on achieving the Millennium Development Goals on maternal health, child mortality and HIV/AIDS. Activities for addressing these Goals are implemented at the regional and national levels, with a specific focus on the health of women and adolescents, HIV/AIDS, and human resources for health. Operates through the provision of capacity-building and other health sector-related technical assistance to organizations in Commonwealth member countries.

Geographical Area of Activity: Commonwealth countries.

Address: Marlborough House, Pall Mall, London SW1Y 5HX, UK.

Telephone: (20) 7747-6460; *Fax:* (20) 7930-1647; *Internet:* www.thecommonwealth .org/stpd/index.html; *e-mail:* info@commonwealth.int.

Co-operation Council for the Arab States of the Gulf

GCC Environmental Award

Established in 1997, based on the resolution of the fourth meeting of the Ministers in charge of environment affairs in Gulf Co-operation Council (GCC) states. Part of the Council's strategy to encourage and further the enhancement of environment awareness and quality in member states through scientific research, innovation, and adherence to environmental regulations, standards and specifications.

Activities: The Award aims to promote environmental awareness in conserving and sustaining environmental resources, and to recognize and encourage those who endeavour to create a better regional environment; encourage environmental activities, as well as individual and collective initiatives which contribute to the protection of the environment and sustainable development; inspire individuals and establishments to innovate research; contribute to the spread of environmental awareness and knowledge among citizen and residents; and emphasize the efforts of industrial establishments committed to environmental standards and specifications. Awards are made within the following categories: the best research in the field of environment; environmental awareness; environment personality; the best educational and research institution which serves environment in each member state; and an industrial establishment, in each state, which complies with the environmental standards and specifications for the best environmental practices.

Geographical Area of Activity: Arab States of the Gulf: Bahrain, Kuwait, Oman, Qatar, Saudi Arabia and United Arab Emirates.

Financial Information: Research prize 50,000 Saudi riyals.

Contact: Sec.-Gen. Jameel Ibrahim Al-Hejailan.

Address: POB 59111, Riyadh 11525, Saudi Arabia.

Telephone: (1) 482-7777; *Fax:* (1) 482-9089; *Internet:* www.gcc-sg.org/award.html.

GULF CO-OPERATION COUNCIL (GCC) FOLKLORE CENTRE

Established in 1983 by the Co-operation Council for the Arab States of the Gulf to collect, document and classify the regional cultural heritage.

Activities: Operates in the following areas: publishing research; sponsoring and protecting regional folklore; providing a database and documentation centre on Gulf folklore; organizing conferences and exhibitions; and promoting traditional culture through educational initiatives.

Geographical Area of Activity: Arab Gulf States.

Publications: Al Ma'thurat Al Sha'biyyah: La Sagesse Populaire (also published in English).

Address: POB 7996, Doha, Qatar.

Telephone: 861999; *Fax:* 867170; *Internet:* www.gccfolklore.org; *e-mail:* folkcent@ qatar.net.qa.

Council of Europe

European Human Rights Prize of the Council of Europe

The Prize rewards individuals' and organizations' contribution to the defence of human rights.

Activities: Operates through an award every three years to an individual, group of people, an institution or an NGO which has played an active part in promoting human rights. Open to people or organizations originating from a state which has signed the European Convention on Human Rights.

Geographical Area of Activity: European Union, Central and Eastern Europe, Mediterranean countries, Iceland, Liechtenstein, Norway and Switzerland.

How to Apply: The Prize is awarded every three years; the last award was made in 2003.

Financial Information: Total prize €20,000.

Contact: Contact Sally-Ann Honeyman.

Address: Parliamentary Assembly, ave de l'Europe, 67075 Strasbourg Cedex, France.

Telephone: 3-88-41-28-58; *Internet:* www.humanrights.coe.int/intro/eng/general /welc2dir.htm; *e-mail:* sally-ann.honeyman@coe.int.

CULTURAL POLICY AND ACTION DEPARTMENT

Action Plan for Russia

Aims to help develop exchanges and co-operation within the Russian Federation at regional level, as well as between the Federation and Council of Europe member states, and to help the Federation develop its cultural policies.

Activities: Supports intergovernmental exchange and co-operation in the Russian Federation and the development of cultural policies, through grants for regional initiatives, seminars and workshops in the areas of cultural policy and regional development, management of cultural organizations, civil society and new partnerships, and cultural diversity and cultural initiatives. Also funds initiatives developing creativity in new media, including training for young media professionals. Grants are targeted at cultural policy-makers and administrators at national, regional and local level, administrators and practitioners of public and private cultural organizations, and civil society organizations. The programme was scheduled to run from 2003–04.

Geographical Area of Activity: Russian Federation.

How to Apply: Applications can be made at any time, preceded by contact with the national Sports Ministry. Projects must be co-financed.

Financial Information: Maximum grant €35,000; average grant €15,000.

Contact: Contact Jean-Philippe Gammel.

Address: 67075 Strasbourg Cedex, France.

Telephone: 3-90-21-46-76; *Fax:* 3-88-41-37-82; *Internet:* www.coe.int/t/e
/cultural_Co-operation/Culture/Assistance_&_Development/m.o.s.a.i.c/; *e-mail:*
jean-philippe.gammel@coe.int.

DEVELOPMENT DEPARTMENT

Aid After Natural and Ecological Disasters

Aims to solve urgent problems faced by victims of natural or ecological disasters.

Activities: Provides local and guarantee funding for urgent projects following
natural or ecological disasters, including professional, health and educational
training, creation of medical centres, schools and social housing, infrastructure
development, and projects aimed at preventing natural disasters.

Geographical Area of Activity: Beneficiaries must be situated in one of the member
countries of the Council of Europe Development Bank.

Financial Information: Grants can be made for up to 50% of total project costs.

Contact: Contact Juan Francisco Seco Guillot.

Address: 55 ave Kléber, 75784 Paris Cedex 16, France.

Telephone: 1-47-55-55-92; *Internet:* www.coebank.org/fr/presentation/frmission
.htm; *e-mail:* eva.schwebel@coebank.org.

Disadvantaged Urban Areas

Aims to strengthen social cohesion in Europe and to improve the quality of life in
disadvantaged urban areas.

Activities: The programme operates through grants, loans and guarantees for
social investment purposes to NGOs, SMEs and local and regional authorities for
the development of cultural and social infrastructures for community, sport,
professional training and information centres, basic medical services, schools,
employment projects and similar activities; and for the development of service
infrastructures, including roads, gas supply, electricity and water services. The
project must be situated in one of the Council of Europe Development Bank (CEB)
member countries, in an area where the unemployment rate is above the national
average, and respect the environment in accordance with the Council of Europe's
conventions.

Geographical Area of Activity: Balkan countries, Central and Eastern Europe,
European Union, Mediterranean countries, Iceland, Liechtenstein, Norway and
Switzerland.

How to Apply: Applications can be made at any time; proposals must be presented
to the government of the country concerned; contact the CEB for information on
the structure of the application form.

Contact: Contact Juan Francisco Seco Guillot.

Address: 55 ave Kléber, 75784 Paris Cedex 16, France.

Telephone: 1-47-55-55-92; *Internet:* www.coebank.org/fr/presentation/frmission
.htm; *e-mail:* ceb@coebank.org.

Environment Protection

Aims to strengthen social cohesion in Europe and protect the European environment.

Activities: The programme operates through the provision of long-term loans to NGOs, SMEs and local and regional authorities for environmental protection activities, including: the reduction and treatment of waste water; the protection of ground water, soil and fight against noise pollution; the filtration of industrial emissions from SMEs; the recycling of waste; and the production of non-polluting and renewable energy. Funded projects must be in accordance with the Council of Europe's conventions and take place in one of the Council of Europe Development Bank (CEB) member countries, concern defined local or regional populations and have private investment.

Geographical Area of Activity: Balkan countries, Central and Eastern Europe, European Union, Mediterranean countries, Iceland, Liechtenstein, Norway and Switzerland.

How to Apply: Applications can be made to the government of the country concerned; contact the CEB for further information on application procedures.

Financial Information: Loans and guarantees are available for up to 50% of the total project costs.

Contact: Contact Juan Francisco Seco Guillot.

Address: 55 ave Kléber, 75784 Paris Cedex 16, France.

Telephone: 1-47-55-55-92; *Internet:* www.coebank.org/fr/presentation/frmission .htm; *e-mail:* eva.schwebel@coebank.org.

Historical Heritage

A loan and guarantee fund established by the Council of Europe Development Bank (CEB) to strengthen social cohesion in Europe and to protect and rehabilitate Europe's historical heritage.

Activities: The fund operates through long-term loans and guarantees to NGOs and other organizations, aimed at protecting Europe's historical heritage. Loans are available for projects which protect and rehabilitate Europe's historical sites, including cleaning buildings, and employment-creation projects related to Europe's heritage sites.

Geographical Area of Activity: Member states of the CEB: Albania, Belgium, Bulgaria, Croatia, Cyprus, Czech Republic, Denmark, Estonia, Finland, France, Germany, Greece, Hungary, Iceland, Italy, Latvia, Liechtenstein, Lithuania, Luxembourg, Malta, Moldova, Netherlands, Norway, Poland, Portugal, Romania, San Marino, Slovakia, Slovenia, Spain, Sweden, Switzerland, former Yugoslav Republic of Macedonia, Turkey and Vatican City.

How to Apply: Applications can be submitted at any time; the project must take place in one of the member states of the CEB.

Financial Information: Loans available for up to 50% of total project costs.

Contact: Contact Juan Francisco Seco Guillot.

Address: 55 ave Kléber, 75784 Paris Cedex 16, France.

Telephone: 1-47-55-55-92; *Internet:* www.coebank.org/fr/presentation/frmission .htm; *e-mail:* ceb@coebank.org.

DIRECTORATE-GENERAL IV—CULTURAL POLICY AND ACTION DEPARTMENT

MOSAIC II—Managing an Open and Strategic Approach in Culture

Launched by the Cultural Policy and Action Department of the Council of Europe in 1998, MOSAIC aims to create a framework for exchanges and co-operation amongst countries in South-Eastern Europe and to assist them in the transition of their cultural policies.

Activities: Aims to encourage a democratic and open approach to cultural policy and decision-making processes, advise decision-makers on how to develop policies to cope with the challenges of democratic transition and the management of cultural diversity, assist in reforming and implementing necessary legislation, encourage a multilateral approach in the co-ordination of policies, partnerships and networks, and move towards a regional multicultural policy and the development of intercultural skills. Funding is available for regional activities, including multilateral debates, seminars and workshops on the role of civil society, training activities and technical assistance; and multilateral activities tackling decentralization, legislation, funding and sponsoring of culture, working conditions of artists, cultural rights of minorities, and cultural management and networks. Target beneficiaries are cultural policy-makers and administrators at national, regional and local level, representatives of the cultural sector, and civil society organizations.

Geographical Area of Activity: Europe.

How to Apply: Applications can be made at any time; interested organizations should first contact their national Sports Ministry. Projects must be co-financed.

Financial Information: Maximum grant awarded €35,000, average grant €15,000.

Contact: Project Man. Jean-Philippe Gammel; Project Asst Frédérique Privat de Fortune.

Address: ave de l'Europe, 67075 Strasbourg Cedex, France.

Telephone: 3-90-21-46-76; *Fax:* 3-88-41-37-82; *Internet:* www.coe.int/t/e /cultural_co-operation/culture/assistance_&_development/m.o.s.a.i.c/; *e-mail:* jean-philippe.gammel@coe.int.

DIRECTORATE OF YOUTH AND SPORT

Solidarity Fund for Youth Mobility

The Fund was established to promote the mobility of disadvantaged young people in Europe.

Activities: The Fund aims to improve disadvantaged young people's international perspective through encouraging them to participate in international activities and make transnational contacts, by providing sums equivalent to the price of the Inter-Rail Card; disadvantaged young people are encouraged to make international railway journeys in order to participate in an international project of an educational character. Projects must include at least 10 individuals from at least two countries, and be for individuals who are: from outer regions and subject to higher travel costs than those living in the centre of Europe; from underdeveloped regions or countries with a high rate of unemployment; learning a crafts profession or activity, but not have the means to pay for the travel costs; and who have an incomplete education and no support at school, with little knowledge of foreign languages as a result.

Geographical Area of Activity: Europe.

How to Apply: Applications should be submitted one month before the project takes place.

Financial Information: Annual budget €100,000 (2003); awards are equivalent to the price of an Inter-Rail Card.

Contact: Contact Birgit Bertsch.

Address: 30 rue Pierre de Coubertin, 67000 Strasbourg, France.

Telephone: 3-88-41-23-04; *Internet:* www.coe.fr/youth/homefr.htm; *e-mail:* birgit .bertsch@coe.int.

SPRINT—SPorts Reform, INnovation and Training

Established in 1991 to provide assistance to reform the sports system in the countries of the former USSR.

Activities: Aims to assist new member countries in accepting common standards and developing appropriate national sports policies and legislation; to promote the influence of sport in general policy; and to achieve increased participation in sporting activities at all levels to improve people's social and health conditions. Funding is provided for intergovernmental and other projects that are active in the fields of legislative reform, democratization of the sports movement, promotion of sport for all, enabling sports associations and clubs to adapt to modern requirements and the market economy, and develop the role of local authorities.

Geographical Area of Activity: Countries of the former USSR.

How to Apply: Interested organizations should apply through the national Sports Ministries; co-financing for projects must be found.

Financial Information: Financed by the Sports Fund of the Council of Europe.

Contact: Contact Diane Murray.

Address: ave de l'Europe, 67000 Strasbourg, France.

Telephone: 3-88-41-35-42; *Internet:* www.coe.int/t/f/coop%e9ration%5fculturelle /sport; *e-mail:* diane.murray@coe.int.

YOUTH DIRECTORATE

European Youth Foundation

Established to demonstrate respect of fundamental freedoms and human rights; the Foundation supports voluntary youth work aimed at promoting mutual understanding, peace and co-operation among people from Europe and the rest of the world.

Activities: The Foundation operates through funding a range of activities related to voluntary youth work, including: documentation, research and studies on youth issues; cultural, educational, humanitarian or social activities at the European level; promotion, primarily through information exchange, of closer co-operation and better understanding among young people in Europe; activities strengthening co-operation and peace in Europe; and encouraging mutual aid in Europe and in developing countries for social, cultural and educational purposes.

Geographical Area of Activity: Europe and developing countries.

How to Apply: Applications can be submitted twice a year.

Financial Information: Annual budget €2,400,000.

Contact: Contact Bente Moller Poulsen.

Address: 30 rue Pierre de Coubertin, 67000 Strasbourg, France.

Telephone: 3-88-41-32-05; *Internet:* www.coe.fr/youth; *e-mail:* bente .moller-poulsen@coe.int.

European Youth Foundation—Action 1

Aims to promote youth co-operation in Europe.

Activities: Works to promote co-operation between young people in Europe through grants for international seminars, conferences, workshops, camps and festivals, organized by young people. Meetings must be organized by a local or national organization or network in partnership with at least three other organizations from different countries or with an international organization; and involve at least four countries. The events themselves must meet the work priorities of the Council of Europe, particularly its youth sector, and bring together participants, at least 75% of whom must be under the age of 30.

Geographical Area of Activity: International.

How to Apply: Grants are awarded twice a year; application forms are available from the Secretariat.

Financial Information: Annual budget €2,400,000 (2003); grants for up to two-thirds of the total cost of the project.

Contact: Contact Bente Moller Poulsen.

Address: 30 rue Pierre de Coubertin, 67000 Strasbourg, France.

Telephone: 3-88-41-32-05; *Internet:* www.coe.fr/youth; *e-mail:* bente .moller-poulsen@coe.int.

European Youth Foundation—Action 2

Aims to promote co-operation and mutual understanding between young people in Europe.

Activities: The programme works through grants to local, national and international organizations and networks operating in partnership and involving at least four countries. Funded activities include: specialist publications, information campaigns, studies and research projects on youth-related issues; production of posters, badges and stickers; development of websites and CD-ROMs; exhibitions or production of audio-visual materials; and newsletters or magazines.

Geographical Area of Activity: Europe.

How to Apply: Grants are awarded twice a year; application forms are available from the Secretariat.

Financial Information: Annual budget €2,400,000 (2003); grants for up to 75% of the total cost of the project.

Contact: Contact Bente Moller Poulsen.

Address: 30 rue Pierre de Coubertin, 67000 Strasbourg, France.

Telephone: 3-88-41-32-05; *Internet:* www.coe.fr/youth; *e-mail:* bente .moller-poulsen@coe.int.

European Youth Foundation—Action 3

Promotes youth co-operation in Europe.

Activities: Aims to develop youth co-operation in Europe through funding capacity building of NGOs, including functioning costs. To be eligible organizations must promote youth participation, have members in at least seven Council of Europe member states, and have received a project grant from the Foundation in the same year in which the application for an administrative grant is made.

Geographical Area of Activity: Europe.

How to Apply: Grants are awarded twice a year.

Financial Information: Annual budget €2,400,000 (2003).

Contact: Contact Bente Moller Poulsen.

Address: 30 rue Pierre de Coubertin, 67000 Strasbourg, France.

Telephone: 3-88-41-32-05; *Internet:* www.coe.fr/youth; *e-mail:* bente .moller-poulsen@coe.int.

European Youth Foundation—Action 4

The programme aims to adapt and open up projects and structures for societal changes, encourage new forms of youth participation and organization, help young people, in particular disadvantaged young people, find ways of meeting the challenges facing them, and contribute to social cohesion, especially by combating social exclusion and problems particularly affecting young people.

Activities: Grants are made to NGOs operating pilot projects in the above categories, and that contribute to youth participation; organize youth activities, by, with or for young people; use an innovative methodology; promote intercultural dialogue and understanding; and have a European dimension, either by involving more than one country and/or by taking the European context into consideration.

Geographical Area of Activity: Europe.

How to Apply: Grants are awarded twice a year; application forms are available from the Secretariat.

Financial Information: Annual budget €2,400,000 (2003); grants of up to 50% of the pilot projects are available.

Contact: Contact Bente Moller Poulsen.

Address: 30 rue Pierre de Coubertin, 67000 Strasbourg, France.

Telephone: 3-88-41-32-05; *Internet:* www.coe.fr/youth; *e-mail:* bente .moller-poulsen@coe.int.

East African Community (EAC)

Established in November 1999, EAC is the regional intergovernmental organization of the Republics of Kenya, Uganda and Tanzania. Its main institutions are the Summit of Heads of State and/or Government; Council of Ministers; Co-ordination Committee; Sectoral Committees; East African Court of Justice; East African Legislative Assembly; and the Secretariat.

Activities: Operates on the basis of a five-year Development Strategy which spells out the policy guide-lines, priority programmes and implementation schedules. The EAC strategy emphasizes socio-economic co-operation with the private sector and civil society in various areas, covering trade, investments and industrial development; monetary and fiscal affairs; infrastructure and services; human resources, science and technology; agriculture and food security; environment and natural resources management; tourism and wildlife management; and health, social and cultural activities. Partnerships developed with NGOs include the signing of a Memorandum of Understanding between EAC and the World Conservation Union (IUCN) under which the two organizations co-operate in the promotion and protection of the environment as well as in the sustainable use of natural resources.

Geographical Area of Activity: Kenya, Tanzania and Uganda.

Contact: Sec.-Gen. Nuwe Amanya-Mushega; Deputy Sec.-Gen., Projects and Programmes Dr Kipyego Cheluget; Deputy Sec.-Gen., Finance and Admin Ali Said Mchumo.

Address: Arusha International Conference Centre (AICC) Bldg, Kilimanjaro Wing, 5th Floor, POB 1096, Arusha, Tanzania.

Telephone: (27) 2504253; *Fax:* (27) 2504255; *Internet:* www.eachq.org; *e-mail:* each@eachq.org.

European Association for the Education of Adults (EAEA)

Founded in 1953 by representatives from a number of European countries, and originally known as the European Bureau of Adult Education, as a transnational, non-profit association. Aims to link and represent European organizations which are directly involved in adult learning, specifically NGOs whose principal aim is the education of adults. Membership includes around 100 organizations in 34 countries.

Activities: Promotes the development of adult learning and encourages co-operation in the field of adult learning at European level, primarily through support for NGOs and national co-ordinating bodies for adult learning. Also lobbies international bodies to adopt policies which respond to the needs of the adult population in Europe. Works in partnership with national and regional governments and international bodies and organizations such as the European Union, the Council of Europe, the International Council for Adult Education (ICAE), United Nations Educational, Scientific and Cultural Organization (UNESCO) and the International Labour Organization (ILO, qq.v.). Maintains additional offices in Girona (Spain), Helsinki (Finland) and Budapest (Hungary).

Geographical Area of Activity: Europe.

Financial Information: Annual budget €137,798 (2002).

Publications: Grundtvig—Message for the Future 2001; Focus on Lifelong Learning 2001; Newsletter.

Contact: Gen. Sec. Ellinor Haase.

Address: 27 rue Liedts, 1030 Brussels, Belgium.

Telephone: (2) 513-52-05; *Fax:* (2) 513-57-34; *Internet:* www.eaea.org; *e-mail:* eaea-main@eaea.org.

European Association for Renewable Energies (EUROSOLAR)

European Solar Prize

Aims to intensify the promotion of solar energy and create a new impetus for its widespread introduction.

Activities: Works to raise awareness of the subject of solar energy and to mobilize the public for a general solar energy movement. Solar Prizes are awarded for outstanding initiatives in the introduction and utilization of solar energy in the following categories: cities and municipalities, industrial and commercial enterprises, associations, solar architecture, media, education and special awards.

Geographical Area of Activity: European Union.

How to Apply: Applications can be made at any time.

Address: Kaiser-Friedrich-Str. 11, 53113 Bonn, Germany.

Telephone: (22) 8362373; *Internet:* www.eurosolar.org/new/index.shtml; *e-mail:* inter_office@eurosolar.org.

European Bank for Reconstruction and Development (EBRD)

The EBRD's mission is to foster market economies in a democratic context.

Activities: Operates in collaboration with local interest groups, NGOs, opinion-makers, business circles, academics, think-tanks, local authorities and other groups, which are encouraged to work with the EBRD, as well as with their own governments, to bring about positive change. The NGO team facilitates dialogue between the EBRD, and NGOs and communities.

Geographical Area of Activity: Europe.

Address: 1 Exchange Square, London EC2A 2JN, UK.

Telephone: (20) 7338-6868; *Fax:* (20) 7338-6102; *Internet:* www.ebrd.org; *e-mail:* ngo@ebrd.com.

ENERGY EFFICIENCY TEAM

Energy Efficiency

The EBRD's mission is to foster market economies in a democratic context; NGOs, opinion-makers, business circles, academics, think-tanks, local authorities and other groups are encouraged to work with the EBRD, as well as with their own governments, to bring about positive change. The NGO team facilitates dialogue between the EBRD and NGOs and communities. The Energy Efficiency programme aims to promote a better use of energy in the countries concerned through the implementation of new structures or restoration of existing equipment.

Activities: Promotes efficient energy use in the countries of Central and Eastern Europe, and the Commonwealth of Independent States (CIS), through the award of loans to NGOs, SMEs and companies. Funded activities include energy-efficient urban lighting systems, production of equipment and materials for efficient energy use, projects on renewable energy, investment in better energy management in hospitals, schools and public buildings, and improving the energy management systems in the production process in industrial companies. Small projects are invited to group together in order to obtain the minimum award of €5,000,000.

Geographical Area of Activity: Central and Eastern Europe, and CIS countries.

How to Apply: Applications can be made at any time.

Financial Information: Minimum award €5,000,000.

Contact: Contact Jacquelin Ligot.

Address: 1 Exchange Square, London EC2A 2JN, UK.

Telephone: (20) 7338-7096; *Internet:* http://europa.eu.int/comm/energy/en/fa_2_en .html; *e-mail:* ligotj@ebrd.com.

European Environment Agency (EEA)

ROYAL AWARDS FOUNDATION

Royal Awards for Sustainability

Founders include the European Environment Agency and the City of Copenhagen; named after the Foundation's two patrons: His Royal Highness Crown Prince Felipe of Spain and His Royal Highness Crown Prince Frederik of Denmark. The Foundation was formerly known as the Prince's Award Foundation.

Activities: Makes annual awards to environment and sustainable development projects, including the Royal Green Food Award which recognizes sustainable agriculture and healthy food initiatives and seeks to increase public awareness and promote participation in the move towards sustainable agricultural practices, the Royal Award for Urban Innovation in Waste Management, which is made to innovative achievements, interventions or projects that are currently in an advanced phase within the area of urban management in European cities.

Geographical Area of Activity: Europe.

Contact: Exec. Dir Mikael Backman; Project Mans Jakob Lund, Simon Storgaard.

Address: Kongens Nytorv 6, 1050 Copenhagen K, Denmark.

Telephone: 33-36-71-21; *Fax:* 33-36-71-99; *Internet:* www.royalawards.org.

European Greenways Association

European Greenways Award

The Award is part of the Joint European Award scheme, which aims to promote sustainable development by providing a platform for political debate and for the exchange of information and knowledge.

Activities: The European Greenways Award concerns greenways or innovative initiatives in this field covering all projects dealing with the implementation, management and maintenance, development, activities on and promotion of greenways. Fields of excellence recognized by the Award include networking, local participation, urban mobility and socio-economic impact; communication and urban integration; landscape treatment and greenway attractiveness; innovative technical solutions, exemplary management and maintenance; preservation, rehabilitation and enhancement of cultural and architectural heritage; services provided to users following user demands and expectations; exemplary promotion of public use of the greenway; and actions in favour of young people and children.

Geographical Area of Activity: European Union, Central and Eastern Europe, and Mediterranean countries.

How to Apply: Grants are awarded throughout the year; participation details are available from the Secretariat and on the website.

Contact: Contact Mr Callebaut.

Address: Gare de Namur, 5000 Namur, Belgium.

Telephone: (8) 122-42-56; *Fax:* (8) 122-90-02; *Internet:* www.aevv-egwa.org/new /french/aevv.html; *e-mail:* ac.louette@aevv-egwa.org.

European Union: African, Caribbean and Pacific (ACP) States

Following ratification of the Cotonou Agreement, a partnership agreement between ACP and the European Union in 2002, ACP put into place a programme for funding civil society organizations aiming to encourage their involvement in the mainstream of political, economic and social life.

Activities: Makes grants for capacity-building activities of civil society organizations and to improve the institutional framework necessary for social cohesion, for the functioning of a democratic society and market economy, and for the emergence of an active and organized civil society.

Geographical Area of Activity: Africa (excluding South Africa), Asia and the Pacific.

Address: 451 ave Georges Henri, 1200 Brussels, Belgium.

Telephone: (2) 743-06-00; *Fax:* (2) 735-55-73; *Internet:* www.acpsec.org; *e-mail:* info@acpsec.org.

ACP CULTURAL FOUNDATION

Established at the third summit meeting of Heads of State and Government of the African, Caribbean and Pacific Group of States (ACP) in Nadi, Fiji in July 2002.

Activities: Set up to support cultural initiatives and projects in the ACP region, in order to promote cultural development and its contribution to society.

Geographical Area of Activity: Africa (excluding South Africa), Asia and the Pacific.

Address: 451 ave Georges Henri, 1200 Brussels, Belgium.

Telephone: (2) 743-06-00; *Fax:* (2) 735-55-73; *Internet:* www.acpsec.org; *e-mail:* info@acpsec.org.

TECHNICAL CENTRE FOR AGRICULTURAL AND RURAL CO-OPERATION (CTA)

Established in 1983 under the Lomé Convention between the African, Caribbean and Pacific Group of States (ACP) and the European Union member states. Since 2000, CTA has operated within the framework of the ACP–European Communities Cotonou Agreement. CTA aims to develop and provide services that improve access to information for agricultural and rural development, and to strengthen the capacity of ACP countries to produce, acquire, exchange and utilize information in this area.

Activities: Programmes are organized around principal themes: developing information management and partnership strategies needed for policy formulation and implementation; promoting contact and exchange of experience; providing ACP partners with information on demand; and strengthening their information and communication capacities. Activities include distributing small grants of €5,000 through the GenARDIS fund, which was established to address gender issues in information and communications technologies in ACP agricultural and rural development.

Geographical Area of Activity: African, Caribbean and Pacific countries.

Address: Postbus 380, 6700 AJ Wageningen, Netherlands.

Telephone: (31) 746-71-00; *Fax:* (31) 746-00-67; *Internet:* www.agricta.org; *e-mail:* cta@cta.int.

European Union: European Commission

DIRECTORATE-GENERAL AGRICULTURE

European Structural Funds: European Agricultural Guidance and Guarantee Fund (EAGGF)

One of the four European Structural Funds and administered by DG Agriculture. EAGGF's Guidance section promotes the adjustment of agricultural structures and rural development measures within the context of the EC rural development policy, which recognizes a number of different roles played by farming, including the preservation of rural heritage. Also provides funding for the Leader+ (q.v.) Community Initiative.

Activities: The Fund promotes measures supporting farming income and the maintenance of viable farming communities in mountainous or less-favoured areas; start-up support for young farmers; improving the structural efficiency of holdings; encouraging the establishment of producers' associations; conversion, diversification, reorientation and improvement in the quality of agricultural production; development of rural infrastructure; encouragement of investment in tourism; and other measures, such as the prevention of natural disasters, village renewal, protection of the rural heritage, development and exploitation of woodland, protection of the environment and countryside, and financial engineering.

Geographical Area of Activity: European Union.

How to Apply: To apply for funding, organizations must contact the national authorities in the relevant country; application procedures vary according to national rules and regulations.

Contact: Contact Rudolf Strohmeier.

Address: 200 rue de la Loi, 1049 Brussels, Belgium.

Telephone: (2) 296-23-41; *Internet:* http://europa.eu.int/comm/agriculture /index_en.htm; *e-mail:* agri-library@cec.eu.int.

INTERREG III

The programme was established in 2000, as a Community Initiative funded by the European Regional Development Fund (q.v.), to strengthen economic and social cohesion in Europe and promote a balanced development in the European Union territory through co-operation activities. The programme is being further developed through the INTERACT programme (q.v.).

Activities: The programme is organized into three Strands: A, B and C (qq.v.). All projects must be clearly transnational, and be organized by at least two or more member states or concerned third countries. A project can only be organized in one member state if it can be demonstrated that there is a significant impact for other member states or third countries. The programme was to run from 2000–06.

Geographical Area of Activity: Europe.

Financial Information: Global budget €4,875,000,000 (2000–06); funding for up to 75% of total project costs is available in Objective 1 countries and up to 50% in other countries. Funded by the European Regional Development Fund.

Contact: Contact Moray Gilland.

Address: 200 rue de la Loi, 1049 Brussels, Belgium.

Telephone: (2) 296-92-89; *Internet:* http://europa.eu.int/comm/regional_policy /interreg3/index_fr.htm; *e-mail:* moray.gilland@cec.eu.int.

INTERREG III A

Part of the European Commission's INTERREG programme; aims to develop trans-frontier co-operation.

Activities: Promotes trans-frontier co-operation through support for common economic, social and trans-border strategies between neighbouring territorial authorities, in all countries located at the internal and external borders of the European Union, including some marine regions. Funded activities include promotion of rural, urban and coastal development; strengthening of entrepreneurship and the development of SMEs; promotion of social inclusion; exchange of human resources and equipment relating to research, teaching, culture, communication and health; support for environmental protection activities; infrastructure development; improved co-operation in the juridical and administrative fields; and the increase of human and institutional trans-border co-operation. The programme was to run from 2000–06.

Geographical Area of Activity: Europe.

Financial Information: Receives part of the INTERREG global budget of €4,875,000,000 (2000–06); between 50% and 75% of total project costs is available.

Contact: Contact Armando Miranda-Cardoso.

Address: 200 rue de la Loi, 1049 Brussels, Belgium.

Telephone: (2) 295-75-58; *Internet:* http://europa.eu.int/comm/regional_policy /interreg3/index_fr.htm; *e-mail:* armando.cardoso@cec.eu.int.

INTERREG III B

Part of the European Commission's INTERREG programme; aims to develop transnational co-operation.

Activities: The programme works to promote a better territorial integration between national, regional and local authorities within regions, in order to establish sustainable, harmonious and balanced development in the European Union and enhance a better integration with the candidate countries and other neighbouring countries. Funding is given for: the development of operational strategies for territorial development at the transnational level, including between cities or urban and rural zones, in order to promote sustainable development; promotion of efficient and sustainable transport systems and better access to the information society, particularly in insular or peripheral regions; and preservation of the environment and good management of natural resources, in particular water. For the regions classified as ultra-peripheral—French overseas departments, Canary Islands, Azores and Madeira—funded projects promote better economic integration and improved co-operation with other member states, and improvement of links and co-operation with neighbouring countries. The programme was to run from 2000–06.

Geographical Area of Activity: Europe.

Financial Information: Receives part of the INTERREG global budget of €4,875,000,000 (2000–06); grants for between 50% and 75% of total project costs are available.

Contact: Contact Mario Rodrigues.

Address: 200 rue de la Loi, 1049 Brussels, Belgium.

Telephone: (2) 296-94-34; *Internet:* http://europa.eu.int/comm/regional_policy /interreg3/index_fr.htm; *e-mail:* mario.rodrigues@cec.eu.int.

INTERREG III C

Part of the European Commission's INTERREG programme; aims to develop inter-regional co-operation.

Activities: Works to increase the efficiency of regional and cohesive development through funding for inter-regional co-operation activities, primarily through the exchange of best practices and networking. Three types of projects are funded: regional framework operations, proposals which consist of a minimum of three smaller projects submitted by a group of regions, which receive grants ranging from €500,000 to €5,000,000; individual inter-regional co-operation projects, aiming at transferring know-how and involving co-operation between at least three countries, which are eligible for grants of between €100,000 and €500,000; and networks of several regions inside and outside the European Union for exchange of implementation methods and development, with grants ranging from €200,000 to €1,000,000. Eligible subjects for project funding include research and technological development, technological development and SMEs, information society, tourism, culture and employment, entrepreneurship and the environment, maritime and coastal co-operation, insular and ultra-peripheral issues, and natural disasters. The programme was to run from 2000–06.

Geographical Area of Activity: Europe.

How to Apply: Priority is given to projects involving regions covered by the Objective 1 and 2 zones, urban development and dissemination of lessons learned from innovative initiatives.

Financial Information: Receives part of the INTERREG global budget of €4,875,000,000 (2000–06); between 50% and 75% of total project costs is available.

Contact: Contact Armando Miranda-Cardoso.

Address: 200 rue de la Loi, 1049 Brussels, Belgium.

Telephone: (2) 295-75-58; *Internet:* http://europa.eu.int/comm/regional_policy /interreg3/index_fr.htm; *e-mail:* armando.cardoso@cec.eu.int.

INTERREG: INTERACT

The programme was launched in 2003, and is part of the EC Initiative Programme INTERREG (q.v.). It is designed to capitalize on the vast pool of experience accumulated through INTERREG in the areas of regional development, cross-border co-operation, transnational co-operation and inter-regional co-operation.

Activities: The programme aims to contribute to the quality of the INTERREG Programme by enabling and encouraging the transfer of experiences and good practice between institutions and individuals in different geographical areas and by creating a platform for the development and establishment of common standards and procedures for the implementation of INTERREG Programmes. The programme was to run from 2002–06.

Geographical Area of Activity: Europe.

Financial Information: Global budget €25,000,000 (2002–06); funded by the EC Structural Funds.

Address: INTERACT Secretariat Vienna, OIR–Managementdienste GmbH, Franz-Josefs-Kai 27, 1010 Vienna, Austria.

Telephone: (1) 533-87-47-31; *Fax:* (1) 533-87-47-66; *Internet:* www.interact-online .net; *e-mail:* interact@oir.at.

Leader+

One of four Community Initiatives financed by European Structural Funds (q.v.), designed to help people in rural areas consider the long-term potential of their local region. The programme encourages the implementation of integrated, high-quality and original strategies for sustainable development, focusing on partnerships and networks of exchange of experience. Follows on from the Leader I and Leader II initiatives; plays a role as a laboratory which aims to encourage the emergence and testing of new approaches to integrated and sustainable development that will influence, complete and/or reinforce rural development policy in the Community.

Activities: The programme is structured around three actions, in addition to technical assistance: Action 1 provides support for integrated territorial development strategies of a pilot nature based on a bottom-up approach (86.75% of the total budget); Action 2 provides support for co-operation between rural territories (10% of the total budget); Action 3 supports networking activities (1.36% of the total budget); and technical assistance support (1.89% of the total budget). Priority areas for support are: making the best use of natural and cultural resources, including enhancing the value of sites; improving the quality of life in rural areas; adding value to local products, in particular by facilitating access to markets for small production units via collective actions; and the use of new know-how and new technologies to make products and services in rural areas more competitive. The beneficiaries of funding are Local Action Groups (LAGs), as well as other collective bodies. LAGs must consist of a balanced and representative selection of partners drawn from different socio-economic sectors in the territory concerned, including NGOs. The Leader+ initiative was to run from 2000–06.

Geographical Area of Activity: European Union.

How to Apply: Application details are available on the website.

Financial Information: Global budget €5,046,500,000 (2000–06); €2,105,100,000 provided by the European Agriculture Guidance and Guarantee Fund Guidance section and the remainder by public and private contributions.

Contact: Contact Rob Peters.

Address: Directorate F, Unit F3, Office L130, 6/197, 1049 Brussels, Belgium.

Telephone: (2) 296-26-24; *Internet:* http://europa.eu.int/comm/agriculture/rur /leaderplus/index_en.htm; *e-mail:* Bente.Munch@cec.eu.int.

Rural Development Programmes: European Agriculture Guidance and Guarantee Fund (EAGGF)

The Fund aims to strengthen the agriculture and forestry sector in developing countries, improve the competitiveness of rural areas and preserve the environmental and rural heritage.

Activities: The Fund supports the development of the agricultural and forestry sectors, through funding for the provision of services in rural areas, encouragement for tourism and craft activities, support for young farmers and vocational training, agri-environmental measures, development and optimal utilization of forests, and compensation for less-favoured areas. Member states are the direct beneficiaries of the Fund, but NGOs also benefit through the national authorities. The programme was to run from 2000–06.

Geographical Area of Activity: European Union.

How to Apply: Applications are co-ordinated through the national programmes, via rural information centres.

Financial Information: Global budget €30,000,000 (2000–06); in Objective 1 regions grants are available for up to 75% of the total project costs, for other regions the maximum amount of funding available is 50%.

Contact: Contact Patrice Baillieux.

Address: 200 rue de la Loi, 1049 Brussels, Belgium.

Telephone: (2) 295-69-61; *Internet:* http://europa.eu.int/comm/agriculture/rur/leg /index_en.htm; *e-mail:* patrice.baillieux@cec.eu.int.

DIRECTORATE-GENERAL DEVELOPMENT

EC–Prep European Community Poverty Reduction Effectiveness Programme

The Programme was established to enhance the European Community's development assistance through intensified collaboration between the European Commission and the UK government's Department for International Development (DFID); aims to halve the number of people living in poverty by 2015.

Activities: Operates through grant support to research projects and studies in the focus areas of European development policy. Priority areas are trade and development, regional migration and co-operation, macro-economic support and equitable access to social services, transport, food security and sustainable rural development, and institutional capacity building. Research focusing on cross-sectoral issues such as human rights, environment, gender, governance, conflict prevention and crisis management related to poverty eradication is also eligible for funding.

Geographical Area of Activity: Africa (excluding South Africa), Asia, Central and South America and the Caribbean, European Union (EU), and other developing countries.

Restrictions: Non-EU-based institutions must make a joint application with an EU partner.

How to Apply: Grants are awarded twice yearly; the selection procedure is organized by consultants Deloitte and Touche.

Financial Information: Annual budget €3,200,000; grants available range from €50,000 to €160,000.

Contact: Contact Françoise Moireau.

Address: 200 rue de la Loi, 1049 Brussels, Belgium.

Telephone: (2) 299-32-00; *Internet:* www.ec-prep.org; *e-mail:* francoise.moreau@cec.eu.int.

Information Unit: Lorenzo Natali Prize for Journalism

Established to reward a journalist or publication for their distinguished efforts to defend human rights and democracy in developing countries, and to encourage the press to write about development and inform the public both in developing countries and in Europe.

Activities: The annual awards are distributed to independent journalists or publications promoting the fight for human rights and democracy in the developing world; selection criteria are that articles must address democracy or human rights as vital elements of development; and must have been published in a European publication or a publication from a developing country.

Geographical Area of Activity: International; developing countries.

Restrictions: Articles written by EC members of staff are not eligible.

How to Apply: The prizes are awarded annually in the spring.

Financial Information: Annual budget €20,000 (2003); two annual prizes of €10,000.

Contact: Contact Maria-Rosa de Paolis.

Address: 200 rue de la Loi, 1049 Brussels, Belgium.

Telephone: (2) 299-30-65; *Internet:* http://europa.eu.int/comm/development /events_2003_en.cfm; *e-mail:* maria-rosa.de-paolis@cec.eu.int.

Raising Awareness of Development Issues

Established to promote audiovisual productions likely to contribute to a better understanding in Europe of the realities of the developing world and of the need for North–South co-operation.

Activities: Support is given for audiovisual productions targeted at as wide an audience as possible, with preference given to productions designed for TV broadcasting and likely to appeal to a non-specialist audience. Productions can include documentaries, educational programmes or programmes aimed at young people, current affairs programmes, magazines and short feature films, on any subject relating to the developing world and North–South co-operation in the economic, social and cultural fields.

Geographical Area of Activity: Developing countries.

Restrictions: No funding for long feature films, nor for political topics or purely ethnographical documentaries.

How to Apply: Grants are awarded annually.

Financial Information: Annual budget €1,000,000 (2003); grants range from €75,000 to €150,000, up to 25% of the total project costs.

Contact: Contact Jacques Goedertier.

Address: 200 rue de la Loi, DG Development A5, 1049 Brussels, Belgium.

Telephone: (2) 296-26-43; *Internet:* http://europa.eu.int/comm/development /index_en.cfm; *e-mail:* jacques.goedertier@cec.eu.int.

DIRECTORATE-GENERAL EDUCATION AND CULTURE

EC–Canada Co-operation in Higher Education

Aims to develop mutual co-operation in languages, culture and institutions between countries in the European Union and Canada, improve the quality of the development of human resources, improve the quality of transatlantic student mobility, encourage the exchange of skills relating to recent innovations in higher education and training establishments, particularly training in new technologies, and create and consolidate partnerships between higher education institutions, trade associations, the public sector and other relevant authorities.

Activities: The programme operates through funding student partnerships and exchange programmes for students, teachers and administrative staff; joint development of curricula and teaching materials; intensive courses; and teaching assignments in a partner institution. Multilateral partnerships must involve at least three active partners in the EC and three in Canada. The programme was to run from 2001–05.

Geographical Area of Activity: Canada and Europe.

Financial Information: Global budget €3,650,000; grants of up to €100,000 for a three-year project; student mobility grants of €12,000 per partner.

Contact: Contact Nicole Versijp.

Address: 200 rue de la Loi, DG Education and Culture A5, 1049 Brussels, Belgium.

Telephone: (2) 296-66-64; *Internet:* http://europa.eu.int/comm/education/Canada /Canada.html; *e-mail:* nicole.versijp@cec.eu.int.

EC–USA Co-operation in Higher Education

Established to promote mutual co-operation between the European Union (EU) and the USA, to improve the quality of the development of human resources and encourage the exchange of competencies, in particular relating to training in new technologies and tele-teaching and the consolidation and creation of partnerships between higher education institutions, training establishments, trade associations, public authorities, the business sector, and other relevant organizations, in the EU and USA.

Activities: Promotes transatlantic co-operation in the fields of higher education and vocational training, through grants for multilateral partnerships, including exchange programmes, joint development of curricula and teaching materials, intensive courses, teaching assignments in partner institutions, and development of international study programmes. Also operates the Fulbright–EU programme, providing six study grants each year for research and lecturing on EU affairs and EU–US relations. Each multilateral partnership must involve at least three active partners in the EU and three in the USA. The programme was to run from 2001–05.

Geographical Area of Activity: Europe and the USA.

How to Apply: Grants are distributed on an annual basis.

Financial Information: Annual budget €3,500,000; grants of €100,000 for a three-year project; student mobility grants of €10,000.

Contact: Contact Augusto Gonzalez.

Address: 200 rue de la Loi, DG Education and Culture A5, 1049 Brussels, Belgium.

Telephone: (2) 296-63-19; *Internet:* http://europa.eu.int/comm/education/ec-usa /usa.html; *e-mail:* augusto.gonzalez@cec.eu.int.

Leonardo da Vinci–2 Pilot Projects

Part of the Leonardo da Vinci programme, established in 2000, promoting professional training. This strand of the overall programme aims to support transnational pilot projects in the field of professional training.

Activities: The programme operates through grants to transnational pilot projects for the development and dissemination of innovation and quality in the field of professional training, including the use of information and communications technologies. Grants are made for the development, establishment and evaluation of pilot projects concerning development and/or dissemination of innovation in the field of professional training, and the development of the quality of professional training in the context of life-long learning. Themes covered by the projects are development of new methods promoting transparency, support for people disadvantaged in the job market, and the development of professional training within companies.

Geographical Area of Activity: Europe.

How to Apply: The project is evaluated at both national level and EC level.

Financial Information: Receives part of the Leonardo da Vinci overall budget of €1,150,000,000; maximum grant €300,000, up to 75% of the costs of the project.

Contact: Contact Marta Ferreira.

Address: 200 rue de la Loi, DG Education and Culture B2, 1049 Brussels, Belgium.

Telephone: (2) 296-26-58; *Internet:* http://europa.eu.int/comm/education/leonardo .html; *e-mail:* leonardo@cec.eu.int.

Leonardo da Vinci–3 Language Competencies

Part of the Leonardo da Vinci programme, established in 2000, promoting professional training. This strand of the overall programme aims to promote linguistic competency in the context of professional training.

Activities: The programme makes grants to transnational projects, including pilot projects, which aim to develop linguistic competence in the area of professional training, particularly where it concerns less well-known and less used languages. Projects should cover the development, evaluation and dissemination of pedagogical methods adapted to the specific needs of the professional and economic sector.

Geographical Area of Activity: Europe.

How to Apply: The project is evaluated at both national level and EC level; support for projects can last for up to three years.

Financial Information: Receives part of the Leonardo da Vinci overall budget of €1,150,000,000; maximum grant €200,000.

Contact: Contact Marta Ferreira.

Address: 200 rue de la Loi, DG Education and Culture B2, 1049 Brussels, Belgium.

Telephone: (2) 296-26-58; *Internet:* http://europa.eu.int/comm/education/leonardo .html; *e-mail:* leonardo@cec.eu.int.

Leonardo da Vinci–4 Transnational Networks

Part of the Leonardo da Vinci programme, established in 2000, promoting professional training. This strand of the overall programme aims to promote transnational networks.

Activities: The programme aims to develop competencies and innovative approaches, improve the analysis and forecast of needs in terms of professional qualifications, and disseminate network experiences. Eligible organizations include local authorities, chambers of commerce, employees and employers' organizations, universities and research organizations.

Geographical Area of Activity: Europe.

How to Apply: The project is evaluated at both national level and EC level; support for projects can last for up to three years.

Financial Information: Receives part of the Leonardo da Vinci overall budget of €1,150,000,000; maximum grant €150,000, up to 50% of the total cost of the project.

Contact: Contact Marta Ferreira.

Address: 200 rue de la Loi, DG Education and Culture B2, 1049 Brussels, Belgium.

Telephone: (2) 296-26-58; *Internet:* http://europa.eu.int/comm/education/leonardo .html; *e-mail:* leonardo@cec.eu.int.

Observation and Analysis: Socrates II—Observation and Innovation

Part of the Socrates II (q.v.) programme; aims to promote studies and analysis relating to educational policies and systems.

Activities: This strand of the Socrates II programme aims to improve the quality and transparency of education systems, and to further the process of educational innovation in Europe through the exchange of information and experience, the identification of good practice, the comparative analysis of policies and systems in this field, and the discussion and analysis of matters of common educational policy. Funding is provided for: the observation of educational systems, policies and innovation; support for studies, analyses, pilot projects, seminars, and exchanges of experts; the organization of and participation in ARION (q.v.) multilateral study visits; the educational network Eurydice; the recognition of diplomas, qualifications and periods of learning, including studies, pilot projects, analyses and the exchange of information and experience, and the NARIC network of national academic recognition information centres; and for innovative initiatives responding to emerging needs, including transnational projects and studies aimed at developing innovation in one or more specific fields of education. The programme was to run from 2000–06.

Geographical Area of Activity: Europe.

How to Apply: Applications should be sent directly to the European Commission.

Financial Information: Annual budget €1,300,000; maximum annual grant €300,000, up to 50% of the total project costs.

Contact: Contact Olivier Brunet.

Address: 200 rue de la Loi, DG Education and Culture A4, 1049 Brussels, Belgium.

Telephone: (2) 295-10-61; *Internet:* http://europa.eu.int/comm/education/socrates /observation/intro_en.html; *e-mail:* olivier.brunet@cec.eu.int.

Partnerships with Civil Society: Projects Organized by Associations and Federations of European Interest

The programme aims to strengthen the dialogue between the European Union (EU) and its citizens with a view to encouraging the emergence of an active and participatory European citizenship and the networking of civil society organizations.

Activities: Operates through awarding grants for debate and reflection projects organized by associations and federations of European interest, to cover the costs of activities and projects with a European focus carried out by these organizations. Eligible themes include the ethnical and spiritual values of European integration, European governance, Europe's cultural diversity and European citizenship.

Geographical Area of Activity: EU.

How to Apply: Selection of beneficiaries is made once a year.. The application proposal must include a programme of the annual activities of the applicant organization, a staff listing including their responsibilities, a list of other funders, and accounts.

Financial Information: Total budget €1,260,000 (2003); maximum grant €25,000, up to 60% of the total project costs.

Contact: Contact Anne-Michele Van Der Elst.

Address: 200 rue de la Loi, DG Education and Culture D2, 1049 Brussels, Belgium.

Telephone: (2) 299-91-58; *Internet:* http://europa.eu.int/infonet/civil_en.htm; *e-mail:* eac-soc-civile@cec.eu.int.

Partnerships with Civil Society: Support for European projects concerning debates between non-governmental organizations

Established to encourage information campaigns and other awareness-raising projects undertaken by various civil society organizations.

Activities: Provides funding to NGOs to enable information and communication projects on a range of issues, including combating unemployment, protecting the environment, promoting equality between men and women, providing aid to developing countries and countering social exclusion and poverty. Funding is provided for seminars, conferences, publications, software products, radio and television broadcasts and the development of networks of NGOs.

Geographical Area of Activity: Europe.

Restrictions: No funding for ongoing costs, overheads, capital investment, or charges for financial services.

How to Apply: Application forms are available on the website.

Financial Information: Annual budget €1,500,000 (2003).

Contact: Contact Anne-Michele Van Der Elst.

Address: VM-2, 4/52, DG Education and Culture D2, 1049 Brussels, Belgium.

Telephone: (2) 299-91-58; *Internet:* http://europa.eu.int/infonet/civil_en.htm; *e-mail:* eac-soc-civile@cec.eu.int.

Preparatory Actions for Co-operation on Cultural Matters

The programme aims to contribute to the creation and/or strengthening of European networks and co-operation platforms, provide for a wide dissemination of results and facilitate the exchange of experiences and good practice in the field of culture.

Activities: Grants are available to projects involving a degree of experimentation, which can serve as the basis for future actions, operated within a European Union (EU) member state. There are four themes under which grants are made: co-operation between member states, including pilot projects, seminars, exchanges of experts and other appropriate actions aimed at improving knowledge and facilitating an innovative exchange of expertise and experience in the field of cultural policy; direct co-operation between cultural operators in countries participating in the cultural programmes, including funding for co-operation activities that encourage structured and lasting co-operation based on efficient management and expertise in terms of content, through umbrella structures; cultural industries involving co-operation activities between the largest number of professional organizations, state or semi-state authorities and operators in the music or publishing sectors; and education and culture, including the development and implementation of methods of teaching music at school, dissemination of the European music culture to children or young people, projects aimed at comparing the education programmes of different conservatoires, development of teaching tools, exchange of good practices between schools, and co-operation projects between exhibition centres and schools, libraries or cultural centres, for work on the visual image.

Geographical Area of Activity: EU.

How to Apply: Application details are available on the website.

Financial Information: Global budget €1,600,000 (2003); grants range from €100,000 to €350,000.

Contact: Contact Fabienne Metayer.

Address: 200 rue de la Loi, DG Education and Culture C2, 1049 Brussels, Belgium.

Telephone: (2) 299-86-43; *Internet:* http://europa.eu.int/eur-lex/en/dat/2003/c_217 /c_21720030912en00070020.pdf; *e-mail:* fabienne.metayer@cec.eu.int.

Socrates II—Accompanying measures

Part of the Socrates II programme (q.v.); established to fund projects and activities that do not fit into any of the specific programme strands of Socrates II.

Activities: Aims to raise awareness of the importance of European co-operation in the field of education, through grants for information and dissemination activities, including: the introduction or strengthening of the European dimension in education; preparation, production or dissemination of pedagogical material dealing with European themes; specific publications related to European co-operation, with an emphasis on the innovative use of new technologies, promotion of equality of opportunity for men and women, and meeting the specific needs of people with disabilities; creation or strengthening of European associations; conferences and seminars addressing European co-operation in the field of education; dissemination and exchange of information about innovative methods of promoting education and the teaching of foreign languages; use of new information technologies for improving European co-operation in the field of education, for example, the teaching of art; and co-operation in the field of research. The programme is open to applications from candidate and associated countries.

Geographical Area of Activity: Europe.

How to Apply: Grants awarded annually.

Financial Information: Receives part of the programme's overall budget of €1,850,000,000; grants available for up to 50% of the project's total costs.

Contact: Contact Anders Hingel.

Address: 200 rue de la Loi, DG Education and Culture A4, 1049 Brussels, Belgium.

Telephone: (2) 296-39-88; *Internet:* http://europa.eu.int/comm/education/socrates /action8.html; *e-mail:* anders.hingel@cec.eu.int.

Socrates II—COMENIUS

Established as part of the Socrates II programme (q.v.) to promote co-operation in the field of school education at all levels.

Activities: Aims to encourage transnational co-operation between schools, improve initial and in-service training of staff involved in the school education sector, and promote language learning and intercultural awareness. Operates through three separate programmes: COMENIUS 1, COMENIUS 2 and COMENIUS 3 (qq.v.). School partnerships must involve at least three partner institutions from different countries.

Geographical Area of Activity: Europe.

How to Apply: Applications must be sent to the relevant Socrates agency; grants are awarded annually.

Financial Information: Receives part of the global Socrates programme budget of €1,850,000,000.

Contact: Contact Bertrand Delpeuch.

Address: 200 rue de la Loi, DG Education and Culture A3, 1049 Brussels, Belgium.

Telephone: (2) 296-87-11; *Internet:* http://europa.eu.int/comm/education/socrates /comenius/index.html; *e-mail:* bertrand.delpeuch@cec.eu.int.

Socrates II—COMENIUS 1

A strand of the COMENIUS initiative, which forms part of the Socrates II programme (q.v.); aims to support transnational school partnerships and the development of transnational co-operation projects.

Activities: Under the programme, grants are available primarily to support co-operation between schools, including transnational school partnerships bringing together pupils and teachers from at least three different countries; language projects, seeking to motivate young people and increase their capacity to speak foreign languages; school development projects, aiming to link school managers and teachers for the exchange of information on a variety of issues, including educating children of migrant workers, Roma (gypsies) and travellers, pupils at risk of social exclusion, and pupils with special educational needs; and language assistant hosting. Funding is also available for preparatory visits.

Geographical Area of Activity: Europe.

How to Apply: Applications must be sent to the relevant Socrates agency; grants are awarded annually.

Financial Information: Receives part of the global Socrates programme budget of €1,850,000,000.

Contact: Contact Bertrand Delpeuch.

Address: 200 rue de la Loi, DG Education and Culture A3, 1049 Brussels, Belgium.

Telephone: (2) 296-87-11; *Internet:* http://europa.eu.int/comm/education/socrates /comenius/index.html; *e-mail:* bertrand.delpeuch@cec.eu.int.

Socrates II—COMENIUS 2

Established as part of the Socrates II programme (q.v.), to promote initial and in-service training for educational staff.

Activities: This strand of the Socrates programme aims to contribute to the professional development of educational staff by supporting European in-service training projects through strengthening the European dimension of the in-service training of teachers, promoting European co-operation between schools, and promoting intercultural activities within schools. Grants are given for in-service training courses, initial teacher training, language assistantships, study programmes, curriculum development and pedagogical strategy development.

Geographical Area of Activity: European Union, and candidate and associated countries.

How to Apply: Applications can be sent to the relevant Socrates agency or to the European Commission; grants are awarded annually.

Financial Information: Receives part of the global Socrates programme budget of €1,850,000,000; annual grants are available for between €20,000 and €100,000.

Contact: Contact Bertrand Delpeuch.

Address: 200 rue de la Loi, DG Education and Culture A3, 1049 Brussels, Belgium.

Telephone: (2) 296-87-11; *Internet:* http://europa.eu.int/comm/education/socrates /comenius/index.html; *e-mail:* bertrand.delpeuch@cec.eu.int.

Socrates II—COMENIUS 3

Established as part of the Socrates II programme (q.v.), to promote networking between schools.

Activities: Aims to enhance networking in order to promote co-operation and innovation at school level, to enable schools to consolidate their European co-operation beyond EC funding and to promote innovation and best practice. Funding is provided for the exchange of information, training of co-ordinators, promotion activities and comparative analysis, and the organization of working groups, seminars and conferences. Priority fields for support are information technologies, language learning, art education, environmental education, combating violence at school, racism and xenophobia, and the education of specific target groups.

Geographical Area of Activity: European Union, and candidate and associated countries.

How to Apply: Grants are awarded annually; pre-selection in March, final selection in November. Applications must be sent to the European Commission via the Socrates Technical Assistance Office.

Financial Information: Receives part of the global Socrates programme budget of €1,850,000,000; annual grants are available for between €50,000 and €150,000.

Contact: Contact Bertrand Delpeuch.

Address: 200 rue de la Loi, DG Education and Culture A3, 1049 Brussels, Belgium.

Telephone: (2) 296-87-11; *Internet:* http://europa.eu.int/comm/education/socrates /comenius/index.html; *e-mail:* bertrand.delpeuch@cec.eu.int.

Socrates II—ERASMUS

A strand of the Socrates II programme (q.v.); aims to promote European co-operation in the field of higher education, and to improve transparency and the academic recognition of studies carried out abroad.

Activities: Operates through three separate programmes: ERASMUS 1 (q.v.), ERASMUS 2 and ERASMUS 3 (q.v.).

Geographical Area of Activity: Europe.

How to Apply: Applications can be submitted to the national Socrates agency in the country concerned or directly to the European Commission.

Financial Information: Receives part of the Socrates II global programme budget of €1,850,000,000.

Contact: Contact Hilde Brandt.

Address: 200 rue de la Loi, DG Education and Culture A2, 1049 Brussels, Belgium.

Telephone: (2) 299-63-80; *Internet:* http://europa.eu.int/comm/education/erasmus .html; *e-mail:* holger.helrer@cec.eu.int.

72

Socrates II—ERASMUS 1

Part of the ERASMUS programme (q.v.), aiming to promote universities' European activities.

Activities: Promotes European-wide activities by universities through grants to universities to develop their European strategy, including: organization of students' and teachers' mobility; intensive programmes bringing together students and staff from different countries to obtain new perspectives and to compare and test teaching methods in an international classroom environment; preparatory visits to develop future co-operation initiatives; curriculum development activities; integrated language courses; and the introduction of the European Credit Transfer System, a method of academic credit allocation.

Geographical Area of Activity: European Union, and candidate and associated countries.

How to Apply: Applications are sent to the European Commission via the national Socrates technical offices.

Financial Information: Receives part of the Socrates II global programme budget of €1,850,000,000.

Contact: Contact Holger Helrer.

Address: 200 rue de la Loi, DG Education and Culture A2, 1049 Brussels, Belgium.

Telephone: (2) 299-19-46; *Internet:* http://europa.eu.int/comm/education/erasmus .html; *e-mail:* holger.helrer@cec.eu.int.

Socrates II—ERASMUS 3

Part of the ERASMUS programme (q.v.), aiming to create thematic networks to improve quality in higher education.

Activities: Aims to develop thematic networks that define and develop a European dimension within a given academic discipline or within other areas of common interest, including administrative issues, through co-operation activities between university faculties and departments, academic or professional associations and other partners. Thematic network projects receiving support concern the development of the European dimension within specific disciplines or frameworks of subjects of mutual interest, leading to curriculum development or other results with a significant impact on a large number of universities.

Geographical Area of Activity: European Union, and candidate and associated countries.

How to Apply: Applications are sent to the European Commission via the national Socrates technical offices; grants are awarded twice a year.

Financial Information: Receives part of the Socrates II global programme budget of €1,850,000,000; average grant €75,000.

Contact: Contact Ettore Deodato.

Address: 200 rue de la Loi, DG Education and Culture A2, 1049 Brussels, Belgium.

Telephone: (2) 296-39-89; *Internet:* http://europe.eu.int/comm/education/erasmus .html; *e-mail:* ettore.deodato@cec.eu.int.

Socrates II—GRUNDTVIG

A strand of the Socrates II (q.v.) programme; aims to promote adult education and other alternative forms of education, through the promotion of life-long learning on a European level through transnational co-operation projects.

Activities: Operates through four sub-programmes; GRUNDTVIG 1 for transnational co-operation projects; GRUNDTVIG 2 for learning partnerships; GRUNDTVIG 3 for mobility projects for the training of educational staff; and GRUNDTVIG 4 to develop network activities (qq.v.).

Geographical Area of Activity: European Union, and candidate and associated countries.

How to Apply: Co-financing must be found for all four sub-programmes.

Financial Information: Receives part of the Socrates II global programme budget of €1,850,000,000.

Contact: Contact Alan Smith.

Address: 200 rue de la Loi, DG Education and Culture A1, 1049 Brussels, Belgium.

Telephone: (2) 295-83-82; *Internet:* http://europa.eu.int/comm/education/socrates/adult/home.html; *e-mail:* alan.smith@cec.eu.int.

Socrates II—GRUNDTVIG 1

Part of the GRUNDTVIG (q.v.) strand of the Socrates II (q.v.) programme; promotes European co-operation projects in adult education.

Activities: Supports transnational co-operation projects in the field of adult education, where institutions and organizations work together, pooling knowledge and experience, in order to achieve concrete and innovative results with European-wide value. Supported projects include pilot activities in strategic areas or teaching tools, priorities including promoting access and individual demand for adult education and life-long learning; developing information and support services for adult learners, including guidance and counselling; elaborating methods of accreditation and recognition of skills and competencies; improving the teaching and learning of European languages and the appreciation of different European cultures; and the development of information and communication technology in the field of adult education, including e-learning.

Geographical Area of Activity: European Union, and candidate and associated countries.

How to Apply: Applications are sent to the European Commission via the national Socrates technical offices.

Financial Information: Receives part of the Socrates II global programme budget of €1,850,000,000; grants range from €50,000 to €150,000 a year.

Contact: Contact Alan Smith.

Address: 200 rue de la Loi, DG Education and Culture A4, 1049 Brussels, Belgium.

Telephone: (2) 295-83-82; *Internet:* http://europa.eu.int/comm/education/socrates/adult/home.html; *e-mail:* alan.smith@cec.eu.int.

Socrates II—GRUNDTVIG 2

Part of the GRUNDTVIG (q.v.) strand of the Socrates II (q.v.) programme; promotes learning partnerships in the field of adult education.

Activities: Provides a framework for the development of small-scale co-operation activities between organizations working in the field of adult education, focusing on the process of adult education. Aims to broaden the participation of smaller organizations that want to include European co-operation in their educational activities. Funding is provided for meetings between partner organizations, staff exchanges, conception of art works, cultural performances, publication and distribution of documentation about co-operation activities, organization of exhibitions and the production and dissemination of information materials, language preparation, and co-operation with other projects.

Geographical Area of Activity: European Union, and candidate and associated countries.

How to Apply: Applications are sent to the European Commission via the national Socrates technical offices.

Financial Information: Receives part of the Socrates II global programme budget of €1,850,000,000.

Contact: Contact Alan Smith.

Address: 200 rue de la Loi, DG Education and Culture A4, 1049 Brussels, Belgium.

Telephone: (2) 295-83-82; *Internet:* http://europa.eu.int/comm/education/socrates /adult/home.html; *e-mail:* alan.smith@cec.eu.int.

Socrates II—GRUNDTVIG 3

Part of the GRUNDTVIG (q.v.) strand of the Socrates II (q.v.) programme; promotes the mobility of training for educational staff in the field of adult education.

Activities: Aims to improve the quality of adult education through facilitating transnational training for educational staff working with adults, in order to promote understanding of life-long learning in Europe and to improve practical teaching, coaching and counselling skills. The programme is open to adult education providers in both the formal and non-formal education system, including community schools; universities carrying out research and/or curriculum development activities in the field of adult education or providing educational opportunities for adult learners; organizations training adult education staff; and non-formal education providers for adults, including NGOs, trade unions, libraries and museums.

Geographical Area of Activity: European Union, and candidate and associated countries.

How to Apply: Applications are sent to the European Commission via the national Socrates technical offices; co-financing must be found.

Financial Information: Receives part of the Socrates II global programme budget of €1,850,000,000.

Contact: Contact Alan Smith.

Address: 200 rue de la Loi, DG Education and Culture A4, 1049 Brussels, Belgium.
Telephone: (2) 295-83-82; *Internet:* http://europa.eu.int/comm/education/socrates
/adult/home.html; *e-mail:* alan.smith@cec.eu.int.

Socrates II—GRUNDTVIG 4

Part of the GRUNDTVIG (q.v.) strand of the Socrates II (q.v.) programme; promotes the development of co-operation networks in the field of adult education.

Activities: Aims to strengthen the links between the different partners involved in adult education to enable long-term stable co-operation and to enhance their understanding of the European dimension of life-long learning. The focus for funding is on two types of networks: thematic networks, which aim to provide a forum for discussion and exchanges on key issues, policy development and research in the area of adult learning; and project networks, which aims to provide a basis for continuing contact between institutions that have participated in past projects and for the dissemination of project results. Funding is provided for the organization of seminars and conferences, information dissemination, comparative studies and recommendations, and project training and management. Networks must involve at least six countries participating in the Socrates project, with at least one partner from a European Union (EU) member state.

Geographical Area of Activity: EU, and candidate and associated countries.

How to Apply: Applications are sent to the European Commission via the national Socrates technical offices; co-financing must be found.

Financial Information: Receives part of the Socrates II global programme budget of €1,850,000,000; grants range from €50,000 to €150,000 a year.

Contact: Contact Alan Smith.

Address: 200 rue de la Loi, DG Education and Culture A4, 1049 Brussels, Belgium.
Telephone: (2) 295-83-82; *Internet:* http://europa.eu.int/comm/education/socrates
/adult/home.html; *e-mail:* alan.smith@cec.eu.int.

Socrates II—LINGUA

A strand of the Socrates II (q.v.) programme; aims to improve language teaching and quantitative and qualitative learning.

Activities: Aims to encourage and support linguistic diversity throughout the European Union (EU), to improve the quality of language teaching and learning, and to promote access to life-long learning opportunities appropriate to each individual's needs. Operates through two sub-programmes; LINGUA 1 for the promotion of language learning; and LINGUA 2, for the development of instruments for language learning and the teaching and assessment of linguistic skills. All official European Community languages are recognized under the programme, as well as Irish and Luxemburgish and the languages of the European Free Trade Association/European Economic Area countries and the pre-accession countries participating in the programme. Priority is given to the development of skills in the less widely used and less widely taught official Community languages.

Geographical Area of Activity: EU, and candidate and associated countries.

How to Apply: Applications are sent to the European Commission via the national Socrates technical offices.

Financial Information: Receives part of the Socrates II global programme budget of €1,850,000,000.

Contact: Contact Sylvia Vlaeminck.

Address: 200 rue de la Loi, DG Education and Culture B4, 1049 Brussels, Belgium.

Telephone: (2) 295-53-85; *Internet:* http://europa.eu.int/comm/education/socrates /lingua.html; *e-mail:* sylvia.vlaeminck@cec.eu.int.

Socrates II—LINGUA 1

A strand of the Socrates II (q.v.) programme; aims to improve language learning through transnational co-operation.

Activities: This strand of the programme aims to raise citizens' awareness of the multilingual character of the European Union (EU) and the advantages of life-long learning, to improve access to language learning resources and increase the support to those learning languages, and to promote the dissemination of information about innovative techniques and good practice in foreign language teaching in Europe among target groups, primarily decision-makers and key educational professionals. Funding is provided for projects raising awareness of the advantages of language learning; initiatives motivating individuals to learn languages; the provision of information on the means and methods available for language learning, including multilingual comprehension and partial competence; facilitating access to language learning; and the exchange and dissemination of information amongst information policy-makers on innovative approaches and key issues in language teaching. Partners must be from three different countries and grants are also available for week-long preparatory visits.

Geographical Area of Activity: EU, and candidate and associated countries.

How to Apply: Applications are sent to the European Commission via the national Socrates technical offices; co-financing must be found. Funded projects cannot last for more than three years.

Financial Information: Receives part of the Socrates II global programme budget of €1,850,000,000.

Contact: Contact Sylvia Vlaeminck.

Address: 200 rue de la Loi, DG Education and Culture B4, 1049 Brussels, Belgium.

Telephone: (2) 295-53-85; *Internet:* http://europa.eu.int/comm/education/socrates /lingua.html; *e-mail:* sylvia.vlaeminck@cec.eu.int.

Socrates II—LINGUA 2

A strand of the Socrates II (q.v.) programme; aims to develop instruments for language learning and teaching and the assessment of linguistic skills.

Activities: The programme aims to: encourage innovation in the development of language learning and teaching tools and for evaluating language learning; encourage the sharing of best practice; provide a wider variety of teaching materials to more clearly defined target groups; encourage the production of language tools for the less widely used and less widely taught languages; support educational approaches that are commercially under-represented or difficult to market on a large scale; encourage the acquisition of sufficient knowledge of foreign languages to meet the requirements of particular situations and contexts; and improve the distribution and availability of products. Funding is provided to projects that either create, refine, adapt or exchange educational media and materials, methods and tools designed to recognize and evaluate language skills, and teaching and study programmes. Priority is given to projects that concern one or more of the needs explored in the EC survey on the development of European language materials for language learning and teaching.

Geographical Area of Activity: European Union, and candidate and associated countries.

How to Apply: Applications are sent to the European Commission via the national Socrates technical offices.

Financial Information: Receives part of the Socrates II global programme budget of €1,850,000,000.

Publications: EC survey available at http://europa.eu.int/comm/education /languages/download/survey.html.

Contact: Contact Sylvia Vlaeminck.

Address: 200 rue de la Loi, DG Education and Culture B4, 1049 Brussels, Belgium.

Telephone: (2) 295-53-85; *Internet:* http://europa.eu.int/comm/education/socrates /lingua.html; *e-mail:* sylvia.vlaeminck@cec.eu.int.

Socrates II—MINERVA

A strand of the Socrates II (q.v.) programme; aims to promote co-operation activities in the field of open and distance learning, and in the use of information and communications technologies in the field of education policy.

Activities: This strand aims to: raise awareness of teachers, students, decision-makers and the public about the impact of open and distance learning and information and communications technologies (ICT) on education; ensure pedagogical considerations are taken into account in the development of didactic products and education services based on ICT and multimedia; and promote access to pedagogical methods and resources as well as to results and good practice in the field. Funding is provided to projects working to promote the understanding of innovation; the conception, development and experimentation in new methods and pedagogical resources; the promotion of access to projects' results and their dissemination; and for activities aiming to enhance the exchange of ideas and experiences.

Geographical Area of Activity: European Union, and candidate and associated countries.

How to Apply: Applications sent to the European Commission via the Socrates Technical Assistance Office; co-financing must be found for projects.

Financial Information: Annual budget €7,000,000.

Contact: Contact Corinne Hermant.

Address: 200 rue de la Loi, DG Education and Culture A3, 1049 Brussels, Belgium.

Telephone: (2) 296-34-55; *Internet:* http://europa.eu.int/comm/education/socrates /minerva/ind1a.html; *e-mail:* corinne.hermant@cec.eu.int.

Socrates and Youth Office: Socrates II—ARION

Forms part of the Socrates II programme (q.v.); promotes study visits for educational decision-makers.

Activities: Supports multilateral study visits bringing together educational policy-makers and specialists for the exchange of information and experience on matters of common interest to the participating countries, particularly in the field of primary and secondary education. Funding is provided for one-week study visits organized around priority themes; teaching, curriculum development and training tools; language teaching; education statistics; dissemination activities; and educational systems and values. The programme is open to European Union candidate and associated countries: Bulgaria, Cyprus, Czech Republic, Estonia, Hungary, Latvia, Lithuania, Malta, Poland, Romania, Slovakia, Slovenia and Turkey.

Geographical Area of Activity: Bulgaria, Cyprus, Czech Republic, Estonia, Hungary, Latvia, Lithuania, Malta, Poland, Romania, Slovakia, Slovenia and Turkey.

How to Apply: Applications must be sent to the relevant Socrates agency; grants are awarded annually.

Financial Information: Receives part of the global Socrates programme budget of €1,850,000,000; awards available of up to €1,000.

Contact: Contact Sophie Masson.

Address: 70 rue de Trèves, DG Education and Culture A4, 59–61, 1040 Brussels, Belgium.

Telephone: (2) 233-01-11; *Internet:* http://europa.eu.int/comm/education/socrates /arion/index.html; *e-mail:* info@socrates-youth.be.

STAGE (Support for Transition in the Arts in Greater Europe)

Established in 2000 to support cultural development in countries of the Caucasus: Armenia, Azerbaijan and Georgia.

Activities: Supports and develops projects centred on cultural and artistic activities in order to help foster democracy in the countries of the Caucasus: Armenia, Azerbaijan and Georgia. Organizes conferences, training and assistance programmes, promotes networking and meetings between people involved in the arts, policy-makers and civil society organizations, and publishes research findings.

Geographical Area of Activity: Countries of the Caucasus: Armenia, Azerbaijan and Georgia.

How to Apply: Applications can be submitted at any time; co-financing for projects must be found.

Financial Information: Average grant €15,000; maximum grant €35,000.

Contact: Project Man. Dorina Bodea.

Address: 67075 Strasbourg Cedex, France.

Telephone: 3-88-41-20-00; *Fax:* 3-88-41-27-81; *Internet:* www.coe.int/t/e /cultural_co-operation/culture/assistance_&_development/s.t.a.g.e; *e-mail:* dorina .bodea@coe.int.

Support for European Discussion Projects Organized by NGOs for 2003

Aims to support discussions by civil society organizations on topics of European integration, including European governance and the future of the European Union (EU), citizenship, social affairs and enlargement.

Activities: Co-funds projects including seminars, conferences, debates, events, networking between NGOs, publications, and innovative and media activities.

Geographical Area of Activity: Central and Eastern Europe, and the EU.

Restrictions: Projects must start between 15 April and 15 December 2003 and be completed by 30 June 2004.

How to Apply: Application forms to be submitted to the European Commission by post, accompanied by required supporting documents, which include budget information, annual accounts, articles of association and the applicant organization's bank details form.

Financial Information: Total budget approx. €1,500,000.

Address: Partnerships with Civil Society Sector, c/o Ilias Sotirchos, VM-2 4/52, 2 rue Van Maerlant, 1049 Brussels, Belgium.

Telephone: (2) 296-54-17; *Fax:* (2) 299-93-02; *e-mail:* eac-soc-civile-@cec.eu.int.

Support of European Integration Activities by Academic Institutions and Other Organizations

Established to promote European integration activities carried out by academic institutions and organizations.

Activities: The programme aims to promote European integration through supporting institutes, study and research centres, organizations and associations, and university networks of teachers, students and researchers carrying out work around priority themes: enlargement; the future of the European Union (EU), including governance, prospects for the European Convention, and reform of the European institutions; economic policy and prospects; the EU and other nations; and sustainable development. Funded projects must have the potential to mobilize, publicize and disseminate and support is given for symposia, debates and meetings, joint projects for studies, reflection or research, and initiatives designed to circulate information, publications, multimedia and internet dissemination.

Geographical Area of Activity: Europe.

How to Apply: Grants are awarded annually.

Financial Information: Annual budget €1,500,000 (2003); maximum grant available €50,000, monthly allowance €1,000.

Contact: Contact Pedro Martinez-Macias.

Address: 200 rue de la Loi, DG Education and Culture A2, 1049 Brussels, Belgium.

Telephone: (2) 299-61-86; *Internet:* europa.eu.int/comm/education/integration /home.html; *e-mail:* eac-a3022@cec.eu.int.

TEMPUS III

The first phase of the Tempus programme was established in 1990 after the fall of the Berlin Wall in 1989, to respond to the needs for Higher Education reform in Central and Eastern European countries. TEMPUS III was to run from 2000–06.

Activities: The programme encourages institutions in the European Union (EU) member states and partner countries to engage in structured co-operation through the establishment of consortia that implement Joint European Projects (JEPs) with a clear set of objectives. The programme also provides Individual Mobility Grants (IMGs) to individuals working in higher education institutions to help them work on certain specified activities in other countries. Additional support is also available for related activities. Eligible institutions and organizations include higher education institutions, NGOs, companies, and public authorities.

Geographical Area of Activity: Central and Eastern Europe, Mediterranean countries, candidate countries and non-EU countries, including Australia, Canada, Cyprus, Iceland, Japan, Liechtenstein, Malta, New Zealand, Norway, Switzerland, Turkey and the USA.

How to Apply: Each year the European Commission invites partner countries to present priority fields; priority is given to micro-projects.

Financial Information: Global budget €250,000,000; size of grant available varies according to the project and country.

Contact: Contact Augusto Gonzalez.

Address: 200 rue de la Loi, DG Education and Culture A5, 1049 Brussels, Belgium.

Telephone: (2) 296-63-19; *Internet:* http://europa.eu.int/comm/education /programmes/tempus.home.html; *e-mail:* augusto.gonzalez@cec.eu.int.

Unit D1–Youth: Support for international non-governmental youth organizations

Established to encourage the development in Europe of international non-governmental youth organizations and to promote activities of European interest involving and/or targeting young people.

Activities: The programme aims to support the operational costs linked to the organization and implementation of projects at European level. Beneficiary organizations must be international NGOs active in at least eight European Union countries, and organizing projects for young people.

Geographical Area of Activity: Austria, Belgium, Bulgaria, Cyprus, Czech Republic, Denmark, Estonia, Finland, France, Greece, Germany, Hungary, Iceland, Ireland, Italy, Latvia, Liechtenstein, Lithuania, Luxembourg, Malta, Netherlands, Norway, Poland, Portugal, Romania, Slovakia, Slovenia, Spain, Sweden, Turkey and UK.

Restrictions: Applications are only accepted from international, non-profit-making NGOs; youth organizations; and organizations with members in at least eight of the eligible countries.

How to Apply: Grants are awarded annually.

Financial Information: Annual budget approx. €1,500,000 (2003); average grant €10,000, maximum grant €25,000, up to 50% of the organization's annual overheads.

Contact: Contact Pierre Mairesse.

Address: Office VM-2, 05/52, 200 rue de la Loi, 1049 Brussels, Belgium.

Telephone: (2) 299-24-72; *Internet:* http://europa.eu.int/comm/education/youth /program/ingyoen.html; *e-mail:* ingyo@cec.eu.int.

Youth, Culture, Training, Media and Information: Leonardo da Vinci

Established in 2000 to reinforce people's abilities, primarily young people, following a professional training; to improve the quality of professional in-service training and the life-long acquisition of abilities and competencies; and to promote and reinforce the contribution of professional training to the innovation process so as to improve competitiveness and entrepreneurship.

Activities: Funding under the programme falls into six categories: international mobility, pilot projects, promotion of linguistic competencies, transnational networks, development of reference tools, and joint actions (see separate entries). The programme was to run from 2000–06.

Geographical Area of Activity: Europe.

How to Apply: Several steps to submit an application; contact the National Agency in the country concerned.

Financial Information: Global budget €1,150,000,000 (2000-06).

Contact: Contact Marta Ferreira.

Address: 200 rue de la Loi, DG Education and Culture B2, 1049 Brussels, Belgium.

Telephone: (2) 296-26-58; *Internet:* http://europa.eu.int/comm/education/leonardo .html; *e-mail:* leonardo@cec.eu.int.

Youth, Culture, Training, Media and Information: Leonardo da Vinci–1 Mobility

Forms part of the Leonardo da Vinci programme, launched in 2000; aims to support transnational mobility projects for people following a professional training, primarily for young people, and for trainers.

Activities: Provides funding for transnational placement projects, allowing individuals following an initial professional training, or students, or newly employed and new graduates, to carry out part of their training in a company or training institute. Project co-ordinators can also receive financial support through organizing placement and exchange programmes.

Geographical Area of Activity: Europe.

How to Apply: The application process is decentralized at the level of the participating countries.

Financial Information: Receives part of the global budget of €1,150,000,000; maximum grant of €5,000 for individual beneficiaries or €25,000 for project co-ordinators.

Address: 200 rue de la Loi, DG Education and Culture B2, 1049 Brussels, Belgium.

Telephone: (2) 296-26-58; *Internet:* http://europa.eu.int/comm/education/leonardo .html; *e-mail:* leonardo@cec.eu.int.

Youth, Culture, Training, Media and Information: Media Plus–Pilot Projects

Established in January 2001 and superseding the Media II programme which ran from 1996–2000; aims to strengthen the competitiveness of the European audiovisual industry and the audiovisual sector in developing countries with a series of support measures. The total global budget for the period 2001–06 is €350,000,000.

Activities: Supports the development of the audiovisual sector through a series of initiatives, including providing funding for pilot projects. Priority fields for the funding of pilot projects are: cinematographic heritage, European audiovisual programme archives, catalogues of European audiovisual works, and digital dissemination of European content through advanced distribution services. Additional attention is paid to pilot projects developing opportunities for distance learning and pedagogical innovation offered by the development of distance learning systems using on-line technology.

Geographical Area of Activity: Europe and developing countries.

How to Apply: Application forms are available from the European Commission by written request.

Financial Information: Programme scheduled for 2001–06; global budget €17,500,000; co-financing available for up to 50% of project costs.

Contact: Head of Unit Jacques Delmoly.

Address: 200 rue de la Loi, 1049 Brussels, Belgium.

Telephone: (2) 295-84-06; *Internet:* http://europa.eu.int/comm/avpolicy/mediapro /media_en.htm; *e-mail:* jacques.delmoly@cec.eu.int.

Youth, Culture, Training, Media and Information: Socrates II

Established to promote the idea of education and training as a life-long process.

Activities: Operates through various programmes: ARION, COMENIUS, ERASMUS, GRUNDTVIG, LINGUA and MINERVA (qq.v.), and was scheduled to run from 2000–06.

Geographical Area of Activity: Europe.

Financial Information: Global budget €1,850,000,000 (2000–06).

Contact: Contact Bertrand Delpeuch.

Address: 200 rue de la Loi, DG Education and Culture A3, 1049 Brussels, Belgium.

Telephone: (2) 296-87-11; *Internet:* http://europa.eu.int/comm/education/socrates .html; *e-mail:* joao.de-santana@cec.eu.int.

DIRECTORATE-GENERAL EDUCATION AND CULTURE—YOUTH UNIT

Youth, Culture, Training, Media and Information: EURO-MED Youth Programme II

Successor to the EURO-MED Youth Programme I; focuses on the three main actions of the YOUTH programme: Action 1 (Youth Exchanges), Action 2 (Voluntary Service) and Action 5 (Support Measures, qq.v.).

Activities: The Programme aims to: facilitate the integration of young people into social and professional life and to stimulate the democratization of civil society in the Mediterranean partner countries; improve mutual understanding and cohesion between young people across the Mediterranean region, based on and committed to mutual respect, tolerance and dialogue between the various cultures; increase the importance of youth organizations, develop young people's active citizenship, especially that of young women, and promote the exchange of information, experience and expertise between youth organizations. Young people (aged between 15 and 25), youth associations and local NGOs, which are legally resident/based in one of the 12 EC Mediterranean partner countries and in the 15 member states of the European Union (EU). Emphasis is given to supporting training activities, particularly in relation to priority themes, including women's role in the development of society, youth exchanges and voluntary service projects. Also provides support to the Euro-Mediterranean Youth Forum, established as a platform for youth organizations from partner countries in the Mediterranean and EU member states, to represent youth movements and act as the interface with authorities responsible for youth matters. Funded projects include a youth exchange bringing together, in Israel, young people from Italy, Germany, the Palestinian Territories and Israel, to discuss various aspects of minority–majority relations in a Europe/Middle East context; a voluntary service initiative providing young Tunisian people with the opportunity to go to work camps in other countries as well as hosting young foreign people in work camps in Tunisia; and a training scheme for youth workers and young people from Belgium, France, Germany, Italy, Jordan, the Palestinian Territories, Tunisia and Turkey, who work with young people with fewer opportunities, to acquire knowledge and skills in general animation techniques and forum theatre, particularly street theatre.

Geographical Area of Activity: EU and 12 Mediterranean partner countries.

How to Apply: Application forms can be downloaded from the website, and can be submitted by any of the project partners based either in an EU member state or in one of the Mediterranean partner countries to the relevant National Agency and/or National Co-ordinator, which then forwards it to the European Commission for project selection.

Financial Information: Total budget €14,000,000 (2002–04).

Contact: Contact Alejandra Martinez Boluda.

Address: 200 rue de la Loi, 1049 Brussels, Belgium.

Telephone: (2) 299-86-75; *Fax:* (2) 299-40-38; *Internet:* http://europa.eu.int/comm/youth/priorities/euromed_en.html; *e-mail:* eac-euromedyouth@cec.eu.int.

Youth, Culture, Training, Media and Information: YOUTH Programme

Established in 2000 as the European Union's mobility and non-formal education programme targeting young people aged between 15 and 25. Incorporates the experiences faced by the former Youth for Europe and European Voluntary Service programmes.

Activities: The Programme is open to young people in 30 European countries, and offers support for group exchanges and individual voluntary work, and support activities. Operates through National Agencies established in all 30 countries participating in the Programme, which assist with the promotion and implementation of the Programme at national level. Also provides support to co-operation activities with other third countries in South-Eastern Europe and the Commonwealth of Independent States. See separate entries for individual programme strands.

Geographical Area of Activity: Austria, Belgium, Bulgaria, Cyprus, Czech Republic, Denmark, Estonia, Finland, France, Germany, Greece, Hungary, Iceland, Ireland, Italy, Latvia, Liechtenstein, Lithuania, Luxembourg, Malta, Netherlands, Norway, Poland, Portugal, Romania, Slovakia, Slovenia, Spain, Sweden, Turkey and UK.

How to Apply: There are five application deadlines each year; see website for details. Projects are selected at both national and European level.

Financial Information: Global budget €520,000,000 (2000–06).

Contact: Contact Gabriella Amoruso.

Address: Technical Assistance Office, 59–61 rue de Trèves, 1040 Brussels, Belgium.

Telephone: (2) 233-01-11; *Fax:* (2) 233-01-50; *Internet:* http://europa.eu.int/comm /youth/program/index_en.html; *e-mail:* youth@cec.eu.int.

Youth, Culture, Training, Media and Information: YOUTH Programme Action 1—Youth for Europe

A strand of the YOUTH Programme (q.v.); aims to promote bilateral, trilateral and multilateral exchanges between Programme countries.

Activities: Provides support for youth exchange activities for groups of between 16 and 60 participants, with priority given to the participation of young people with fewer opportunities, including those from a less-privileged cultural, geographical or socio-economic background, or with disabilities, and young people for whom the exchange is their first European experience. In exceptional cases participants who are under 15 or over 25 can be included, if there are good reasons and their number is strictly limited. Supported exchanges should contribute to the young people's education process and increase their awareness of the European/international context in which they live.

Geographical Area of Activity: Austria, Belgium, Bulgaria, Cyprus, Czech Republic, Denmark, Estonia, Finland, France, Germany, Greece, Hungary, Iceland, Ireland, Italy, Latvia, Liechtenstein, Lithuania, Luxembourg, Malta, Netherlands, Norway, Poland, Portugal, Romania, Slovakia, Slovenia, Spain, Sweden, Turkey and UK.

Restrictions: No funding for statutory meetings of organizations, holiday travel, language courses, school class exchanges, academic study trips, performance tours, competitions, exchange activities which can be classed as tourism, and exchange activities which aim to make financial profit.

How to Apply: Application forms are available from the National Agencies and can be downloaded from the European Commission websites. For a bilateral or trilateral exchange, the sending and host groups apply separately to their respective National Agencies. For a multilateral exchange, the host group (co-ordinating group) applies, on behalf of all the partners, to its National Agency. If the multilateral exchange is itinerant, any of the partner groups (co-ordinating groups) can apply to its National Agency on behalf of all the partners. European youth organizations which are based in one of the Programme countries and have member branches in at least eight Programme countries may apply directly to the European Commission; they may also apply through their national branches to the relevant National Agency.

Financial Information: Receives part of the YOUTH Programme global budget of €520,000,000 (2000–06); co-financing is required.

Contact: Contact Gabriella Amoruso.

Address: Technical Assistance Office, 59–61 rue de Trèves, 1040 Brussels, Belgium.

Telephone: (2) 233-01-11; *Fax:* (2) 233-01-50; *Internet:* http://europa.eu.int/comm /youth/program/guide/action1_en.html; *e-mail:* youth@cec.eu.int.

Youth, Culture, Training, Media and Information: YOUTH Programme Action 2—European Voluntary Service (EVS)

A strand of the YOUTH Programme (q.v.); supports non-formal education opportunities for young people through transnational voluntary service which directly and actively involves young people in activities designed to meet the needs of society in a wide range of fields. The Action is based on three fundamental principles: to provide a non-formal intercultural learning experience for young people, encouraging their social integration and active participation, improving their employability and giving them opportunities to show solidarity with other people; to support the development of local communities; and to encourage the establishment of new partnerships and the exchange of experience and good practice between partners.

Activities: Support is given to volunteer service projects which allow a young person to be a volunteer in another country for a specified period, normally between six and 12 months, for work in the fields of the environment, arts and culture, activities with children, young people or the elderly, heritage, or sports and leisure. Priority is given to projects that target young people with fewer opportunities who otherwise would not have easy access to the Programme; introduce voluntary service activities as a new element to existing partnerships and/or create new partnerships between organizations/associations/structures active in the social, cultural, youth or environmental fields; involve organizations which have not yet participated in EVS; involve a new area of activity, or have innovative features; and support the development of local communities. Activities must take place in a country other than where the volunteer lives, be non-profit-making and unpaid, bring an added value to the local community, not involve job substitution, and last for a limited period (maximum 12 months). Projects involving just two countries are dealt with directly by the National Agencies in the Programme countries. One of the countries involved in an EVS project must be a European Union member state.

Geographical Area of Activity: Austria, Belgium, Bulgaria, Cyprus, Czech Republic, Denmark, Estonia, Finland, France, Germany, Greece, Hungary, Iceland, Ireland, Italy, Latvia, Liechtenstein, Lithuania, Luxembourg, Malta, Netherlands, Norway, Poland, Portugal, Romania, Slovakia, Slovenia, Spain, Sweden, Turkey and UK.

How to Apply: After a partnership is established, the sending and approved host organizations prepare their respective applications for funding, completing the application forms together. They are then sent to the National Agencies in the sending and host countries by the deadlines indicated in the available User's Guide. Volunteers should be involved in the preparation of the applications as much as possible, allowing them to influence the content of the project.

Financial Information: Receives part of the YOUTH Programme global budget of €520,000,000 (2000–06); co-financing is required.

Contact: Contact Gabriella Amoruso.

Address: Technical Assistance Office, 59–61 rue de Trèves, 1040 Brussels, Belgium.

Telephone: (2) 233-01-11; *Fax:* (2) 233-01-50; *Internet:* http://europa.eu.int/comm /youth/program/guide/action2_en.html; *e-mail:* youth@cec.eu.int.

Youth, Culture, Training, Media and Information: YOUTH Programme Action 3—Youth Initiatives

A strand of the YOUTH Programme (q.v.); aims to support young people's initiative and creativity, through providing young people with the chance to try out ideas through initiatives which give them an opportunity to be directly and actively involved in planning and realizing projects in their local community.

Activities: Support is provided to Group Initiatives created and run by a group of at least four young people aged between 15 and 25, for between three months and one year, which represent innovative examples of the contributions that young people want to make to their local community. Grants are awarded within three priority areas: Priority 1 projects are run by young people with fewer opportunities, and from a less-privileged cultural, geographical or socio-economic background, and which benefit the local community where they take place; Priority 2 projects are run by any young people and must benefit young people with fewer opportunities and from a less-privileged cultural, geographical or socio-economic background; and Priority 3 projects are initiatives run by groups of young people and which benefit mainly the members of the group. Support is also provided for networking activities following completion of a Group Initiative, and for Future Capital projects. Future Capital projects enable ex-volunteers to pass on the experience and skills acquired during their European Voluntary Service (EVS) to the local community and other young people, including starting up a professional activity, one-off projects and personal development projects. Grants are also awarded within three priority areas: Priority 1 projects must be of benefit to other young people or a local community, including one-off projects, or those starting up a professional activity encouraging local development; Priority 2 projects are one-off or personal development projects which are integrated into a specific project aiming at increasing employability; and Priority 3 projects are personal development projects which are connected with the experience acquired during EVS.

Geographical Area of Activity: Austria, Belgium, Bulgaria, Cyprus, Czech Republic, Denmark, Estonia, Finland, France, Germany, Greece, Hungary, Iceland, Ireland, Italy, Latvia, Liechtenstein, Lithuania, Luxembourg, Malta, Netherlands, Norway, Poland, Portugal, Romania, Slovakia, Slovenia, Spain, Sweden, Turkey and UK.

How to Apply: Application forms can be requested from the National Agencies or downloaded from the European Commission's website. Applications should be submitted by the deadlines stipulated in the available User's Guide.

Financial Information: Receives part of the YOUTH Programme global budget of €520,000,000 (2000–06). Group Initiatives: maximum award for Priority 1 projects €10,000, maximum award for Priority 2 projects €7,500, and maximum award for Priority 3 projects €5,000. Future Capital projects: maximum award for Priority 1 projects €5,000, maximum award for Priority 2 projects €3,750, and maximum award for Priority 3 projects €2,500.

Contact: Contact Gabriella Amoruso.

Address: Technical Assistance Office, 59–61 rue de Trèves, 1040 Brussels, Belgium.

Telephone: (2) 233-01-11; *Fax:* (2) 233-01-50; *Internet:* http://europa.eu.int/comm/youth/program/guide/action3_en.html; *e-mail:* youth@cec.eu.int.

Youth, Culture, Training, Media and Information: YOUTH Programme Action 4—Joint Actions

A strand of the YOUTH Programme (q.v.); aims to promote a Europe of knowledge focusing on themes that are not limited to one field alone, i.e. education, training or youth policy. Carried out in co-operation with the Socrates and Leonardo da Vinci programmes (qq.v.).

Activities: Supports youth initiatives that aim to create European-level conditions under which learners of all ages are able to acquire the experience, knowledge and skills they need to live, work and actively participate in society and that extend beyond the scope of a single Programme strand. Also supports actions that aim to encourage the development of innovative approaches to analyzing and solving problems which cut across several areas.

Geographical Area of Activity: Austria, Belgium, Bulgaria, Cyprus, Czech Republic, Denmark, Estonia, Finland, France, Germany, Greece, Hungary, Iceland, Ireland, Italy, Latvia, Liechtenstein, Lithuania, Luxembourg, Malta, Netherlands, Norway, Poland, Portugal, Romania, Slovakia, Slovenia, Spain, Sweden, Turkey and UK.

How to Apply: Calls for proposals are published in the Official Journal of the European Communities.

Financial Information: Receives part of the YOUTH Programme global budget of €520,000,000 (2000–06); co-financing is required.

Contact: Contact Gabriella Amoruso.

Address: Technical Assistance Office, 59–61 rue de Trèves, 1040 Brussels, Belgium.

Telephone: (2) 233-01-11; *Fax:* (2) 233-01-50; *Internet:* http://europa.eu.int/comm/youth/program/guide/action4_en.html; *e-mail:* youth@cec.eu.int.

Youth, Culture, Training, Media and Information: YOUTH Programme Action 5—Support Measures

A strand of the YOUTH Programme (q.v.); aims to help all those involved in youth activities or interested in youth matters to prepare and develop projects and initiatives within the context of the YOUTH Programme.

Activities: The Support Measures programme has two principal aims: to assist the development of the three major Actions of the YOUTH programme (Youth for

Europe, European Voluntary Service and Youth Initiatives, qq.v.) through the support of training, co-operation and information projects; and to contribute to achieving the objectives of the YOUTH Programme as well as fostering and strengthening European youth policy. Applications are accepted from youth organizations, groups of young people, youth leaders and mentors for nine types of activity: practical training experience or job shadowing; feasibility visits; contact-making seminars; study visits; seminars; training courses; youth information; transnational partnerships and networks; and support for quality and innovation.

Geographical Area of Activity: Austria, Belgium, Bulgaria, Cyprus, Czech Republic, Denmark, Estonia, Finland, France, Germany, Greece, Hungary, Iceland, Ireland, Italy, Latvia, Liechtenstein, Lithuania, Luxembourg, Malta, Netherlands, Norway, Poland, Portugal, Romania, Slovakia, Slovenia, Spain, Sweden, Turkey and UK.

How to Apply: Application forms are available from the National Agencies and can be downloaded from the European Commission's website, and should be submitted by the deadlines stipulated in the available User's Guide. National Agencies provide assistance for completing applications. One of the partner organizations must take the lead in submitting the application as well as in implementing the project. European youth organizations which are based in one of the Programme countries and have member branches in at least eight Programme countries may apply directly to the European Commission.

Financial Information: Receives part of the YOUTH Programme global budget of €520,000,000 (2000–06); maximum grant available €100,000, up to 75% of the project's total costs.

Contact: Contact Gabriella Amoruso.

Address: Technical Assistance Office, 59–61 rue de Trèves, 1040 Brussels, Belgium.

Telephone: (2) 233-01-11; *Fax:* (2) 233-01-50; *Internet:* http://europa.eu.int/comm /youth/program/guide/action5_en.html; www.training-youth.net; *e-mail:* youth@ cec.eu.int.

DIRECTORATE-GENERAL EMPLOYMENT AND SOCIAL AFFAIRS

Action Programme to Combat Discrimination: Support to European-level NGOs

The Programme was established by Council decision 2000/750/EC of 27 November 2000, which provided the legal framework for the Programme's implementation.

Activities: Under the Programme grants are available to NGOs which are working towards advancing the rights of groups facing discrimination, within five main areas: advocacy work for developing anti-discrimination legislation at national level; monitoring discrimination; strategic litigation; campaigning against discrimination; and setting up efficient organizations. The Programme was to run from 2003–05 and approximately five grants of €100,000 each were to be made to European-level organizations during the period.

Geographical Area of Activity: European Union, Bulgaria and Romania.

Financial Information: Total budget approx. €500,000 (2003–05); maximum grant available €100,000.

Address: 200 rue de la Loi, 1049 Brussels, Belgium.

Internet: http://europa.eu.int/comm/employment_social/fundamental_rights/prog/calls_en.htm.

Analysis and Studies on the Social Situation, Demography and Family

Aims to promote the development of benchmarking, exchanges in analyzing and improving the European Union's (EU) knowledge on social phenomena and their changing patterns in the social situation, including demographic trends.

Activities: Funded activities include studies and research, analysis and conferences, through grants to associations, local and regional authorities, universities and research organizations. The grant themes change each year; in 2003 the priority themes were: the social situation in the enlarged EU; family and children issues; time use and living conditions; migration in the context of demographic trends; and the situation of people with disabilities in residential institutions.

Geographical Area of Activity: EU and Central and Eastern European countries.

How to Apply: Selection of beneficiaries is made once a year; application details are available on the website.

Financial Information: Annual budget €500,000; grants are available for up to 80% of the project's eligible costs.

Contact: Contact Katri Rahkola.

Address: 200 rue de la Loi, DG Employment and Social Affairs E1, 1049 Brussels, Belgium.

Telephone: (2) 299-32-05; *Internet:* http://europa.eu.int/comm/employment_social/tender_en.htm#proposals; *e-mail:* katri.rahkola@cec.eu.int.

Community Initiatives Unit: EQUAL

Part of the European Union's (EU) strategy for securing more and better jobs and for ensuring that no one is denied access to them. Funded by the European Social Fund (ESF, q.v.), EQUAL tests new ways of tackling discrimination and inequality experienced by those in work and those looking for a job. EQUAL co-finances activities in all EU member states, is a follow-up to the previous Community initiatives Adapt and Employment and aims to build on their results. EQUAL differs from the ESF mainstream programmes for its emphasis on innovation and active co-operation between member states. The first of two calls for proposals for EQUAL projects in the member states took place during the first half of 2001, with the next one scheduled for mid-2004.

Activities: Operates through Development Partnerships (DPs) on a geographical or sectoral level to tackle discrimination and inequality in employment matters, which are fed into individual country Community Initiative Programmes; and European Thematic Networks, composed of a steering group, a liaison group and working groups, which include NGOs and are responsible for identifying, adapting and presenting good practice, and for products and events related to the thematic questions established in the work programme. The current European

Thematic Networks are: Employability; Entrepreneurship; Adaptability; Equal Opportunities; and Asylum Seekers. There are four principal types of action under which funding is available: setting up of DPs in the sector or territory, and transnational co-operation; implementation of the work programmes of the DPs; thematic networking, dissemination of good practices, and making an impact on national policy; and technical assistance.

Geographical Area of Activity: EU.

Restrictions: DPs must involve transnational co-operation with at least one other DP from a different member state, and may also include co-operation with similar projects from a non-member state funded under the PHARE, Euro-Mediterranean Partnership (MEDA) or TACIS programmes (qq.v.).

How to Apply: Responsibility for the implementation of the Community Initiative programmes in the member states lies with the national authorities.

Financial Information: EU contribution to EQUAL of €3,026,000,000 matched by national funding; programme funding ranges from 50% to 75% of the project's total costs.

Address: 200 rue de la Loi, 1049 Brussels, Belgium.

Fax: (2) 299-45-26; *Internet:* http://europa.eu.int/comm/employment_social/equal /index.cfm; *e-mail:* empl-equal-info@cec.eu.int.

Community Programme on Gender Equality—2001–2005: Women's Organizations

One of this Pogramme's aims is to cover the annual running costs and activities of women's organizations in Europe.

Activities: Provides support to women's organizations in Europe not covered by the European Women's Lobby and to assist women who are victims of trafficking in Europe. Funding is provided for transnational projects concerning the transfer of experience and information, exchanges of personnel, joint development of products, processes, strategies and methodology, awareness-raising activities, and the dissemination of information. Projects must be co-ordinated by partners from at least three member states or countries from the European Economic Area (EEA).

Geographical Area of Activity: European Union and EEA countries.

How to Apply: Grants are awarded annually.

Financial Information: Available grants range from €250,000 to €500,000.

Contact: Contact Rosa Novo-Cid-Fuentes.

Address: 200 rue de la Loi, DG Employment and Social Affairs G1, 1049 Brussels, Belgium.

Telephone: (2) 295-16-09; *Internet:* http://europa.eu.int/comm/employment_social /equ_opp/fund_en.html; *e-mail:* equop@cec.eu.int.

European Structural Funds: European Social Fund (ESF)

One of the four European Structural Funds and administered by DG Employment and Social Affairs. The Fund focuses on vocational training and employment aids in order to promote equality, stability and growth in employment. It is the sole contributor to Objective 3 programmes and the EQUAL (q.v.) Community Initiative and so is the only fund available to NGOs situated outside the Objective 1 and 2 regions.

Activities: The Fund provides assistance for: the development of active labour policies to fight unemployment, to prevent long-term unemployment, to facilitate the reintegration of the long-term unemployed into the labour market and to support the occupational integration of young people and of people returning to the labour market; the promotion of social inclusion and equal opportunities for all in accessing the labour market; the development of education and training systems as part of a life-long learning policy to enhance and sustain employability, mobility and integration into the labour market; the improvement of systems to promote a skilled, trained and adaptable workforce, to foster innovation and adaptability in work organization, to support entrepreneurship and employment creation and to boost human potential in research, science and technology; and greater participation of women in the labour market, including their career development and access to new job opportunities and entrepreneurship and reducing segregation in the labour market. Financed measures are complementary to national employment policies and each member state establishes a development plan identifying the best ways in which ESF funding can help improve national employment and human resources policies in line with European employment strategy. Particular emphasis is placed on the improvement of systems to promote a skilled, trained and adaptable workforce and to increase the participation of women in the labour market. There are provisions within ESF regulations for the participation of NGOs in ESF-supported programmes through the provision of small grants schemes, with an emphasis on promoting social inclusion, through improving employability and the education of the most disadvantaged groups and by fighting discrimination and inequality in access to the labour market.

Geographical Area of Activity: European Union.

How to Apply: To apply for funding, organizations must contact the national authorities in the relevant country; application procedures vary according to national rules and regulations.

Address: 200 rue de la Loi, 1049 Brussels, Belgium.

Fax: (2) 295-49-18; *Internet:* http://europa.eu.int/comm/employment_social /esf2000/index.htm#sf; *e-mail:* empl-info@cec.eu.int.

Innovating Measures under European Social Fund—ESF—Strand 1

Operates under Article 6 of ESF regulations, supporting innovative measures that promote new approaches and identify examples of good practice which can subsequently improve implementation of ESF operations. Strand 1 projects relate to the theme: adaptation to the new economy within the framework of social dialogue.

Activities: Projects supported under this allocation include pilot projects, studies, exchanges of experience and information activities, operated by NGOs, training organizations, companies and local authorities. In 2003 priority issues were: anticipation of economic and social change, use of Information Society tools in the framework of social dialogue, new approaches to corporate social responsibility, modernization of work organization, and promotion of life-long learning.

Geographical Area of Activity: European Union.

How to Apply: Grants are awarded at the beginning of the year; a direct funding programme, applicants should apply directly to the European Commission.

Financial Information: Annual budget €30,000,000; grants of up to 75% of the project's total cost, ranging from €300,000 to €3,000,000 over two years.

Contact: Contact Lisbeth Bahl-Poulsen.

Address: 200 rue de la Loi, DG Employment and Social Affairs C4, 1049 Brussels, Belgium.

Telephone: (2) 299-54-47; *Internet:* http://europa.eu.int/comm/employment_social /esf2000/article_6-fr.htm; *e-mail:* lisbeth.bahl-poulsen@cec.eu.int.

Non-Discrimination Law Programme—Combating Discrimination

The grant programme targets transnational actions for the development of policy and/or legal responses to the fight against discrimination in the European accession countries (excluding Turkey).

Activities: Aims to develop organizations' capacity to prevent and address discrimination effectively, in particular by strengthening organizations' means of action through support for the exchange of information and good practice, while taking into account the specific characteristics of the different forms of discrimination. Grants are available for: developing the case for collecting data on discrimination at European and national level; developing monitoring and assessment tools; developing close co-operation between public authorities at all levels and civil society as a whole with the view of mainstreaming equality into all policies; and actions in favour of the promotion of Roma integration in education and in employment.

Geographical Area of Activity: European accession countries.

How to Apply: Application forms, budget forms and guide-lines on applying for a grant are available on the website.

Financial Information: Global budget €1,000,000; grants range from €35,000 to €45,000, up to 80% of the project's total costs.

Contact: Contact Flaminia Bussacchini.

Address: 200 rue de la Loi, 1049 Brussels, Belgium.

Internet: http://europa.eu.int/comm/employment_social/fundamental_ rights/; *e-mail:* antidiscrimination@cec.eu.int.

Support to European Non-Governmental Organizations Fighting Racism

Established in 2003 to support the operating costs of organizations active in the fight against racism, xenophobia and anti-Semitism.

Activities: Grants are available for NGOs, associations, unions, universities and federations to support their ongoing annual programmes, rather than one-off projects, in the fight against racism, xenophobia and anti-Semitism. Priority areas in the programme are: the development of training and educational materials in the field of anti-racism and anti-Semitism; the production of publications and materials to raise awareness, deepen understanding and stimulate debate on the issues of racism, xenophobia and anti-Semitism; thematic studies on issues concerning racism, xenophobia and anti-Semitism; stimulation of the exchange of views, problems and possible solutions, related to problems of racism, xenophobia and anti-Semitism with a Community dimension, involving stakeholders at national, regional and local level; capacity building, in particular reinforcing the involvement of small NGOs, new NGO networks and NGOs in the applicant and candidate countries at European level; and conferences and seminars concerning racism, xenophobia and anti-Semitism. Particular priority is given to activities which focus on issues affecting the Roma community in Europe. Applicant organizations should operate primarily in the field of combating racism, xenophobia and anti-Semitism and be active at a European level and be able to show that their activities cover at least five European Union (EU) countries.

Geographical Area of Activity: EU.

Financial Information: Total budget €100,000.

Address: VP/2003/29, Office J37 5/23, 1049 Brussels, Belgium.

Telephone: (2) 296-94-88; *Internet:* http://europa.eu.int/comm/employment_social /fundamental_rights/pdf/prog/calls/glines.

DIRECTORATE-GENERAL ENLARGEMENT

PHARE (Poland and Hungary Assistance for Economic Restructuring)

The programme is one of the three pre-accession instruments financed by the European Communities to assist the applicant countries of central Europe in their preparations for joining the European Union. Originally created in 1989 to assist Poland and Hungary, the programme encompasses the 10 candidate countries of central and eastern Europe, Bulgaria, Czech Republic, Estonia, Hungary, Latvia, Lithuania, Poland, Slovakia, Romania and Slovenia, aiming to help them through a period of significant economic restructuring and political change.

Activities: PHARE works through different programmes: cross-border programmes, national programmes, multi-beneficiary programmes, and horizontal programmes. The current phase of the programme was to run from 2000–06.

Geographical Area of Activity: Bulgaria, Czech Republic, Estonia, Hungary, Latvia, Lithuania, Poland, Slovakia, Romania and Slovenia.

How to Apply: Grants are awarded several times each year.

Financial Information: Annual budget €1,600,000; up to 100% of project costs available.

Address: Enlargement/PHARE Information Centre, 1000 Brussels, Belgium.

Telephone: (2) 296-58-28; *Internet:* http://europa.eu.int/comm/enlargement/pas /phare/index.htm; *e-mail:* helmuth.lohan@cec.eu.int.

PHARE (Poland and Hungary Assistance for Economic Restructuring) Enlargement Information Programme

Part of the PHARE initiative (q.v.).

Activities: Aims to inform the general public about the European institutions and enlargement policy, through funding for communication activities. The Programme was to run from 2002–06.

Geographical Area of Activity: European Union and candidate countries (Bulgaria, Cyprus, Czech Republic, Estonia, Hungary, Latvia, Lithuania, Malta, Poland, Romania, Slovakia, Slovenia and Turkey).

How to Apply: Applications are submitted through the national EC representative.

Financial Information: Receives part of the global PHARE budget of €150,000,000 (2002–06).

Contact: Contact Ben Nieuwenhuis.

Address: 200 rue de la Loi, DG Enlargement Information Unit, 1049 Brussels, Belgium.

Telephone: (2) 295-85-49; *Internet:* http://europa.eu.int/comm/enlargement/pas /phare/programmes/multi-bene/; *e-mail:* benedictus.nieuwenhuis@cec.eu.int.

PHARE (Poland and Hungary Assistance for Economic Restructuring) Multi-Beneficiary Drugs Programme
Part of the PHARE initiative (q.v.).

Activities: The Programme aims to support the development of effective drugs policies in Central and Eastern Europe, counter the supply and illegal trafficking of drugs and promote cross-border co-operation, through funding for technical projects in the field of policy development and co-operative projects between NGOs.

Geographical Area of Activity: European Union and Central and Eastern Europe.

How to Apply: Grants are awarded annually.

Financial Information: Global budget €10,000,000.

Contact: Contact Henk Visser.

Address: 200 rue de la Loi, DG Enlargement B2, 1049 Brussels, Belgium.

Telephone: (2) 299-85-52; *Internet:* http://europa.eu.int/comm/enlargement/pas /phare/programmes/multi-bene/drugs.htm; *e-mail:* henk.visser@cec.eu.int.

PHARE (Poland and Hungary Assistance for Economic Restructuring) Multi-Beneficiary Programmes: Consensus III—Social Protection Reform and Social *Acquis* Implementation
The programme evolved out of Consensus I which was launched in June 1995 and was established to support the sustainability of social protection reform in Central and Eastern Europe.

Activities: The programme focuses on designing an inter-institutional social protection reform policy, preparing adequate tools for its implementation and encouraging exchanges of experience on a multi-country basis. Involves monitoring social policy developments in the candidate countries and guiding the social security reform process depending on each country's needs and state of progress. Since 2000 assistance for adopting and implementing the social *acquis* has been supported under PHARE national programmes, following the priorities set out in each country's Accession Partnership. Consensus III acts as a bridge between this and the previous Consensus programmes. Grants are made to support twinning projects that: strengthen institutions responsible for the implementation of the social *acquis*; strengthen social protection systems so as to facilitate adoption and implementation of the *acquis*; enhance dialogue between governments and social partners, NGOs and the public in general about reforming and modernizing social protection and adopting the social *acquis*; and prepare the way for a strongly reinforced social dimension in the PHARE programmes.

Geographical Area of Activity: European Union candidate countries.

Financial Information: Total budget €18,120,000.

Address: Charleroi 3/8, 170 rue de la Loi, 1049 Brussels, Belgium.

Fax: (2) 299-17-77; *Internet:* http://europa.eu.int/comm/enlargement/pas/phare /programmes/multi-bene/consensus3.htm; *e-mail:* enlargement@cec.eu.int.

PHARE (Poland and Hungary Assistance for Economic Restructuring) Multi-Beneficiary Programmes: Drugs Programme

The Programme was launched in 1992; initially directed towards Bulgaria, the Czech Republic, Hungary, Poland, Romania and Slovakia, it now also includes Albania, Bosnia and Herzegovina, Estonia, former Yugoslav Republic of Macedonia, Latvia, Lithuania and Slovenia. Aims to support the Central and Eastern European countries (CEECs) in developing effective drugs policies and measures consistent with the European Union (EU) Drugs Strategy, to counter the supply and illicit trafficking in drugs, and to reduce the demand for drugs.

Activities: The Programme is the main PHARE mechanism for supporting the development of the institutional capacity of the 10 candidate countries of Central and Eastern Europe, and the PHARE partner countries of Albania, Bosnia and Herzegovina and the former Yugoslav Republic of Macedonia, and for developing multi-disciplinary and co-ordinated drugs strategies, in line with the EU Drugs Strategy. Also works to facilitate the development of integrated and co-ordinated strategies in the field of drugs, based on a balanced approach between drugs demand reduction and drugs supply reduction. Grants are made for projects that: develop information systems for the collection, analysis and distribution of objective, comparable and reliable data on drugs, in line with the methodology of the European Monitoring Centre for Drugs and Drug Addiction (EMCDDA); prepare the integration of the candidate countries from Central and Eastern Europe into the EMCDDA; strengthen drugs demand reduction strategies in the partner countries; reinforce drugs demand reduction networks in all partner countries and link them with EU networks as well as strengthening experts' capacity in this field; enhance the basis of civil society, particularly NGOs, in prevention activities; develop measures in the field of precursor control, in line with EU standards; establish/improve effective administrative procedure and training in the field of illicit drugs control; develop a legal and institutional framework and strengthen the capacity to combat synthetic drugs, in line with EU standards; strengthen co-operation and the development of common approaches among law enforcement personnel of CEECs and EU member states; strengthen drugs law enforcement capacities in South-Eastern Europe with a view to curbing drugs-trafficking along the Balkan Route; and develop anti-money-laundering measures, according to international and EU standards.

Geographical Area of Activity: EU candidate countries.

Contact: Contact Michael Sorensen.

Address: Charleroi 3/8, 170 rue de la Loi, 1049 Brussels, Belgium.

Fax: (2) 299-17-77; *Internet:* http://europa.eu.int/comm/enlargement/pas/phare/programmes/multi-bene/drugs.htm; *e-mail:* michael.sorensen@cec.eu.int.

PHARE (Poland and Hungary Assistance for Economic Restructuring) Multi-Beneficiary Programmes: Justice and Home Affairs Programme

The initial Programme started in 1996; the current Programme aims to raise the legislation, institutions, procedures, training provisions and practices of the candidate countries to European Union (EU) standards, with the aim of the effective implementation of the justice and home affairs *acquis*.

Activities: Grants are made in support of projects that focus on the adoption and implementation of measures in the following areas: the rule of law, in particular the independence of the judiciary; the judiciary, including international judicial co-operation in civil and penal matters; asylum; migration and visa policy, procedures and practices; external border control and management; organization of the police; the penitentiary system; and organized crime. There are also four specific projects, covering the reinforcement of the rule of law; judicial co-operation in penal matters; training of judges in Community law; migration policy and external border management. Support is also given for missions to the candidate countries to assess needs and progress.

Geographical Area of Activity: EU candidate countries.

Contact: Contact Massimo Serpieri.

Address: Charleroi 3/8, 170 rue de la Loi, 1049 Brussels, Belgium.

Fax: (2) 299-17-77; *Internet:* http://europa.eu.int/comm/enlargement/pas/phare/programmes/multi-bene/jha.htm; *e-mail:* massimo.serpieri@cec.eu.int.

PHARE (Poland and Hungary Assistance for Economic Restructuring) Multi-Beneficiary Programmes: PHARE Access Programme

The Programme was developed to strengthen and prepare the civil society sector in the candidate countries for European Union (EU) accession and to help them put into practice the Copenhagen criteria based on the rule of law, human rights and the respect and protection of minority communities. Central to the Programme is the belief that NGOs should play a greater role in representing citizens' interests and increasing their participation in the development of society. It replaced the PHARE LIEN partnership programme, which had been active since 1993.

Activities: Support is given for projects in the fields of environmental protection, socio-economic development and social activities, although assistance priorities are defined country-by-country based on the situation in each individual country. Co-financing grants are provided for transnational macro-projects and local micro-projects carried out by NGOs. The Programme also includes a networking facility, providing funding to NGOs in the candidate countries to enable them to participate in activities organized at EU level, including travel and subsistence costs for attending events.

Geographical Area of Activity: EU and the candidate countries.

How to Apply: Macro-projects must be carried out in partnership with organizations from at least two different countries, with the lead organization based in one of the candidate countries. The project proposal is submitted to the European Commission delegation in the lead country. Micro-projects can be carried out by a single organization based in one of the candidate countries.

Financial Information: Budget €20,000,000 (2002–03); maximum grant for macro-projects €200,000; maximum grant for micro-projects €50,000, up to 80% of the total budget in both cases.

Contact: Task Man. Mirko Puig.

Address: Charleroi 3/8, 170 rue de la Loi, 1049 Brussels, Belgium.

Telephone: (2) 295-37-60; *Fax:* (2) 296-95-01; *Internet:* http://europa.eu.int/comm /enlargement/pas/phare/programmes/multi-bene/access2000.htm; *e-mail:* mirko .puig@cec.eu.int.

PHARE (Poland and Hungary Assistance for Economic Restructuring) Multi-Beneficiary Programmes: Small Projects Programme

The Programme aims to provide grant support to projects which fall outside the direct scope of national or multi-beneficiary PHARE programmes but which support implementation of the PHARE programme in general and which contribute to closer European integration.

Activities: Grants are available to NGOs for events such as conferences, seminars, congresses, symposia, fairs, or workshops, related to the enlargement of the European Union (EU) and more particularly to the Accession criteria defined by the European Council in 1993 in Copenhagen and the 31 chapters of the Accession negotiations. Funded events should have the objective of raising awareness on European integration and the enlargement process in the candidate countries of Central and Eastern Europe; supporting and publicizing the efforts of these candidate countries to join the EU; and increasing the visibility of the EU in these candidate countries.

Geographical Area of Activity: EU or countries eligible for funding from the PHARE programme: Bulgaria, Czech Republic, Estonia, Hungary, Latvia, Lithuania, Poland, Romania, Slovakia and Slovenia.

How to Apply: Applications must be submitted using the standard application form attached to the Guide-lines for Applicants available on the website.

Financial Information: Total budget €2,100,000; minimum grant available €15,000, maximum grant €50,000.

Contact: Contact Benedicte Bronchart.

Address: Charleroi 3/8, 170 rue de la Loi, 1049 Brussels, Belgium.

Fax: (2) 295-95-40; *Internet:* http://europa.eu.int/comm/enlargement/pas/phare /programmes/multi-bene/smallproj.htm; *e-mail:* benedicte.bronchart@cec.eu.int.

PHARE (Poland and Hungary Assistance for Economic Restructuring) Small Projects Programme—SPP

Part of the PHARE programme (q.v.); aims to raise awareness in the PHARE countries of European integration, pre-accession strategies and enlargement, contribute to closer integration between the European Union (EU) and Eastern European countries, and increase the visibility of the EU in pre-accession countries.

Activities: Provides financial support to information projects promoting goodwill and greater awareness about EU activities in the PHARE countries, including seminars, summer schools, meetings, lectures, symposia, fairs and workshops.

Geographical Area of Activity: EU and Central and Eastern Europe.

How to Apply: Grants awarded annually.

Financial Information: Global budget €5,000,000; grants available up to €50,000, up to a maximum of 50% of total project costs.

Contact: Contact Benedicte Bronchart.

Address: 200 rue de la Loi, DG Enlargement D4, 1049 Brussels, Belgium.

Telephone: (2) 295-98-98; *Internet:* http://europa.eu.int/comm/enlargement/pas /phare/programmes/multi-bene/smallproj.htm; *e-mail:* benedicte.bronchart@cec .eu.int.

Pilot Programme on the Impact of Enlargement in Border Regions

Established by the European Commission's DG Enlargement Unit to support preparatory actions to support vulnerable labour forces in European Union regions bordering on the candidate countries, specifically in border regions of Austria, Finland, Germany, Greece and Italy.

Activities: The Programme aims to increase the occupational and geographical mobility of those potentially and currently working in small and medium-sized businesses of sectors affected by enlargement, in particular the most vulnerable groups, such as unskilled workers. Grants are available for qualification programmes for the most vulnerable groups in economic sectors and regions most likely to be affected by enlargement, particularly projects providing opportunities for young people. Specific priorities are to enable and facilitate: institutionalized contacts and co-operation between training institutions and business; community development in affected sectors and regions, including across the border; the development of sustainable training programmes corresponding to the needs of the border regions; continuous information/awareness for employees and workers on qualification programmes in border regions; creation of awareness and transfer of knowledge of new skills to vulnerable groups of the labour force in certain border regions and sectors; and training of trainers to provide continuous training to the labour force in border regions.

Geographical Area of Activity: Border regions of Austria, Finland, Germany, Greece and Italy.

Financial Information: Total budget €5,000,000; grants available range from €500,000 to €1,000,000.

Contact: Contact Judith Novak.

Address: 170 rue de la Loi, DG Enlargement D4, 1049 Brussels, Belgium.
Telephone: (2) 295-98-35; *Fax:* (2) 299-17-77; *Internet:* http://europa.eu.int/comm
/enlargement/borderregions/pdf/2003/calls2/call_for_proposal_notice;   *e-mail:*
elarg-empl@cec.eu.int.

DIRECTORATE-GENERAL ENVIRONMENT

Accidental Marine Pollution
Aims to support the efforts of European Union (EU) member states to improve
their capabilities for responding to major pollution incidents at sea involving oil or
other hazardous substances, and to create the conditions for effective mutual
assistance and co-operation.
Activities: Aims to support activities on the control and reduction of pollution
caused by hydrocarbons released in the sea, through funding community
information provision, training programmes, pilot projects, and international co-
operation activities. Priority fields of action are: responding to oil pollution, aerial
surveillance, bioremediation, illicit discharges from ships, analysis of major
accidents, and techniques and methods of response and rehabilitation. The
programme was scheduled to run from 2000–06.
Geographical Area of Activity: EU.
Financial Information: Global budget €7,000,000 (2000–06).
Contact: Contact Pia Bucella.
Address: 200 rue de la Loi, DG Environment B4: Civil Protection, 1049 Brussels,
Belgium.
Telephone: (2) 296-95-14; *Internet:* http://europa.eu.int/comm/environment/civil
/funds.htm; *e-mail:* pia.bucella@cec.eu.int.

Action Programme Promoting European Environmental NGOs
Aims to provide support to NGOs acting for the protection of the environment that
contribute to the continuing of the development and set-up of Environmental
Community policy and legislation in all regions of Europe, and to promote
systematic involvement of NGOs at all stages of policy shaping, by ensuring
relevant representation in stakeholder consultation meetings and public
hearings.
Activities: Supports environmental NGOs in Europe, through the provision of
operational costs rather than project grants, with selection based on NGOs':
sustainable multiplier effect at European level; contribution to transnational co-
operation; capacity to promote dialogue and co-operation; capacity to favour a
multisector approach to environmental issues; and promotion of the EC's
environmental policy. The Programme was scheduled to run from 2002–06.
Geographical Area of Activity: Europe, including European Union candidate
countries and Balkan countries.
How to Apply: Applications are invited annually, at the beginning of the year.
Financial Information: Global budget €32,000,000 (2002-06).
Contact: Contact Annika Agerblad.

Address: 200 rue de la Loi, 1049 Brussels, Belgium.

Telephone: (2) 296-91-00; *Internet:* http://europa.eu.int/comm/environment /funding/finansup.htm; *e-mail:* annika.agerblad@cec.eu.int.

Euro-Mediterranean Partnership (MEDA): SMAP—Small and Medium Term Priority Environmental Action Plan Mediterranean

Part of the MEDA Programme; the principal financial instrument of the Euro-Mediterranean Partnership.

Activities: Aims to protect the Mediterranean environment and to contribute to the sustainable development of the region, through funding for awareness-raising activities, including campaigns and documentation centres; capacity building and partnership building; education and training programmes; transfer of appropriate and environmentally sound technologies and know-how; and networking to promote North–North, South–South and North–South co-operation. Priority areas are integrated management of water, waste management, hot spots, integrated management of coastal areas, and the fight against desertification.

Geographical Area of Activity: Mediterranean countries: Algeria, Cyprus, Egypt, Israel, Jordan, Lebanon, Malta, Morocco, Palestinian Autonomous Areas, Syria, Tunisia and Turkey.

Financial Information: Annual budget €20,000,000 (2003); grants for regional projects between €1,000,000 and €5,000,000.

Contact: Contact Athena Mourmouris.

Address: 200 rue de la Loi, DG Environment A4, 1049 Brussels, Belgium.

Telephone: (2) 296-39-51; *Internet:* http://europa.eu.int/comm/environment/smap /home.html; *e-mail:* athena.mourmouris@cec.eu.int.

Grants in the Field of the Environment

The grant programme was established to ensure the implementation of existing environmental legislation and integrate environmental concerns into all relevant policy areas.

Activities: Grants are made to organizations to complement European environmental policy in the fields of: civil society, to strengthen awareness raising and the provision of information to citizens within the areas of climate change, nature and biodiversity, environment and health, and natural resources and waste; nature and biodiversity; climate change and energy; chemicals; radiation protection; enlargement and neighbouring countries; and development and global biodiversity. Funded activities include audiovisual productions, public events, and information campaigns.

Geographical Area of Activity: European Union, Central and Eastern Europe, and Mediterranean countries.

How to Apply: Applications are accepted annually.

Financial Information: Annual budget €1,200,000 (2003); grants available for up to 75% of the total project costs.

Contact: Contact Valérie Drezet.

Address: 200 rue de la Loi, 1049 Brussels, Belgium.

Telephone: (2) 296-00-38; *Internet:* http://europa.eu.int/comm/environment /funding/general/index_en.htm; *e-mail:* valerie.drezet-humez@cec.eu.int.

LIFE III: LIFE–Environment

Forms part of the LIFE programme (q.v.), launched in 1992. This strand of the programme was launched in 2000 and aims to support the development of innovative techniques relating to the environment.

Activities: The programme aims to bridge the gap between research and development results and their large-scale application. It works to achieve its objectives through providing co-financing for demonstration projects and the dissemination of results within five eligible areas: land-use development and planning; water management; reduction of the environmental impact of economic activities; waste management; and reduction of the environmental impact of products through an integrated product policy. Funded projects include: decontamination of treated wood waste; local environmental management plans; integrated initiatives to promote sustainable development and sustainable tourism; mobility and environment-friendly transport; action to combat the greenhouse effect and air pollution: promotion of ecological construction; sustainable development strategies in urban and rural areas; reducing the environmental impact of pig farming; integrated management of coastal areas and river basins; sustainable forest management; and the re-use of waste information technology (IT) equipment.

Geographical Area of Activity: European Union (EU), and Mediterranean and Baltic countries (Algeria, Bosnia-Herzegovina, Croatia, Cyprus, Egypt, Israel, Jordan, Lebanon, Malta, Morocco, Baltic shoreline of Russia, Syria, Tunisia, Turkey and Palestinian Autonomous Areas), and participating Central and Eastern European EU accession candidate countries (Estonia, Latvia, Hungary, Romania, Slovenia and Slovakia).

Restrictions: No funding for research or investment in existing technologies or infrastructure.

How to Apply: Each year a call for proposals is published in the Official Journal (OJEC), and the member states and third countries send the Commission their project proposals. The Commission publishes the closing date in the OJEC and evaluates the proposals. The Commission is responsible for the financial control and monitoring of the implementation of LIFE projects. Accompanying measures ensure the on-site monitoring of projects and dissemination of results.

Financial Information: The EU has allocated approx. €300,000,000 for the programme for the period 2000–04. Grants are available for up to 30% of the project costs for projects generating substantial net revenue and up to 50% in other cases.

Publications: Searchable on-line database of funded projects.

Contact: Head of Unit Bruno Julien; Contact Angelo Salsi.

Address: BU5, 200 rue de la Loi, 1049 Brussels, Belgium.

Telephone: (2) 295-61-33; *Fax:* (2) 296-95-56; *Internet:* http://europa.eu.int/comm /environment/life/contact/home.htm; *e-mail:* bruno.julien@cec.eu.int.

LIFE III: LIFE–Third Countries

Forms part of the LIFE programme (q.v.), launched in 1992. This strand of the programme was launched in 2000 and aims to contribute to the establishment of capacities and administrative structures needed in the environmental sector and in the development of environmental policy and action programmes in third countries bordering on the Mediterranean and the Baltic Sea as well as Central and Eastern European European Union accession candidate countries.

Activities: The programme funds technical assistance projects carried out in specified third countries in the Mediterranean and the Baltic Sea area as well as Central and Eastern European countries, which contribute to the implementation of regional and international guide-lines and agreements; promote sustainable development at international, national or regional level; and provide solutions to major environmental problems in the region and the relevant sector. Priority is given to projects which will promote co-operation at the trans-frontier, transnational or regional level. Funded projects include: sustainable traffic development; creation of an environmental information, awareness and training centre; environmental action plans; introduction of national provisions concerning air pollution and waste; integrated management of the rural environment; creation of natural tourist parks; measures to combat forest fires; and establishment of pilot desertification monitoring systems.

Geographical Area of Activity: European Union (EU), and Mediterranean and Baltic countries (Algeria, Bosnia-Herzegovina, Croatia, Cyprus, Egypt, Israel, Jordan, Lebanon, Malta, Morocco, Baltic shoreline of Russia, Syria, Tunisia, Turkey and Palestinian Autonomous Areas), and participating Central and Eastern European accession candidate countries (Estonia, Latvia, Hungary, Romania, Slovenia and Slovakia).

How to Apply: Each year a call for proposals is published in the Official Journal (OJEC), and the member states and third countries send the Commission their project proposals. The Commission publishes the closing date in the OJEC and evaluates the proposals. The Commission is responsible for the financial control and monitoring of the implementation of LIFE projects. Accompanying measures ensure the on-site monitoring of projects and dissemination of results.

Financial Information: The EU has allocated approximately €38,000,000 for the programme for the period 2000–04. Grants are available for up to 75% of the total project costs.

Publications: Searchable on-line database of funded projects.

Contact: Head of Unit Bruno Julien; Contact Angelo Salsi.

Address: BU5, rue de la Loi 200, 1049 Brussels, Belgium.

Telephone: (2) 295-61-33; *Fax:* (2) 296-95-56; *Internet:* http://europa.eu.int/comm/environment/life/contact/home.htm; *e-mail:* bruno.julien@cec.eu.int.

LIFE Unit—Unit D1: LIFE–Nature

Forms part of the LIFE programme (q.v.), launched in 1992. This strand of the programme was launched in 2000 and aims to promote flora and fauna conservation.

Activities: The programme aims to conserve or restore natural habitats and wild flora and fauna species, as listed in the Birds Directive (79/409/EEC) and the

Habitats Directive (92/43/EEC), and to establish the Natural 2000 network to preserve biodiversity by maintaining or restoring natural habitats of Community importance. The programme funds a range of nature conservation projects, reflecting the diversity of natural environments in Europe, including: land acquisition to protect areas of special importance; restoration of riverbanks and wetland habitats; reintroduction of grazing; preservation of Baltic boreal coastal meadows; protection of almost extinct and declining species (brown bears, European black vultures, European mink, bats, etc.); ecological land management contracts with groups of farmers; restoration of biodiversity destroyed by farming; and the reintroduction of spontaneous processes to recreate natural landscapes.

Geographical Area of Activity: European Union (EU), and Mediterranean and Baltic countries (Algeria, Bosnia-Herzegovina, Croatia, Cyprus, Egypt, Israel, Jordan, Lebanon, Malta, Morocco, Baltic shoreline of Russia, Syria, Tunisia, Turkey and Palestinian Autonomous Areas), and participating Central and Eastern European EU accession candidate countries (Estonia, Latvia, Hungary, Romania, Slovenia and Slovakia).

How to Apply: Projects must concern Special Protection Areas or Sites of Community Importance. Each year a call for proposals is published in the Official Journal (OJEC), and the member states and third countries send the Commission their project proposals. The Commission publishes the closing date in the OJEC and evaluates the proposals. The Commission is responsible for the financial control and monitoring of the implementation of LIFE projects. Accompanying measures ensure the on-site monitoring of projects and dissemination of results.

Financial Information: The EU has allocated approximately €300,000,000 for the programme for the period 2000–04. Grants are available for up to 50% of the project costs. Exceptionally, for projects concerning priority natural habitats or priority species defined in the Habitats Directive, the Commission can finance up to 75% of the project's eligible costs.

Publications: Searchable on-line database of funded projects.

Contact: Head of Unit Bruno Julien; Contact Angelo Salsi.

Address: BU 9 02/1, 1049 Brussels, Belgium.

Telephone: (2) 295-61-33; *Fax:* (2) 296-95-56; *Internet:* http://europa.eu.int/comm /environment/life/contact/home.htm; *e-mail:* bruno.julien@cec.eu.int.

LIFE Unit—Unit D1: LIFE III

Launched in 1992, LIFE (The Financial Instrument for the Environment) is one of the spearheads of European Community environment policy. It co-finances environmental initiatives in the European Union (EU) and a number of third countries bordering on the Mediterranean and the Baltic Sea and in participating Central and Eastern European accession candidate countries. In the framework of sustainable development, the programme aims to contribute to the implementa-tion, development and enhancement of the Community environmental policy and legislation as well as the integration of the environment into other EU policies. It also promotes new solutions to environmental problems faced by the EU and works towards the implementation of Community policy, defined by the Sixth Action Programme for the Environment, based on a practical approach.

Activities: LIFE programmes fall under three strands: LIFE–Nature, LIFE–Envi-ronment and LIFE–Third Countries (qq.v.).

Geographical Area of Activity: EU, Mediterranean and Baltic countries (Algeria, Bosnia and Herzegovina, Croatia, Cyprus, Egypt, Israel, Jordan, Lebanon, Malta, Morocco, Baltic shoreline of Russia, Syria, Tunisia, Turkey and Palestinian Autonomous Areas), and participating Central and Eastern European EU accession candidate countries (Estonia, Latvia, Hungary, Romania, Slovenia and Slovakia).

How to Apply: Each year a call for proposals is published in the Official Journal (OJEC), and the member states and third countries send the Commission their project proposals. The Commission publishes the closing date in the OJEC and evaluates the proposals. The Commission is responsible for the financial control and monitoring of the implementation of LIFE projects. Accompanying measures ensure the on-site monitoring of projects and dissemination of results.

Financial Information: Current phase (2000–04) has a budget of €640,000,000; approx. €1,490,000,000 committed since 1992.

Contact: Head of Unit Bruno Julien; Contact Angelo Salsi.

Address: BU 9 02/1, 1049 Brussels, Belgium.

Telephone: (2) 295-61-33; *Fax:* (2) 296-95-56; *Internet:* http://europa.eu.int/comm /environment/life/contact/home.htm; *e-mail:* bruno.julien@cec.eu.int.

DIRECTORATE-GENERAL EXTERNAL RELATIONS

Euro-Mediterranean Partnership (MEDA): Euro-Mediterranean Foundation

Scheduled to be launched by the European Commission in July 2004; aims to promote a dialogue of cultures and civilizations, and to raise awareness of the Barcelona Process through intellectual, cultural and civil society exchanges.

Activities: The Foundation is expected to focus on five areas: promoting dialogue with Islam, in particular experiences of the European version of Islam; the issue of rising illegal immigration; accelerating co-operation between SMEs and development of entrepreneurship in the Mediterranean region; increasing scientific co-operation between Mediterranean and European universities; and the development of Euro-Mediterranean co-operation in the field of defence policy. The Foundation will support projects based in Egypt, Israel, the Lebanon and Maghreb countries.

Geographical Area of Activity: Europe and the Mediterranean region.

Address: 200 rue de la Loi, 1049 Brussels, Belgium.

Information for Third Countries

Aims to promote the work of the European Community and improve the image of the European Union (EU) in non-member countries.

Activities: Grants are given to NGOs, universities and schools, Chambers of Commerce and industry, for projects promoting the image of the EU in non-member countries, and the development of effective communication and information activities. NGOs can apply through a delegation of the European Commission in the country where the project is to be carried out.

Geographical Area of Activity: International.

How to Apply: Applications may be submitted at any time.

Financial Information: Annual budget €5,000,000 (2003).

Contact: Contact Saturnino Munoz-Gomez.

Address: 200 rue de la Loi, DG External Relations I5, 1049 Brussels, Belgium.

Telephone: (2) 299-93-32; *Internet:* http://europa.eu.int/comm/external_relations /index.htm; *e-mail:* saturnino.munoz@cec.eu.int.

New Transatlantic Agenda (NTA)

Established in December 1995 at the European Union (EU)–US Summit in Madrid, jointly signed by then European Commission President Santer, Spanish Prime Minister González, as President of the European Council, and US President Clinton. Aims to develop the transatlantic relationship, moving from one of consultation to one of joint action in four major fields: promoting peace and stability, democracy and development around the world; responding to global challenges; contributing to the expansion of world trade and closer economic relations; and building bridges across the Atlantic. The NTA is accompanied by a Joint EU–US Action Plan.

Activities: Works to develop co-operation between the EU and the USA, through grants for initiatives which promote a greater awareness, understanding and positive perception of the EU in the USA; focus on globalization of the economy and EU–US relations; concern extraterritoriality, jurisdiction and inter-dependence; and combat computer-related crime. Funded activities include public awareness raising, analysis and studies, and recommendations.

Geographical Area of Activity: EU and North America.

How to Apply: Grants are awarded annually.

Financial Information: Annual budget €160,000 (2003); maximum grant €40,000.

Contact: Contact Eric Hayes.

Address: 200 rue de la Loi, DG External Relations C1, 1049 Brussels, Belgium.

Telephone: (2) 299-16-99; *Internet:* http://europa.eu.int/comm/external_relations /us/new_transatlantic_agenda/index.htm; *e-mail:* eric.hayes@cec.eu.int.

DIRECTORATE-GENERAL FISHERIES

European Structural Funds: Financial Instrument for Fisheries Guidance (FIFG)

One of the four European Structural Funds and administered by DG Fisheries.

Activities: FIFG funds structural measures in the fisheries sector, fulfilling two major objectives: to contribute to the aims of the common fisheries policy, and to strengthen economic and social cohesion. Eligible actions are mainly directed towards developing infrastructure and promoting industrial change, including fleet modernization, fish farming and marketing.

Geographical Area of Activity: European Union.

How to Apply: To apply for funding, organizations must contact the national authorities in the relevant country; application procedures vary according to national rules and regulations.

Contact: Contact Chiara Gariazzo.

Address: 200 rue de la Loi, 1049 Brussels, Belgium.

Telephone: (2) 299-92-55; *Fax:* (2) 299-30-40; *Internet:* http://europa.eu.int/comm /fisheries/policy_en.htm.

DIRECTORATE-GENERAL HEALTH AND CONSUMER PROTECTION

Health, Consumer Protection and Social Policy: Support to European Consumer Organizations

Established to support the activities of European consumer organizations.

Activities: Aims to support the promotion, presentation and defence of consumers' interests at European Community level, through supporting the annual running costs of consumers' organizations. Applicant organizations must be NGOs, aim to promote and protect the interests and health of consumers, and be mandated to operate at European level.

Geographical Area of Activity: European Union.

How to Apply: Grants are awarded annually.

Financial Information: Annual budget €1,500,000 (2003); up to 50% of the total project costs available.

Contact: Contact Arturo Montforte.

Address: 200 rue de la Loi, 1049 Brussels, Belgium.

Telephone: (2) 295-51-41; *Internet:* http://europa.eu.int/comm/dgs /health_consumer/library/tenders/call08-09-intro_en.html; *e-mail:* arturo .montforte@cec.eu.int.

Programme of Community Action on Public Health

The Programme brings together eight former programmes on public health: cancer, AIDS, drug dependence, rare diseases, pollution-related diseases, health monitoring, health information and injury prevention. Aims to improve public health information, enhance co-ordinated responses to health threats, and prevent the spread of disease.

Activities: Within different programme strands, funding is provided to initiatives relating to monitoring and rapid reaction public health initiatives, and the co-ordination of activities by non-profit organizations active in the field of health. The programme was to run from 2003–06.

Geographical Area of Activity: Europe.

How to Apply: Grants awarded annually.

Financial Information: Global budget €312,000,000 (2003–06); grants available range from €100,000 to €1,000,000.

Contact: Contact Horst Kloppenburg.

Address: Plateau du Kirchberg, 2920 Luxembourg, Luxembourg.

Telephone: 4301-33926; *Internet:* http://europa.eu.int/comm/health; *e-mail:* horst .kloppenburg@cec.eu.int.

Programme of Community Action on Public Health—Strand 1

Forms part of the European Commission's general Programme of Community Action on Public Health, promoting the improvement of public health information.

Activities: Operates through grants for health information initiatives, including the promotion of information exchange on communicable and non-communicable diseases, development of dialogue between member states and stakeholders on health issues, and the exchange of information and best practice.

Geographical Area of Activity: Europe.

How to Apply: Grants awarded annually.

Financial Information: Receives part of the global programme budget of €312,000,000; grants available range from €250,000 to €500,000, up to 70% of the total project costs.

Contact: Contact Josepha Wonner.

Address: rue Alcide de Gaspéri, DG Health and Consumer Protection F2, 2920 Luxembourg, Luxembourg.

Telephone: 4301-33007; *Internet:* http://europa.eu.int/comm/health; *e-mail:* josepha.wonner@cec.eu.int.

Programme of Community Action on Public Health—Strand 2

Forms part of the European Commission's general Programme of Community Action on Public Health, promoting the implementation of strategies responding to threats to health, in particular communicable diseases.

Activities: Aims to support initiatives designed to respond to health threats, through grants for a range of activities, including: strategies for preventing, exchanging information on and responding to non-communicable disease threats, including gender-specific and rare diseases; exchanging information on vaccination and immunization strategies; developing methods for reducing antibiotic resistance; and protecting human health from possible adverse effects of environmental factors.

Geographical Area of Activity: Europe.

How to Apply: Grants awarded annually.

Financial Information: Receives part of the global programme budget of €312,000,000; grants available range from €300,000 to €500,000, up to 70% of the total project costs.

Contact: Contact Henriette Chamouillet.

Address: Plateau du Kirchberg, DG Health and Consumer Protection G2, 2920 Luxembourg, Luxembourg.

Telephone: 4301-38135; *Internet:* http://europa.eu.int/comm/health; *e-mail:* henriette.chamouillet@cec.eu.int.

Programme of Community Action on Public Health—Strand 3

Forms part of the European Commission's general Programme of Community Action on Public Health, supporting public health promotion, education, information and training.

Activities: Operates in the field of public health promotion, education, information and training, through grants to organizations carrying out awareness-raising activities on life-style and health, including nutrition, drugs, tobacco, alcohol and physical exercise; developing strategies to counter health inequalities and assessing the impact of socio-economic factors on health; assessing the effect of the environment on health; analyzing the success of public health strategies; and encouraging relevant training activities.

Geographical Area of Activity: Europe.

How to Apply: Grants awarded annually.

Financial Information: Receives part of the global programme budget of €312,000,000; grants available range from €250,000 to €500,000, up to 70% of the total project costs.

Contact: Contact Josepha Wonner.

Address: rue Alcide de Gaspéri, DG Health and Consumer Protection F2, 2920 Luxembourg, Luxembourg.

Telephone: 4301-33007; *Internet:* http://europa.eu.int/comm/health; *e-mail:* josepha.wonner@cec.eu.int.

Programme of Community Action on Public Health—Strand 4

Forms part of the European Commission's general Programme of Community Action on Public Health, promoting transversal projects in the field of public health.

Activities: The programme is run in close collaboration with the member states, funding initiatives in the following areas: networking activities; development and implementation of health promotion and disease prevention projects, involving NGOs, pilot projects and networks of national institutions; activities relating to legislation; the promotion of NGO co-operation at European Union level; and meetings and information exchange between public health experts.

Geographical Area of Activity: Europe.

How to Apply: Grants awarded annually.

Financial Information: Receives part of the global programme budget of €312,000,000; grants available range from €250,000 to €500,000, up to 70% of the total project costs.

Contact: Contact Josepha Wonner.

Address: rue Alcide de Gaspéri, DG Health and Consumer Protection F2, 2920 Luxembourg, Luxembourg.

Telephone: 4301-33007; *Internet:* http://europa.eu.int/comm/health; *e-mail:* josepha.wonner@cec.eu.int.

DIRECTORATE-GENERAL OF HUMAN RIGHTS

European Commission against Racism and Intolerance (ECRI)

Established following a decision of the first Summit of Heads of State and Government of the member States of the Council of Europe, held in Vienna in October 1993, and strengthened by a decision of the second Summit held in Strasbourg in October 1997. ECRI's task is to combat racism, xenophobia, anti-Semitism and intolerance at the level of greater Europe and from the perspective of the protection of human rights.

Activities: Undertakes activities in three programme areas: country-by-country approach; work on general themes; and ECRI and civil society. In the first area of activity, ECRI analyses the situation regarding racism and intolerance in each of the member states, in order to advise governments on measures to combat these problems. General themes include the preparation of policy recommendations and guide-lines on issues of importance for combating racism and intolerance. Also collects and disseminates examples of good practices relating to these issues. Under the third programme area, ECRI aims to disseminate information and raise awareness of the problems of racism and intolerance among the general public. Collaborates with four NGO networks: UNITED for Intercultural Action, the Internet Centre Anti-Racism in Europe (ICARE), the European Network Against Racism (ENAR) and the European Research Centre on Migration and Ethnic Relations (ERCOMER), and organizes national roundtable meetings.

Geographical Area of Activity: Europe.

Publications: Annual Report.

Contact: Exec. Sec. Isil Gachet.

Address: 67075 Strasbourg Cedex, France.

Telephone: 3-88-41-20-00; *Fax:* 3-88-41-39-87; *Internet:* www.coe.int/t/e /human_rights/ecri.

DIRECTORATE-GENERAL INFORMATION SOCIETY

Eumedis 1

The programme aims to develop a Euro-Mediterranean information society.

Activities: Operates through launching pilot regional co-operation projects in the field of the information society, and creating collaborative actions between European and Mediterranean research networks. Funded activities include: the development of a regional health-care network; pilot projects for Euro-Mediterranean electronic commerce; pilot projects in the areas of tourism and cultural heritage; pilot projects on information technology (IT) research; and pilot projects in the field of education, including production of innovative and multilingual course materials, the design of Euro-Mediterranean, computer-assisted, research and education programmes and public databases in regional priority areas. Projects must involve at least two European Union partners and a group of Mediterranean partner organizations as large as possible.

Geographical Area of Activity: Mediterranean countries.

110

How to Apply: Grants are awarded annually; seven copies of the project proposal must be submitted, in English or in French.

Financial Information: Global budget €45,000,000; minimum grants €1,000,000, up to 80% of the project's total costs.

Contact: Contact Bruno Ferlito.

Address: 200 rue de la Loi, DG Information Society F4, 1049 Brussels, Belgium.

Telephone: (2) 298-45-55; *Internet:* http://europa.eu.int/ispo/eumedis /versionfrancaise/i_eumedis_def_fr.html; *e-mail:* bruno.ferlito@cec.eu.int.

Medici

Established not as a grant-making organization but as a mechanism to enhance cultural co-operation.

Activities: The programme promotes partnerships and co-operation between museums, cultural organizations and industry, through an open frame permitting the exchange of experience and co-operation, and the development of economic activities creating job opportunities linked with cultural employment. Open to participation by European museums and cultural heritage organizations, universities and research centres, public and private organizations and industry. It is also open to non-European institutions which have an interest in European culture.

Geographical Area of Activity: European Union.

Restrictions: No grants awarded.

How to Apply: Open to applications at any time.

Contact: Contact Mario Verdese.

Address: 200 rue de la Loi, 1049 Brussels, Belgium.

Telephone: (2) 296-35-18; *Internet:* www.medicif.org; *e-mail:* mario.verdese@cec .eu.int.

DIRECTORATE-GENERAL JUSTICE AND HOME AFFAIRS

AGIS—Programme on Police and Judicial Co-operation in Criminal Matters

A framework programme combining five previous programmes (Grotius–Criminal, Stop II, Oisin II, Hippokrates and Falcone), and preparatory actions to stop drugs-trafficking. Aims to develop a European criminal judicial area and the introduction of European instruments; strengthen networking and mutual co-operation activities on subjects of common interest to the member states in the field of justice and security; improve and adapt training and technical and scientific research; and encourage member states to set up co-operative activities with the candidate countries, other third countries and appropriate regional and international organizations.

Activities: Provides grants to universities, training centres, research organizations, NGOs and other organizations to support vocational training activities; joint exchange programmes and traineeships; research, specialized studies, including operational feasibility studies and assessment; and co-operation and networking between judicial authorities in order to prevent and fight crime. In 2003 the priority fields were the European judicial area, strengthening co-operation between organizations, preventing and fighting organized crime, preventing drugs-trafficking, victim assistance, threat assessment, comparability of information and statistics. The programme was scheduled to run from 2003–07.

Geographical Area of Activity: Central and Eastern Europe, and the European Union.

How to Apply: Following consultation with the annual call text and work programme; applications are accepted annually at the beginning of the year. Projects must involve at least three partners (private or public) from different member states.

Financial Information: Global budget €65,000,000 (2003–07).

Contact: Contact Brian Lucas.

Address: 200 rue de la Loi, DG Justice and Home Affairs B5, 1049 Brussels, Belgium.

Telephone: (2) 299-10-57; *Internet:* http://europa.eu.int/comm/justice_home /funding/agis/wai/funding_agis_en.htm; *e-mail:* jai-agis@cec.eu.int.

European Fund for Refugees

The Fund aims to analyze and evaluate the conditions for the reception of asylum seekers, displaced people and refugees; support the voluntary return of refugees, displaced people and asylum seekers; help build the capacity of the organizations within the member states and at European level which are active in the fields covered by the Fund; and disseminate best practices to opinion-formers at national and European level.

Activities: The Fund supports the development of services relating to the reception and voluntary repatriation of refugees and displaced people, through grants to organizations involved in the following activities: creation and improvement of infrastructures, development of a more equitable and efficient administrative process; provision of subsistence means and support to particularly vulnerable categories of refugees and displaced people, including young people, victims of tortures or rapes requiring specific medical treatment; and public information, assistance and advice, training and education. Priorities in 2002 were voluntary return projects, issues surrounding protection for people with special needs or in special circumstances, reception conditions and health care, and the integration of vulnerable people. Transnational projects should involve at least two different member states.

Geographical Area of Activity: Africa (excluding South Africa), Asia, Central and Eastern Europe, Central and South America and the Caribbean, and the Pacific.

How to Apply: Grants are awarded annually.

Financial Information: Annual budget €2,000,000; grants range from €40,000 to €400,000, up to 80% of the project's total costs.

Contact: Contact Anne Boillot.

Address: 200 rue de la Loi, DG Justice and Home Affairs A2, 1049 Brussels, Belgium.
Telephone: (2) 299-20-61; *Internet:* http://europa.eu.int/comm/justice_home /funding/refugee/funding_refugee_en.htm; *e-mail:* anne.boillot@cec.eu.int.

INTI—Pilot Projects 2003—Integration of Third Country Nationals
A programme launched in 2003 to fund projects promoting the integration in the European Union (EU) member states of people who are not citizens of the EU.
Activities: Grants of up to 80% of the project's total costs are available to NGOs, local and regional authorities, associations, and SMEs for the support of initiatives promoting integration in EU member states of people who are not citizens of the EU, and for promoting dialogue with civil society, the development of integration models, the dissemination of best practices in the field, and the establishment of European-level networks. Projects must involve the collaboration of at least three member states, and can involve accession countries and/or other third countries although they are not eligible to receive funding under the framework.
Geographical Area of Activity: EU member states and accession countries.
How to Apply: Application details and guide-lines are available on the website.
Financial Information: Total budget €4,000,000; grants of up to 80% of the project's total costs.
Contact: Contact Helene Urth.
Address: LX46-6/50, DG Justice and Home Affairs A2, 1049 Brussels, Belgium.
Telephone: (2) 296-12-38; *Fax:* (2) 298-03-06; *Internet:* http://europa.eu.int/comm /justice_home/funding/inti/docs/appel_inti_2003_en; *e-mail:* jai-inti@cec.eu.int.

DIRECTORATE-GENERAL REGIONAL POLICY

European Structural Funds: European Regional Development Fund (ERDF)
One of the four European Structural Funds and administered by DG Regional Policy. The Fund co-finances actions to help reduce gaps in socio-economic development between various regions and member states. It is the primary contributor to programmes under Objectives 1 and 2, as well as the sole funder of the INTERREG III (q.v.) Community Initiative, and may contribute up to 75% of funding for the URBAN initiative (q.v.) in Objective 1 regions.
Activities: The Fund provides support for: productive investments to create and safeguard permanent jobs; investments in infrastructure; indigenous development, including local development and employment initiatives and the activities of small and medium-sized enterprises; innovative measures and technical assistance in regions under Objective 1 and areas under Objective 2; and investment linked to the environment. NGOs can only receive funding from ERDF if they are situated in an Objective 1 or Objective 2 area. The types of NGO projects given support by the Fund include urban regeneration projects in the areas of housing, employment, training and the environment, including pollution and conservation projects. Also supports innovative actions, including the

development of regional economies based on knowledge and technological innovation; e-Europe, which aims to promote the information society for the purpose of regional development; and regional identity and sustainable development initiatives.

Geographical Area of Activity: European Union.

How to Apply: NGOs wishing to apply for funding must apply through the regional authority responsible for the functioning and implementation of the Structural Funds' programmes.

Contact: Contact Jean-Charles Leygues.

Address: 1049 Brussels, Belgium.

Telephone: (2) 296-06-34; *Fax:* (2) 296-60-03; *Internet:* http://europa.eu.int/comm /regional_policy/; *e-mail:* regio-info@cec.eu.int.

URBAN II

Established to promote the economic and social regeneration of cities and neighbourhoods in crisis in order to promote sustainable urban development.

Activities: Aims to promote the formulation and implementation of innovative strategies for sustainable economic and social regeneration of small and medium-sized towns and cities as well as distressed urban neighbourhoods in larger cities, and to enhance and exchange knowledge and experience in relation to sustainable urban regeneration and development in the European Union (EU). Funding is provided for mixed use and environmentally friendly brownfield redevelopment, entrepreneurship and employment schemes, integration of excluded people and the affordable access to basic services, integrated public transport and communications, waste minimizing and treatment, development of the potential of information society technologies, and improvements in governance. The population of each urban area must be at least 10,000.

Geographical Area of Activity: EU.

How to Apply: The award procedure is decentralized and depends on the policy of the national and local managing authorities.

Financial Information: Global budget €700,000,000 (2000–06); minimum award of €500 per inhabitant; funded by the European Regional Development Fund (q.v.).

Contact: Contact Marcello Roma.

Address: 200 rue de la Loi, DG Regional Policies B2, 1049 Brussels, Belgium.

Telephone: (2) 295-82-56; *Internet:* http://europa.eu.int/comm/regional_policy /urban2/index_en.html; *e-mail:* mireille.grubert@cec.eu.int.

DIRECTORATE-GENERAL TRANSPORT AND ENERGY

Intelligent Energy for Europe (STEER)

The programme was launched in 2003 to support initiatives relating to all energy aspects of transport, the diversification of fuels and the promotion of renewable fuels and energy efficiency in transport, including the preparation of legislative measures and their applications.

Activities: Within the field of energy and transport, grants are awarded to organizations for a variety of activities, including: the promotion of sustainable development and security of energy supply; the creation, enlargement or reorganization of structures and instruments for sustainable energy development; the promotion of sustainable energy systems and equipment in order to accelerate their penetration of the market and to stimulate investment in this area; the development of information, education and training structures and the promotion and dissemination of know-how and best practice in this area; the monitoring of the implementation and the impact of Community initiatives and support measures; and the evaluation of the impact of projects funded under the programme.

Geographical Area of Activity: Europe.

How to Apply: Grants awarded annually.

Financial Information: Annual budget €31,000,000; grants are available for up to 50% of total project costs.

Address: 200 rue de la Loi, DG Transport and Energy D2, 1049 Brussels, Belgium.

Telephone: (2) 296-79-90; *Internet:* http://europa.eu.int/comm/energy/res /intelligent_energy/index_en.htm; *e-mail:* hans-jakob.mydske@cec.eu.int.

EUROPEAID CO-OPERATION OFFICE

Actions Undertaken by NGOs in Favour of Developing Countries

Aims to consolidate the role of NGOs through co-financing arrangements with European NGOs which are involved in encouraging the European public to support development, alleviating poverty, and enhancing the target group's quality of life and own inherent development capacities.

Activities: The programme consists of two main elements: support for European NGOs and their partners in developing countries, through grants for diverse development activities (90% of the total budget), and funding for awareness-raising activities through education and information campaigns (10% of budget). Funded projects include the construction of schools, free clinics, health programmes, information programmes, staff training and capacity-building activities.

Geographical Area of Activity: Europe and developing countries.

Restrictions: NGOs from developing countries cannot apply directly for funding; applications must be through a European NGO.

How to Apply: Applications are accepted once a year in March. Contact the information officer at EuropeAid in charge of the region covered; co-financing can be in the form of block grants, programmes or individual project funding.

Financial Information: Annual budget €200,000,000; grants are available for up to 75% of project costs.

Contact: Contact Aristotelis Bouratsis.

Address: 200 rue de la Loi, EuropeAid Co-operation Office F2, 1049 Brussels, Belgium.

Telephone: (2) 299-92-44; *Internet:* http://europa.eu.int/comm/europeaid/projects /ong_cd/index_fr.htm.

Aid for Population and Healthcare in Developing Countries

Aims to empower women, men and young people to make an informed choice about the number of children they have, contribute to the creation of the socio-cultural, economic and educational environment that allows this free choice, particularly by the condemnation of violence, mutilations and sexual abuse, and the development and reform of health systems in order to improve the accessibility and quality of health care.

Activities: Provides support for the development of population policies and programmes in developing countries, through grants to health care development initiatives, aimed primarily at young people and pregnant women; support for health-care promotion projects; improvement of health-care services in the areas of maternity, family planning, and the prevention and treatment of transmissible diseases; support to information and education campaigns raising awareness of population issues; and family planning services and information campaigns about family planning methods.

Geographical Area of Activity: Asia, Central and South America, and European Union and Mediterranean countries.

How to Apply: Projects must be co-financed; applications are accepted annually.

Financial Information: Annual budget €8,000,000.

Contact: Contact Marc de Brucker.

Address: 200 rue de la Loi, EuropeAid Co-operation Office F4, 1049 Brussels, Belgium.

Telephone: (2) 299-28-17; *Internet:* http://europa.eu.int/comm/europeaid/projects /index_en.htm; *e-mail:* marc.debrucker@cec.eu.int.

Aid to Uprooted People in Developing Countries

The programme follows emergency aid support, as part of the long-term development phase of affected countries, and aims to provide aid to refugees, displaced people and repatriated people who have left their countries in bad circumstances for their own safety and essential needs.

Activities: Grants are made to partnership projects of NGOs active in the following areas: placement of refugees in a host country; replacement of refugees in a third country; temporary or definitive placement of displaced people in their country; socio-economic integration of refugees, repatriated and displaced people in the host country or region, social reintegration in civil life of demobilized combatants, their families and communities; and assistance to local populations in host territories.

Geographical Area of Activity: Asia, Central and South America, and European Union countries.

How to Apply: NGOs may contact the EC delegations in the countries involved in reconstruction to propose their projects. Projects should be submitted by at least two NGOs, and be implemented over 2–3 years or more; the European Commission might ask the NGOs to work under the co-ordination of a specialized consultant.

Financial Information: Annual budget €40,000,000; project grants of up to €2,000,000.

Address: 200 rue de la Loi, EuropeAid Co-operation Office F4, 1049 Brussels, Belgium.

Telephone: (2) 296-66-07; *Internet:* http://europa.eu.int/europeaid/projects/eidhr /index_fr.htm; *e-mail:* thierry.dudermel@cec.eu.int.

ALBAN

Aims to encourage students, postgraduates and professionals from Central and South America to study in European Union (EU) countries, to promote the excellence of higher education in Europe, and to promote the employability of nationals from Central and South America in their own countries.

Activities: The programme awards mobility grants to graduate professionals from Central and South America for study and specialization within EU countries. The first grants were awarded for the 2003–04 academic year.

Geographical Area of Activity: Central and South America, and EU countries.

How to Apply: Application forms available on the website.

Financial Information: Budget 2002–05 €42,500,000; average annual grants €19,200, up to a maximum of 75% of the cost of the training.

Contact: Contact Maria Almeida Teixeira.

Address: 200 rue de la Loi, EuropeAid Co-operation Office E4, 1049 Brussels, Belgium.

Telephone: (2) 299-11-11; *Internet:* http://europa.eu.int/comm/europeaid/projects /alban/index_fr.htm; *e-mail:* europeaid-infoalban@cec.eu.int.

ALFA II

Aims to enhance co-operation and mutual enrichment of practices in higher education between the European Union (EU) and Central and South America, and to develop co-operation activities, university networks and student exchanges.

Activities: Provides support to academic projects related to the economic and social sciences, through two programmes: co-operation for institutional management and co-operation for scientific and technological training. Grants are for a range of network and co-operation activities, including the development of common research projects, the improvement, adaptation and harmonization of curricula, and the development of curricula for advanced training, including PhDs and masters courses. The programme was scheduled to run from 2000–05.

Geographical Area of Activity: Central and South America, and EU countries. Eligible countries from Central and South America are: Argentina, Bolivia, Brazil, Chile, Colombia, Costa Rica, Cuba, Ecuador, El Salvador, Guatemala, Honduras, Mexico, Nicaragua, Panama, Paraguay, Peru, Uruguay and Venezuela.

How to Apply: Grant decisions are made in January of each year.

Financial Information: Global budget €42,000,000 (2000–05).

Contact: Contact Maria Almeida Teixeira.

Address: 200 rue de la Loi, EuropeAid Co-operation Office E4, 1049 Brussels, Belgium.

Telephone: (2) 299-11-11; *Internet:* http://europa.eu.int/comm/europeaid/projects /alfa/index_fr.htm; *e-mail:* maria-esmeralda.almeida-teixeira@cec.eu.int.

Antipersonnel Landmines

Aims to eliminate land-mines and eradicate their social and economic effects on populations.

Activities: The programme operates through grants to NGOs and research organizations aiming to raise the public's awareness of the dangers and of the fight against antipersonnel land-mines. Funded activities include elaboration of a system of geographical information on land mines; marking and identification of mined fields; setting up of awareness campaigns; mine clearance training and provision of equipment; assistance for the victims of land mines; and research into a more profitable technology of mine detection and elimination. Priority is currently given to projects in South-Eastern Europe. The programme was to run from 2002–04.

Geographical Area of Activity: Africa, excluding South Africa, the Caribbean, Central and Eastern Europe, the Pacific, and the European Union.

How to Apply: Selection of beneficiaries is made once a year.

Financial Information: Annual budget €16,000,000.

Contact: Contact Thierry Dudermel.

Address: 200 rue de la Loi, EuropeAid Co-operation Office F3, 1049 Brussels, Belgium.

Telephone: (2) 299-66-07; *Internet:* http://europa.eu.int/comm/external_relations /mine/intro/index.htm; *e-mail:* thierry.dudermel@cec.eu.int.

Asia Information and Communications Technology (ICT)

Aims to advance mutually beneficial co-operation between countries of the European Union (EU) and Asia, and to promote the full utilization of European Information and Communications Technology (ICT) for applications in the following areas of activity: agriculture, education, health, transport, society, tourism, intelligent manufacturing and electronic commerce.

Activities: Initiatives funded under the programme include: Get-in-Touch and Keep-in-Touch activities, linking organizations to find solutions to adaptation and adaptability issues between Europe and Asia; university courses searching for solutions to problems posed by ICT; intensification of direct communication connections and electronic traffic between Europe and Asia; liaison between European ICT programmes, task forces and workshops; promotion of understanding of European and Asian regulatory and legislative organizational structures; and practical demonstration projects. Grants are available for associations, universities, SMEs, local and regional authorities, and research organizations, and projects must involve three participating partners: two from EU countries and one Asian partner. Participating countries in Asia are Afghanistan, Bangladesh, Bhutan, Brunei, Cambodia, India, Indonesia, Laos, Malaysia, Maldives, Nepal, Pakistan, the Philippines, Sri Lanka, Thailand, Timor Leste and Vietnam.

Geographical Area of Activity: EU and Asia (Afghanistan, Bangladesh, Bhutan, Brunei, Cambodia, India, Indonesia, Laos, Malaysia, Maldives, Nepal, Pakistan, the Philippines, Sri Lanka, Thailand, Timor Leste and Vietnam).

How to Apply: Two annual deadlines for submission of applications.

Financial Information: Global budget €25,000,000; grants of between 50% and 80% of the project's total costs, between €200,000 and €400,000.

Contact: Contact Massimiliano Dragoni.

Address: 200 rue de la Loi, EuropeAid Co-operation Office D2, 1049 Brussels, Belgium.

Telephone: (2) 295-85-24; *Internet:* http://europa.eu.int/comm/europeaid/projects /asia-itc/html/main.htm; *e-mail:* europeaid-asia-itc@cec.eu.int.

Asia and Latin America (ALA): Asia Pro Eco Programme

Launched in 2002, the Programme is one of a series of initiatives by the European Union (EU) designed to promote mutual benefit and understanding between the member states and Asia. The Programme aims to improve environmental performance and technology partnership in economic sectors, and promote sustainable responsible investment.

Activities: The Programme aims to promote policies, technologies and practices that promote cleaner, more resource-efficient, sustainable solutions to environmental problems in Asia. Grants are available to public and non-profit organizations for a range of related activities, including organization of working conferences, diagnostic studies, policy advice, feasibility studies, technology partnership and demonstration activities in the field of environment. Open to projects involving organizations from the 15 member states of the EU and 17 Asian states, Afghanistan, Bangladesh, Bhutan, Cambodia, China (with the exception of Hong Kong and Macao), India, Indonesia, Laos, Malaysia, Maldives, Nepal, Pakistan, Philippines, Sri Lanka, Thailand, Timor Leste and Vietnam. Brunei, Hong Kong, Macao and Singapore may be considered as project participants, but are not eligible to receive funding under this Programme.

Geographical Area of Activity: Member states of the EU and Afghanistan, Bangladesh, Bhutan, Cambodia, China (with the exception of Hong Kong and Macao), India, Indonesia, Laos, Malaysia, Maldives, Nepal, Pakistan, Philippines, Sri Lanka, Thailand, Timor Leste and Vietnam.

How to Apply: Information on how to apply is available on the website.

Financial Information: Total programme budget €82,300,000, including an EC contribution of €31,500,000.

Address: 28 rue Belliard, 1040 Brussels, Belgium.

Fax: (2) 298-48-63; *Internet:* http://europa.eu.int/comm/europeaid/projects /asia-pro-eco/index_en.htm; *e-mail:* europeaid-asia-pro-eco@cec.eu.int.

Asia and Latin America (ALA): Asia Urbs Programme

Established by the European Union (EU) as an instrument of decentralized co-operation (city–to–city) in 1998, following the New EU Strategy Toward Asia released by the European Commission in 1994, which had the main objectives of promoting mutual understanding between Asia and Europe, supporting the alleviation of poverty, and developing economic partnerships. This strategy was revised and updated in 2001 as Europe and Asia as a Strategic Framework for Enhanced Partnerships.

Activities: Aims to encourage local governments to join forces, share experience and knowledge, and effect a project in conjunction with civil society organizations, in order to help local communities improve their urban environment, contribute to the sustainability of their activities, and improve understanding between people and organizations at local and international level. The Programme's objectives are: to provide co-funding to local government partnerships to undertake urban development projects; and encourage the networking of these projects to share knowledge and experience with the ultimate goal of promoting capacity building for local government, to involve civil society in decision-making, and to encourage an approach to urban management in a sustainable way, environmentally, socially, and economically, to promote poverty alleviation. Pilot projects are co-funded by the Programme and encouraged to exchange information and experience through networking and Asia Urbs seminars.

Geographical Area of Activity: EU, South and South-East Asia, and People's Republic of China.

Restrictions: All local government and other organizations intending to be Partners or Associated Partners in a project must be based in one of the eligible countries in the EU, or in South/South-East Asia or China.

How to Apply: Annual call for proposals with at least one deadline; grant applications should be submitted within the timeframes given.

Address: 41 rue de la Loi, 3/49, 1049 Brussels, Belgium.

Telephone: (2) 298-47-31; *Fax:* (2) 298-48-63; *Internet:* http://europa.eu.int/comm /europeaid/projects/asia-urbs/; *e-mail:* europeaid-asia-urbs@cec.eu.int.

CARDS—Community Assistance for Reconstruction, Development and Stabilization

The programme takes over from the former OBNOVA programme; aims to provide reconstruction funding aid for the return of refugees; to support democracy and the rule of human rights; promote sustainable economic development and social development; and to foster transnational co-operation between the countries of the European Union (EU), Central and Eastern Europe, Balkans and Mediterranean.

Activities: Provides support for the stabilization and association process in South-Eastern European countries, through funding for regional co-operation and good neighbourhood projects and trans-border initiatives; rebuilding of infrastructure and other individual or collective facilities; consolidation of democracy and civil society; return of refugees, displaced persons and former soldiers into employment; preparation of the production process for economic recovery; development of the private sector, including small businesses; and the strengthening of NGOs, cultural organizations and educational institutions. Eligible countries are Albania, Bosnia and Herzegovina, Serbia and Montenegro and the former Yugoslav Republic of Macedonia. The programme is also open to the participation of organizations in Cyprus, Malta, Turkey and countries in Central and Eastern Europe. It was to run from 2000–06.

Geographical Area of Activity: EU, Central and Eastern Europe, Balkan and Mediterranean countries.

How to Apply: Grants are distributed several times each year, according to calls for proposals. The programme also acts flexibly to answer urgent needs; initial contact must be through the EC national delegation.

Financial Information: Global budget €4,650,000,000 (2000-06); minimum grant for small projects €100,000, minimum grant for large projects €1,000,000.

Contact: Contact Carmen Falkenberg.

Address: 200 rue de la Loi, 1049 Brussels, Belgium.

Telephone: (2) 296-42-41; *Internet:* http://europa.eu.int/comm/external_relations /index.htm; *e-mail:* carmen.falkenberg-ambrosio@cec.eu.int.

CARDS—Community Assistance for Reconstruction, Development and Stabilization: Calls for Proposals in the Fields of Justice and Home Affairs

Established by the European Commission, under its CARDS programme (q.v.), to support the provision of advice, training and the setting up of networking and co-operation mechanisms in the fields of justice and home affairs in the CARDS beneficiary countries.

Activities: Grants are available to NGOs within four programme areas: establishment of European Union-compatible legal, regulatory and institutional frameworks in the fields of asylum, migration and visa matters; development of reliable and functioning policing systems, and enhancement of methods of combating main criminal activities and police co-operation; development of a reliable and functioning prison system respecting fundamental rights and standards, and enhancement of regional networking and co-operation; and the establishment of an independent, reliable and functioning judiciary, and the enhancement of judicial co-operation, primarily in criminal matters. Financed activities include: regional and national thematic meetings, conferences, round tables with NGOs and representatives of civil society, police and security services, financial services, professional organizations, members of the judicial system, lawyers, prison and other law enforcement staff; specialist expert missions and gaps and needs analysis sessions; capacity-building activities: training sessions, study visits, and technical assistance; and establishment of information networks, libraries and support groups in order to pool information, enhance co-operation and facilitate co-ordinated action. All activities should take place in one or more of the Balkan countries.

Geographical Area of Activity: CARDS beneficiary countries: Balkan countries.

How to Apply: Guide-lines for proposals and preliminary application forms are available on the website.

Financial Information: Total budget €13,000,000; funded from the budget of the CARDS Regional Programme.

Contact: Head of Unit Colin Wolfe.

Address: L-41 02/110, EuropeAid Co-operation Office A3, 1 rue de Genève, 1049 Brussels, Belgium.

Internet: http://europa.eu.int/comm/europeaid/tender/data/aof41018.doc; *e-mail:* stephane.mechati@cec.eu.int.

CARDS—Community Assistance for Reconstruction, Development and Stabilization/OBNOVA: Democratic Stabilization and Civil Society Support in the Western Balkans

The programme aims to promote democracy and civil society in the Western Balkans, through support to civil society organizations, with the aim of helping to reduce cross-border crime, including regional actions to help fight trafficking in human beings and anti-corruption initiatives.

Activities: Up to six grants are awarded under this programme to activities carried out to support regional anti-trafficking and anti-corruption projects in the CARDS countries of the Western Balkans, for programmes running for up to 18 months.

Geographical Area of Activity: Western Balkans: Albania, Bosnia and Herzegovina, Bulgaria, Croatia, Cyprus, Czech Republic, Estonia, Hungary, Latvia, Lithuania, Malta, Poland, Romania, Serbia and Montenegro, Slovakia, Slovenia, the former Yugoslav Republic of Macedonia; and Turkey.

How to Apply: Guide-lines and application forms are available on the website.

Financial Information: Total budget €1,500,000; maximum grant available €500,000, minimum grant €250,000, up to 90% of the total project costs.

Contact: Contact Jacques van de Moortele.

Address: 28 rue Belliard, 1040 Brussels, Belgium.

Internet: http://europa.eu.int/comm/europeaid/tender/index_en.htm; *e-mail:* jacques.van-de-moortele@cec.eu.int.

Decentralized Co-operation

Aims to promote an approach to development which places the agent at the centre of the project implementation process so as to adapt projects to people's needs; support sustainable development initiatives undertaken by European Union (EU) decentralized co-operation agents and developing countries, whilst promoting participative development in response to initiatives developed by people in developing countries, the diversification and strengthening of civil society and the democratization of grassroots organizations, and the mobilization of decentralized co-operation agents in the European Community and in developing countries.

Activities: The programme seeks to encourage European and Southern NGO participation in the decentralization of EU-ACP development co-operation through grants to NGOs, local and regional authorities and research organizations. In 2002–03 financed projects focused on strengthening of institutions and the agent's capacity for action, promotion of North–South dialogue, increasing participation of decentralized co-operation programmes, and improving communication with civil society and networking. Priority is given to projects presented by organizations from developing countries. The programme was to run from 2002–06.

Geographical Area of Activity: Africa (excluding South Africa), Asia, Central and South America and the Caribbean, the Pacific, EU, Mediterranean countries, and other developing countries.

How to Apply: Contact the information officer at the Brussels Headquarters, as well as the EC delegation in the country where the project will take place.

Financial Information: Annual budget €5,800,000; grants available between €200,000 and €1,000,000.

Contact: Contact Efterpi Verigaki.

Address: 200 rue de la Loi, EuropeAid Co-operation Office F2, 1049 Brussels, Belgium.

Telephone: (2) 296-62-14; *Internet:* http://europa.eu.int/comm/europeaid/projects /ong_cd/index_fr.htm; *e-mail:* efterpi.verigaki@cec.eu.int.

Directorate D—Asia: Asia Link Programme

An EC initiative to promote regional and multilateral networking between higher education institutions in European Union (EU) member states and South Asia, South-East Asia and the People's Republic of China; aims to support the creation of new partnerships and new sustainable links between European and Asian higher education institutions, and to reinforce existing partnerships.

Activities: The Programme promotes regional and multilateral networking between higher education institutions in Europe, South and South-East Asia and China. Eligible countries are the 15 member states of the EU and 17 Asian countries. Partnerships must involve higher education institutions from at least two different EU member states and two different eligible Asian countries. Grants are made within three categories: Asia-Link Human Resource Development, Asia-Link Curriculum Development, and Asia-Link Institutional and Systems Development for the following types of activity: upgrading and enhancement of the skills and mobility of postgraduate students, teaching staff and administrators of higher education institutions through the provision of in-country and overseas training; promotion of the exchange of experience and encouragement of mutual knowledge and recognition of study programmes and reciprocal access to higher education; encouragement of the creation of a basis for future development, including common curricula and courses/modules, agreements on credit transfer and mutual degree recognition, and reciprocal access to higher education; increasing the availability of information about the EU higher education system in the participating Asian countries in order to enhance the attractiveness of European higher education; providing Asian students with a broader choice of study-abroad opportunities; and raising awareness of opportunities in the sector and development of links that can ultimately lead to mutually beneficial economic co-operation. Institutions and organizations from Brunei, Hong Kong, Macao and Singapore can also participate as associated/external partners, provided that they cover the costs of their own participation.

Geographical Area of Activity: EU member states and 17 Asian countries: Afghanistan, Bangladesh, Bhutan, Cambodia, People's Republic of China, India, Indonesia, Laos, Malaysia, Maldives, Nepal, Pakistan, Philippines, Sri Lanka, Thailand, Timor Leste and Vietnam.

Restrictions: No funding for scholarships or individual researchers.

How to Apply: Application details and guide-lines for applicants are available on the website.

Financial Information: Total budget €10,000,000; maximum grant available €300,000, minimum grant €200,000.

Address: L-41, 02/44, 1049 Brussels, Belgium.

Fax: (2) 298-48-63; *Internet:* http://europa.eu.int/comm/europeaid/projects /asia-link/index_en.htm; *e-mail:* europeaid-asia-link@cec.eu.int.

Environment: Tropical Forests and Environment in Developing Countries

Established to stimulate sustainable development and the integration of environmental protection in the development process.

Activities: The programme aims to: support activities undertaken within developing countries to enable the population of those countries to integrate environmental protection and the concepts of sustainable development into their daily lives; and promote the sustainable preservation and management of tropical forests that have a local importance, for example, for the prevention of soil erosion, or an international importance, for example linked to climatic change and losses of biological diversity. Funding is provided to NGOs for pilot projects that are likely to contribute to sustainable development; the development of operational tools likely to promote sustainable development; statistical analyses; and the assessment of the environmental impact of projects, programmes, strategies and sustainable development policies and their impact on social and economic development.

Geographical Area of Activity: Developing countries.

How to Apply: Application details are available on the website.

Financial Information: Annual budget €40,000,000 (2003); minimum grant €500,000, up to 80% of the total project costs.

Contact: Contact Franck Jacobs.

Address: 200 rue de la Loi, EuropeAid Co-operation Office F4, 1049 Brussels, Belgium.

Telephone: (2) 296-50-50; *Internet:* http://europa.eu.int/comm/europeaid/projects /index_en.htm; *e-mail:* franck.jacobs@cec.eu.int.

Euro-Mediterranean Partnership (MEDA): The Euro-Mediterranean Youth Action Programme

Launched in 1999, as part of the EC's Euro-Mediterranean Partnership, the Programme was scheduled to run until 2006. The Programme aims to facilitate the integration of young people into social and professional life and stimulate the democratization of the civil society of the Mediterranean partner countries, specifically through improving mutual comprehension and cohesion between young people across the Mediterranean basin, based on and committed to mutual respect, tolerance and dialogue between the various cultures.

Activities: The Programme targets young people in the Mediterranean partner countries of the EC, primarily through supporting capacity building of youth organizations, developing active citizenship of young people, especially young women, and promoting the exchange of information, experience and expertise between youth organizations. Activities funded include training courses and exchanges, and voluntary service initiatives. The Programme is open to young people (aged between 15 and 25), youth associations and local NGOs, which are legally resident or based in one of the 12 Mediterranean partner countries and in the 15 member states of the European Union (EU).

Geographical Area of Activity: EU and 12 Mediterranean partner countries (Algeria, Cyprus, Egypt, Israel, Jordan, Lebanon, Malta, Morocco, Palestinian Autonomous Areas, Syria, Tunisia and Turkey).

How to Apply: Applications can be submitted by any of the project partners, i.e. a sending or host group, or an organization based either in a EU member state or in one of the Mediterranean partner countries. It submits the application on behalf of all partners to the relevant National Agency and/or National co-ordinator, which then forwards it to the European Commission for project selection. Projects must be multilateral, with partners from at least four countries, at least two EU member states and two Mediterranean partner countries. There are three application deadlines each year.

Financial Information: Total budget €6,000,000.

Contact: Contact Alejandra Martinez Boluda.

Address: 200 rue de la Loi, 1049 Brussels, Belgium.

Telephone: (2) 299-86-75; *Fax:* (2) 299-40-38; *Internet:* http://europa.eu.int/comm /youth/priorities/euromed_en.html; *e-mail:* eac-euromedyouth@cec.eu.int.

Euro-Mediterranean Partnership (MEDA): Euromed Visitors Programme

Launched in 1998, as part of the EC's Euro-Mediterranean Partnership, the Programme allows representatives from the media and civil society from Mediterranean partner countries to acquaint themselves with the European Union (EU) and to acquire knowledge about the Euro-Mediterranean Partnership, particularly with respect to their specific field of activity.

Activities: The Programme organizes a one-week visit to Brussels where groups of 15 visitors from media and civil society organizations in Mediterranean partner countries hear presentations and debate different aspects of the EU, its history, treaties, institutions and key issues. The visitors also have the opportunity to have direct exchanges with EU officials, Members of the European Parliament, and to visit its major institutions (European Commission, Council of the EU and the European Parliament).

Geographical Area of Activity: EU and Mediterranean countries.

Financial Information: Grants of €25,000 are available for each visitor.

Address: 200 rue de la Loi, 1049 Brussels, Belgium.

Internet: http://europa.eu.int/comm/europeaid/projects/med/regional /mediavisits_en.htm.

Euro-Mediterranean Partnership (MEDA) II

The MEDA programme is the principal financial instrument of the Euro-Mediterranean Partnership, which aims to: turn the Mediterranean basin into an area of dialogue, exchange and co-operation guaranteeing peace, stability and prosperity; strengthen political dialogue; develop economic and financial co-operation; increase the social, cultural and human dimension; and by 2010 establish a free-trade area. It makes economic transition and free trade the central issue of European Union (EU) financial co-operation with the Mediterranean region. The partnership was launched at the 1995 Barcelona Conference between the EU and its 12 Mediterranean partners (called the Barcelona Process). The partners are Morocco, Algeria, Tunisia (Maghreb); Egypt, Israel, Jordan, Palestinian Autonomous Areas, Lebanon, Syria (Mashrek), Turkey, Cyprus and Malta; Libya currently has observer status at certain meetings. MEDA II, which was scheduled to run from 2000–06, follows the first MEDA programme, which ran from 1995–99.

Activities: Support from the programme is available to bilateral and regional co-operation projects. Bilateral project priorities are to support economic transition, aiming to prepare for the implementation of free trade through increasing competitiveness with a view to achieving sustainable economic growth, in particular through development of the private sector; and the strengthening of the socio-economic balance, aiming to alleviate the short-term costs of economic transition through appropriate measures in the field of social policy. Regional and multilateral co-operation project priorities are to strengthen activities in support of decentralized co-operation, in line with the Barcelona declaration, including addressing the requirements of the civil society Partnership for Peace programme. The Commission's External Relations Directorate-General is responsible for drawing up the strategy papers and the three-year indicative programmes. Based on this input, the Commission's EuropeAid Co-operation Office establishes the annual financing plans and manages the projects and programmes from the identification to the evaluation phase. The national and regional programmes take account of the priorities determined with the Mediterranean partners, in particular the conclusions of economic dialogue, and define the main goals, guide-lines and priority sectors of Community support in the fields concerned.

Geographical Area of Activity: EU and Mediterranean countries.

How to Apply: Grants are awarded annually.

Financial Information: Global budget €5,350,000,000 (2000-06).

Contact: Contact Zusanne Deignier.

Address: 200 rue de la Loi, 1049 Brussels, Belgium.

Telephone: (2) 299-07-09; *Internet:* http://europa.eu.int/cimm/external_relations /med_mideast/intro/; *e-mail:* zusanne.deignier@cec.eu.int.

European Initiative for Democracy and Human Rights (EIDHR)

Established to support activities in the fields of human rights, democratization and conflict prevention. The Initiative integrates all budget lines concerning human rights, democratization, international criminal tribunals and conflict prevention.

Activities: The Initiative operates through funding targeted projects, general calls for proposals and micro-projects, supporting activities in the field of human rights, democratization and conflict prevention. Priority themes are: support to strengthen democratization, good governance and the rule of law; activities in support of the abolition of the death penalty; support to the fight against torture and impunity and for international tribunals and criminal courts; and combating racism and xenophobia and discrimination against minorities and indigenous people.

Geographical Area of Activity: International.

How to Apply: Grants are awarded annually.

Financial Information: Annual budget €100,000,000; minimum grant €300,000.

Contact: Contact Timothy Clarke.

Address: 200 rue de la Loi, EuropeAid Co-operation Office F3, 1049 Brussels, Belgium.

Telephone: (2) 296-17-04; *Internet:* http://europa.eu.int/comm/europeaid/projects/eidhr/index_en.htm; *e-mail:* timothy.clarke@cec.eu.int.

European Initiative for Democracy and Human Rights (EIDHR): EC Support for the Rehabilitation of Victims of Torture

An initiative of the European Initiative for Democracy and Human Rights (EIDHR, q.v.), following adoption by the EC of a Communication in May 2001 which recommended a focus on the fight against torture and the rehabilitation of torture victims. Aims to influence third countries to take effective measures against torture and ill-treatment and to ensure the prohibition of torture and ill-treatment.

Activities: Grants are made to European Union (EU)-based NGOs providing rehabilitation to torture victims within the EU or in the accession countries, either individually or in partnership with other organizations, or for institutional strengthening. Rehabilitation services eligible for support, include psychotherapy and other psychiatric assistance, medical care, and social rehabilitation. Grants for institutional strengthening can be made for training of professionals and volunteers, development of managerial capacity, development of monitoring systems, development of fundraising capabilities, strengthening of partnerships with national health authorities, and public awareness building.

Geographical Area of Activity: EU and accession countries.

Restrictions: No grants for individual sponsorships, individual scholarships, one-off conferences or projects supporting single political parties.

How to Apply: Applications must be submitted on the official application form available on the website.

Financial Information: Total budget €11,500,000 (2003–04); minimum grant €300,000, maximum grant €1,500,000.

Address: 200 rue de la Loi, 1049 Brussels, Belgium.

Internet: http://europa.eu.int/comm/europeaid/tender/gestion/cont_typ/st /index_en.htm.

European Initiative for Democracy and Human Rights (EIDHR): EIDHR Microprojects Israel

Established by the European Commission as part of its European Initiative for Human Rights (EIDHR) to support the development of human rights in the West Bank/Gaza Strip and East Jerusalem area.

Activities: Aims to improve the capacity of local NGOs in the West Bank/Gaza Strip and East Jerusalem in terms of human resources, financial management, research and planning skills, and the strengthening of communication between civil society organizations and networks. Grants ranging from €15,000 to €50,000 are available for: projects promoting good governance and enhancing mechanisms of participatory governance at national and local councils level, including public awareness and campaigns, reporting on due process as well as taking legal actions pertaining to violations of laws, training of human rights field workers and researchers, mobilizing the local community in the prospective field, promoting dialogue on good governance at the formal and informal levels and in local councils, and combating corruption; and projects aimed at strengthening the legal system and its institutions, including enhancing the capacity of the legal profession, promoting the role of the Palestinian Bar Association, and developing legal and constitutional policies through research and inter-institutional activism.

Geographical Area of Activity: West Bank/Gaza Strip and East Jerusalem.

How to Apply: Application guide-lines are available on the website.

Financial Information: Total budget €500,000; minimum grant available €15,000, maximum grant €50,000.

Contact: Head of Social and Civil Society Sector Raffaella Iodice de Wolff.

Address: European Commission Technical Assistance Office West Bank and Gaza, George Adam Smith 5, POB 22207, Mount of Olives, Jerusalem, Israel.

Internet: http://europa.eu.int/comm/europeaid/projects/eidhr/calls-for -proposals/cfp-micro-gaza-guidelines_en; *e-mail:* mailto@delwbg.cec.eu.int.

European Initiative for Democracy and Human Rights (EIDHR): European Union Election Assistance and Observation

The programme was established to support electoral processes in developing countries without a stable democracy, as part of the European Initiative for Democracy and Human Rights (EIDHR, q.v.).

Activities: Aims to ensure the good functioning of democratic processes in third countries that do not have a stable democracy through grants for training of personnel taking part in electoral observation missions and projects providing access to the media during electoral campaigns. Specific attention is given to the increase in the visibility of the European Union in international observation missions and to projects presented by organizations with experience in the field of electoral observation and which involve more than one country.

Geographical Area of Activity: Africa (excluding South Africa), Asia, Central and South America and the Caribbean.

Restrictions: No grants for individuals, one-off conferences or projects exceeding 36 months.

How to Apply: Grants are awarded annually at the end of the year.

Financial Information: Annual budget €4,500,000.

Contact: Contact Victor Madeira Dos Santos.

Address: 200 rue de la Loi, EuropeAid Co-operation Office F3, 1049 Brussels, Belgium.

Telephone: (2) 299-08-54; *Internet:* http://europa.eu.int/comm/europeaid/projects/eidhr/elections_fr.htm; *e-mail:* victor.madeira-dos-santos@cec.eu.int.

European Programme for the Reconstruction and Development of South Africa (EPRD)

The Programme aims to support the South African government in its work of redeveloping and reconstructing the country.

Activities: Aims to provide support for the South African government's economic policies and programmes for integrating the South African economy into the global economy and trade standards; promote economic reform, support the private sector, supply social services and basic infrastructures for poor people; reinforce democracy, institution building, protection of human rights, good public governance and participation of civil society in the development process; and support the political reforms aiming at better living conditions and access to social services. Grants are made for basic social services, including education, health, water supply and purification; development of the private sector; democratization and good governance; and regional integration. Priority is given to projects targeting South Africa's poorest people. The Programme was to run from 2000–06.

Geographical Area of Activity: South Africa.

How to Apply: Applications are accepted at any time; projects should be initiated by partner organizations and proposed to the DG Development and the EC Delegation in South Africa.

Financial Information: Global budget €885,500,000 (2000–06); grants are available for between 25% and 100% of project costs.

Contact: Contact Mark Leysen.

Address: 200 rue de la Loi, EuropeAid Co-operation Office C4, 1049 Brussels, Belgium.

Telephone: (2) 299-26-20; *Internet:* http://europa.eu.int/comm/development_old/region/region_en.htm; *e-mail:* mark.leysen@cec.eu.int.

European Union–China Small Project Facility

Established to support the reform process in China and to contribute to the reinforcement of European Union (EU)-China co-operation activities. The programme is administered by a management agency in China.

Activities: Aims to support the reform process in China through the award of small grants to NGO projects of high quality and relevance both to the reform process and EC–China relations. Grants are made to NGOs in China carrying out small

129

projects of limited duration, in the fields of: social and economic reform, including legislative framework; World Trade Organization (WTO) accession-related issues and practices; environmental protection; higher education; promotion of good governance; and the promotion of mutual understanding through media and cultural initiatives. Proposals in other areas may be considered if the project is consistent with the priorities and objectives of the EU in China. The programme was to run from 2002–07.

Geographical Area of Activity: People's Republic of China.

Restrictions: No grants for humanitarian aid, equipment, science and technology projects, nor where projects overlap with main projects.

How to Apply: Applications can be submitted at any time.

Financial Information: Global budget €1,000,000; maximum grant available €100,000.

Contact: Contact Saintiago Herrero-Villa.

Address: 200 rue de la Loi, 1049 Brussels, Belgium.

Telephone: (2) 299-42-37; *Internet:* www.delchn.cec.eu.int/en/co-operation/spf .htm; *e-mail:* saintiago-herrero.villa@cec.eu.int.

European Union–China Training Programme on Village Governance

The programme aims to develop co-operation between the European Union (EU) and China to enhance the understanding and observance of the law on the part of villagers and elected representatives in their administrative and managerial functions, and to promote the development of village self-governance.

Activities: The Programme operates through providing technical assistance and funding to develop village self-governance in China, and through raising the level of democratic elections for Village Committees and democratic management, and improving the transparency and accountability of existing laws and regulations. Funded activities include teacher training in village electoral practices; strengthening of institutions in collaboration with the Ministry of Civil Affairs; providing scholarships for joint studies and data collection by Chinese and European researchers on village governance; dissemination of training and informal educational materials; exposure to international election techniques and local governance practices; organization of twinning activities between China and the EU; and research projects.

Geographical Area of Activity: People's Republic of China.

How to Apply: Applications are invited annually.

Financial Information: Global budget €14,000,000.

Contact: Contact Timothy Clarke.

Address: 200 rue de la Loi, 1049 Brussels, Belgium.

Telephone: (2) 295-17-04; *Internet:* www.delchn.cec.eu.int/en/co-operation /village_governance.htm; *e-mail:* timothy.clarke@cec.eu.int.

European Union Partnership for Peace Programme

Aims to strengthen relations between Israelis and Palestinians on the popular level in areas such as culture, education, media, research and the business community, and to support civil society initiatives in both countries that promote peace and conflict resolution.

Activities: The Programme aims to support the Middle East peace process principally through grants to strengthen NGOs and co-operation between Arab and Israeli NGOs, and for the creation of pressure groups that promote issues of regional and common concern. Preference is given to projects that include organizations from more than one country involved in the Middle East peace process, preferably involving at least one Arab and one Israeli civil society partner.

Geographical Area of Activity: Middle East.

How to Apply: Grants are awarded annually; applications should be sent to the EC Delegations in Gaza, Israel or Jordan.

Financial Information: Annual budget €4,000,000; grants range from €100,000 to €500,000, average up to 80% of the total project costs.

Contact: Contact Andreas Havelka.

Address: 200 rue de la Loi, EuropeAid Co-operation Office B2, 1049 Brussels, Belgium.

Telephone: (2) 295-89-45; *Internet:* http://europa.eu.int/comm/external_relations /mepp/index.htm.

European Union Partnership for Peace Programme: Middle East Peace Projects

A strand of the European Union Partnership for Peace programme (q.v.), aims to help re-create the conditions for re-launching the peace process and providing a solid foundation at civil society level for a just and lasting peace in the Middle East.

Activities: Aims to strengthen and increase direct civil society relationships and co-operation based on equality and reciprocity between Arabs and Israelis, including the Arab–Palestinian minority in Israel. Grants are made to support activities and initiatives assisting in the implementation of the peace roadmap in areas likely to have a direct impact on people's everyday lives and welfare, focusing on practical activities promoting communication and understanding. Eligible projects can be in various fields, including capacity building, co-operation of universities' student groups and other educational institutions, health, agriculture, environment, community co-operation, and rural development. Special priority is given to projects that promote non-violence and the development of a culture of tolerance, moderation and understanding, and media projects, creating channels of communication. Grants are available to NGOs, public-sector organizations, local authorities, media-related companies, research institutions, universities, schools and other education-related organizations, which have their headquarters in the European Unions or one of the beneficiary countries of the grants programme: Algeria, Cyprus, Egypt, Israel, Jordan, Lebanon, Malta, Morocco, Syria, Tunisia, Turkey and West Bank/Gaza.

131

Geographical Area of Activity: Algeria, Cyprus, Egypt, Israel, Jordan, Lebanon, Malta, Morocco, Syria, Tunisia, Turkey and West Bank/Gaza.

Financial Information: Total budget €5,800,000 (2003); maximum grant available €500,000, up to 80% of the project's total costs.

Address: 200 rue de la Loi, EuropeAid Co-operation Office B2, 1049 Brussels, Belgium.

Telephone: (2) 295-89-45; *Internet:* http://europa.eu.int/comm/europeaid/tender /forecast/.

FED/BUDGET: PROINVEST Business Development Services Activities

A programme of the ACP Group (African, Caribbean and the Pacific group of countries) and the European Commission, to promote investment and technology flows to enterprises operating within key sectors in the ACP States through support for business development support activities proposed by intermediary organizations. The programme is managed by the PROINVEST Management Unit on behalf of the European Commission.

Activities: Grants for the promotion of business development services are available in two areas: capacity building and *ad-hoc* training for ACP intermediaries, including the provision of investment promotion related capacity building and *ad-hoc* training assistance to intermediaries for developing or extending the range of their investment promotion related business development services; and the reinforcement of investment promotion agencies at regional level, including the provision of capacity building and *ad-hoc* training assistance to Investment Promotion Agencies (IPAs) and Export Promotion Zones (EPZs). Grants are available to organizations in ACP countries, and must involve at least two organizations from two different ACP countries.

Geographical Area of Activity: ACP countries (Africa, excluding South Africa, Caribbean and the Pacific).

How to Apply: Applications must be submitted using the standard application form attached to the guide-lines for applicants available on the website, whose format and instructions must be strictly observed. For each submission, one signed original application and five copies must be supplied by the applicant.

Financial Information: Total budget €870,000; maximum grant available €70,000.

Contact: Man. Patrick Keene.

Address: PROINVEST Management Unit, Centre for the Devt of Enterprise—CDE, 52 ave Herrmann-Debroux, 1160 Brussels, Belgium.

Telephone: (2) 679-18-50; *Fax:* (2) 679-18-70; *Internet:* www.proinvest-eu.org; *e-mail:* infos@proinvest-eu.org.

FED/BUDGET: PROINVEST Private Sector Advocacy and Policy Dialogue Initiatives

A programme of the ACP Group (African, Caribbean and the Pacific group of countries) and the European Commission, to promote investment and technology flows to enterprises operating within key sectors in the ACP States through support to intermediary organizations and professional associations and the development of inter-enterprise partnerships. The programme is managed by the PROINVEST Management Unit on behalf of the European Commission.

Activities: Grants are made for a number of activities related to enterprise development, including: policy dialogue strategy planning, for the preparation of proposals for action plans aiming at promoting public-private initiatives related to the improvement of the investment environment and climate (including public-private partnership approaches); development of investment policy proposals, including activities related to the development of initial action plans/strategy papers into fully substantiated policy proposals ready for submission to regional/national authorities and the reinforcement of intermediary organizations in the field of policy dialogue; and the implementation of policy proposals and lobbying activities, including the provision of technical assistance to ACP intermediaries in the course of lobbying regional/national authorities to introduce specific improvements in the regional/national investments in environment and climate, as well as implementation of specific policy proposals. Grants are available to organizations in ACP countries, and projects must involve at least two organizations from two different ACP countries.

Geographical Area of Activity: ACP countries (Africa, excluding South Africa, Caribbean and the Pacific).

How to Apply: Applications must be submitted using the standard application form attached to the guide-lines for applicants available on the website, whose format and instructions must be strictly observed. For each submission, one signed original of the application and five copies must be supplied by the applicant.

Financial Information: Total budget €1,520,000; maximum grant available €50,000.

Contact: Man. Patrick Keene.

Address: PROINVEST Management Unit, Centre for the Devt of Enterprise—CDE, 52 ave Herrmann-Debroux, 1160 Brussels, Belgium.

Telephone: (2) 679-18-50; *Fax:* (2) 679-18-70; *Internet:* www.proinvest-eu.org; *e-mail:* infos@proinvest-eu.org.

Food Aid and Food Security

Established to help ensure people have access to an appropriate diet as well as improving the accessibility and availability of food products to local populations, in accordance with their local food habits, production and trade systems, in particular in times of crisis.

Activities: Operates through making grants to development projects aiming to provide food security in developing countries, primarily Afghanistan, Angola, Armenia, Azerbaijan, Bangladesh, Bolivia, Burkina Faso, Cape Verde, Ethiopia, Georgia, Haiti, Honduras, Kyrgyzstan, Liberia, Madagascar, Malawi, Mauritania, Mozambique, Nicaragua, Niger, North Korea, Palestinian Autonomous Areas, Peru, Rwanda, Sierra Leone, Somalia, Sudan, Tajikistan and Yemen. Grants are awarded within the fields of food aid and support for food security, and early warning systems and storage programmes. Funded activities include promotion of food security in favour of the populations of developing regions and countries;

raising of the nutritional level of people from developing countries; promotion of food independence and the fight against poverty; storage programmes; and preparatory visits and training.

Geographical Area of Activity: International; developing countries. Priority countries: Afghanistan, Angola, Armenia, Azerbaijan, Bangladesh, Bolivia, Burkina Faso, Cape Verde, Ethiopia, Georgia, Haiti, Honduras, Kyrgyzstan, Liberia, Madagascar, Malawi, Mauritania, Mozambique, Nicaragua, Niger, North Korea, Palestinian Autonomous Areas, Peru, Rwanda, Sierra Leone, Somalia, Sudan, Tajikistan and Yemen.

How to Apply: Applications are invited annually.

Financial Information: Annual budget €455,000,000; grants available for up to 75% of the total cost of the project.

Contact: Contact Chantal Hebberecht.

Address: 200 rue de la Loi, EuropeAid Co-operation Office F5, 1049 Brussels, Belgium.

Telephone: (2) 299-25-77; *Internet:* http://europa.eu.int/comm/europeaid/projects /foodsec/index_en.htm; *e-mail:* chantal.hebberecht@cec.eu.int.

Health and Education: North–South Co-operation Against Drug Abuse

Established with the aim of preventing and reducing the abusive consumption and illegal production of drugs, and of controlling drugs-trafficking.

Activities: Operates in the field of drug prevention, through grants to activities concerned with: the assessment of the drugs phenomenon and the establishment of an integrated strategy in co-operation with UNIDCP—UN International Drug Control Programme; epidemic studies and research into the frequency, distribution and causes of drug addiction; information, education and awareness raising; social rehabilitation for people addicted to drugs; identification of national prevention strategies about illegal drugs production; development of rural zones by the creation of new agricultural and industrial initiatives; and economic, social and environmental rehabilitation and training.

Geographical Area of Activity: International.

How to Apply: Applications can be submitted at any time; projects concerning Central and South America, Asia and Mediterranean countries should contact DG External Relations, and projects based in Africa, the Caribbean and Pacific region should contact DG Development.

Financial Information: Annual budget €1,600,000 (2003); maximum grant €1,000,000 for up to 100% of the total project costs.

Contact: Contact Cinzia Brentari.

Address: 200 rue de la Loi, EuropeAid Co-operation Office F4, 1049 Brussels, Belgium.

Telephone: (2) 295-67-66; *Internet:* http://europa.eu.int/comm/europeaid/projects /index_en.htm; *e-mail:* cinzia.brentari@cec.eu.int.

PHARE (Poland and Hungary Assistance for Economic Restructuring)/ISPA (Instrument for Structural Policies for Pre-Accession)/SAPARD (Special Accession Programme for Agriculture and Rural Development): PROINVEST Organization of Sector Partnership Initiatives

A programme of the ACP Group (Africa, Caribbean and the Pacific group of countries) and the European Commission, to promote the organization of sector partnership initiatives. The programme is managed by the PROINVEST Management Unit on behalf of the European Commission.

Activities: Grants are made within four areas: sub-sector partnership meetings, for ACP and European Union (EU) intermediary organizations willing to initiate and organize sub-sector partnership meetings, in order to facilitate South–South and North–South Investment and Inter-Enterprise Co-operation Agreements (I&ICAs) in the selected sub-sector, encourage co-operation between EU and ACP Intermediary Organizations (IOs), and strengthen the capacity of intermediary organizations to organize sub-sector partnership initiatives meetings in ACP; sector on sub-sector partnership missions in ACP countries, including support to ACP intermediary organizations for the organization of sector or sub-sector partnership missions in ACP regions/countries; inter-enterprise twinning–mentoring initiatives, involving support to ACP and EU intermediary organizations for the identification of specific opportunities of twinning–mentoring activities between EU and ACP enterprises and for the organization of tailored twinning–mentoring/partnership missions; and ACP partnership missions in the EU or ACP countries, consisting of support for the identification and selection of ACP companies to attend Investment and Inter-Enterprise Co-operation Agreements (I&ICAs) promotion events in EU and ACP countries in order to increase inward flows of investment, technology, know-how and managerial skills. Proposals must be submitted by groupings of at least three private, public and semi-public intermediary organizations from three ACP countries and at least three intermediary organizations from three member states of the EU.

Geographical Area of Activity: ACP countries (Africa, excluding South Africa, Caribbean and the Pacific) and the EU.

How to Apply: Applications must be submitted using the standard application form attached to the guide-lines for applicants available on the website, whose format and instructions must be strictly observed. For each submission, one signed original application and five copies must be supplied by the applicant.

Financial Information: Total budget €2,065,000.

Contact: Man. Patrick Keene.

Address: PROINVEST Management Unit, Centre for the Devt of Enterprise—CDE, 52 ave Herrmann-Debroux, 1160 Brussels, Belgium.

Telephone: (2) 679-18-50; *Fax:* (2) 679-18-70; *Internet:* www.proinvest-eu.org; *e-mail:* info@proinvest-eu.org.

Rehabilitation and Reconstruction in ACP (African, Caribbean and Pacific) Countries

Set up to support rehabilitation and reconstruction activities in communities affected by war, social unrest or natural disasters in the ACP countries.

Activities: Support is given to organizations active in the following areas: material and functional rehabilitation of basic infrastructure services, including healthcare and education, mine clearing, social integration and the demobilization of military forces; rehabilitation of refugees, repatriated and displaced people; and the restoration of local institutions' capacities. The programme was to run from 2000–05.

Geographical Area of Activity: ACP countries (Africa, excluding South Africa, Caribbean and the Pacific).

How to Apply: Applications can be submitted at any time, via the EC delegation in the country concerned.

Financial Information: Grants are available for up to 75% of the total project costs; funded by the European Development Fund.

Contact: Contact Jeffrey Tudor.

Address: 200 rue de la Loi, EuropeAid Co-operation Office C4, 1049 Brussels, Belgium.

Telephone: (2) 299-17-60; *Internet:* http://europa.eu.int/comm/development /index_en.cfm; *e-mail:* jeffrey.tudor@cec.eu.int.

Rehabilitation and Reconstruction in Afghanistan

A technical assistance programme targeting the rehabilitation and reconstruction of Afghanistan. It is complementary to emergency aid and long-term development aid and forms part of the global strategy of the European Union to contribute to stabilization in the region.

Activities: Aims to finance the rehabilitation, reconstruction and re-establishment of civil society and the free media in Afghanistan.

Geographical Area of Activity: Afghanistan.

How to Apply: Applications can be submitted at any time directly to the EC delegation.

Financial Information: Grants are available for up to 75% of the total project costs.

Contact: Contact Thierry Dudermel.

Address: 200 rue de la Loi, EuropeAid Co-operation Office F4, 1049 Brussels, Belgium.

Telephone: (2) 296-66-07; *Internet:* http://europa.eu.int/comm/development /index_en.htm; *e-mail:* thierry.dudermel@cec.eu.int.

Rehabilitation and Reconstruction: Rehabilitation and Reconstruction in Developing Countries

Established as a technical assistance programme to support rehabilitation and reconstruction projects in developing countries.

Activities: Supports rehabilitation and reconstruction projects in developing countries, following war, social unrest or natural disasters to restore the functioning of the economy and institutional capacity. Funded activities include material and functional rehabilitation of basic infrastructure services, including healthcare and education, through mine clearing, social integration and the demobilization of military forces; rehabilitation of refugees, repatriated and displaced people; and the restoration of the capacity of local institutions. The management of projects is organized according to geographical regions: Asia, Central and South America and the Middle East and is additional to the Rehabilitation and Reconstruction in ACP Countries programme.

Geographical Area of Activity: Developing countries.

How to Apply: Applications can be submitted at any time, through the EC delegation based in the country concerned.

Financial Information: Annual budget €8,000,000 (2003); grants for up to 75% of the total project costs.

Contact: Contact Thierry Dudermel.

Address: 200 rue de la Loi, EuropeAid Co-operation Office F4, 1049 Brussels, Belgium.

Telephone: (2) 296-66-07; *Internet:* http://europa.eu.int/comm/development /index_en.cfm; *e-mail:* thierry.dudermel@cec.eu.int.

Support for ACP Cultural Events in the European Union—PAMCE

Established to increase opportunities for ACP (Africa, excluding South Africa, the Caribbean and the Pacific) cultural events; to attract a wider audience for artists from these countries; and to promote their activities within European countries.

Activities: Aims to promote the activities of artists from ACP countries, through grants for: exhibitions of works by ACP artists, authors and cultural works; the development of cultural events devoted to ACP cultures; admission of ACP artists into major European cultural events; and to develop production networks in ACP countries and distribution networks within European Union member states.

Geographical Area of Activity: ACP countries (Africa, excluding South Africa, the Caribbean and the Pacific).

How to Apply: Applications are accepted twice yearly for up to 40% of the project's total costs.

Financial Information: Global budget €2,600,000; grants available range from €50,000 to €150,000.

Contact: Contact Joelle Guenier.

Address: 200 rue de la Loi, EuropeAid Co-operation Office C4, 1049 Brussels, Belgium.

Telephone: (2) 295-59-81; *Internet:* http://europa.eu.int/comm/development /index_en.cfm; *e-mail:* joelle.guenier-amsallem@cec.eu.int.

TACIS (Technical Assistance to the Commonwealth of Independent States)

Launched by the EC in 1991, to provide grant-financed technical assistance to 13 countries of Eastern Europe and Central Asia (Armenia, Azerbaijan, Belarus, Georgia, Kazakhstan, Kyrgyzstan, Moldova, Mongolia, Russia, Tajikistan, Turkmenistan, Ukraine and Uzbekistan), aiming to enhance the transition process in these countries.

Activities: Aims to promote the understanding and appreciation of democracy and market-oriented social and economic systems by cultivating links and lasting relationships between public, private and community organizations and individuals in the republics of the former USSR, Mongolia and the European

Union (EU). Funding is provided for national programmes, small project programmes, cross-border and inter-state programmes for the following activities: economic policy advice and government organization advice; training and distance learning methods; studies, pre-investment plans, market research and analysis, and feasibility studies; and technical assistance and expertise for the establishment of new legal and regulatory frameworks, including restructuring banks, employment offices, social service institutions and training centres. The programme was to run from 2000–06.

Geographical Area of Activity: EU and Eastern Europe and Central Asia (Armenia, Azerbaijan, Belarus, Georgia, Kazakhstan, Kyrgyzstan, Moldova, Mongolia, Russia, Tajikistan, Turkmenistan, Ukraine and Uzbekistan).

How to Apply: Grants are awarded several times a year.

Financial Information: Global budget €3,140,000,000.

Contact: Contact Annika Floren.

Address: 200 rue de la Loi, EuropeAid Co-operation Office A6, 1049 Brussels, Belgium.

Telephone: (2) 299-31-36; *Internet:* http://europa.eu.int/comm/external_relations /ceeca/tacis/index.htm; *e-mail:* annika.floren@cec.eu.int.

TACIS (Technical Assistance to the Commonwealth of Independent States) Cross-Border Co-operation Small Projects and Micro-Projects

Established by the European Commission in 1996 to foster small-scale co-operation projects between local and regional authorities and civil society organizations, in the cross-border areas of the Newly Independent States (NIS—Belarus, Moldova, Russia and Ukraine) and neighbouring areas in the candidate countries and European Union (EU) countries.

Activities: Aims to promote co-operation projects between the NIS (Belarus, Moldova, Russia and Ukraine) and neighbouring areas in the candidate countries and EU countries, particularly projects aiming to resolve a common problem, which develop skills, and are active in the fields of administrative reform, local economic development, social welfare, the environment and energy efficiency. Funding is provided for network development, environmental protection projects and the management of natural resources, support of the private sector, and economic development projects. Projects must include at least two partners at the EU/NIS border and three partners at the EU/Eastern Europe border. The programme maintains branch offices in Chisinau, Kiev, Minsk and St Petersburg.

Geographical Area of Activity: EU and the NIS countries (Belarus, Moldova, Russia and Ukraine) and neighbouring candidate countries.

How to Apply: Grants are awarded annually; applications for micro-projects (grants up to €50,000) can be submitted at any time.

Financial Information: Annual budget €6,700,000 (2002); grants range from €50,000 to €200,000. Total grants awarded €25,400,000 (1996–2001).

Publications: Application Form; Guide-lines; Procedures Manual.

Contact: Contact Jyrki Wessman.

Address: 200 rue de la Loi, 1049 Brussels, Belgium.

Telephone: (2) 299-37-51; *Internet:* http://europa.eu.int/comm/europeaid/projects /tacis_cbc_spf/programmes/index_en.htm; *e-mail:* jyrki.wessman@cec.eu.int.

TACIS (Technical Assistance to the Commonwealth of Independent States) Institution Building Partnership Programme (IBPP)

This strand of the TACIS programme (q.v.) provides support to civil society organizations and local initiatives.

Activities: The Programme provides support in five areas: Public Administration Reform Issues, such as citizen-oriented services, financial management, and human resources management; Economic Development Issues, including development of trade, assistance to SMEs, public/private partnerships, initiatives to reduce unemployment, vocational training, and socio-economic development, including the promotion of social dialogue and consumer protection; social issues, such as the social reintegration of marginalized groups, the promotion of sustainable health and social care, on behalf, for example, of elderly people, people with HIV/AIDS, disadvantaged women and other disadvantaged groups of the local population; Urban Management Issues, including urban utilities, waste management, wastewater management, transport and energy supply, urban/regional planning, health and education services, housing services and tourism services; and Environmental Issues, including environmental pollution, energy efficiency and eco-tourism. Applications can be made by organizations within three categories: NGOs in the health or social sector, consumers associations, community-based organizations, and environmental protection groups; non-profit professional organizations such as associations of SMEs or entrepreneurs, Chambers of Commerce, trade associations, and trade unions; and local and regional authorities.

Geographical Area of Activity: PHARE (Central and Eastern Europe) and TACIS countries.

How to Apply: A call for proposals is launched once a year by the European Commission; announced in the EC Official Journal and on the EuropeAid website. Proposals can be submitted by eligible organizations from the European Union, TACIS or PHARE countries.

Financial Information: Global budget €10,000,000; annual budget €5,400,000 (2002); grants available range from €100,000 to €200,000, up to 80% of the project's total costs.

Address: L-41, AIDCO Unit A3, 2/110, 1049 Brussels, Belgium.

Fax: (2) 296-04-23; *Internet:* http://europa.eu.int/comm/europeaid/index_en.htm; *e-mail:* europeaid-ibpp@cec.eu.int.

TACIS (Technical Assistance to the Commonwealth of Independent States) Seminars Programme

Established to support the organization of conferences and seminars within the framework of the implementation of the TACIS (q.v.) programme.

Activities: The eligible themes for the organization of conferences and seminars are: poverty reduction; gender disparities; human rights; justice and home affairs, including customs and border security, crime prevention, illegal trafficking, and anti-corruption; health; education; research; the environment; and culture. The Programme mainly targets the participation of CIS countries, although seminars can be organized in PHARE countries or in European Union (EU) member states if they are in the interest of the European Commission and CIS partner states and related to the aims of the TACIS programme. The maximum duration of each funded project is six months.

Geographical Area of Activity: Primarily CIS, but also EU and PHARE (Central and Eastern European) countries.

How to Apply: Grants are awarded annually.

Financial Information: Annual budget €400,000 (2003); grants range from €10,000 to €50,000, up to 80% of the eligible project costs.

Contact: Contact Antoinette Nicolo.

Address: 200 rue de la Loi, EuropeAid Co-operation Office A3, 1049 Brussels, Belgium.

Telephone: (2) 299-07-43; *Internet:* http://europa.eu.int/comm/external_relations /ceeca/tacis/index.htm; *e-mail:* antoinette.nicolo@cec.eu.int.

URB–AL II

Established to promote the development of direct and lasting partnerships between local communities of Europe and Central and South America.

Activities: Organized around existing thematic co-operation networks designed to resolve the practical problems of local urban development, the programme aims to strengthen exchanges, contact and decentralized co-operation between cities, regions and other local authorities and local communities of the European Union (EU) and Central and South America. Sector network themes are: local finance; fight against urban poverty; urban housing; promoting the role of women in local decision-making bodies; towns and the information society; and citizens' urban safety. Funding is provided for the co-ordination of thematic networks and their strengthening; joint projects; and biennial meetings.

Geographical Area of Activity: EU and Central and South America; eligible countries are: Argentina, Bolivia, Brazil, Chile, Colombia, Costa Rica, Cuba, Ecuador, El Salvador, Guatemala, Honduras, Mexico, Nicaragua, Panama, Paraguay, Peru, Uruguay and Venezuela.

How to Apply: Applications must be made through the network co-ordinator.

Financial Information: Global budget €50,000,000 (2002–06); maximum network grant €500,000, maximum joint project grant €250,000. Co-financing for projects must be found for approx. 50% of the total project costs.

Contact: Head of Unit Riccardo Gambini; Co-ordinator Berith Andersson; Sec. Jimena Bastidas de Janon.

Address: J-54 4/13, EuropeAid Co-operation Office E3, 1049 Brussels, Belgium.

Telephone: (2) 298-46-38; *Fax:* (2) 299-10-80; *Internet:* http://europa.eu.int/comm /europeaid/projects/urbal/index_fr.htm; *e-mail:* europeaid-urb-al@cec.eu.int.

EUROPEAN COMMUNITY HUMANITARIAN OFFICE (ECHO)

ECHO is the EC office charged with co-ordinating humanitarian activities, for the benefit of people in developing countries, African, Caribbean and Pacific states and other third countries which are victims of natural catastrophes and man-made crises (including wars and conflicts) or of comparable exceptional situations.

Activities: ECHO covers the full costs of humanitarian operations, as well as co-financing activities together with other funding agencies, international organizations and the European Union member states. Community-financed humanitarian activities can be implemented at the request of international organizations and bodies, NGOs, member states, beneficiary third countries, or on the European Commission's own initiative. Projects are undertaken for the period of time required to tackle the resulting humanitarian needs, as well as for demining activities, including awareness raising among local people of the threat posed by anti-personnel mines. Assistance provided includes medical teams and equipment, medicines, tents, food, various kinds of emergency equipment, diesel generators and fuel. Also provides specific and highly targeted food aid, supplied to meet humanitarian needs, to people facing serious food shortages as a result of a catastrophe (such as drought, floods or an earthquake). The funds are also used for the purchase of any products or materials required to carry out humanitarian actions, including house and shelter construction for the affected populations, short-term rehabilitation and reconstruction works (notably of infrastructure and equipment), external personnel costs (whether expatriate or local), storage, international and national haulage, logistical support, distribution of relief supplies and any other activity aimed at facilitating access to the people for whom the aid is destined. ECHO's mandate includes grants and funding of training and studies in the humanitarian field, activities designed to highlight the community character of the aid, and information and awareness-raising actions. These actions are targeted, in particular, towards public opinion in Europe and in those third countries where the Community is funding significant humanitarian work. ECHO also awards service contracts to organizations operating in its areas of activity.

Geographical Area of Activity: International; developing countries.

How to Apply: Application forms available on the website.

Financial Information: Total budget €442,000,000 (2003); funded by the general EC budget and the European Development Fund.

Contact: Commissioner for Development and Humanitarian Aid Poul Nielson.

Address: G-1, 4/305, 1049 Brussels, Belgium.

Internet: http://europa.eu.int/comm/echo/index_en.htm.

Dipecho

Aims to protect communities that are threatened by natural disasters, and to promote sustainable development.

Activities: The programme aims to both prevent and prepare for natural disasters through making grants at three levels: short-term operations, including activities aimed at reducing human losses and material damage and carrying out assistance and rehabilitation operations; reducing the impact of a disaster on communities and their environment; and addressing the vulnerability of communities, by developing their ability to face disasters. Funded projects include on-site training of managers and local technicians, strengthening of the management and institutions involved in preparing for disasters, and helping local authorities establish affordable disaster preparation technologies. The programme operates through a network of experts and technical officers who organize training on humanitarian assistance techniques, throughout South Asia, South-East Asia, Central America and the Caribbean.

Geographical Area of Activity: South Asia, South-East Asia, Central America and the Caribbean.

Financial Information: Annual budget €10,000,000; grants are made for approximately 25% of the total project budget.

Contact: Contact Laure Boutinet.

Address: 200 rue de la Loi, 1049 Brussels, Belgium.

Telephone: (2) 299-01-11; *Internet:* http://europa.eu.int/comm/echo/en/index_en .html; *e-mail:* echo-info@cec.eu.int.

EUROPEAN NGO CONFEDERATION FOR RELIEF AND DEVELOPMENT (CONORD)

Formerly known as the Liaison Committee of Development NGOs (CLONG), represents approximately 1,200 European Union (EU)-based development and humanitarian NGOs.

Activities: As of 2003, CONORD was in the process of restructuring its activities. Prior to this, initiatives had included the TRIALOG project, which aimed to integrate development and humanitarian NGOs from the EU accession countries, whose priorities in terms of development co-operation do not always match those presently accepted in the EU, through a series of seminars, study visits, policy papers, lobbying and advocacy work and dissemination of information through publications.

Geographical Area of Activity: European Union and accession countries.

Contact: Board of Directors: Frans Polman (Pres.); Justin Kilcullen, Carol Rask (Vice-Pres); Bart Bode (Sec.); Giampiero Alhadeff (Treas.); Dir Oliver Consolo.

Address: 10 square Ambiorix, 1040 Brussels, Belgium.

Telephone: (2) 27438760; *Fax:* (2) 27438761.

EUROPEAN STRUCTURAL FUNDS

The objective of the Structural Funds is to achieve social and economic cohesion throughout the European Union (EU). Resources are targeted at actions that help bridge the gaps between the more and less developed regions and promote equal employment opportunities between different social groups. There are four Structural Funds: the European Regional Development Fund, the European Social Fund, the European Agricultural Guidance and Guarantee Fund and the

Financial Instrument for Fisheries Guidance (qq.v.). There are also four related Community initiatives: INTERREG III, Leader+, URBAN, and EQUAL (q.v.), which benefit from 5.3% of Community funding under the Structural Funds.

Activities: The Structural Funds provide financial support for NGO activities such as training, work with unemployed people, young people, immigrants and disabled people, as well as work in rural areas and deprived urban areas. There are three Community objectives: Objective 1, promoting the development and structural adjustment of regions whose development is lagging behind; Objective 2, supporting the economic and social conversion of areas facing structural difficulties; and Objective 3, supporting the adaptation and modernization of policies and systems of education, training and employment. Regions must be designated as Objective 1 or 2 regions in order to receive financial support; Objective 1 and 2 regions are found in all member states and all regions are eligible for support under Objective 3.

Geographical Area of Activity: EU.

How to Apply: To apply for funding, organizations must contact the national authorities in the relevant country; application procedures vary according to national rules and regulations.

Financial Information: Total Structural Funds budget €195,000,000,000 (2000–06).

Address: 1049 Brussels, Belgium.

EUROSTAT—STATISTICAL OFFICE OF THE EUROPEAN UNION

MEDSTAT

Established as part of the MEDA programme, within its economic and financial co-operation strand, to promote co-operation between European Union (EU) and Mediterranean partner countries in the field of statistics.

Activities: Promotes co-operative activities between EU and Mediterranean partner countries in the field of statistics, through grants for harmonization and institutional capacity building; improvement of the exchange of data between different national and regional systems; concentration of efforts on satisfying users' needs; provision of references on statistical information systems in the Euro-Mediterranean region, and awareness raising amongst policy makers for the statistical dimension in policy strategies regarding socio-economic policies and good governance.

Geographical Area of Activity: EU and Mediterranean countries.

How to Apply: Grants are awarded annually.

Financial Information: Total global budget €30,000,000 (2002–05).

Contact: Contact José Pessanha.

Address: EUROSTAT C3, 2920 Luxembourg, Luxembourg.

Telephone: 4301-35054; *Internet:* http://europa.eu.int/comm/external_relations /euromed/meda.htm#1; *e-mail:* jose.pessanha@cec.eu.int.

INFORMATION CENTRE ENLARGEMENT

TACIS (Technical Assistance to the Commonwealth of Independent States) BISTRO

Part of the TACIS programme, which aims to stimulate partnerships between the European Union (EU) and the Commonwealth of Independent States (CIS).

Activities: Aims to promote the exchange of know-how between the EU, Armenia, Georgia, Kazakhstan, Russia and Ukraine to promote the transition process to democratic society and a market economy, to support institutional reforms, support the private sector and economic development, and support societal development and meet the consequences of transition. Funding is provided for fact-finding missions to access European know-how, organizations of meetings and workshops, organization of professional training seminars for students, sectoral and regional research, and professional training. Projects should include partners from the EU and CIS.

Geographical Area of Activity: European Union and the CIS.

Restrictions: No funding for individual sponsorships for participation in workshops, seminars, conferences and congresses; individual scholarships; feasibility studies or business plans.

How to Apply: Applications should be prepared on the basis of the instructions and guide-lines introduced in the Call for Project Proposals and addressed to the Head of the Operations Section. Project applications should consist of a Terms of Reference and Project Summary, and be submitted with a covering letter; four copies in English and one copy in Russian; and an electronic version in English.

Financial Information: Global budget €38,000,000; financed from the TACIS budget of the Newly Independent States.

Contact: Contact Lena Karnovich.

Address: Delegation of the European Commission in Russia, Kadashevskaya Naberezhnaya, 14/1, Moscow, Russian Federation.

Telephone: (095) 721-20-02; *Fax:* (095) 721-20-40; *Internet:* www.eur.ru/en/index .htm; *e-mail:* lena.karnovich@cec.eu.int.

PROJECT MANAGEMENT OFFICE

European Union–China Human Rights Small Project Facility

Established by the European Commission to promote human rights in the People's Republic of China, and to encourage the continuing growth of civil society organizations and the strengthening of the rule of law in China. The programme is administered by a management agency in China.

Activities: The programme operates through providing small grants to NGOs and other civil society organizations for the organization of conferences, workshops and seminars with a central theme of human rights, the promotion of civil society or the strengthening of the rule of law in China. Eligible activities include training, translations, publications, exhibitions, expert missions or other information dissemination activities which would help the development of EC–China human rights dialogue. Priority areas include: prevention of torture and the rehabilitation of victims; reduction in the use of the death penalty;

protection of workers' rights; participation of people in public policy issues; anti-discrimination activities promoting the rights of disadvantaged and vulnerable groups, including minority communities; freedom of expression and freedom of the press; and economic, social and cultural rights.

Geographical Area of Activity: People's Republic of China.

How to Apply: Grants are awarded annually.

Financial Information: Global budget €840,000; maximum grant available €100,000.

Contact: Contact Françoise Collet.

Address: Delegation of the European Commission to China, 15 Dongzhimenwai, Sanlitun, 100600 Beijing, People's Republic of China.

Telephone: (10) 65326733; *Internet:* www.delchn.cec.eu.int/en/co-operation/hrspf .htm; *e-mail:* hrspf@hotmail.com.

SECRETARIAT-GENERAL

Organizations Advancing the Idea of Europe

Established to promote the idea of the European Union (EU), and to raise public commitment to the activities carried out by the European institutions.

Activities: The programme operates through grants to cultural organizations promoting the idea of Europe, for annual running costs and project activities. Organizations should be based in more than one member state, or carry out their regular activities in co-operation with organizations in other member states.

Geographical Area of Activity: EU.

How to Apply: Grants awarded annually.

Financial Information: Annual budget €2,000,000 (2003); projects should have at least 20% funding from sources outside the EU bduget.

Contact: Contact Adam Buick.

Address: 200 rue de la Loi, Secretariat-General G2, 1049 Brussels, Belgium.

Telephone: (2) 296–73-28; *Internet:* http://europa.eu.int/comm/secretariat_general /sgc/subvention/fr/subv.htm; *e-mail:* esther.dams@cec.eu.int.

Protection of Sites of Nazi Concentration Camps

Aims to keep the memory of the victims of the Nazi concentration camps alive and to promote the study of the phenomenon from an historical perspective.

Activities: Grants are made to non-profit organizations working to preserve the sites of concentration camps, preserving deportation archives, producing multi-lingual publications, and organizing guided visits at sites.

Geographical Area of Activity: Europe.

How to Apply: Grants are awarded annually.

Financial Information: Annual budget €350,000 (2003); average grant awarded €11,500, up to 80% of the total project costs.

Contact: Contact Adam Buick.

Address: 200 rue de la Loi, Secretariat-General C3, 1049 Brussels, Belgium.

Telephone: (2) 296-73-28; *Internet:* http://europa.eu.int/comm/secretariat_general /sgc/subvention/fr/subv.htm; *e-mail:* esther.dams@cec.eu.int.

Youth, Culture, Training, Media and Information: Prince

Established to promote the exchange of information and to raise awareness about European enlargement, primarily focusing on marginalized target groups.

Activities: Operates through grants to civil society organizations carrying out information and awareness-raising activities on behalf of marginalized groups in society, including young people, rural populations, and elderly people, as well as the general public and small businesses. Projects must be transnational and involve at least three European Union (EU) member states.

Geographical Area of Activity: EU and Central and Eastern Europe.

Restrictions: No funding for pilot projects, projects with a solely national scope, and projects that have already received Community funding.

How to Apply: Grants are awarded annually.

Financial Information: Total budget €5,500,000 (2003); grants range from €100,000 to €300,000, for up to 75% of the project's total costs.

Contact: Contact Georges Ingber.

Address: Office CHAR/614, 200 rue de la Loi, BREY 7/226, 1049 Brussels, Belgium.

Telephone: (2) 295-59-81; *Internet:* http://europa.eu.int/comm/enlargement /communication/index.htm#call; *e-mail:* georges.ingber@cec.eu.int.

OTHER PROGRAMMES

Afghan Refugees in Pakistan Programme

The Programme was established to support activities aiming to improve the living conditions of the Afghan population in Pakistan.

Activities: Grants are available to NGOs for activities based in Pakistan that aim to improve the living conditions of Afghan refugees, including vocational training of Afghan men and women in different trades, preparing them for a sustainable return to Afghanistan, particularly its urban areas, and for the delivery of community social services, particularly for women.

Geographical Area of Activity: Pakistan.

How to Apply: Application details available on the website.

Financial Information: Global budget €2,000,000.

Contact: Contact Karl Harbo.

Address: c/o Delegation of the European Commission to Pakistan, House 9, St 88, Sector G 6/3, POB 1608, Islamabad, Pakistan.

Telephone: (51) 2271828; *Fax:* (51) 2822604; *Internet:* http://europa.eu.int/comm /europeaid/cgi/frame12.pl.

European Union–ACP Programme on Reproductive Health

A joint European Union–African, Caribbean and Pacific group of countries (ACP) programme launched in 2002 in partnership with the UN Population Fund and the International Planned Parenthood Federation to strengthen work on sexual and reproductive health in the developing world.

Activities: The Programme helps target countries in the developing world with support for family planning and advice on population, health and sexual matters. Also aims to reinforce the capacity of countries to provide a wide range of services including pre- and post-natal care, assisted births, family planning, prevention and treatment of sexually transmitted diseases, including HIV and AIDS, and information and advice to young people vulnerable to unwanted pregnancies and unsafe abortions.

Geographical Area of Activity: Developing countries.

Financial Information: Total budget €32,000,000.

Address: c/o UNFPA, 220 East 42nd St, New York, NY 10017, USA.

Internet: www.unfpa.org.

Health, Consumer Protection and Social Policy: DAPHNE

Set up to develop measures for combating violence against children, adolescents and women; aims to support and encourage organizations active in the fight against violence to work together, and to support the raising of public awareness of the fight against violence and the prevention of violence against children, young people, and women, including the victims of trafficking for the purposes of sexual exploitation.

Activities: The programme operates through funding transnational projects to set up and reinforce multi-disciplinary networks and to ensure the exchange of information and best practice; the development of pilot projects in the field of violence prevention and protection of children, young people and women; transnational public awareness initiatives; encouragement of information campaigns in co-operation with member state governments; development of a Community-wide information source to assist and inform NGOs of information relevant to the field of violence, its prevention and the support of victims; studies in the field of violence and sexual abuse and means of their prevention; and improvement of the recognition, reporting and management of the consequences of violence. In 2003, funding priorities were the adaptation and transfer of existing results to other countries, languages or target groups; development of indicators to measure the extent of violence and the impact on society and health; and street children in the European Union (EU).

Geographical Area of Activity: EU, Central and Eastern Europe, Mediterranean countries, and European Economic Area countries.

How to Apply: Applications are invited from NGOs and non-profit organizations with an innovative transferable project, involving partners from two different countries; grants are awarded annually in March.

Financial Information: Annual budget €5,000,000; grants are available for between €30,000 and €125,000, up to 80% of total project costs.

Contact: Contact Patrick Trousson.

147

Address: 200 rue de la Loi, 1049 Brussels, Belgium.

Telephone: (2) 296-58-03; *Internet:* http://europa.eu.int/comm/justice_home /project/daphne/fr/index.htm; *e-mail:* patrick.trousson@cec.eu.int.

European Union: European Parliament

COMMITTEE ON DEVELOPMENT AND CO-OPERATION/EDUCATION INTERNATIONAL

Education for All

Launched in 2000 by Education International and the European Parliament's Committee on Development and Co-operation, led by the European Parliament's Vice-Chairman, Max van den Berg, MEP. Initially aims to campaign on a resolution which proposes to double the European Union (EU) budget for primary education in developing countries and to make countries within the EU commit more resources, and not words, to give children everywhere a free quality education.

Activities: Campaigns to promote Education For All, by gathering together contributions from development organizations, education unions and NGOs, in the form of petition letters and case-studies on education projects in developing countries, to demonstrate projects initiated at local level and the needs of children and teachers in developing countries.

Geographical Area of Activity: International.

Address: 5 blvd du Roi Albert II, 1210 Brussels, Belgium.

Telephone: (2) 224-06-11; *Fax:* (2) 224-06-06; *Internet:* www.europeforeducation .org; *e-mail:* contribute@europeforeducation.org.

HUMAN RIGHTS UNIT

Sakharov Prize for Freedom of Thought

Established in 1988 to recognize people and organizations that have defended human rights and freedom against intolerance, fanaticism and hate. The annual prize of €50,000 is awarded at a formal sitting in Strasbourg, which falls on or around 10 December, the day on which the UN Universal Declaration of Human Rights was signed in 1948.

Activities: The Prize is awarded in recognition of the outstanding work of either an individual or organization in the defence of human rights and freedom of speech and thought, including all intellectual or artistic activities and activities committed to the defence of human rights, fundamental rights, respect of international law and freedom of science.

Geographical Area of Activity: International.

How to Apply: To be considered, applicants must have the support of at least 25 members of the European Parliament that take the initiative of the proposing candidate. Applications must be submitted before September of each year.

Financial Information: Annual prize €50,000.

Contact: Contact Andrea Subhan.

Address: rue Wiertz, BP 1047, 1047 Brussels, Belgium.

Telephone: (2) 284-25-84; *Internet:* www.europarl.eu.int/comparl/afet/droi /sakharov/default_en.htm; *e-mail:* asubhan@europarl.eu.int.

Foundation for the Philippine Environment (FPE)

Established in January 1992 following the collective efforts of the Philippine government, NGOs, and the US government paved the way for the funding of FPE; the first grant-making institution to environmental organizations in the Philippines.

Activities: Aims to reverse the rapid destruction of the Philippines' natural resources by initiating programmes and activities that strengthen the role of NGOs, people's organizations, and local communities in the responsible management of the ecosystem. Operates an Action Grants Programme which aims to help NGOs and people's organizations acquire the skills/capabilities and develop the technology and mechanisms to define and implement appropriate strategies on biodiversity conservation and sustainable resource management; generate deeper understanding or wider education on biodiversity conservation; and establish a common perspective of national and global environmental trends and how these relate to community-based environment concerns and endeavours. Also maintains three regional offices.

Geographical Area of Activity: Philippines.

How to Apply: Application guide-lines and criteria are available on the website.

Financial Information: Start-up funding from the United States Agency for International Development (USAID) through its Natural Resources Management Programme (NRMP); total endowment approx. US $22,000,000.

Contact: Board of Trustees: Vitaliano Nanagas II (Chair.).

Address: 77 Matahimik St, Teachers' Village, Quezon City 1101, Philippines.

Telephone: (2) 927-2186; *Internet:* www.fpe.ph.

Global Development Network

A global network of research and policy institutes working together to address the problems of national and regional development.

Activities: Activities include supporting multidisciplinary research in social sciences; promoting the generation of local knowledge in developing and transition countries; producing policy-relevant knowledge on a global scale; building research capacity to advance development and alleviate poverty; facilitating knowledge sharing among researchers and policy-makers; and disseminating development knowledge to the public and policymakers. Promotes multidisciplinary research and building research capacity in developing and transition countries through regional research competitions in the seven regions of sub-Saharan Africa, Middle East and North Africa, South Asia, East Asia, Central and South America, Central and Eastern Europe and the Commonwealth of Independent States, funding policy-relevant research projects. Also carries out global research projects which encourage networking among researchers from different countries, and distributes the annual Global Development Awards. Holds conferences and runs GDNet, which provides on-line networking tools and services to support researchers from developing countries in their work and helps disseminate their research.

Geographical Area of Activity: Developing countries.

Publications: GDN Funding Opportunities Newsletter; Annual Report.

Contact: Dir Lyn Squire.

Address: 2600 Virginia Ave, NW, Suite 1112, Washington, DC 20037, USA.

Telephone: (202) 338-6350; *Fax:* (202) 338-6826; *Internet:* www.gdnet.org; *e-mail:* gdni@gdnet.org.

Global Development Awards

Established by the Global Development Network (q.v.); one of the world's largest international contests for researchers on development.

Activities: Operates as an annual awards programme, distributing prizes totalling approximately US $400,000. There are two main categories for the Awards: Japanese Award for Most Innovative Development Project, awarded to development and research projects that hold the greatest promise for benefiting the poor in developing countries; and the Japanese Award for Outstanding Research on Development for development projects and research that hold the greatest promise for improving understanding of development. Medals are also awarded to researchers who submit the best research papers on the selected research themes. The programme is open only to scholars and practitioners based in developing countries, with an emphasis on recognizing and supporting the work of younger researchers at the start of their careers.

Geographical Area of Activity: Developing countries.

Restrictions: Only open to researchers and practitioners based in developing countries.

How to Apply: Multi-disciplinary panels of experts select finalists in the three categories. All the short-listed candidates receive funded places to the Annual Conference, where they present their research to an international audience of policy-makers and researchers. The Awards are thematically organized, generally mirroring the theme of the upcoming Annual Conference, so that finalists' papers are presented in a context of international research and analysis of that theme. The final selection is made by the judging panels at the conference and the prizes awarded to the winners in a formal ceremony.

Financial Information: Funding for the Awards provided by the government of Japan, Merck Corporation, government of Italy, International Bank for Reconstruction and Development (IBRD—World Bank), and the government of India; approx. US $400,000 distributed annually in prizes.

Contact: Dir Lyn Squire.

Address: 2600 Virginia Ave, NW, Suite 1112, Washington, DC 20037, USA.

Telephone: (202) 338-6350; *Fax:* (202) 338-6826; *Internet:* www.gdnet.org /activities/gdn_competitions/global_development_awards/; *e-mail:* gdni@gdnet .org.

The Global Fund to Fight AIDS, Tuberculosis and Malaria

The Fund was established to attract, manage and disburse additional resources through a public–private partnership that aims to make a sustainable and significant contribution to the reduction of infections, illness and death, thereby mitigating the impact caused by HIV/AIDS, tuberculosis and malaria in countries in need, and contributing to poverty reduction as part of the United Nation's Millennium Development Goals. The concept for an international funding mechanism to fight HIV/AIDS, tuberculosis, and malaria began at the Okinawa G8 Summit in July 2000. At the urging of UN Secretary-General Kofi Annan and many national leaders, the idea for the Fund was unanimously endorsed in June 2001 at the first UN General Assembly Special Session to focus on HIV/AIDS. In July 2001 at its meeting in Genoa, G8 leaders committed US $1,300,000,000 to the Fund.

Activities: Grants are available for prevention, treatment, care, and support initiatives focusing on HIV/AIDS, tuberculosis and malaria. Country proposals are accepted from a Country Co-ordination Mechanism (CCM) that includes broad representation from government agencies, NGOs, community-based organizations, private-sector institutions and bilateral and multilateral agencies. In addition, other organizations, such as country or regionally based academic institutions that can facilitate and support the programmes are also eligible. Proposals from groups of organizations from multiple countries can also be accepted in order to address cross-border issues related to the three diseases. Such proposals need to have the support of the CCMs in the countries involved.

Geographical Area of Activity: International.

How to Apply: Guide-lines for applying for funds, calls for proposals and application forms are available on the website.

Financial Information: Target annual budget between US $7,000,000,000 and US $10,000,000,000; as of July 2003 total funds committed approx. US $1,700,000,000.

Publications: Annual Report.

Contact: Chair. Dr Chrispus Kiyonga; Deputy Chair. Seiji Morimoto; Exec. Dir Richard G. A. Feachem.

Address: 53 ave Louis-Casai, 1216 Geneva–Cointrin, Switzerland.

Telephone: (22) 7911700; *Fax:* (22) 7911701; *Internet:* http://www.theglobalfund .org; *e-mail:* info@theglobalfund.org.

Inter-American Development Bank (IDB)

CULTURAL CENTER

Cultural Development Program

Carries out the cultural activities of the Cultural Center of the Inter-American Development Bank (IDB); aims to stimulate communities to initiate projects to preserve their cultural heritage.

Activities: The Program provides small matching grants to community-based, innovative projects in Central and South America and the Caribbean to promote community cultural development through technical training, recovering traditions, conservation of cultural heritage, and youth education. In 2003, 46 projects received funding from a total of 23 countries: Argentina, Barbados, Belize, Bolivia, Chile, Colombia, Costa Rica, Dominican Republic, Ecuador, El Salvador, Guatemala, Guyana, Honduras, Jamaica, Mexico, Nicaragua, Panama, Paraguay, Peru, Suriname, Trinidad and Tobago, Uruguay and Venezuela. Also organizes travelling exhibitions.

Geographical Area of Activity: Central and South America and the Caribbean, including Argentina, Barbados, Belize, Bolivia, Chile, Colombia, Costa Rica, Dominican Republic, Ecuador, El Salvador, Guatemala, Guyana, Honduras, Jamaica, Mexico, Nicaragua, Panama, Paraguay, Peru, Suriname, Trinidad and Tobago, Uruguay and Venezuela.

Restrictions: No grants to individuals.

How to Apply: Applications must be submitted to the IDB Representative in each member country.

Financial Information: Grants range from US $1,000 to US $5,000; annual total grants approx. US $150,000; all projects must have local match funding.

Publications: Annual Report.

Contact: General Co-ordinator Felix Angel; Program Asst Elba Agusti.

Address: 1300 New York Ave, NW, Washington, DC 20577, USA.

Telephone: (202) 623-3774; *Fax:* (202) 623-3192; *Internet:* www.iadb.org/EXR /cultural/NEW.html; *e-mail:* elbaa@iadb.org.

INTER-AMERICAN CULTURE AND DEVELOPMENT FOUNDATION (IACDF)

Established by the Inter-American Development Bank (IDB).

Activities: The Inter-American Culture and Development Foundation (IACDF), scheduled for launch in 2004, aims to promote cultural and creative initiatives and projects in Central and South America and the Caribbean.

Geographical Area of Activity: Central and South America and the Caribbean.

Address: 1300 New York Ave, NW, Washington, DC 20577, USA.

Internet: www.iadb.org.

INTER-AMERICAN WORKING GROUP ON YOUTH DEVELOPMENT (IAWGYD)

Formed in November 1995 as a consortium of international donor organizations that support new approaches to positive youth development and participation in Central and South America and the Caribbean. Member organizations are the Canadian International Development Agency, Global Meeting of Generations, Inter-American Development Bank, Inter-American Foundation, Inter-American Institute for Co-operation on Agriculture, International Youth Foundation, LEADAmericas, Organization of American States, Pan American Health Organization, Partners of the Americas, UNESCO, UN Youth Unit, United States Agency for International Development, United States Peace Corps and Youth Service America.

Activities: The consortium exchanges information on best practices, jointly mobilizes technical and financial resources, collaborates on specific projects and advocates for effective youth policies.

Geographical Area of Activity: Central and South America and the Caribbean.

Address: 1300 New York Ave, NW (Stop W502), Washington, DC 20577, USA.

Telephone: (202) 623-1060; *Internet:* www.iadb.org/exr/mandates/youth/wg.htm; *e-mail:* bidjuventud@iadb.org.

Partnership for Promoting Youth Development and Participation

Implemented by the International Youth Foundation, a member agency of the Inter-American Working Group on Youth Development (IAWGYD).

Activities: Aims to promote the personal development of low-income youth (aged between 14 and 28, with particular emphasis on those under the age of 24) as active participants and volunteers in the development process, and to strengthen projects operated by or on behalf of young people. Initially the programme has funded four pilot projects in Ecuador, Guatemala, Paraguay and Trinidad and Tobago, which concentrate on developing youth enterprise initiatives, promoting local youth development activities, mobilizing financial support and disseminating best practice. Local administering partner organizations (LAPs) in each country will channel financial support to both youth-directed and mentor/practitioner-directed projects.

Geographical Area of Activity: Central and South America and the Caribbean; initially Ecuador, Guatemala, Paraguay and Trinidad and Tobago.

Financial Information: Pilot project costs US $1,139,500.

Contact: Pres. and Chief Exec. Rick Little.

Address: 34 Market Place, Suite 800, Baltimore MD 21202, USA.

Telephone: (410) 347-1500; *Fax:* (410) 347-1188; *Internet:* www.iadb.org/exr/pipeline/rg5825.htm.

OFFICE OF EXTERNAL RELATIONS

Special Programs Section: IDB Youth and Development Outreach Program

Established in 1995 to respond more effectively to the needs of young people in Central and South America and the Caribbean and promote their participation and leadership in the development process. The Program's four principal aims are to: advocate youth development and participation as an integral part of development; empower young people to become involved in their personal development and that of their communities; mainstream youth development and participation throughout Inter-American Development Bank (IDB) operations; and promote inter-organizational partnerships to advance youth development and participation.

Activities: Promotes the development and active participation of Central and South American and Caribbean youth in the development process with emphasis on participation and leadership, entrepreneurial development, technology, and community service, through establishing alliances with the public and private sectors, NGOs and young people themselves. Provides support to capacity-building initiatives, including training initiatives and projects that develop the managerial, entrepreneurial and leadership skills of young people; a regional network of over 8,000 IDB youth delegates established during a youth forum in Israel in 1995; outreach and communication to raise public awareness; inter-agency mainstreaming, including co-operation with other IDB departments and institutions; and policy advocacy and formulation. The Program also represents IDB in the Inter-American Working Group on Youth Development (IAWGYD), a consortium of international donor agencies that supports new approaches to positive youth development and participation in Central and South America and the Caribbean.

Geographical Area of Activity: Central and South America and the Caribbean.

Address: 1300 New York Ave, NW, Washington, DC 20577, USA.

Telephone: (202) 623-1060; *Internet:* www.iadb.org/exr/mandates/youth/yp.htm; *e-mail:* bidjuventud@iadb.org.

PROLEAD—PROGRAM FOR THE SUPPORT OF WOMEN'S LEADERSHIP AND REPRESENTATION

Women's Leadership for Good Governance in Central America

Launched by the Inter-American Development Bank (IDB) in 1998, in conjunction with the United Nations Development Fund for Women (UNIFEM), the Inter-American Commission of Women of the Organization of American States (OAS/CIM), the United Nations Development Programme (UNDP), and the United Nations Children's Fund (UNICEF, qq.v.); aims to promote women's leadership in every sector and at every level.

Activities: Aims to contribute to increasing women's citizen participation and access to leadership positions in public and civic life in Central and South America and the Caribbean, and to promote organizational capacity building in the region,

157

by promoting networks to foster linkages and information exchange, and by sharing successful experiences and best practices, both in and outside the region. The second phase of the Program targeted civil society organizations in Costa Rica, El Salvador, Guatemala, Honduras, Nicaragua and Panama for projects on women's leadership and good governance issues.

Geographical Area of Activity: Central and South America and the Caribbean.

Financial Information: Initial funding from IDB (US $3,250,000), the government of Norway (US $350,000) and the government of Sweden (US $120,000). Funding for the second phase of the Program included a grant of US $950,000 from the Netherlands government.

Address: 1300 New York Ave, NW (Stop W0502), Washington, DC 20577, USA.

Telephone: (202) 623-2509; *Fax:* (202) 623-1463; *Internet:* www.iadb.org/sds /prolead/site_5_e.htm; *e-mail:* prolead@iadb.org.

SUSTAINABLE DEVELOPMENT DEPARTMENT

Social Policy Dialogue Project

The Social Development Division (SDS/SOC) supports Inter-American Development Bank (IDB) operations and helps to identify and promote new opportunities for Bank action in social development that will accelerate growth and improve the well-being of people in Central and Latin America and the Caribbean.

Activities: Working in tandem with the Bank's operational departments, the Division offers technical advice on priority issues for women and indigenous groups through the Women in Development Unit and the Indigenous Peoples and Community Development Unit, and gives similar assistance in the areas of early childhood development, health, labour markets, urban development, violence prevention and control, and the formulation of social policy. The three main areas of operation are: the production of inputs for decision-makers through data collection on socially excluded groups, and research and diagnostic studies about the causes and consequences of social exclusion in the region; capacity building through training of excluded communities on leadership and project development of projects and through co-ordination with other multilateral institutions; and best practices identification and project development through researching and seeking best practices on design, implementation and supervision of projects that promote social inclusion, including consultation with socially excluded communities.

Geographical Area of Activity: Central and South America and the Caribbean.

Address: 1300 New York Ave, NW, Washington, DC 20577, USA.

Internet: www.iadb.org/sds/soc/publication/gen_2483_1920_e.htm; *e-mail:* webmaster@iadb.org.

Special Programs: Financing and Disseminating Best Practices in the Prevention of Child Labor

Established in 2002 by the Sustainable Development Department of the Inter-American Development Bank to support the fight against child labour in Central and South America and the Caribbean.

Activities: Grants are available to NGOs, public organizations, community organizations or trade associations working in the areas of child labour, poverty reduction, youth development, labour markets or related fields on projects that offer innovative strategies to combat child labour in Central and South America and the Caribbean. Funding is available for between one and two years.

Geographical Area of Activity: Central and South America and the Caribbean.

Financial Information: Grants range from €20,000 to €80,000.

Contact: Dept Chief Exec. Mayra Buvinic.

Address: SDS/SOC, 1300 New York Ave, NW (Stop W502), Washington, DC 20577, USA.

Telephone: (202) 623-3533; *Fax:* (202) 623-1576; *Internet:* www.iadb.org/sds/soc /publication/gen_63_3098_e.htm; *e-mail:* mayrab@iadb.org.

Inter-Governmental Authority on Development (IGAD)

The mandate of IGAD is to co-ordinate the efforts of member states to advance their development goals in the priority areas of economic co-operation, political and humanitarian affairs and food security and environmental protection. Aims to achieve regional co-operation and economic integration through promotion of food security, sustainable environmental management, peace and security, intra-regional trade and development of improved communications infrastructure.

Activities: Works in co-operation with NGOs to achieve its aims, including peace-building efforts in the IGAD member countries. Current projects include: Promotion of Training and Credit Schemes for Trades People in Artisanal Fisheries in IGAD member states; Promoting Sustainable Production of Drought Tolerant High Yielding Crop Varieties Through Research and Extension; Regional Livestock Development Programme for Eastern Africa; Household Energy Project; Promotion of Community Based Natural Resources Management; Capacity Building In Integrated Water Resources Management; Promoting Environmental Education and Training in the IGAD Region; Enhancing Disaster Risk Management Capability in the IGAD Region; and a Pilot Programme for the Reintegration and Rehabilitation of Refugee Returnees, Internally Displaced Persons and Affected Host Communities.

Geographical Area of Activity: Africa: Djibouti, Eritrea, Ethiopia, Kenya, Somalia, Sudan and Uganda.

Contact: Contact Prof. Benson Mochoge.

Address: POB 2653, Djibouti, Djibouti.

Telephone: 354050; *Fax:* 356994; *Internet:* www.igad.org; *e-mail:* igad@intnet.dj.

International Association for the Promotion of Co-operation with Scientists from the New Independent States of the former Soviet Union (INTAS)

An independent international association formed by the European Union (EU), EU member states and other countries, including EU candidate countries and Switzerland, acting to preserve and promote the valuable scientific potential of the former USSR partner countries through East–West Scientific co-operation.

Activities: Currently supporting research in the countries of the former USSR under the Sixth Framework Programme 2002–06, consisting of grants for research projects and networks.

Geographical Area of Activity: Armenia, Azerbaijan, Belarus, Georgia, Kazakhstan, Kyrgyzstan, Moldova, Russia, Tajikstan, Turkmenistan, Ukraine and Uzbekistan; and INTAS member countries: EU member states, Bulgaria, Cyprus, Czech Republic, Estonia, Hungary, Iceland, Israel, Latvia, Lithuania, Malta, Norway, Poland, Romania, Slovakia, Slovenia, Switzerland and Turkey.

Financial Information: Maximum grant available up to €25,000.

Contact: Exec. Sec. Jaak Sinnaeve.

Address: 58/8 ave des Arts, 1000 Brussels, Belgium.

Telephone: (2) 549-01-11; *Fax:* (2) 549-01-56; *Internet:* www.intas.be; *e-mail:* intas@intas.be.

Innovation Grants

Aims to promote the development, utilization and marketing of INTAS research in INTAS member states (EU member countries, candidate countries and Switzerland) and the Newly Independent States of the former USSR.

Activities: Grants are made to enable researchers to exploit the results of their research and to bring them to the market in the INTAS member states and the countries of the former USSR, with an emphasis on innovative products, technologies, services and strategies of a significant economic and/or social value.

Geographical Area of Activity: Countries of the former USSR and INTAS member states.

How to Apply: Application details and on-line application forms are available on the website.

Contact: Exec. Sec. Jaak Sinnaeve.

Address: 58/8 ave des Arts, 1000 Brussels, Belgium.

Telephone: (2) 549-01-11; *Fax:* (2) 549-01-56; *Internet:* www.intas.be; *e-mail:* intas@intas.be.

Research Projects and Networks

A programme promoting collaborative research projects between groups of scientists and networks in the INTAS member countries (European Union—EU member countries, candidate countries and Switzerland) and countries of the New Independent States of the former USSR.

Activities: The programme supports the collaboration of INTAS member countries and scientists from the former USSR, through support for research projects and networks. There are three types of call for proposals: Open Calls, for research projects and networks not restricted in scope; Thematic Calls, for research projects addressing specific problems; and Collaborative Calls, for research projects jointly defined and funded by INTAS and a co-funding organization. The size of the grant available depends on the number of participating teams of researchers from countries of the former USSR.

Geographical Area of Activity: Countries of the former USSR, EU and Central and South-Eastern Europe.

How to Apply: Application details and on-line application forms are available on the website.

Financial Information: Maximum grant €300,000 for research projects and €150,000 for network grants.

Contact: Exec. Sec. Jaak Sinnaeve.

Address: 58/8 ave des Arts, 1000 Brussels, Belgium.

Telephone: (2) 549-01-11; *Fax:* (2) 549-01-56; *Internet:* www.intas.be; *e-mail:* intas@intas.be.

Young Scientist Fellowships

Seeks to provide incentives for young scientists in countries of the former USSR to remain in science through the award of fellowships.

Activities: The programme is open to all scientists in countries of the former USSR under the age of 36 in all fields of science, to enable them to advance their careers through international collaboration; stabilize their position and continue their research in these countries; and establish contact between INTAS research teams and research teams in countries of the former USSR and create collaborations for future research. Fellowships are awarded for both PhD and post-doctoral study.

Geographical Area of Activity: Countries of the former USSR.

How to Apply: Application details and on-line application forms are available on the website.

Financial Information: Maximum fellowship €16,400 for PhD students and €20,400 for post-doctoral fellows.

Contact: Exec. Sec. Jaak Sinnaeve.

International Association for the Promotion of Co-operation with Scientists

Address: 58/8 ave des Arts, 1000 Brussels, Belgium.

Telephone: (2) 549-01-11; *Fax:* (2) 549-01-56; *Internet:* www.intas.be; *e-mail:* intas@intas.be.

International Bank for Reconstruction and Development (IBRD—World Bank)

Environment: Critical Ecosystems Partnership Fund (CEPF)

A joint initiative of the Environment Department of the World Bank, Conservation International, the Japanese government, the MacArthur Foundation and the Global Environment Facility (GEF, q.v.). The Fund's goal is to ensure that civil society is engaged in biodiversity conservation.

Activities: The Fund aims to dramatically advance conservation of Earth's biodiversity hotspots by providing funding and technical assistance to non-governmental, community and grassroots organizations working to save the diversity of life in hotspots in the developing world, i.e. places rich in unique plants, and animals at enormous risk. Supported initiatives should also ultimately contribute to poverty alleviation and economic prosperity. The Fund develops an investment strategy, or ecosystem profile, for each ecosystem before grant disbursement begins, and funded projects must be linked to one of the strategic directions articulated in the relevant ecosystem profile to be eligible for funding.

Geographical Area of Activity: International, focusing on biodiversity crisis regions in the developing world.

Restrictions: No grants to directly fund government agency activities, the purchase of land, involuntary resettlement of people, capitalization of a trust fund or the alteration of any physical cultural property.

How to Apply: Applying for grants is a two-part process; applicants must first submit a letter of inquiry, and if invited, applicants then submit a more detailed proposal.

Financial Information: Total revenue US $20,284,256, total expenditure US $15,009,103, total grants US $11,119,187 (Jan. 2001–June 2002).

Publications: Annual Report.

Contact: Chair. CEPF Donor Council James D. Wolfensohn; Exec. Dir and Senior Vice-Pres. Jorgen Thomsen; Grant Dir Africa Nina Marshall; Grant Dir Asia Judy Mills; Grant Dir Central and South America Michele Zador.

Address: 1919 M St, NS, Suite 600, Washington, DC 20036, USA.

Telephone: (202) 912-1808; *Fax:* (202) 912-1045; *Internet:* www.cepf.net; *e-mail:* cepfsupport@caconservation.org.

Global Urban Partnership

Launched in 1997 by the World Bank, in association with several partners. Aims to create a vehicle for an analytical and cross-sectoral focus on urban development, viewing the city as a whole unit of analysis rather than an agglomeration of sectors. The Partnership seeks to engage local stakeholders as drivers of strategic thinking and the development process for their cities; it also works to organize external technical assistance, funding and advice by donors, development agencies, and other partners in a way that is strategically coherent and ordered to meeting the priority needs of the city as a whole.

Activities: Collaborates with community-level, national and international organizations, other donor agencies, the private sector, NGOs, community-based organizations, academics and others in the urban field. Activities include involvement in the Cities Alliance (q.v.); and the Street Children Initiative, focused on the post-conflict environments and transition economies of Eastern Europe and countries of the former USSR (the Europe and Central Asia—ECA—Region), which produces information on the magnitude and characteristics of the problems of street children in the region, examining issues such as drug use, prostitution, human trafficking, disease, abuse and child labour and translating lessons into tools with which to address the street child phenomenon in the region. Also carries out collaborative research, including the Rapid Economic Growth of Cities and Survival of the Urban Poor programme.

Geographical Area of Activity: International.

Financial Information: Funded from World Bank Trust Fund commitments, other donors and private foundations.

Publications: Urban Age (quarterly magazine).

Address: 1818 H St, NW, Washington, DC 20433, USA.

Telephone: (202) 473-1000; *Fax:* (202) 477-6391; *Internet:* www.worldbank.org /html/fpd/urban/urb_part/urb_part.htm; *e-mail:* urbanweb@worldbank.org.

Grants Facility for Indigenous Peoples

Launched by the World Bank in June 2003 to provide small grants for indigenous peoples' development activities; governed by an advisory board of indigenous leaders, donor agencies, governments, representatives of the UN Permanent Forum on Indigenous Issues, and the World Bank.

Activities: The fund was established to provide seed grants averaging approximately US $30,000 to indigenous peoples' organizations working on issues of indigenous peoples' development.

Geographical Area of Activity: International.

Financial Information: Total budget US $700,000 (2003); average grant US $30,000, co-financing of a minimum of 20% of the project's total costs is required.

Address: 1818 H St, NW, Washington, DC 20433, USA.

Telephone: (202) 473-1000; *Fax:* (202) 477-6391; *Internet:* www.worldbankimflib .org.

AIDS CAMPAIGN TEAM FOR AFRICA

Multi-Country HIV/AIDS Programme (MAP) for Africa

Launched in September 2000 by the World Bank to address the financial and organizational shortcomings that had characterized the fight against HIV/AIDS in Africa, by committing substantial resources and leveraging co-financing on a country-by-country basis through the International Partnership Against AIDS in Africa (IPAA).

Activities: Grants are available to African countries to support projects that dramatically increase access to HIV/AIDS prevention, care, and treatment programmes, with emphasis on vulnerable groups (such as youth, women of childbearing age, and other groups at high risk). The specific development objectives of each individual country project provide the basis for the Programme and are agreed upon at the time of appraisal of the national projects. A key target of MAP resources is to channel direct support to community organizations, NGOs, and the private sector for local HIV/AIDS initiatives.

Geographical Area of Activity: Africa.

How to Apply: In order to qualify for MAP assistance, governments must provide: satisfactory evidence of a strategic approach to HIV/AIDS, developed in a participatory manner; existence of a high-level HIV/AIDS co-ordinating body, with broad representation of key stakeholders from all sectors, including people living with HIV/AIDS; commitment to quick implementation arrangements, including channeling grant funds for HIV/AIDS activities directly to communities, civil society, and the private sector; and agree to use multiple implementation agencies, especially NGOs and community-based organizations.

Financial Information: Two initial World Bank donations totalling US $1,000,000,000.

Address: Room J5-282, 1818 H St, NW, Washington, DC 20433, USA.

Telephone: (202) 458-0606; *Fax:* (202) 522-7396; *Internet:* www.worldbank.org/afr/aids/map.htm; *e-mail:* actafrica@worldbank.org.

BANK–NETHERLANDS PARTNERSHIP PROGRAMME (BNPP)

Operates as an agreement between the Netherlands Ministry of Foreign Affairs (MFA) and the World Bank to provide financing and a priority setting framework for all new projects and programmes of a global and regional (GRI) nature as well as for a Consultancy Trust Fund (CTF) financed by the Ministry of Foreign Affairs. The Netherlands is one of the largest donors of trust fund resources to the World Bank.

Activities: The Programme currently prioritizes environment, water resource management, renewable energy, gender, governance, poverty, urban development, health, water and sanitation programmes, education and culture and development and rural development, as well as other initiatives related to the World Trade Organization (WTO) and the UN. Initiatives funded by the Programme include the Governance Knowledge Sharing Programme (GKSP, q.v.).

Geographical Area of Activity: International.

Financial Information: Basic BNPP funding is approx. US $18,750,000, of which US $5,500,000 is applied to the CTF and approx. US $13,250,000 to the GRI.

Contact: Co-ordinator Cora Shaw; Cofinancing Analyst Ekaterina Kan.

Address: 1818 H St, NW, MSN 4-416, Washington, DC 20433, USA.

Internet: www1.worldbank.org/publicsector/bnpp/.

BANK–NETHERLANDS WATER PARTNERSHIP (BNWP)

Water and Energy Department: Water Supply and Sanitation

BNWP was established in 2000, as an operational instrument to stimulate innovative approaches to water resources management in World Bank operations and the broader development community. In 2001 the Partnership was extended to cover water supply and sanitation.

Activities: The programme's activities enhance performance of World Bank operations in the water supply and sanitation sector and support a broad sector reform agenda with a strong poverty focus. The partnership works through various units within the World Bank, including the regional operations and central operational support units and the Water and Sanitation Capacity Building Programme of the World Bank Institute, and engages with a broad array of partners, including national, state or local governments, NGOs, community groups, and the private sector. Supported projects should have a clear focus on: poverty alleviation; South–South co-operation; scaling up of innovative practices; and gender issues. Grants are awarded for both projects and activities, and grants for activities cannot exceed US $50,000.

Geographical Area of Activity: Developing countries.

How to Apply: Proposals from outside the World Bank Group (WBG) will be considered if submitted through a WBG staff member/proponent who will take on the standard task management responsibilities, including implementation, monitoring, and financial and progress reporting.

Financial Information: Total funding from the Netherlands Ministry of Foreign Affairs US $8,400,000; maximum grant available US $50,000, co-financing for projects is encouraged but not essential.

Contact: Programme Man. Jan G. Janssens.

Address: 1818 H St, NW, Washington, DC 20433, USA.

Telephone: (202) 458-7796; *Fax:* (202) 522-3228; *Internet:* http://wbln0018 .worldbank.org/water/bnwp.nsf; *e-mail:* bnwp@worldbank.org.

CONSULTATIVE GROUP TO ASSIST THE POOREST (CGAP)

CGAP/IFAD Rural Pro-Poor Innovation Challenge

The Consultative Group to Assist the Poorest (CGAP) is a consortium of 29 bilateral and multilateral donor agencies who support micro-finance, aiming to improve the capacity of micro-finance institutions to deliver flexible, high-quality financial services to the very poor on a sustainable basis. The CGAP/IFAD Rural Pro-Poor Innovation Challenge operates as a partnership between IFAD (the International Fund for Agricultural Development) and CGAP (the Consultative Group to Assist the Poor) to support innovations in rural and micro-finance, through supporting the development of financial products and methodologies for very poor people or difficult to reach rural populations, to reduce their vulnerability and increase their economic well-being.

Activities: The Challenge operates through providing flexible funding awards to promote micro-finance innovation that deepens rural poverty outreach and its impact. In 2003, five awards of up to US $50,000 were made. Previous awards have been made to human rights and micro-credit organizations based in Albania, Honduras, India, Kyrgyzstan, Mexico, Moldova, Nepal, Peru and Togo for a range of activities including rural credit programmes, community banking and credit and loan services.

Geographical Area of Activity: International; developing countries.

Financial Information: Annual budget approx. US $250,000 (2003).

Contact: Dir Elizabeth Littlefield; Capacity-Building Product Man. Leslie Barcus.

Address: 1818 H St, NW, Washington, DC 20433, USA.

Telephone: (202) 473-9594; *Fax:* (202) 522-3744; *Internet:* www.cgap.org/html /mfis_funding.html; *e-mail:* cgap@worldbank.org.

CONSULTATIVE GROUP ON INTERNATIONAL AGRICULTURAL RESEARCH (CGIAR)

An initiative of the World Bank, launched in 1971; aims to achieve sustainable food security and reduce poverty in developing countries through scientific research and research-related activities in the fields of agriculture, forestry, fisheries, policy, and environment.

Activities: Pursues its objectives primarily through supporting 16 research centres, which operate as autonomous institutions; now known as Future Harvest Centers. At the national level, CGIAR works with National Agricultural Research Systems (NARS) and NGOs to devise policies, conduct research, and ensure that research results move from laboratories to farmers' fields. Approximately 300 NGOs are engaged in collaborative research programmes with the CGIAR research centres. Regionally, CGIAR supports the growth of regional federations of agricultural research institutions, and forums such as the Asia Pacific Association of Agricultural Research Institutions (APAARI), Association of Agricultural Research Institutions in the Near East and North Africa (AARINENA), Forum on Agricultural Research in Africa, and the Latin America and Caribbean Forum on Agricultural Research, and their interaction with other similar organizations. On a global level, CGIAR served as a catalyst in the establishment of the Global Forum on Agricultural Research to explore, establish, and implement collaborative programmes for sustainable food security amongst NGOs, farmers' organizations, the private sector, local and national governments, national research systems, advanced research organizations, and international centres.

Geographical Area of Activity: Developing countries.

Financial Information: Co-sponsored by the World Bank, the United Nations Food and Agriculture Organization (FAO), IFAD and the United Nations Development Programme (UNDP); total income US $337,000,000 (2001).

Contact: Chair. Ian Johnson.

Address: CGIAR Secretariat, World Bank, MSN G6-601, 1818 H St, NW, Washington, DC 20433, USA.

Telephone: (202) 473-8951; *Fax:* (202) 473-8110; *Internet:* www.cgiar.org; *e-mail:* cgiar@cgiar.org.

King Baudouin Award

Established in 1981, following CGIAR's receipt in 1980 of the King Baudouin International Development Prize for its contribution to the qualitative and quantitative improvement of food production in the world. Using funds received from the King Baudouin International Development Prize, the CGIAR established its own King Baudouin Award, presented every two years, to acknowledge and stimulate agricultural research and other activities and to recognize an achievement stemming from the work of a research centre.

Activities: The Award is intended to recognize the application, use and impact of a particular technology, material or knowledge developed by international research centres in the field of agricultural research, as well as significant research achievements with great potential impact.

Geographical Area of Activity: Developing countries.

Address: CGIAR Secretariat, World Bank, MSN G6-601, 1818 H St, NW, Washington, DC 20433, USA.

Telephone: (202) 473-8951; *Fax:* (202) 473-8110; *Internet:* www.cgiar.org/who /wwa_baudouin.html; *e-mail:* cgiar@cgiar.org.

CORPORATE STRATEGY UNIT

Development Marketplace Team: Development Marketplace

Established by the World Bank to promote innovation in development and to nurture creative solutions in poverty reduction.

Activities: The programme promotes innovative development ideas through early stage seed funding, and linking social entrepreneurs with poverty fighting ideas to partners with resources to help implement their vision. Operates on two levels, globally and nationally/regionally: the Global Development Marketplace is held every 18–24 months in Washington, DC, USA and includes a global competition as well as a knowledge forum; Country Innovation Days are replicas of the global programme but on a smaller scale, also including a competition and a knowledge forum addressing national/regional development issues. Organizations eligible to apply for funding include NGOs, bilateral and multinational development organizations, individuals, academic institutions, governments, foundations and private-sector businesses. The theme for the Global Competition in 2003 was Making Services Work for Poor People, in the areas of health, education, water and sanitation, infrastructure (roads and transportation), energy, financial services, including micro-finance, small business and micro-enterprise support, information and communications technology, social protection, conservation and ecosystem services, or any other project that improves delivery of services to poor people.

Geographical Area of Activity: International.

How to Apply: Proposals must be submitted in partnership with at least one other organization; themes criteria and application procedures are announced on the website.

Financial Information: Total awards since 1998 approx. US $16,000,000.

Address: World Bank, 1818 H St, NW, Washington, DC 20433, USA.

Internet: www.developmentmarketplace.org; *e-mail:* dminfo@caworldbank.org.

DEVELOPMENT GRANT FACILITY (DGF)

The Development Grant Facility of the World Bank was established in 1997 to integrate the overall strategy, allocations and management of the World Bank's grant-making activities under one umbrella mechanism.

Activities: DGF co-ordinates the World Bank's overall grant-making strategy, in accordance with the Bank's development work and as a complement to its lending and advisory services. Grants are made to encourage innovation, catalyze partnerships and to broaden the scope of the Bank's services. The total grant budget of US $157,000,000 in 2003 covered 48 grant programmes.

Geographical Area of Activity: International.

How to Apply: Each grant proposal must have a Bank sponsor to be considered against the institutional priorities of the Bank-wide DGF Council.

Financial Information: Total budget US $157,000,000 (2003).

Address: 1818 H St, NW, Washington, DC 20433, USA.

Internet: www.worldbank.org/dgf.

Association for the Development of Education in Africa (ADEA)

ADEA was established with support from the Africa Region of the World Bank in 1988 to nurture donor co-ordination in education; initially known as Donors to African Education (DAE).

Activities: Aims to further African capacity building and development of country-led partnerships with education donors, in support of the UN Special Initiative on Africa (UNSIA) and the follow-up to the targets set at the April 2000 Dakar World Education Forum of providing Education for All by 2015. Activities include the annual Africa Education Journalism Award; meetings every two years on education policy, bringing together African Ministers of Education, representatives of development agencies, researchers and other education professionals in a professional environment; ongoing research into the education system in Africa; development of effective policy responses to the challenges and dangers that the HIV/AIDS epidemic poses for education systems; and a programme of Intra-African exchanges, including study visits and the exchange of expertise. Also operates the Communication for Education and Development (COMED) programme that promotes the use of communication in support of education, implemented with the World Bank and the West African News Media and

Development Centre (WANAD), and with co-funding from the Norwegian Education Trust Fund, which aims to build ministerial capacities for communication and improved media understanding of education issues.

Geographical Area of Activity: Africa.

Financial Information: Annual budget US $3,400,000 (2003).

Publications: ADEA Newsletter (quarterly); Secretariat and working group publications; and other reports, papers and publications.

Contact: Steering Cttee Chair. Ahlin Byll-Cataria; Alternate Chair. Hon. Lesao Archibald Lehohla.

Address: 7–9 rue Eugène-Delacroix , 75116 Paris, France.

Telephone: 1-45-03-77-57; *Fax:* 1-45-03-39-65; *Internet:* www.adeanet.org.

International Institute for Educational Planning (IIEP): Capacity Building for Educational Planning and Management

A World Bank-funded programme, implemented by the International Institute for Educational Planning (IIEP), established to strengthen the capacity of countries to plan and manage their education systems.

Activities: Aims to develop, co-ordinate and support capacity-building efforts in developing countries, paying special attention to institution building, and to expanding institutional co-operation among developing countries and between developing and developed countries. Support is given to: strengthen core training materials in educational planning; strengthen and modernize course materials for special-purpose training programmes delivered at within-country and sub-regional levels; expand capacity-building programmes focused on technical skills delivered via consortia of education ministries; improve the quality of schools through capacity building of school leaders; improve educational management capacities in Francophone Africa; design and implement interactive satellite training courses in partnership with the World Bank's Global Development Learning Network; deliver policy forums on the policy and planning implications of e-learning; improve school mapping procedures and district-level planning in countries in transition; develop approaches for enhancing ethics and for avoiding corruption in education; build IIEP's capacity to act as a broker institution for the delivery of capacity-building initiatives; and to build faculty capacity for the Eastern European Center for Economic Research and Graduate Education in Economics (CERGE–EI) Institute in order to respond to the region's critical needs and training for a diverse group of leaders in economics. IIEP also maintains an office in Buenos Aires, Argentina.

Geographical Area of Activity: Developing countries.

Restrictions: No grants, fellowships of direct support to individuals.

Financial Information: Annual budget US $10,500,000 (2003).

Contact: World Bank Contact Ernesto P. Cuadra; Governing Board Chair. Dato'Asiah bt. Abu Samah; Dir Gudmund Hernes.

Address: 7–9 rue Eugène-Delacroix, 75116 Paris, France.

Internet: www.unesco.org/iiep.

ENVIRONMENT DEPARTMENT

World Bank/WWF (World Wide Fund for Nature) Alliance for Forest Conservation and Sustainable Use

The WB-WWF Alliance is a strategic, performance-based, global partnership, formed in response to a crisis: the continued depletion of the world's forest biodiversity, the loss of forest-based goods and services essential for sustainable development, and the resulting severe impacts on the livelihoods of the rural poor. The Alliance is working with governments, the private sector, and civil society to create 50 million hectares (124 million acres) of new protected areas of forest, and aims to help ensure that a similar amount of existing protected areas come under effective management by 2005. In the same timeframe, the Alliance aims to have 200 million hectares (495 million acres) of the world's production forests under independently certified management.

Activities: To meet its three challenges, the Alliance supports the small-scale activities of NGOs, local community organizations, governments, the private sector, scientific and policy research institutes, through stimulating investment opportunities in protected areas and promoting the improvement of forest management practices. Supported projects include workshops in management effectiveness, illegal logging and creative financing mechanisms for sustainable management and forest law enforcement. The Alliance is currently active in 22 countries in Africa, East Asia and the Pacific, Central and South America and the Caribbean, and South Asia.

Geographical Area of Activity: Africa, South Asia, East Asia and the Pacific, Central and South America, and the Caribbean.

How to Apply: Project proposals must be developed in consultation with local World Bank and/or WWF representatives. Proposals are then evaluated by the Alliance.

Publications: Annual Report; Protected Areas reports; Sustainable Forest Management reports.

Contact: World Bank Alliance Co-ordinator Christian Peter; World Wildlife Fund Alliance Co-ordinator Stephen Kelleher.

Address: World Bank, 1818 H St, NW, Washington, DC 20433, USA.

Internet: www.forest-alliance.org; *e-mail:* wbwwfalliance@worldbank.org.

ENVIRONMENT AND SOCIAL SECTOR UNIT—AFRICA REGION (AFTES)

Managing the Environment Locally in Sub-Saharan Africa (MELISSA)

Established in 1966, managed by the Environment and Social Sector Unit—Africa Region (AFTES) of the World Bank and hosted by the Council for Scientific and Industrial Research in Pretoria, South Africa; aims to support and facilitate the improvement of the local environment through partnership development and knowledge management, in order to contribute to finding the balance between social equity, economic advancement and sustainable development to ensure improved living conditions and a better quality of life for urban, peri-urban and rural citizens.

172

Activities: Aims to facilitate the acquisition, absorption, and dissemination of decentralized environmental management knowledge in sub-Saharan Africa through participatory action learning, capacity building and networking to promote partnerships for effective local environmental governance. The programme funds local organizations and decentralized structures, including urban and rural municipalities; provincial and regional departments; community-based organizations, NGOs, co-operatives, youth groups, women's organizations, farmers' groups, school development associations, health committees and research and training institutions.

Geographical Area of Activity: Sub-Saharan Africa, including Benin, Burkina Faso, Côte d'Ivoire, Gambia, Ghana, Madagascar, Mali, Nigeria, Senegal, South Africa, Tanzania, Uganda and Zimbabwe.

How to Apply: Apply directly by submitting a proposal request; application guidelines are available on the programme website.

Financial Information: Funded by the European Commission and Norwegian and Swedish governments.

Publications: KERN Forum proceedings; *KERN InfoBriefs; KERN papers; African Journal of Environmental Assessment and Management—AJEAM* (2 a year).

Address: MELISSA Programme Co-ordinator, World Bank Office in South Africa, POB 12629, Hatfield, 0028 Pretoria, South Africa.

Telephone: (12) 349-2994; *Fax:* (12) 349-2080; *Internet:* www.melissa.org; *e-mail:* melissa@melissa.org.

ENVIRONMENT UNIT

Development Grant Facility (DGF): Forest Partnerships Programme

Forms part of the World Bank's Forest Strategy seeking to address the challenges of harnessing the economic potential of forests to reduce poverty, integrating forests into sustainable economic development, and protecting vital local and global values.

Activities: The Programme works through establishing major partnerships with NGOs; in 2003 partnerships were developed with the World Bank/WWF Alliance for Forest Conservation and Sustainable Use, Forest Trends, the Amazon Network on Forests and the World Business Council for Sustainable Development (WBCSD) Forum on Forests.

Geographical Area of Activity: International.

Financial Information: Annual budget US $5,000,000 (2003).

Contact: World Bank Contact David S. Cassells.

Address: World Bank, 1818 H St, NW, Washington, DC 20433, USA.

Telephone: (202) 473-1376; *Internet:* www.worldbank.org; www.forest.trends.org.

EUROPE AND CENTRAL ASIA REGION–SOCIAL SECTOR DEVELOPMENT NETWORK

Caspian Environment Programme Priority Investment Portfolio Project (CEP–PIPP)

Implemented by the United Nations Development Programme (UNDP), the Priority Investment Portfolio Project (PIPP) was initiated within the framework of the Caspian Environment Programme and as a component of the Global Environment Facility (GEF) Project Addressing Trans-boundary Environmental Issues in the Caspian Environment Programme. Aims to increase the number and quality of priority environmental investments that have a positive trans-boundary environmental impact and that contribute to economic growth of the Caspian littoral countries of Azerbaijan, Iran, Kazakhstan, Russia and Turkmenistan.

Activities: The Project consists of four major sub-components: Investment Identification and Pre-preparation, supporting the identification and pre-preparation of investment projects, with priority given to trans-boundary environmental issues in the areas of industrial pollution prevention and mitigation directly affecting the Caspian waters (including pollution from the oil industry), and the recovery of sturgeon stocks and their habitat; Institutional Strengthening and Training for Project Preparation, including the training of national focal points (NFP) and other national personnel on project preparation, project cycles, finance, management and supervision, and training or seminars for NFPs and other senior national personnel on the role of investments in implementing the national policy agenda; Matched Small Grants Programme for Trans-boundary Issues, advancing the implementation of small-scale priority projects as quickly as possible in order to take curative or preventative actions, as well as to develop the capacity for future activities, with around 5–10 small-scale or pilot projects developed into larger scale investment opportunities, or projects that can be replicated in other locations around the Caspian Sea; and Project Management, to ensure transparency and the maximum use of resources by establishing a Baku-based Project Manager at the CEP Project Co-ordination Unit (PCU), who is responsible for all co-ordination among the NFPs, Caspian Regional Thematic Centres, and the PCU, and establishing contacts with one lead local consultant on a part-time basis in each Caspian state to assist the NFP in implementation of the project.

Geographical Area of Activity: Azerbaijan, Iran, Kazakhstan, Russia and Turkmenistan.

Restrictions: Only open to NGOs, government and private-sector organizations from Azerbaijan, Iran, Kazakhstan, Russia and Turkmenistan.

How to Apply: Application form available to download from the website.

Contact: Steering Cttee Chair. Gouseyn Bagirov.

Address: Room 108, 3rd Entrance, Government House, U. Hadjibeyov St 40, Baku 370016, Azerbaijan.

Telephone: (12) 97-17-85; *Fax:* (12) 97-17-86; *Internet:* www.caspianenvironment .org; *e-mail:* caspian@caspian.in-baku.com.

HUMAN DEVELOPMENT NETWORK—HEALTH, NUTRITION AND POPULATION DEPARTMENT

Population and Reproductive Health Capacity Building Programme

Forms part of the World Bank's support for population and reproductive health activities; co-ordinated by the Bank's Human Development Network—Health, Nutrition and Population Department. Aims to build the capacity of civil-society organizations to develop and implement culturally appropriate interventions in the sensitive fields of population and reproductive health, leading to healthier behaviour at individual and community levels, and improved reproductive health outcomes.

Activities: The Programme aims to develop the capacity of grassroots NGOs working in population, reproductive health, safe motherhood, female genital mutilation and other women's and adolescents' health issues, through grants to international and regional NGOs for assistance to grassroots NGOs in developing countries. International and regional NGOs with links to grassroots NGOs in developing countries can apply for grant funds to act as grant-making and technical assistance intermediaries.

Geographical Area of Activity: Developing countries.

How to Apply: Information on how to apply from the Human Development Network—Health, Nutrition and Population Department.

Financial Information: Annual budget US $16,500,000 (2003).

Contact: Contact Janet Nassim.

Address: World Bank, 1818 H St, NW, Washington, DC 20433, USA.

Telephone: (202) 473-7024; *Internet:* www1.worldbank.org/hnp/; *e-mail:* healthpop@worldbank.org.

LATIN AMERICA AND CARIBBEAN REGION

Brazil Rain Forest Unit: Pilot Programme to Conserve the Brazilian Rain Forest

Established in 1992 as a partnership of the Brazilian Government, Brazil's civil society, the international community and the World Bank, amidst concern about the deforestation of Brazil's humid rain forests in the Amazon and on the Atlantic coast. The Programme is administered by the World Bank's Brazil Rain Forest Unit in the Central and South America and Caribbean Region.

Activities: Aims to demonstrate ways towards conservation and sustainable use of the natural resources of the rain forests, through helping community groups obtain information, participate in policy formulation, contribute to programme design, and exchange ideas through two coalitions of NGOs: the Amazon Working Group (GTA), and the Atlantic Forest Network (RMA). Funding is given to Brazilian NGOs and community organizations experienced in locally-based efforts to conserve the Brazilian rain forest. The Programme is currently operating within five focal areas: to test and demonstrate conservation and sustainable development, through support for demonstration, forest and floodplain management projects; to protect the environment and conserve resources, in the areas of indigenous lands, extractive reserves, and rain forest corridors; to strengthen institutions for environmental management, through its natural resources policy; to build capacities to take on environmental policy and management responsibilities, in the fields of fire prevention, through the GTA and the RMA; and produce and apply scientific knowledge, including supporting science centres and directed research, new cross-cutting initiatives, running a sustainable production project, and an Atlantic Forest sub-programme.

Geographical Area of Activity: Brazil.

How to Apply: Further information on applications available on the Programme website and from the World Bank country office in Brasília, Brazil.

Financial Information: Funded in part by bilateral funds, the Brazilian and Netherlands governments, and by a trust fund created by the G-7 countries (Canada, France, Germany, Italy, Japan, UK and USA). Total funds approx. US $347,000,000.

Contact: Team Leader Joseph Leitmann.

Address: World Bank, 1818 H St, NW, Washington, DC 20433, USA.

Internet: www.worldbank.org/rfpp; *e-mail:* jleitmann@worldbank.org.

MARGARET MCNAMARA MEMORIAL FUND

Margaret McNamara Memorial Fund

Founded in 1981 in memory of Margaret Graig McNamara, honorary president of the World Bank Family Network (WBFN) from 1972 to 1981; aims to support the education of women from developing countries who are committed to improving the lives of women and children in a developing country.

Activities: Supports the education of women in developing countries, through awarding approximately six annual grants of US $11,000. Beneficiaries must have a record of service to women and/or children in their country and be a resident of the USA at the time the application is submitted.

Geographical Area of Activity: Developing countries and USA.

Address: 1818 H St, NW, MSN H2-204, Washington, DC 20433, USA.

e-mail: mmmf@caworldbank.org.

MIDDLE EAST AND NORTH AFRICA REGION

**Rural Development, Water and Environment Department:
Mediterranean Technical Assistance Programme Pilot NGO Small
Grants Facility (METAP SGF)**

The Mediterranean Technical Assistance Programme (METAP) was founded in 1990, to bring together countries in the Mediterranean region and multilateral donors to assist beneficiary countries in project preparation and strengthen their capacity in regional environmental management. METAP is implemented jointly by UN Resident Missions and the World Bank Rural Development, Water and Environment Group, Middle East and North Africa Region.

Activities: Aims to reduce the effects of environmental degradation in the Mediterranean region, through grants to small-scale innovative activities initiated by community-based NGOs in Albania, Algeria, Bosnia and

Herzegovina, Croatia, Cyprus, Egypt, Jordan, Lebanon, Libya, Morocco, Syria, Slovenia, Tunisia, Turkey, and West Bank and Gaza. Supported activities have ranged from project preparation to institutional strengthening, policy development, training, establishment of regional networks, and local empowerment in various sectors of the environment. The current phase of METAP is to operate as a regional programme, through the identification of a regional priority, which is then assessed at country and regional levels for strategy development and regional project design. Funding proposals are then developed by METAP for submission to potential donors for funding of the regional programme or activity, which have country and regional level activities. Countries determine their own priorities for country level implementation within the scope of the regional programme.

Geographical Area of Activity: Albania, Algeria, Bosnia and Herzegovina, Croatia, Cyprus, Egypt, Jordan, Lebanon, Libya, Morocco, Syria, Slovenia, Tunisia, Turkey, and West Bank and Gaza.

How to Apply: See World Bank website.

Financial Information: In its previous three phases, METAP provided approx. US $60,000,000.

Address: Mail Stop H8-801, 1818 H St, NW, Washington, DC 20433, USA.

Telephone: (202) 473-2194; *Fax:* (202) 477-1374; *Internet:* www.worldbank .org; www.metap.org; *e-mail:* askmna@worldbank.org.

NGO AND CIVIL SOCIETY UNIT, SOCIAL DEVELOPMENT DEPARTMENT

Small Grants Programme

Established by the World Bank in 1983 to promote dialogue and disseminate information about development.

Activities: Operates through making grants to support civic engagement activities by local civil society organizations The Programme aims to promote the empowerment of citizens to give them greater ownership of development processes, and grants are made for activities related to this purpose. Activities should also promote dialogue and disseminate information for the empowerment of marginalized and vulnerable groups, and enhance partnerships with key players in support of the development process, including government agencies, civil society organizations, multilateral and bilateral agencies, foundations, and the private sector. No grants are distributed from the Head Office and grants are made through over 60 national country offices.

Geographical Area of Activity: International.

How to Apply: All grant decisions are made through participating World Bank Country Offices once a year. Interested NGOs and other civil society organizations must contact the local World Bank Country Office.

Financial Information: Funded by the Development Grant Facility (q.v.) of the World Bank; total grants US $2,500,000 (2002).

Address: World Bank, 1818 H St, NW, Washington, DC 20433, USA.

Internet: www.worldbank.org/ngos.

POST-CONFLICT UNIT, SOCIAL DEVELOPMENT DEPARTMENT

Post-Conflict Fund (PCF)

The Fund was established in 1997 to enhance the Bank's ability to support countries in transition from conflict to sustainable peace and economic growth.

Activities: Aims to help countries in transition from conflict situations, through providing support for reconstruction efforts, including planning, piloting and analysis of ground-breaking activities, by governments and partner organizations, including institutions, NGOs, UN agencies, transitional authorities, and other civil society institutions. Partner organizations include Co-operative Assistance and Relief Everywhere (CARE), International Federation of Red Cross and Red Crescent Societies (IFRC), Canadian Centre for International Studies and Co-operation (CECI), World Links Organization, African Women Alliance for Mobilizing Action, South African Center of Conflict Resolution, and Groupe de Recherches et d'Echanges Technologiques. Priority is given to funding innovative projects. An on-line database allows users to search PCF-funded projects by country, region, status and theme. In 2002 the Fund distributed grants in 36 countries.

Geographical Area of Activity: Developing countries.

Financial Information: Total grants US $7,000,000 (2002); average grant US $643,000. Total grants since 1997 US $50,900,000.

Publications: Guidelines and Procedures; Application Form.

Address: World Bank, 1818 H St, NW, Washington, DC 20433, USA.

Internet: www.worldbank.org/postconflict.

PREM NETWORK PUBLIC SECTOR BOARD

Governance Knowledge Sharing Programme (GKSP)

Funded under the World Bank Netherlands Partnership Programme (BNPP), the Programme seeks to encourage governance knowledge sharing through new tools, media and learning.

Activities: The Programme provides funding for innovative projects that aim to stimulate local demand for better governance, and to improve existing World Bank projects for sharing governance knowledge. Grants are made to NGOs, governments, academics, students, media organizations and other partners for projects that make governments more informed consumers of development assistance and raise demand for public sector reform through empowering civil society and the private sector with increased public information and discussion.

Geographical Area of Activity: International.

How to Apply: Application forms can be downloaded from the website or completed on-line; proposals should have a sponsor from within the World Bank.

Contact: Management Board Chair. Helen Sutch; Implementation Team: Bill Moore, Ranjana Mukherjee.

Address: World Bank, 1818 H St, NW, Washington, DC 20433, USA.

Telephone: (202) 473-5261; *Fax:* (202) 522-7132; *Internet:* www.worldbank.org /publicsector/bnpp; *e-mail:* gksp@worldbank.org.

PRIVATE PARTNERSHIP IN INFRASTRUCTURE UNIT (INFPI)

Global Partnership on Output-Based Aid (GPOBA)

Established in January 2003 by the United Kingdom's Department for International Development (DFID) and the World Bank, GPOBA is a multi-donor trust fund administered by the World Bank. It aims to provide increased access to reliable basic infrastructure and social services to the poor in developing countries through the wider use of Output-Based Aid (OBA) approaches.

Activities: GPOBA demonstrates and documents OBA methods of supporting the sustainable delivery of basic services (water, sanitation, electricity, tele-communications, transportation, health and education) to those least able to afford them and to those currently without access. Supports pilot demonstration projects and related activities to identify and disseminate lessons of experience on the design and implementation of OBA schemes, including the targeting of eligible beneficiaries, definition of performance requirements, the determination of payment structures, and the design of monitoring arrangements. Operates through delegating service delivery to a third party, typically private companies and NGOs, under contracts that tie disbursement of the public funding to the services or outputs actually delivered.

Geographical Area of Activity: International.

How to Apply: Application forms can be downloaded from the website.

Contact: Contact Clive G. Harris.

Address: I9-905, 1818 H St, NW, Washington, DC 20433, USA.

Fax: (202) 522-3481; *Internet:* www.gpoba.org; *e-mail:* gpoba@worldbank.org.

PUBLIC–PRIVATE INFRASTRUCTURE ADVISORY FACILITY (PPIAF) PROGRAMME MANAGEMENT

Public–Private Infrastructure Advisory Facility (PPIAF)

Launched in July 1999, at the joint initiative of the governments of Japan and the United Kingdom, in close conjunction with the World Bank. Operates as a multi-donor technical assistance facility aimed at helping developing countries improve the quality of their infrastructure through private-sector involvement.

Activities: PPIAF operates through providing technical assistance to governments related to private-sector involvement in infrastructure development activities, policy, regulatory and institutional reforms, pioneering transactions, and consensus and capacity building. Eligible infrastructure services include gas transmission and distribution, water and sewerage, solid waste, electricity, telecommunications, ports, airports, railways and roads. Open to applications from NGOs, academia, developing country governments, international financial institutions, bilateral and multilateral donors.

Geographical Area of Activity: Developing countries.

How to Apply: Applications can come from any source, but country-specific activities require formal endorsement from the beneficiary government. Applicants can download an application form on-line or apply directly to PPIAF Programme Management.

Financial Information: Donors include the governments of Canada, Japan, Norway, Switzerland and the UK, and the United Nations Development Programme and the World Bank.

Publications: Annual Report.

Contact: Governed by a Programme Council made up of representatives of the donor agencies.

Address: c/o World Bank, Mail Stop 19-900, 1818 H St, NW, Washington DC 20433, USA.

Telephone: (202) 458-5588; *Fax:* (202) 522-7466; *Internet:* www.ppiaf.org; *e-mail:* info@cappiaf.org.

RURAL DEVELOPMENT, WATER AND ENVIRONMENT GROUP

Palestinian NGO Project (PNGO Project)

A World Bank-financed project, managed by the Welfare Association Consortium, to assist Palestinian NGOs in providing needed services to the poor, the marginalized and the disadvantaged in the West Bank and Gaza. The Project Management Organization (PMO) is made up of a consortium of the Welfare Association, the British Council and the UK-based Charities Aid Foundation.

Activities: The second phase of the Project aims at strengthening the capacity of NGOs to deliver sustainable services to poor and marginalized Palestinians, while supporting the overall professional and strategic development of the NGO Sector in Palestine. Under the Partnership Development Programme grants are awarded for 5–8 service delivery projects implemented by lead NGOs in partnership with smaller NGOs or CBOs. Projects are expected to be implemented over a period of two years with an average budget of US $1,000,000 and an estimated sub-grant size of US $50,000–$100,000, with the aims of improving the technical capacity of smaller NGOs in delivering quality services; to support access by these NGOs to increased levels of funding; to expand the reach of larger NGOs to marginalized communities through a larger network of field-based NGOs; and to promote best practice as a core project strategy. Under the Development Grant Programme, grants are awarded to medium capacity NGOs that have demonstrated the ability to manage quality projects during the first phase and that demonstrate clear potential for greater impact and sustainability. Grants for projects range from US $50,000 to US $300,000 with 7% of the total budget allocated for tailor-made capacity building and institutional development to the recipient NGO. Also operates a Sector Support Programme, aiming to develop the NGO sector's strategic approach to meeting the needs of the poor and provides technical support and funding to improve project monitoring and evaluation.

Geographical Area of Activity: Palestinian Autonomous Areas.

Restrictions: Only applications from NGOs are accepted.

How to Apply: Application forms must be completed within a specific time frame.

Financial Information: Established as a US $14,900,000 project funded by the World Bank (US $10,000,000), the government of Italy (US $2,100,000), the government of Saudi Arabia (US $2,500,000), and the Welfare Association (US $300,000). In July 2001 the World Bank and the Welfare Association implemented the second phase of the Project for a total amount of US $8,000,000, with an additional commitment of US $2,500,000 from the Saudi Fund and US $2,500,000 from DFID (British Development Assistance Department for International Development).

Publications: PNGO Project Newsletter.

Contact: Contact Dr Mohammed Shadid.

Address: Welfare Association Consortium, Al Fityani Bldg, Dahiat al-Barid, POB 2173, Ramallah, Palestinian Autonomous Areas.

Telephone: (2) 2347771; *Fax:* (2) 2347776; *Internet:* www.pngo-project.org; *e-mail:* mshadid@capngo-project.org.

TRANSPORT AND URBAN DEVELOPMENT DEPARTMENT

Cities Alliance

Established in 1999 with initial support from the World Bank and the United Nations Centre for Human Settlements (UN-Habitat), the political heads of the four leading global associations of local authorities and 10 governments; Canada, France, Germany, Italy, Japan, Netherlands, Norway, Sweden, the UK and the USA; the Asian Development Bank joined the Cities Alliance in March 2002. Operates as an alliance of cities and their development partners created to foster new tools, practical approaches and knowledge sharing to promote local economic development and a direct attack on urban poverty. Its activities support the implementation of the Habitat Agenda.

Activities: Organizes its activities around three strategic objectives: to build political commitment and shared vision, principally the Cities Without Slums action plan adopted as a new international development target by the UN Millennium Summit; create a learning alliance to fill knowledge gaps, through developing networks of cities to share their City Development Strategy experience; and catalyze city-wide and nation-wide impacts, working in partnership with local and national authorities. Funding is available for NGOs, community organizations and private-sector organizations working in partnership with local authorities.

Geographical Area of Activity: International, including Bangladesh, Brazil, Bulgaria, Cambodia, People's Republic of China, Egypt, El Salvador, Ethiopia, India, Indonesia, Kenya, Madagascar, Mauritania, Morocco, Mozambique, Nepal, Nigeria, Pakistan, Philippines, Rwanda, South Africa, Vietnam and Yemen.

How to Apply: Application guide-lines available on the website; all proposals must be approved by the government of the recipient country and sponsored by at least one Alliance member. Proposals must include co-financing, combining seed funding from the Alliance with at least 20% of financing from the cities themselves as well as from other sources.

Publications: Annual Report.

Address: Mailstop F-4P-400, 1818 H St, NW, Washington, DC 20433, USA.

Telephone: (202) 473-9233; *Fax:* (202) 522-3224; *Internet:* www.citiesalliance.org; *e-mail:* info@cacitiesalliance.org.

TRUST FUND CO-ORDINATION, RESOURCE MOBILIZATION AND CO-FINANCING

Japan Social Development Fund (JSDF)

Established by the Japanese Government and the World Bank in June 2000, aiming to assist World Bank clients to effectively tackle the poverty and social consequences that resulted from the 1997–99 global economic and financial crises.

Activities: Works through initiating and supporting innovative programmes which have high potential for ameliorating the deterioration in the affected countries' situations, supports initiatives which have positive prospects of developing into sustainable activities over the long term; and assists programmes designed and implemented by local populations and civil society. Grants are made through two programmes: project grants are designed to provide direct relief measures to the poor, available to organizations in World Bank member countries; and capacity building grants available to NGOs, local community organizations and/or local institutions. Support is given to a range of community development activities including women's development, child protection, community development, restoring health services, and improving educational opportunities for disadvantaged groups.

Geographical Area of Activity: Developing countries.

How to Apply: Project grants are available to organizations in World Bank member countries whose 1999 GNP per head does not exceed US $1,445; capacity building grants are available to low-income and lower middle-income countries (as defined in the 2000–01 World Development Report).

Financial Information: Total grants US $36,000,000 (2001).

Address: World Bank, 1818 H St, NW, Washington, DC 20433, USA.

Internet: www.worldbank.org/rmc/jsdf/index.htm; *e-mail:* jsdf@worldbank.org.

UNITED NATIONS DEVELOPMENT PROGRAMME (UNDP)

Special Programme for Research and Training in Tropical Diseases (TDR)

Established in 1975 and co-sponsored by the United Nations Development Programme (UNDP), the World Bank and the World Health Organization (WHO), it aims to help co-ordinate, support and influence global efforts to combat a portfolio of major diseases of the poor and disadvantaged, including African trypanosomiasis, dengue, leishmaniasis, malaria, schistosomiasis, tuberculosis, Chagas disease, leprosy, lymphatic filariasis, and onchocerciasis.

Activities: Grants are made to support goal-oriented research, and are made within the following categories: collaborative research; project development; research training; re-entry initiatives; capacity strengthening; research and development; and capacity strengthening for malaria research in Africa.

Geographical Area of Activity: Developing countries.

How to Apply: Scientific work-plans should be studied before applications are submitted.

Contact: Dir Dr C. Morel.

Address: c/o WHO, 1211 Geneva 27, Switzerland.

Telephone: (22) 7913725; *Fax:* (22) 7914854; *Internet:* www.who.int/tdr/; *e-mail:* tdr@who.int.

WATER AND SANITATION PROGRAMME (WSP)

Participatory Hygiene and Sanitation Transformation (PHAST)

Launched in Africa as a pilot initiative in 1993, jointly by the Water and Sanitation Programme, the United Nations Children's Fund (UNICEF) and the World Health Organization (WHO); aims to enhance the participation of women, men, and children in the development process. Beyond teaching hygiene and sanitation concepts the objective of PHAST is to enable people to overcome barriers to change.

Activities: Initially operated as an 18-month pilot programme in collaboration with NGOs, and the governments of Botswana, Kenya, Uganda and Zimbabwe, organizing training initiatives which allowed participants, once they had returned to their countries, to organize national and district training workshops, adapt the methods and tools they had acquired to their local situations, and field-test them leading to the development of hygiene promotion programmes in each of the participating countries. The Programme has now been expanded to include other developing countries.

Geographical Area of Activity: Developing countries.

Contact: Programme Man. Walter Stottmann.

Address: 1818 H St, NW, Washington, DC 20433, USA.

Telephone: (202) 473-9785; *Fax:* (202) 522-3313; *Internet:* www.wsp.org/english /activities/hygiene-promo.html; *e-mail:* info@wsp.org.

WORLD BANK INSTITUTE

Joint Japan/World Bank Group Scholarship Programme (JJ/WBGSP)

Funded by the Japanese government and administered by the World Bank Institute, the Programme awards scholarships to individuals from World Bank member countries to undertake graduate studies at universities renowned for their development research and teaching.

Activities: Operates through its Regular Programme, awarding scholarships to students for training and graduated degree study at more than 160 universities in more than 40 countries. Scholars may study at universities in World Bank member countries, except their own country. Also operates a Partnership Programme, in conjunction with 11 universities, aiming to help scholars receive specialized training aiming towards a master's degree in key areas of development, such as economic policy management or infrastructure management. The Programmes seek promising candidates from the public sector in developing countries, such as central banks and ministries of finance and planning.

Geographical Area of Activity: International.

Financial Information: Funded by the government of Japan; total funding US $10,159,937 (2002).

Contact: Steering Cttee Chair. Frannie A. Léautier; Deputy Chair. Yuzo Harada; Admin. Abdul-Monem Al-Mashat.

Address: JJ/WBGSP Secretariat, 1818 H St, NW, Washington, DC 20433, USA.

Internet: www.worldbank.org/wbi/scholarships/.

Robert S. McNamara Fellowships Programme

Established in 1982 to award fellowships for full-time study or research at the postgraduate level in fields related to economic development, to be carried out at a recognized institution in a World Bank member country other than the applicant's home country.

Activities: The Programme has been restructured into a master's degree in public policy at Woodrow Wilson School of Public and International Affairs, Princeton University.

Geographical Area of Activity: International.

Financial Information: Funded by a US $1,000,000 contribution from the World Bank and US $1,800,000 from the governments of Bangladesh, People's Republic of China, India, Kuwait, Nigeria, Pakistan, Peru and Serbia and Montenegro. The interest from the endowment funds is approx. US $200,000 a year.

Address: World Bank, 1818 H St, NW, Washington, DC 20433, USA.

Internet: www.worldbank.org/wbi/scholarships.

WORLD LINKS

Began in 1997 as a World Bank initiative; a global learning network linking thousands of students and teachers around the world via the Internet for collaborative projects and integration of technology into learning.

Activities: The organization provides a set of educational technology-related services, specifically geared towards Ministries of Education, NGOs and international development agencies working in developing countries, services ranging from basic school connectivity solutions, to teacher professional development, and training programmes for both policy-makers and local communities interested in launching educational technology initiatives.

Geographical Area of Activity: Botswana, Brazil, Burkina Faso, Chile, Colombia, Costa Rica, El Salvador, Gambia, Ghana, India, Mauritania, Mozambique, Palestinian Autonomous Areas, Paraguay, Peru, Philippines, Senegal, South Africa, Turkey, Uganda and Zimbabwe.

Contact: Exec. Dir Hans Hoyer.

Address: 1211 Connecticut Ave, NW, Suite 406, Washington, DC 20036, USA.

Telephone: (202) 462-9234; *Fax:* (202) 462-9736; *Internet:* www.world-links.org; *e-mail:* info@world-links.org.

International Center for Human Rights and Economic Development—Rights and Democracy

Created by Canada's Parliament in 1988 to encourage and support the universal values of human rights and the promotion of democratic institutions and practices around the world. Works with individuals, organizations and governments in Canada and abroad to promote the human and democratic rights defined in the UN's International Bill of Human Rights.

Activities: The Center's programmes currently focus on five themes: democratic development, women's human rights, globalization and human rights, the rights of indigenous peoples, and international human rights advocacy. In the field of democratic development supports civil society participation, advocates the recognition of the right to democracy, works to strengthen human rights institutions and facilitates capacity building of partners during strategic periods of democratic transitions; in the field of women's rights works to defend and promote the integration of women's human rights within the UN system and other international and regional organizations and advocates in favour of the implementation of international human rights instruments; in the field of globalization of human rights works with Canadian and international non-governmental coalitions on key cross-cutting issues such as the right to food, the impact of foreign investment and information and communications technologies on human rights; in the area of the rights of indigenous peoples facilitates the participation of indigenous organizations in democratic processes in specific countries and their access to international organizations for the promotion of their rights; and in the field of international human rights advocacy facilitates the access and participation of NGOs, particularly from developing countries, in regional and international forums.

Geographical Area of Activity: International.

Contact: Pres. Jean-Louis Roy.

Address: 1001 de Maisonneuve Blvd East, Suite 1100, Montréal, QC H2L 4P9, Canada.

Telephone: (514) 283-6073; *Fax:* (514) 283-3792; *Internet:* www.ichrdd.ca; *e-mail:* ichrdd@ichrdd.ca.

John Humphrey Award

An annual award administered by the International Center for Human Rights and Economic Development—Rights and Democracy to an organization or individual from any country or region of the world, including Canada, for exceptional achievement in the promotion of human rights and democratic development. The Award is named after the Canadian John Peters Humphrey, the human rights law professor who prepared the first draft of the Universal Declaration of Human Rights.

Activities: The Award, made to individuals or organizations for their exemplary work in the field of human rights and democratic development, consists of a prize of C $25,000 as well as a speaking tour of Canadian cities to help increase awareness of the recipient's human rights work.

Geographical Area of Activity: International.

How to Apply: Applications should include: a letter describing the nominee, their work and why they merit the Award; a curriculum vitae or organizational profile; supporting documentation such as articles written by or about the nominee; and referees (with addresses and phone numbers), who may be contacted by members of the jury for more detailed information.

Financial Information: Annual award of C $25,000.

Address: 1001 de Maisonneuve Blvd East, Suite 1100, Montréal, QC H2L 4P9, Canada.

Telephone: (514) 283-6073; *Fax:* (514) 283-3792; *Internet:* www.ichrdd.ca/; *e-mail:* ichrdd@ichrdd.ca.

International Centre for the Study of the Preservation and Restoration of Cultural Property (ICCROM)

An intergovernmental organization established in Rome in 1959, following a decision made at the ninth UNESCO General Conference in New Delhi in 1956; has a world-wide mandate to promote the conservation of both movable and immovable heritage in all its forms. Its membership currently comprises over 100 member states, as well as 103 associate members from among the world's leading conservation institutions.

Activities: Aims to improve the quality of conservation as well as raise people's awareness of its importance. Operates in five spheres of activity: Training, Information, Research, Co-operation and Advocacy, developing information tools and resources for conservation organizations, developing collaborative projects, organizing professional training activities, providing technical advice and technical assistance.

Geographical Area of Activity: International.

Contact: Dir-Gen. Nicholas Stanley-Price.

Address: Via di San Michele 13, 00153 Rome, Italy.

Telephone: (06) 585531; *Internet:* www.iccrom.org; *e-mail:* info@iccrom.org.

International Co-operation for Development and Solidarity (CIDSE—Co-opération internationale pour le développement et la solidarité)

An alliance of 14 Catholic development organizations from Europe and North America established in 1967; aims to co-ordinate the work of national Catholic development organizations and provide more effective aid to the South. The members are Broederlijk Delen, CAFOD, Comité Catholique Contre la Faim et pour le Développement (CCFD), CORDAID, Entraide et Fraternité, Fastenopfer der Schweizer Katholiken, Koordinierungsstelle, Manos Unidas, Misereor, Organisation Catholique Canadienne pour le Développement et la Paix, Scottish Catholic International Aid Fund, Trocaire, and Volontari nel Mondo.

Activities: Operates in the fields of advocacy, European Union/trade/food security, social justice, debt/adjustment, peace and conflict, development and development education in Africa, Asia and the Pacific, Central and South America, and Cambodia, Laos and Vietnam. Exchanges information among member organizations, lobbies governments, intergovernmental and multilateral organizations, provides funding to community-based development projects that aim to involve local people, and publishes reports and lobbying papers.

Geographical Area of Activity: Developing countries of the southern hemisphere.

Publications: Newsletter; Annual Report; publications on trade and development, debt, development policy and other relevant issues.

Contact: Sec.-Gen. Christiane Overkamp.

Address: 16 rue Stévin, 1000 Brussels, Belgium.

Telephone: (2) 230-77-22; *Fax:* (2) 230-70-82; *Internet:* www.cidse.org; *e-mail:* postmaster@cidse.org.

International Coral Reef Action Network (ICRAN)

Established in 2000 by the founding partners: United Nations Environment Programme (UNEP), WorldFish Center, World Resources Institute (WRI), UNEP–World Conservation Monitoring Center (WCMC), Global Coral Reef Monitoring Network (GCRMN), International Coral Reef Initiative (ICRI) Secretariat, Coral Reef Alliance (CORAL), as a public–private response to ICRI's Call to Action and to help implement the Framework for Action, the internationally agreed blueprint for conservation of coral reefs.

Activities: In 2003, following donations of US $3,000,000 from USAID and the UN Foundation, the Network launched a US $30,000,000 appeal to establish a Coral Reef Fund to ensure sustainable financing for coral reef conservation and management. The Fund's purpose is to develop flexible financing and innovative public–private partnerships to help sustain coral reefs and the people who depend upon them across local, regional and global levels. The Network's other activities, in co-operation with partner organizations, include advocacy campaigns, production of educational materials, and empowerment of local communities in the management of coral reefs, through highlighting and demonstrating replicable activities and providing support to achieve a multiplying effect on the ground.

Geographical Area of Activity: International.

Contact: Asst. Dir Kristian Teleki.

Address: c/o UNEP–WCMC, 219 Huntingdon Rd, Cambridge CB3 0DL, UK.

Telephone: (1223) 277314; *Fax:* (1223) 277136; *Internet:* www.icran.org; *e-mail:* icran@icran.org.

International Coral Reef Initiative (ICRI)

Initiated at the Small Island Developing States conference in 1994, by the governments of Australia, France, Jamaica, Japan, Philippines, Sweden, UK and USA, alongside the International Bank for Reconstruction and Development (IBRD—World Bank) and the United Nations Environment Programme (UNEP). ICRI is a voluntary partnership of developing countries, donor counties, development banks, international environmental and development agencies, scientific associations, the private sector and NGOs, linked by a global Secretariat.

Activities: An environmental partnership that brings stakeholders together with the objective of sustainable use and conservation of coral reefs for future generations, allowing representatives of over 80 developing countries with coral reefs to sit in equal partnership with major donor countries and development banks, international environmental and development agencies, scientific associations, the private sector and NGOs, to decide on the best strategies to conserve the world's coral reef resources. Also aims to catalyze the development and funding of regional programmes and projects.

Geographical Area of Activity: International.

Address: 20 ave de Ségur, 75302 Paris 07 SP, France.

Telephone: 1-42-19-20-21; *Internet:* www.environnement.gouv.fr/icri/site_icri /au%20sujet%20de%20l'icri/about.html.

International Council for Local Environmental Initiatives (ICLEI)

An international association of local governments implementing sustainable development; aims to build and serve a world-wide movement of local governments to achieve tangible improvements in global environmental and sustainable development conditions through cumulative local actions.

Activities: Organizes campaigns on issues of environmental sustainability, including the Local Agenda 21 campaign, which aims to generate tangible results and increase standards of local performance at the local level through: the institution of broad-based participatory planning processes aimed at achieving sustainable development; the global Cities for Climate Protection campaign (CCP), which aims to reduce the emissions that cause global warming and air pollution; and the Water Campaign, launched at Global Cities 21 ICLEI World Congress in June 2000. Also provides training and technical services to local governments, distributes the annual Local Initiatives Awards (q.v.), organizes international conferences and events, and lobbies on sustainable development with the aim of building an international policy environment that is supportive and responsive to local-level initiatives.

Geographical Area of Activity: International.

Publications: Initiatives Newsletter.

Contact: Dir Mary Pattenden.

Address: City Hall, West Tower, 16th Floor, Toronto, ON M4K 1X4, Canada.

Telephone: (416) 392-0273; *Fax:* (416) 392-1478; *Internet:* www.iclei.org/; *e-mail:* liawards@iclei.org.

Local Initiatives Awards

Established by the International Council for Local Environmental Initiatives to give international recognition to the outstanding environmental achievements of local governments working in co-operation with community partners. The new awards are carried out with the support of the Saitama Prefectural Government in Japan.

Activities: Five annual awards are made under the programme: Excellence in Governance for Sustainable Development; Excellence in Land Resources Management; Excellence in Freshwater Management; Excellence in Atmospheric Protection; and Excellence in Waste Management.

Geographical Area of Activity: International.

How to Apply: Application forms are available on the website.

Contact: Dir Mary Pattenden.

Address: City Hall, West Tower, 16th Floor, Toronto, ON M4K 1X4, Canada.
Telephone: (416) 392-0273; *Fax:* (416) 392-1478; *Internet:* www.iclei.org/liawards; *e-mail:* liawards@iclei.org.

International Development Research Center (IDRC)

Established in 1970 by the Canadian government to help developing countries find long-term solutions to the social, economic and environmental problems they face. Aims to assist scientists in developing countries to identify sustainable long-term, practical solutions to pressing development problems; to mobilize and strengthen the research capacity of developing countries, particularly capacity for policies and technologies that promote healthier and more prosperous societies, food security, biodiversity, and access to information; to develop links among developing country researchers, and provide them access to the results of research around the globe, in particular through developing and strengthening the electronic networking capacity of institutions in developing countries that receive IDRC funding; and to ensure that the products from the activities it supports are used by communities in the developing world, and that existing research capacity is used effectively to solve development problems.

Activities: Aims to find sustainable solutions to the social, economic and environmental problems faced by developing countries, through funding the work of scientists working for universities, private enterprise, government, and non-profit organizations in developing countries. Also provides support to regional research networks and institutions in the developing world. Maintains additional offices in Cairo, Dakar, Delhi, Montevideo, Nairobi, and Singapore.

Geographical Area of Activity: Developing countries.

Financial Information: Total budget C $135,300,000 (2000–01).

Publications: Annual Report.

Contact: Pres. Maureen O'Neil.

Address: POB 8500, Ottawa, ON K1G 3H9, Canada.

Telephone: (613) 236-6163; *Fax:* (613) 238-7230; *Internet:* www.idrc.ca; *e-mail:* info@idrc.ca.

Acacia Initiative—Communities and the Information Society in Africa Programme Initiative

An international programme, conceived and led by the International Development Research Centre, which aims to empower sub-Saharan communities with the ability to apply information and communications technologies (ICTs) to their own social and economic development.

Activities: Operates as an integrated programme of research and development and demonstration projects to address issues of applications, technology, infrastructure, policy, and governance. Operates within three programme modalities: ICT Policy Research, Technology Research and Development and Knowledge Generation for Enhanced Appropriation; and supports and develops projects within each of these modalities according to the following themes: Poverty

194

Reduction, Gender, People Development, Partnerships, Opportunities, Networks, and Learning and Development. Also operates a Research and Development Small Grants Programme which aims to promote an active ICT research environment in Africa for issues related to ICT based development applications, policy research and their impacts.

Geographical Area of Activity: Sub-Saharan Africa.

How to Apply: All information on the application process, including deadlines for project submission and proposal review dates, is available on the website.

Publications: ACACIA Newsletter (quarterly).

Contact: Contact Morenike Ladikpo.

Address: 250 Albert St, POB 8500, Ottawa, ON KIG 3H9, Canada.

Telephone: (613) 236-6163 ext: 2164; *Fax:* (613) 567-7749; *Internet:* http://network .idrc.ca/ev.php?url_id=5895&url_do=do_topic&url_section=201;   *e-mail:* acaciar-d@idrc.ca.

AFRICAN ECONOMIC RESEARCH CONSORTIUM (AERC)

Established in July 1988, initially as an initiative of the International Development Research Center (IDRC); a public not-for-profit organization devoted to advanced policy research and training. AERC's principal objective is to strengthen local capacity for conducting independent, rigorous inquiry into problems pertinent to the management of economies in sub-Saharan Africa.

Activities: Aims to: enhance the capacity of locally based researchers to conduct policy-relevant economic inquiry; promote retention of such capacity; and encourage its application in the policy context. Operates a small grants programme, providing funding to groups of individuals drawn from both academia and policy institutions to conduct research on a limited number of pertinent themes, including poverty, income distribution and labour market issues, trade, regional integration and sectoral policies, macroeconomic policies, stabilization and growth, and finance, resource mobilization and investment. Also provides a peer review support system, holds biannual research workshops, and provides training grants for PhD study. Brings together 16 funders, 12 of whom are members of the Consortium.

Geographical Area of Activity: Sub-Saharan Africa.

Financial Information: Funded by UK Department for International Development, International Development Research Centre of Canada, John D. and Catherine T. MacArthur Foundation, Ministry of Foreign Affairs, Denmark, Ministry of Foreign Affairs, Netherlands, Norwegian Agency for Development Co-operation, the Rockefeller Foundation, Swedish International Development Agency, Swiss Agency for Development Co-operation, US Agency for International Development, the International Bank for Reconstruction and Development (IBRD—World Bank), Ministry of Foreign Affairs, France, African Capacity Building Foundation, African Development Bank, the European Commission, and the Ford Foundation.

Publications: AERC Newsletter (annual); *Research Newsletter* (annual).

Contact: Exec. Dir Prof. William Lyakurwa; Exec. Asst Jacqueline Macakiage; Sec. Amyrose Opiyo.

Address: 8th Floor, International House, POB 62882, 00200 City Square, Nairobi, Kenya.

Telephone: (2) 228057; *Fax:* (2) 21930; *Internet:* www.aercafrica.org/; *e-mail:* exec .dir@aercafrica.org.

ECONOMY AND ENVIRONMENT PROGRAMME FOR SOUTHEAST ASIA (EEPSEA)

Established in May 1993 to support training and research in environmental and resource economics, with the goal of strengthening local capacity for the economic analysis of environmental problems so that researchers can provide sound advice to policy-makers across its 10 member countries: Cambodia, People's Republic of China, Indonesia, Laos, Malaysia, Papua New Guinea, Philippines, Sri Lanka, Thailand, and Vietnam.

Activities: The Programme awards grants ranging from C $24,000 to C $35,000 for research projects, generally within four areas: management of forests and wetlands; policy instruments for control of urban pollution; resource pricing; and economy-wide and global issues. Researchers, or teams of researchers, may be affiliated with a university, government or NGO and grants are normally made to that institution. Most applicants attend one of EEPSEA's courses before or in conjunction with their research project. Also provides training awards, typically related to EEPSEA-funded research projects. The Programme also maintains a secretariat in the Philippines.

Geographical Area of Activity: Cambodia, People's Republic of China, Indonesia, Laos, Malaysia, Papua New Guinea, Philippines, Sri Lanka, Thailand and Vietnam.

How to Apply: Proposals are sent to experts for written review. Those recommended for further consideration must then be revised and presented in a working group meeting at the next EEPSEA biannual meeting. Further revisions are usually called for, until the project is judged satisfactory and a grant approved. After approval, interim findings are presented and critiqued every six months until the project is completed.

Financial Information: Funded by a Sponsors Group, whose members each commit at least C $100,000 a year: the International Development Research Centre, Canada, Swedish International Development Agency, and the Canadian International Development Agency. Research grants range from C $24,000 to C $35,000.

Publications: Research reports, technical papers and special papers; Annual Report.

Contact: Dir Dr David Glover.

Address: Tanglin, POB 101, Singapore 912404, Singapore.

Telephone: 6235-1344; *Fax:* 6831-6854; *Internet:* www.eepsea.org; *e-mail:* dglover@idrc.org.ca.

SECRETARIAT OF INSTITUTIONAL SUPPORT FOR ECONOMIC RESEARCH IN AFRICA (SISERA)

A multi-donor structure created in July 1997, with a mission to reinforce African centre capacity in research and management.

Activities: Aims to develop African research through providing core institutional grants and seed funding, support to collaborative thematic research, enhancement of managerial capacity building and centre integration in the international scientific community through institutional links, exchange of researchers and connectivity. Core grants are typically for research support facilities, individual research projects, staff training, seminars, participation in academic meetings and/or publication costs, whilst seed funding is given for institutions classified as Emerging Centres. SISERA's steering committee comprises representatives of the US Agency for International Development, the Economic Commission for Africa, African Development Bank, Economic Research Consortium, International Development Research Centre, and the North Association of African Universities.

Geographical Area of Activity: Africa.

Financial Information: Maximum research grant C $300,000 over two years; maximum seed grant C $50,000 over two years.

Publications: Activity Report.

Address: c/o International Devt Research Centre, West and Central Africa Regional Office, BP 11007, CD Annexe, Dakar, Senegal.

Telephone: 864-00-00 ext. 2231; *Fax:* 825-32-55; *e-mail:* stall@idrc.org.sn.

Strategies and Analyses for Growth and Access (SAGA) Programme: SAGA Research Competition

The Programme was established for the period 2001–06 by the US Agency for International Development (USAID) and is administered by SISERA. The Programme aims to develop African capacity to produce high quality, policy-oriented research on key issues affecting economic growth and access in sub-Saharan Africa.

Activities: A research competition programme designed to support research projects carried out by African economic research institutes. Aims to strengthen the internal workings of an institute so that its ability to function effectively as an institute is increased, and to strengthen an institute's visibility in providing the analytical underpinnings for various government policy-making activities. The emphasis is on capacity utilization rather than capacity building. The competition is open to researchers or team of researchers of SISERA and non-SISERA member institutions.

Geographical Area of Activity: Sub-Saharan Africa.

How to Apply: Proposals must be submitted through SISERA member institutes in the relevant country.

Financial Information: Maximum annual grant available US $40,000; approximately 5–8 grants awarded annually for the duration of the programme.

Contact: Contact Catherine Daffe.

Address: c/o International Devt Research Centre, West and Central Africa Regional Office, BP 11007, CD Annexe, Dakar, Senegal.

Telephone: 864-00-00; *Fax:* 825-32-55; *e-mail:* cdaffe@idrc.org.sn.

International Federation of Red Cross and Red Crescent Societies

ProVention Consortium

Originally the ProVention secretariat was administered by the Disaster management Facility of the International Bank for Reconstruction and Development (the World Bank). In 2003 the Consortium transferred its secretariat to the International Federation of Red Cross and Red Crescent Societies. The Consortium was initiated as a global coalition of governments, international organizations, academic institutions, the private sector and civil society organizations dedicated to increasing the safety of vulnerable communities and to reducing the impact of disasters in developing countries.

Activities: Aims to help developing countries build sustainable and successful economies and to reduce the human suffering that too often results from natural and technological catastrophes. Consortium projects focus on the links between disasters, poverty and the environment, and fall into four general categories: hazard and risk identification, risk reduction, risk sharing/transfer, and information sharing, with some projects involving a mix of categories. Funding is provided for research projects, pilot and demonstration projects, education and training activities, and workshops and conferences. The Applied Research Grants for Disaster Risk Reduction programme awards grants of up to US $5,000 for creative research designed to reduce disaster impacts; and focuses on the links between disasters, poverty and the environment, falling into three general categories: hazard and risk identification; risk reduction; and risk sharing/transfer.

Geographical Area of Activity: Developing countries.

Publications: Conference papers and reports.

Address: POB 372, 1211 Geneva 19, Switzerland.

Telephone: (22) 7304222; *Fax:* (22) 7330395; *Internet:* www.proventionconsortium .org; *e-mail:* provention@ifrc.org.

International Institute of Tropical Agriculture (IITA)

Founded in 1967 with a mandate for improving food production in the humid tropics and to develop sustainable production systems. It became the first African link in the world-wide network of agricultural research centres supported by the Consultative Group on International Agricultural Research (CGIAR, q.v.).

Activities: The Institute aims to enhance the food security, income and well-being of resource-poor people in sub-Saharan Africa by conducting research and related activities to increase agricultural production, improve food systems, and sustainably manage natural resources, in partnership with national and international stakeholders. Conducts research, germplasm conservation, training, and information exchange activities in partnership with regional bodies and national programmes, including universities, NGOs, and the private sector. The research agenda addresses crop improvement, plant health, and resource and crop management within a food systems framework, targeted at the identified needs of four major agro-ecological zones: the dry savanna, the moist savanna, the humid forests, and the mid-altitude savanna. Research focuses on smallholder cropping and post-harvest systems and on the following food crops: cassava, cowpea, maize, plantain and banana, soybean, and yam.

Geographical Area of Activity: Sub-Saharan Africa.

Contact: Dir-Gen. P. Hartmann.

Address: c/o Lambourn (UK) Ltd, Carolyn House, 26 Dingwall Rd, Croydon CR9 3EE, UK.

Internet: www.iita.org.

International Maritime Organization (IMO)

In 1948 an international conference in Geneva adopted the IMO Convention formally establishing IMO (the original name was the Inter-Governmental Maritime Consultative Organization, or IMCO, but the name was changed in 1982 to IMO); the Convention entered into force in 1958 and the Organization met for the first time the following year. IMO aims to provide machinery for co-operation among governments in the field of governmental regulation and practices relating to technical matters of all kinds affecting shipping engaged in international trade; and to encourage and facilitate the general adoption of the highest practicable standards in matters concerning maritime safety, efficiency of navigation and prevention and control of marine pollution from ships.

Activities: Activities carried out by IMO include distribution of funds through a trust fund established in 1998 to mark IMO's 50th anniversary, which established an additional teaching chair at the World Maritime University in Sweden and financed fellowships for the training of seafarers. Also awards the annual International Maritime Prize to the individual or organization judged to have made the most significant contribution to the work and objectives of IMO, and awards fellowships under its Technical Co-operation Programme. Also grants consultative status to NGOs whose goals and activities relate to IMO's mandate.

Geographical Area of Activity: International.

Address: 4 Albert Embankment, London SE1 7SR, UK.

Telephone: (20) 7735-7611; *Fax:* (20) 7587-3210; *Internet:* www.imo.org.

International Monetary Fund (IMF)

IMF Civic Programme

An international organization of 184 member countries, established to promote international monetary co-operation, exchange stability, and orderly exchange arrangements; to foster economic growth and high levels of employment; and to provide temporary financial assistance to countries to help ease balance-of-payments adjustment. The IMF established its Civic Programme in 1994, principally to help the poor in the host city of Washington, DC, and its surrounding area, as well as those in developing countries. The Programme supports child, youth, and family projects; adult and community projects; and international projects. Priority is given to non-profit programmes that enable persons to become self-sufficient.

Activities: The Programme allocates approximately two-thirds of its donations to help improve economic and social conditions in the host city region, where nearly all IMF employees and their families reside. The balance is donated to international non-profit organizations with records of success in assisting poor families in low-income countries. Staff also volunteer for IMF-funded projects, through the INVOLVE initiative.

Geographical Area of Activity: International: developing countries.

How to Apply: Application form available on the website.

Address: Civic Programme Advisory Committee, 700 19th St, NW, Washington, DC 20431, USA.

Telephone: (202) 623-7000; *Fax:* (202) 589-7085; *Internet:* www.imf.org/external /np/cpac/index.htm; *e-mail:* communityrelations@imf.org.

International Organization for Migration (IOM)

Established in 1951 as an intergovernmental organization to resettle European displaced persons, refugees and migrants, IOM now encompasses a variety of migration management activities throughout the world, working with both migrants and governments to provide humane responses to migration challenges.

Activities: Provides expertise, programme design and implementation support to address migration management needs in the countries of Eastern Europe and Central Asia (countries of the former USSR, excluding the Baltic Countries). Provides a mechanism for information exchange among the region's IOM Missions, disseminates resources on best international practices, facilitates programme development, makes grants to special projects, including gender-based initiatives, assists voluntary returnees, collaborates with governments, and provides emergency and post-crisis assistance.

Geographical Area of Activity: Eastern Europe and Central Asia (excluding the Baltic Countries).

Contact: Dir-Gen. Brunson McKinley; Deputy Dir-Gen. Ndioro Ndiaye.

Address: 17 route des Morillons, 1211 Geneva 19, Switzerland.

Telephone: (22) 7179111; *Fax:* (22) 7986150; *Internet:* www.iom.int; *e-mail:* info@iom.int.

Japan International Co-operation Agency (JICA)

Capacity Development for Science and Mathematics

A partnership between the Association for Development Education in Africa (q.v.), the Japan International Co-operation Agency, and the governments of Ghana, Kenya, and South Africa.

Activities: The project aims to enhance and expand science and mathematics education in Africa, and to strengthen and develop the network of experts and volunteers already established by JICA, through supporting the capacity building of NGOs.

Geographical Area of Activity: Africa.

How to Apply: Application details are available on the website.

Address: Global Issues Division, Planning and Evaluation Department, 2-1 Yoyogi, Shibuya-ku, Tokyo 151-8588, Japan.

Telephone: (3) 5352-5130; *Fax:* (3) 5352-5490; *Internet:* www.jica.go.jp; *e-mail:* kojima.takeharu@jica.go.jp.

Latin American Association of Development Financing Institutions (ALIDE)

Established to promote the cohesion, strengthening and participation of financial institutions in the social and economic development of the Central and South American and Caribbean region.

Activities: Promotes social and economic development of the Central and South American and Caribbean region, through activities in the fields of technical assistance, training, teaching, studies and research, technical meetings, information and documentation, promotion of projects and investment.

Geographical Area of Activity: Central and South America and the Caribbean.

Restrictions: Co-operation is only made through member organizations.

Financial Information: Financed by its members and international co-operation organizations and agencies and from revenue-generating services.

Publications: Boletín ALIDE; Anales de la Asamblea General; Memoria Anual; Data Bank; Revista Alide; Alidenoticias; Directorio de Instituciones de Financiamiento Internacional.

Contact: Sec.-Gen. Rommel Acevedo.

Address: Apdo Postal 3988, Lima 100; Paseo de la República 3211, Lima 27, Peru.

Telephone: (1) 4422400; *Fax:* (1) 4428105; *Internet:* www.alide.org.pe; *e-mail:* sg@alide.org.pe.

League of Arab States

ARAB LEAGUE EDUCATIONAL, CULTURAL AND SCIENTIFIC ORGANIZATION (ALECSO)

Established in 1970 by the League of Arab States to promote and co-ordinate educational, cultural and scientific activities at the regional and national levels in the Arab world and to strengthen ties between Arab neighbours, co-ordinate policies and promote common interests. Its membership extends to 22 states.

Activities: Helps to evolve and implement new approaches and strategies of educational, cultural and scientific development that are commensurate with Arab realities, needs and priorities. Activities include: co-ordinating Arab endeavour in the fields of education, culture and science; exploring new areas of Arab co-operation in the fields of education, culture and science, to mobilize Arab energies and resources in these fields; assisting in solution of problems which confront the Arab countries in the fields of education, culture and science; preserving, restoring and safeguarding Arabic–Islamic heritage in the fields of manuscripts, antiquities and historical sites; promoting the collection and dissemination of information in the fields of education, culture and science; promoting research and studies; organizing training courses which involve educational, cultural and scientific orientation and assimilation; supporting Arabization projects in African and Arab countries; publishing periodicals, encyclopedias, lexicons, books, information and publicity materials; and co-operating with Arab and international organizations for the exchange of information and experience in the fields of education, culture and science. In 1974 ALECSO initiated a programme for the protection of the environment of the Red Sea and Gulf of Aden, which evolved into the Regional Organization for the Conservation of the Environment of the Red Sea and Gulf of Aden—PERSGA in September 1995.

Geographical Area of Activity: Arab region.

Financial Information: Total budget US $17,000,000 (2002).

Address: POB 1120, Tunis, Tunisia.

Telephone: (71) 784-466; *Fax:* (71) 784-965; *Internet:* www.slis.uwm.edu/ALECSO; *e-mail:* alecso@email.ati.tn.

Micronutrient Initiative

Established in 1992, following a pledge by leaders attending the World Summit for Children in 1990 to protect the world's children from micronutrient malnutrition. Until 2001 the organization operated as a secretariat within the International Development Research Centre (IDRC), and run by a committee comprising its main donors: the Canadian International Development Agency (CIDA), the United Nations Children's Fund (UNICEF), the International Bank for Reconstruction and Development (the World Bank), the US Agency for International Development (USAID) and the IDRC. Currently operates as an independent organization developing and supporting partnerships in food fortification, supplementation, research and development.

Activities: The Initiative supports and promotes food fortification and supplementation programmes in Asia, Africa and Central and South America and provides technical and operational support in those countries where micronutrient malnutrition is most prevalent. Carries out its work in partnership with other international agencies, governments and industry. Operates through four regional desks: South Asia; Africa; East Asia and Central and South America; and Global. Maintains regional offices in New Delhi and Johannesburg. Within each identified region, the Initiative supports national programmes that expand the fortification of staple foods and provide dietary supplementation, with a particular focus on vitamin A supplementation. Research proposals are invited from governments, research institutions, development agencies, NGOs and food industry organizations.

Geographical Area of Activity: Africa, East Asia, South Asia, Central and South America, and international.

Financial Information: Founding donors include CIDA, IDRC, UNICEF, USAID and the World Bank.

Address: POB 56127, 250 Albert St, Ottawa, ON K1R 7ZI, Canada.

Telephone: (613) 782-6800; *Fax:* (613) 782-6838; *Internet:* www.micronutrient.org; *e-mail:* mi@micronutrient.org.

Nordic Council of Ministers

Nordic Cultural Fund

The Nordic Cultural Fund was established in 1967 following an agreement between the Nordic countries to support cultural co-operation in the broadest sense between the Nordic countries.

Activities: Promotes culture in the Nordic region through making grants to cultural projects in the Nordic region or Nordic projects outside the Nordic region. Grants are awarded in the areas of art, theatre, music and dance, literature, song and new media. Education, research and trans-sectoral projects can also be supported, but must have a clear connection with culture. Projects must involve at least three Nordic countries or autonomous areas (the Faroe Islands, Greenland and the Åland Islands). Priority is given to funding projects that consist of activities for and with children and young people, promote the understanding of Nordic languages, promote the use of new media, aim to reduce xenophobia and racism, and have broad popular appeal.

Geographical Area of Activity: Primarily Nordic countries, Denmark, Finland, Iceland, Norway, Sweden, and the autonomous areas (the Faroe Islands, Greenland and the Åland Islands).

How to Apply: Guide-lines available on the website.

Financial Information: Annual grants approx. 25,000,000 Danish kroner.

Contact: Special Adviser Mats Jönsson; Advisers Kjell Austin, Heli Hirsch; Admin. Sec. Marilou Pehrson.

Address: Store Strandstraede 18, 1255 Copenhagen K, Denmark.

Telephone: 33-96-02-46; *Fax:* 33-32-56-36; *Internet:* www.nordiskkulturfond.dk/; *e-mail:* mj@norden.org.

Nordic Grant Scheme for Network Co-operation with the Baltic Countries and North-West Russia

The aim of the scheme is to develop long-term co-operation projects in the fields of higher education and research, and in the voluntary sector, between the Nordic region and neighbouring countries; designed to promote development throughout the region.

Activities: Grants are made to collaboration projects, via network building between academic institutions or NGOs in the Nordic countries and neighbouring states, particularly where the projects strengthen the voluntary sector in neighbouring states and involve adult education. Grants can be for long-term collaboration initiatives, seminars, conferences and network meetings, and must involve the participation of at least two Nordic organizations and at least one organization from a neighbouring state. Priorities for collaborative initiatives between NGOs are health and social welfare, children and young people, and women and equality.

Geographical Area of Activity: Nordic countries: Denmark, Finland, Iceland, Norway and Sweden; and neighbouring Baltic countries: Estonia, Latvia, Lithuania and North-West Russia.

How to Apply: Application forms are available on the website.

Financial Information: Total budget approx. 13,000,000 Danish kroner (2001); maximum grant available 250,000 Danish kroner.

Contact: Contact Riitta Lampola.

Address: Store Strandstraede 18, 1255 Copenhagen K, Denmark.

Telephone: 33-96-02-00; *Fax:* 33-96-02-02; *Internet:* www.norden.org; *e-mail:* initials@nmr.dk.

NORDPLUS

The programme aims to promote intensive and wide-ranging co-operation amongst universities of the Nordic countries, and increase the mobility of students and of university teaching staff.

Activities: The programme operates through awarding: student mobility grants for full-time students for one year of study at a university in another Nordic country, and academic staff mobility grants; and organizing short study visits for academic staff and university administrators, and joint intensive study courses for both staff and students.

Geographical Area of Activity: Nordic countries: Denmark, Finland, Iceland, Norway and Sweden.

Address: Store Strandstraede 18, 1255 Copenhagen K, Denmark.

Telephone: 33-96-02-00; *Fax:* 33-96-02-02; *Internet:* www.norden.org; *e-mail:* initials@nmr.dk.

SLEIPNIR

SLEIPNIR is the Nordic Council of Ministers' travel grants programme for young artists in the Nordic countries; aims to increase the mobility of young artists in the Nordic countries and encourage them to operate across the entire Nordic region, the Baltic states and North-West Russia.

Activities: Grants are available to young artists, under the age of 36, practising in the fields of theatre, dance, visual art, design, architecture, music, film, video and literature. The grants are for use outside the country of origin for artists who have already undergone training in their particular field.

Geographical Area of Activity: Nordic countries: Denmark, Finland, Iceland, Norway and Sweden.

Restrictions: No funding for organizations.

Financial Information: Annual grants approx. €250,000.

Address: Store Strandstraede 18, 1255 Copenhagen K, Denmark.

Telephone: 33-96-02-00; *Fax:* 33-96-02-02; *Internet:* www.norden.org; *e-mail:* initials@nmr.dk.

NORDIC YOUTH COMMITTEE (NUK)

The Youth Committee is an advisory body for the Nordic Council of Ministers and administers a grant scheme on its behalf.

Activities: Grants are made to youth projects and umbrella organizations, in the form of organizational support and project funding. Projects must include participation from youth organizations from at least three Nordic countries. Organizations from countries in the Baltic Sea Region are also eligible for funding if the proposed project is to take place in a Nordic country.

Geographical Area of Activity: Nordic countries: Denmark, Finland, Iceland, Norway and Sweden.

How to Apply: There are no fixed deadlines and application forms are sent out after receipt of an initial letter.

Address: Store Strandstraede 18, 1255 Copenhagen K, Denmark.

Telephone: 33-96-02-00; *Fax:* 33-96-02-02; *Internet:* www.norden.org; *e-mail:* initials@nmr.dk.

SNS—NORDIC FOREST RESEARCH COMMITTEE

Established by the Nordic Council of Ministers to promote research into the diverse functions of the forests in sustainable forestry, as well as to advise the Nordic Council of Ministers on questions concerning forests and forestry research.

Activities: Aims to contribute to the socially, economically and ecologically responsible management and utilization of forests and timber resources in the Nordic region, through funding research co-operation, related to forestry, forests and other wooded areas (landscapes, parks, urban trees and marginal land), the utilization of wood and other forest products, as well as the non-commercial values of the forests. Research projects must involve at least three Nordic countries. Countries in the adjacent areas (mainly Estonia, Latvia, Lithuania and North-West Russia) are also eligible, as long as at least two Nordic countries also participate. Also funds pilot projects, networking activities, and the preparation of applications to the European Union framework programme.

Geographical Area of Activity: Nordic region.

Financial Information: Funded by the Nordic Council of Ministers; total budget 2,600,000 Norwegian krone (2004).

Publications: SNS's Strategic Plan 2001-2003; Scandinavian Journal of Forest Research (bi-monthly journal); *The Multiple Functions of the Forest* (research report).

Contact: Contact Olav Gislerud.

Address: SNS Secretariat, c/o Research Council of Norway, POB 2700, St Hanshaugen, 0131 Oslo, Norway.

Telephone: 22-03-71-08; *Fax:* 22-03-71-04; *Internet:* www.nordicforestresearch .org; *e-mail:* sns@rcn.no.

SUSTAINABLE DEVELOPMENT–NEW BEARINGS FOR THE NORDIC COUNTRIES

Established to focus on efforts to integrate environmental considerations and sustainable development in six important sectors: energy, transport, agriculture, business and industry, fisheries, and forestry.

Activities: The strategy adopted by the Nordic Council of Ministers aims to integrate environmental considerations and sustainable development into all sectors, with an initial focus on five essential cross-sectoral issues: climate change, biological diversity, the sea, chemicals, and food safety. Also aims to support initiatives to strengthen public participation in activities promoting sustainable development, in co-operation with local authorities, business and industry, and NGOs.

Geographical Area of Activity: Nordic countries.

Financial Information: Total budget 4,400,000 Danish kroner (2003).

Contact: Contact person in the Nordic Council of Ministers: Loa Bogason.

Address: Store Strandstraede 18, 1255 Copenhagen K, Denmark.

Internet: www.norden.org.

Nordic Environment Finance Corporation (NEFCO)

Nordic Development Fund (NDF)

Established in 1989 as a multilateral Nordic development financing organization with offices in Helsinki, Finland, as part of co-operation in the development assistance area between the five Nordic countries— Denmark, Finland, Iceland, Norway and Sweden.

Activities: Grants long-term credits on concessional terms to poor developing countries, for high-priority projects, which promote economic and social development in developing countries. NDF's lending strategy is governed by the principles of the Nordic countries' bilateral development assistance with a special focus on poverty reduction. Financial support is also provided for private-sector activities in developing countries without government guarantee.

Geographical Area of Activity: Developing countries: Bangladesh, Benin, Bolivia, Burkina Faso, Ethiopia, Ghana, Guatemala, Honduras, Laos, Malawi, Mongolia, Mozambique, Nepal, Nicaragua, Philippines, Senegal, Tanzania, Uganda, Vietnam and Zambia.

Financial Information: Total capital €330,000,000; financed through the development assistance budgets for the Nordic countries..

Contact: Pres. Jens Lund Sørensen; Senior Vice-Pres. Carin Wall; Vice-Pres. Per Eldar Søvik; Special Adviser Siv Ahlberg.

Address: POB 185, 00171 Helsinki, Finland.

Telephone: (9) 1800451; *Fax:* (9) 6221491; *Internet:* www.ndf.fi; *e-mail:* info@ndf.fi.

North American Commission for Environmental Co-operation (CEC)

North American Fund for Environmental Co-operation (NAFEC)

An international organization created by the governments of Canada, Mexico and the USA under the North American Agreement on Environmental Co-operation (NAAEC). CEC aims to address regional environmental concerns, help prevent potential trade and environmental conflicts, and to promote the effective enforcement of environmental law. The Agreement complements the environmental provisions of the North American Free Trade Agreement (NAFTA). CEC created the North American Fund for Environmental Co-operation (NAFEC) in 1995 as a means to fund community-based projects in Canada, Mexico and the USA that promote the goals and objectives of CEC.

Activities: NAFEC supports NGO projects that: are community-based (involving a clearly defined community of stakeholders who actively participate in the design and implementation of the project); respond to a specific issue or problem and lead to concrete results; reflect co-operative and equitable partnerships between or among organizations from different sectors and/or countries within North America; meet the objectives of CEC (by complementing the current CEC programme); strengthen and build the capacities of local people, organizations and institutions; emphasize sustainability; link environmental, social and economic issues; and leverage additional support, but are unlikely to obtain full funding from other sources. In 2003 the grant theme was environmental assessment and monitoring relating to human health.

Geographical Area of Activity: Canada, Mexico and the USA.

How to Apply: Proposals must be submitted prior to annual deadlines and in the required format, according to the NAFEC Call for Proposals which is available on the website. Proposals are reviewed by the NAFEC staff and Selection Committee; the Selection Committee, which consists of two representatives from each country, makes the final decision to approve or decline a proposal.

Financial Information: Total grants C $664,200 (2003).

Address: 393 St Jacques West, Suite 200, Montréal, QC H2Y 1N9, Canada.

Telephone: (514) 350-4357; *Fax:* (514) 350-4314; *Internet:* www.cec.org/grants /index.cfm?varlan=english; *e-mail:* NAFEC@ccemtl.org.

North Atlantic Treaty Organization (NATO)

Manfred Wörner Fellowship

Established in 1995, at the ministerial meeting of NATO Foreign Ministers, in honour of the memory of the late Secretary-General of NATO.

Activities: Awards an annual fellowship of €20,000 for research by individuals or institutions in the following areas: the process of NATO enlargement; NATO as a provider of stability and security in the Euro-Atlantic region; NATO's relations with Russia and/or Ukraine; the development of the Partnership for Peace and the Euro-Atlantic Partnership Council; relations between NATO and other international organizations, particularly in the context of peace support operations; the Transatlantic link and the development of the European Security and Defence Identity; NATO's role in the field of conflict prevention and crisis management; regional co-operation, including NATO's South-East Europe Initiative, the Mediterranean Dialogue, and initiatives in the Caucasus and Central Asia; co-operation on Stability Pact Issues; NATO's policy and objectives of defence, arms control, disarmament, and non-proliferation; global humanitarian mine action; civil emergency planning and disaster preparedness; and developments relating to the challenges of international terrorism. The Fellowship is open to applications from the academic community, including think-tanks, research centres and institutes, and the media, including applications jointly proposed by an individual or institution from at least one NATO country and one Partner country combined.

Geographical Area of Activity: NATO countries and candidate countries.

Restrictions: The Fellowship is not intended to support research in aid of obtaining an academic degree.

How to Apply: Application forms available from NATO or the appropriate national office listed in the annexe to the NATO Manfred Wörner Fellowship brochure.

Financial Information: Annual fellowship of €20,000.

Address: NATO Academic Affairs Officer, blvd Leopold III, 1110 Brussels, Belgium.

Fax: (2) 707-54-57; *Internet:* www.nato.int/acad/fellow/mw00e.htm; *e-mail:* academics@hq.nato.int.

OFFICE OF INFORMATION AND PRESS

Outreach and Partner Relations Section: Co-sponsorship with Partner Countries on Security-related Issues

Part of NATO's information programme which aims to support public discussion in Partner Countries of a wide range of security-related subjects to encompass NATO's contribution to European security, including democratic control of armed forces and the principles of defence reform, including educational projects and projects which promote regional contacts and co-operation.

Activities: Provides discretionary grants, up to a maximum of US $10,000, to promote the dissemination in Partner Countries of reliable information on the role and policies of the Alliance and to generate open debate about security in the Euro-Atlantic area. Both NGOs and universities in Partner Countries involved in these activities are eligible for financial support. NATO also provides organizational advice, possible speakers as well as information materials. Projects typically focus on different aspects of NATO's role in European security or on issues relevant to establishing democratic control of armed forces and defence reform.

Geographical Area of Activity: NATO Partner Countries.

Restrictions: No support for regular salary costs (which would have been incurred even if the activity had not taken place), nor for the costs of any cultural programmes which may take place on the margins of a conference.

How to Apply: Applications must be submitted in either English or French, and include a completed application form (available to download on the website), a project proposal, draft programme, a detailed budget, a list of proposed participants, a covering letter written on the applicant organization's letterhead officially requesting co-sponsorship support from the NATO Office of Information and Press.

Financial Information: Maximum grant available US $10,000; grants range from US $2,000 to US $8,000, normally available for up to 50% of the project's total costs.

Contact: Senior Programme Co-ordinator Dr Peter Lunak.

Address: NATO Headquarters, 1110 Brussels, Belgium.

Telephone: (2) 707-50-37; *Fax:* (2) 707-46-67; *Internet:* www.nato.int/structur/oip/sponsors/intro.htm; *e-mail:* p.lunak@hq.nato.int.

SCIENTIFIC AND ENVIRONMENTAL AFFAIRS DIVISION

NATO Science Programme

The Programme was founded in 1958, with the establishment of the NATO Science Committee, following the recommendations of a Committee on Non-Military Co-operation in NATO. The report of the Committee asserted that progress in the fields of science and technology can be decisive in determining the security of nations and their positions in world affairs, and stated that science and technology was an area of special importance to the Atlantic community.

Activities: Supports scientists of the countries of the Euro-Atlantic Partnership Council (EAPC) in co-operative science, and research infrastructure development, with the purpose of stimulating the co-operation essential for progress in science, of protecting the human resources of the scientific community in Partner Countries, and contributing to overall peace and security. Specific sub-programmes are: Research Infrastructure, Co-operative Science and Technology, Science for Peace, NATO–Russia Science, and Science Fellowships. Scientists of Mediterranean Dialogue Countries are also eligible for support for collaborative activities.

Geographical Area of Activity: Europe: countries of the EAPC.

How to Apply: Application details vary within the sub-programmes; see website for further details.

Address: 1110 Brussels, Belgium.

Telephone: (2) 707-41-11; *Fax:* (2) 707-42-32; *Internet:* www.nato.int/science; *e-mail:* science@hq.nato.int.

Norwegian Council for Higher Education/The Research Council of Norway

Co-operation Programme with South-Eastern Europe—Research and Higher Education

Established by the Norwegian Council for Higher Education and The Research Council of Norway, in conjunction with the Norwegian Ministry of Foreign Affairs.

Activities: The Programme aims to initiate, develop and fund collaboration within higher education and research between universities, university colleges and research institutions in South-Eastern Europe and corresponding Norwegian institutions.

Geographical Area of Activity: Norway and South-Eastern Europe.

Financial Information: Annual budget 15,000,000 Norwegian krone.

Address: POB 7800, 5020 Bergen, Norway.

Telephone: 55-30-88-00; *Fax:* 55-30-88-01; *Internet:* www.siu.no; *e-mail:* siu@siu.no.

Organisation for Economic Co-operation and Development (OECD)

OECD DEVELOPMENT CENTRE

NGOs and Civil Society

The OECD Development Centre is a specialized unit within OECD which groups 30 member countries sharing a commitment to democratic government and the market economy. Maintains active relationships with approximately 70 other countries, NGOs and civil society organizations.

Activities: The co-ordinating unit for OECD's relations with NGOs and civil society, resources available to NGOs include a library and an on-line database of publications and country-by-country analysis of development NGOs.

Geographical Area of Activity: International.

Publications: Working briefs, reports, directories of NGOs and other publications.

Address: 94 rue Chardon Lagache, 75775 Paris Cedex 16, France.

Fax: 1-45-24-79-43; *Internet:* www.oecd.org; *e-mail:* cendev.contact@oecd.org.

Organization of African Unity (OAU)

OAU promotes accelerated socio-economic integration of the continent, in order to achieve greater unity and solidarity between African countries and peoples; aims to build a united and strong Africa and develop partnerships between governments and all segments of civil society, in particular women, young people and the private sector, in order to strengthen solidarity and cohesion amongst the peoples of Africa. Also promotes peace, security and stability on the continent as a prerequisite for the implementation of the development and integration agenda of the Union.

Activities: Develops programmes and collaborates with international organizations, UN agencies and NGOs with the aim of promoting socio-economic development in Africa. Programmes are run by the different directorates, which include Rural Economy and Agriculture; Human Resources, Science and Technology; Economic Affairs; Women, Gender and Development; and Afro-Arab Co-operation. Initiatives include the Special Emergency Assistance Fund for Drought and Famine in Africa (SEAF), the Fund for Emergency Assistance to Refugees, the Afro-Arab Cultural Institute, and specialist women's empowerment programmes, including women and education, women and health, and women and poverty eradication. OAU also makes educational and research awards.

Geographical Area of Activity: Africa.

Contact: Interim Chair. Amara Essy.

Address: POB 3243, Roosevelt St, W21 K19, Addis Ababa, Ethiopia.

Telephone: (1) 517700; *Fax:* (1) 517844; *Internet:* www.african-union.org.

AFRICAN COMMISSION ON HUMAN AND PEOPLES' RIGHTS

Established by the African Charter on Human and Peoples' Rights which came into force on 21 October 1986 after its adoption in Nairobi in 1981 by the Assembly of Heads of States and Governments of the Organization of African Unity (OAU). The Commission is charged with ensuring the promotion and protection of human and peoples' rights throughout the African Continent.

Activities: The Commission has three major functions: the promotion of human and peoples' rights; the protection of human and peoples' rights; and the interpretation of the African Charter on Human and Peoples' Rights. Operates by collecting documents, undertaking studies and research on African problems in the field of human and peoples' rights, organizes seminars, symposia and conferences, disseminates information, encourages national and local organizations concerned with human and peoples' rights and, should the case arise, gives its views or makes recommendations to governments.

Geographical Area of Activity: Africa.

Publications: Directory of NGOs.
Address: 90 Kairaba Ave, POB 673, Banjul, Gambia.
Telephone: 392962; *Fax:* 390764; *Internet:* www.achpr.org; *e-mail:* achpr@achpr
.org.

Organization of American States (OAS)

INTER-AMERICAN AGENCY FOR CO-OPERATION AND DEVELOPMENT (IACD)

Established at the beginning of 2000 to promote new and more effective forms of co-operation between the member states of the Organization of American States (OAS) and to enhance partnerships with the private sector and civil society. The Agency is governed by a nine-member Management Board of officials selected from among the member states, as well the Executive Secretariat for Integral Development, which together manage all of the technical co-operation and training activities of the OAS.

Activities: Activities relating to NGOs include the Fellowships programme and FEMCIDI—Special Multilateral Fund of CIDI (q.v.). Also administers Special Funds; horizontal co-operation funds established by member and permanent observer states, private-sector entities and foundations to enhance the hemisphere's ability to apply best practices in various technical areas as broadly as possible. Participating countries include , Argentina, Brazil, Israel, Korea, Mexico, Peru, Spain, Uruguay, and the USA. IACD's Best Practices/Rapid Response Fund is a new programme that aims to expand the delivery of technical co-operation to member states, and promote new forms of inter-American co-operation by mobilizing human, technical and financial resources and by creating new partnerships with other multilateral and regional development institutions, bilateral donor agencies, the private sector, educational and research institutes, and NGOs.

Geographical Area of Activity: OAS member states: Antigua and Barbuda, Argentina, Bahamas, Barbados, Belize, Bolivia, Brazil, Canada, Chile, Colombia, Costa Rica, Cuba, Dominica, Dominican Republic, Ecuador, El Salvador, Grenada, Guatemala, Guyana, Haiti, Honduras, Jamaica, Mexico, Nicaragua, Panama, Paraguay, Peru, St Lucia, St Vincent and the Grenadines, St Kitts and Nevis, Suriname, Trinidad and Tobago, USA, Uruguay, Venezuela.

Contact: Dir-Gen. L. Ronald Scheman.

Address: 1889 F St, NW, Washington, DC 20006, USA.

Telephone: (202) 458-3510; *Fax:* (202) 458-3526; *Internet:* www.iacd.oas.org; *e-mail:* agency@iacd.oas.org.

Department of Information Technology for Human Development: Fellowships

The Inter-American Agency for Co-operation and Development is an umbrella body administering one of the hemisphere's biggest groupings of fellowships for both academic study and for professional training.

Activities: Over several hundred fellowships are available annually for graduate studies and research, fellowships for undergraduate studies at universities through the region and awards for specialized, short-term training at educational institutions and training centres in OAS member and observer states. Also co-finances fellowships through a broad-based consortium of universities, operates an educational portal for e-learning, which includes a programme of electronic fellowships (e-fellowships) as a cost-effective mechanism for expanding fellowship and learning opportunities, and seeks partnerships with other agencies involved in the award and financing of fellowships and mechanisms to facilitate access to educational loans to supplement the fellowship programmes.

Geographical Area of Activity: North, Central and South America.

How to Apply: Information on fellowships and how to apply is available from the National Liaison Office (ONE) of the country of origin, or the appropriate office of the General Secretariat of OAS.

Address: Division of Human Devt, 1889 F St, NW, Washington, DC 20006, USA.

Telephone: (202) 458-3510; *Fax:* (202) 458-3526; *Internet:* www.educoas.org/.

FEMCIDI—Special Multilateral Fund of CIDI

Established to finance co-operation projects presented by the OAS member states.

Activities: The Fund finances co-operation projects carried out by NGOs and public-sector organizations. Under the Strategic Plan for Partnership for Development 2002–05, the eight priority lines of action that aim to make a significant impact on the development of the countries of the region are: social development and generation of productive employment; education; economic diversification and integration, trade liberalization and market access; scientific development, and exchange and transfer of technology; strengthening of democratic institutions; sustainable development of tourism; sustainable development and the environment; and culture. The priority areas in which the member states present projects should directly relate to the most important development needs at the national or regional level. Funding is available for both national and multinational projects.

Geographical Area of Activity: Antigua and Barbuda, Bahamas, Barbados, Belize, Brazil, Chile, Costa Rica, Dominica, Dominican Republic, El Salvador, Grenada, Guatemala, Guyana, Haiti, Honduras, Jamaica, Mexico, Nicaragua, Panama, Paraguay, St Kitts and Nevis, Saint Lucia, St Vincent and the Grenadines, Suriname, Trinidad and Tobago, Uruguay and the USA.

How to Apply: The first stage in the application process is the presentation of a project concept, which describes the objective, methodology, and ability to meet the objective; the contribution the project will make to regional or national development; and the approximate amount required to finance the project. The member states that have presented profiles with the most promising concepts will be invited to prepare complete proposals. During this second stage of the programming cycle, consultations will take place between the proposers of the projects and the Inter-American Agency for Co-operation and Development in order to improve the quality of the project, as well as to apply the best practices and the experience of other national and international organizations. The third and final stage consists of a technical evaluation of each project proposal by the Non-Permanent Specialized Committees (CENPES), groups which are composed of specialists elected each year to comply with this function.

Financial Information: Funded through voluntary contributions from the OAS member states. Annual budget approx. US $9,000,000; maximum grant available US $500,000.

Address: 1889 F St, NW, Washington, DC 20006, USA.

Telephone: (202) 458-3510; *Fax:* (202) 458-3526; *Internet:* www.iacd.oas.org /template-ingles/aboutprojects.htm; *e-mail:* agency@iacd.oas.org.

INTER-AMERICAN COMMISSION OF WOMEN (CIM)

A specialized organization of the Organization of American States (OAS) established in 1928 at the Sixth International Conference of American States in Havana, Cuba; the first official intergovernmental agency in the world created expressly to ensure recognition of the civil and political rights of women. It aims to make the participation and support of women a legitimate and indispensable part of governance and international consensus building in the Americas.

Activities: Through its delegates in each country, CIM provides support and recognition to national women's movements at governmental level, with NGOs, and with grassroots organizations. Also, within the OAS, lobbies on behalf of women's movements throughout the Americas and helps to foster inter-American co-operation. Activities include promoting the mobilization, training, and organization of women to achieve equal participation in civil, political, economic, social, and cultural leadership positions; and establishing close ties of co-operation with those inter-American organizations, world organizations and public and private agencies whose activities affect women. Also distributes grants through its Seed Fund (q.v.).

Geographical Area of Activity: North, Central and South America.

Contact: Pres. Yadira Henríquez; Vice-Pres. Florence Ievers; Exec. Sec. Carmen Lomellin.

Address: 1889 F St, NW, Washington, DC 20006, USA.

Telephone: (202) 458-6084; *Fax:* (202) 458-6094; *Internet:* www.oas.org; *e-mail:* secretariapermanente@oas.org.

Seed Fund

A start-up funding programme of the Inter-American Commission on Women (q.v.); established in 1991 to provide member states with access to resources to support women's advocacy work so as to improve their social status and help to meet women's most urgent needs.

Activities: Provides start-up funding to multinational and national advocacy projects in participating countries, primarily in the fields of health, education, employment, elimination of violence, elimination of poverty and the participation of women in the structures of power and decision-making. In 2001 and 2002 preference was given to projects aimed at implementing the Inter-American

Programme on the Promotion of Women's Human Rights and Gender Equity and Equality, including training programmes for community organizations, vocational training for low-income rural women, entrepreneurship development for rural women, and citizen participation and leadership for young people. Sixty per cent of the Seed Fund is used for implementation of multinational projects and 40% for national projects. Multinational projects should involve at least three participating countries.

Geographical Area of Activity: Central, South and North America.

How to Apply: Closing date for the submission of projects is 31 March of the second year of each two-year project.

Financial Information: Grants for multinational projects up to US $30,000; grants for national projects up to US $15,000. Co-financing of projects is required.

Address: 1889 F St, NW, Washington, DC 20006, USA.

Internet: www.oas.org; *e-mail:* spcim@oas.org.

INTER-AMERICAN MUSIC COUNCIL (CIDEM—CONSEJO INTERAMERICANO DE MÚSICA)

Founded in 1956 by the General Secretariat of the Organization of American States. in compliance with Resolution IX of the First Meeting of the Inter-American Cultural Council, which refers to the creation of an inter-American musical organization that will function with a permanent character, centralize inter-American musical activities and work closely with the International Music Council of the United Nations Educational, Scientific and Cultural Organization (UNESCO). CIDEM is the special advisory entity of the Inter-American Council for Education, Science and Culture.

Activities: CIDEM aims to: promote the interchange and diffusion of works, performers, composers, and general information concerning all fields of music; convoke periodic meetings to consider problems concerning music education; and encourage activity in the field of musicology, folkloric research, music composition, inter-American music festivals, publication, distribution and diffusion of American music. Distributes awards and fellowships to young musicians, including the Robert Stevenson History of Latin American Music and Musicology Award with a first prize of US $5,000; co-founded the Latin American Center for Graduate Studies in Music (LAMC); and funds concert series and performances.

Geographical Area of Activity: Central, South and North America.

Contact: Sec.-Gen. Efrain Paesky.

Address: 1889 F St, NW, 2nd Floor, Washington, DC 20006, USA.

Telephone: (202) 458-3706; *Internet:* www.oas.org.

PAN AMERICAN DEVELOPMENT FOUNDATION (PADF)

Democracy and Civil Society

Established in 1962 through a co-operative agreement between the Organization of American States and private enterprise, to create partnerships to assist the least advantaged people in Central and South America and the Caribbean and to empower them to rebuild their lives.

Activities: Aims to strengthen democracy by improving governments' and NGOs' institutional capacity, managerial expertise and financial independence, and to promote greater citizen participation. The Foundation trains mayors and their local staffs through exchange programmes, study tours and intensive short-term courses with municipal officials from the USA. Also provides technical assistance in strategic/participatory planning, administration, finance management and project design and implementation; and provides in-kind donations, including computers, school buses, fire-trucks, ambulances and tools, as well as specialized medical equipment suited to local needs.

Geographical Area of Activity: Central and South America and the Caribbean.

Contact: Chair. César Gaviria; Vice-Chair. Luigi Einaudi; Pres. Frank D. Gomez; First Vice-Pres. Ruth Espey-Romero; Sec. Yolanda Mellon Suarez; Treas. Maston N. Cunningham; Exec. Dir John Sanbrailo.

Address: 2600 16th St, NW, 4th Floor, Washington, DC 20009-4202, USA.

Telephone: (202) 458-3969; *Fax:* (202) 458-3969; *Internet:* www.padf.org; *e-mail:* padf-dc@padf.org.

Disaster Assistance and Reconstruction Programme

Established in 1962 through a co-operative agreement between the Organization of American States (OAS) and private enterprise, to create partnerships to assist the least advantaged people in Central and South America and the Caribbean and to empower them to rebuild their lives.

Activities: The Programme enables private-sector donors to address the most critical needs of disaster victims with Emergency Shelter Packages, designed to provide shelter, food, clean water and other items in the immediate aftermath of a disaster, through collaboration with OAS offices in each country to obtain quick, duty-free entry of these supplies. Works in partnership with local government, community organizations and NGOs, businesses, and individuals; activities include re-establishing food production through the provision of improved seeds and plant material; reconstruction of farm-to-market roads, irrigation systems, and potable water equipment; soil conservation programmes; and disaster preparedness at a regional and national level. Also partners with the Association of American Chambers of Commerce in Latin America (AACCLA) on natural disaster prevention, preparedness and response in Central and South America and the Caribbean.

Geographical Area of Activity: Central and South America and the Caribbean.

Contact: Chair. César Gaviria; Vice-Chair. Luigi Einaudi; Pres. Frank D. Gomez; First Vice-Pres. Ruth Espey-Romero; Sec. Yolanda Mellon Suarez; Treas. Maston N. Cunningham; Exec. Dir John Sanbrailo.

Address: 2600 16th St, NW, 4th Floor, Washington, DC 20009-4202, USA.
Telephone: (202) 458-3969; *Fax:* (202) 458-6316; *Internet:* www.padf.org; *e-mail:* padf-dc@padf.org.

Raising Family Incomes

Established in 1962 through a co-operative agreement between the Organization of American States and private enterprise, to create partnerships to assist the least advantaged people in Central and South America and the Caribbean and to empower them to rebuild their lives.

Activities: The programme operates through vocational training programmes designed to make low-income people become self-sufficient, providing technical assistance and equipment to training facilities where educational opportunities are limited, to enable students of all ages to gain marketable skills, raise the local pool of qualified job applicants and improve the training institution's capacity to teach. Also operates a sustainable forestry programme, partnering with community-based farming organizations to raise the incomes of small producers through sustainable agricultural practices that promote soil conservation and reforestation; and an employment-generation programme focusing on generating jobs for disadvantaged people through micro-enterprise development, skills training, agricultural improvements, natural resource conservation and expansion of community infrastructure.

Geographical Area of Activity: Central and South America and the Caribbean.

Contact: Chair. César Gaviria; Vice-Chair. Luigi Einaudi; Pres. Frank D. Gomez; First Vice-Pres. Ruth Espey-Romero; Sec. Yolanda Mellon Suarez; Treas. Maston N. Cunningham; Exec. Dir John Sanbrailo.

Address: 2600 16th St, NW, 4th Floor, Washington, DC 20009-4202, USA.

Telephone: (202) 458-3969; *Fax:* (202) 458-6316; *Internet:* www.padf.org; *e-mail:* padf-dc@padf.org.

TRUST FOR THE AMERICAS

Information and Communications Technologies for Development Initiative

A foundation, established in 1997, to foster partnership among companies, foundations, governmental bodies, and academic institutions operating in the Americas; the Trust's mission reflects the central goals of the Organization of American States and its mandates: mobilizing resources to confront extreme poverty and to promote democracy through actions that are environmentally, economically and socially sustainable. The Initiative was created in response to the mandates in the Québec Summit's Connectivity Agenda for the Americas.

Activities: The Initiative aims to create a bridge in the digital divide, democratizing access to training in the new information and communications technology, and to develop relevant points of access for disadvantaged groups in society, including low-income youth, disabled people, small businesses, women, indigenous communities and victims of wars. Current programmes, run in conjunction with host NGOs, are Technology for People with Disabilities, Small Business, Women Leaders in Technology; and Empowering Youth through Technology.

Geographical Area of Activity: North, Central and South America.

Contact: Board of Directors: César Gaviria (Sec.-Gen.); Enrique Segura (Pres.); June Langston DeHart (Vice-Pres.); and 8 others; Exec. Dir Linda H. Eddelman.

Address: 1889 F St, NW, 7th Floor, Washington, DC 20006, USA.

Telephone: (202) 458-3661; *Fax:* (202) 458-3904; *Internet:* www.trustfortheamericas.org.

Transparency and Governance Initiative

A foundation, established in 1997, to foster partnerships among companies, foundations, governmental bodies, and academic institutions operating in the Americas; the Trust's mission reflects the central goals of the Organization of American States and its mandates: mobilizing resources to confront extreme poverty and to promote democracy through actions that are environmentally, economically and socially sustainable.

Activities: The Initiative currently seeks to create awareness of corruption and to promote ethics in the media, through convening conferences in partnership with NGOs, academic institutions, the media and international and governmental organizations; running training programmes for journalists from the print and electronic media in techniques relating to coverage of governance, finance and corruption; and running a Children's Ethics Media Programme to develop materials promoting civic virtue, tolerance and negotiation skills.

Geographical Area of Activity: North, Central and South America.

Contact: Board of Directors: César Gaviria (Sec.-Gen.); Enrique Segura (Pres.); June Langston DeHart (Vice-Pres.); and 8 others; Exec. Dir Linda H. Eddelman.

Address: 1889 F St, NW, 7th Floor, Washington, DC 20006, USA.

Telephone: (202) 458-3661; *Fax:* (202) 458-3904; *Internet:* www.trustfortheamericas.org.

Organization of Arab Petroleum Exporting Countries (OAPEC)

TECHNICAL AFFAIRS DEPARTMENT

OAPEC Award for Scientific Research

Aims to encourage research in the petroleum industry by awarding two annual prizes to individuals or groups of individuals; OAPEC was established in 1968 as an instrument of Arab co-operation whose objective is to provide support to the Arab oil industry.

Activities: The Award consists of two annual prizes of 5,000 and 3,000 Kuwaiti dinars, which aim to fulfil OAPEC's objective of promoting research by individuals in the petroleum industry. In 2004, the selected research theme was Activation of Mature Fields and Boosting their Productivity, and the awardees are expected to demonstrate every relevant method to activate the extraction of oil from mature fields, and consequently increase the reserves to be extracted and to maintain production levels as well as life expectancy of the field, whilst also maintaining its economies for as long as possible.

Geographical Area of Activity: Arab states.

Restrictions: Institutions and organizations are not eligible.

How to Apply: Application form available on the website.

Financial Information: Two annual awards of 5,000 and 3,000 Kuwaiti dinars.

Address: POB 20501, 13066 Safat, Kuwait.

Telephone: 4844500; *Fax:* 4815747; *Internet:* www.oapecorg.org/; *e-mail:* oapec@qualitynet.net.

Organization of Eastern Caribbean States (OECS)

ENVIRONMENT AND SUSTAINABLE ENERGY UNIT

Small Projects Facility

Supports the main objectives of OECS' Environment and Sustainable Energy Unit, whilst also aiming to provide greater flexibility and responsiveness to local needs and circumstances.

Activities: The programme provides technical and financial assistance to a wide range of activities undertaken by member states and community organizations, in the areas of: Biodiversity Management and Protected Areas; Environmental Planning and Management; and Environmental Awareness and Education. Supported activities include eco-tourism initiatives, beach rehabilitation, and training in co-management and community involvement in sustainable development.

Geographical Area of Activity: Anguilla, Antigua and Barbuda, British Virgin Islands, Dominica, Grenada, Montserrat, St Kitts and Nevis, St Lucia, and St Vincent and the Grenadines.

Financial Information: Funded by the UK Department for International Development and the Canadian International Development Agency.

Address: The Morne, POB 1383, Castries, St Lucia.

Telephone: 452-1847; *Fax:* 452-2194; *Internet:* www.oecsnrmu.org/progs.htm; *e-mail:* oecsnr@candw.lc.

Organization of the Petroleum Exporting Countries (OPEC)

ABU DHABI FUND

Established in July 1971 by the government of Abu Dhabi; commenced operations in September 1974.

Activities: Operates through providing economic aid, in the form of loans, grants or capital participation projects, to Arab, African, Asian and other developing countries, and to engage in other activities which support these objectives.

Geographical Area of Activity: Developing countries.

Contact: Dir-Gen. Saeed Khalfan Mattar Al-Rumaithi.

Address: Tourist Area Saeed Ghobash Bldg, POB 814, Abu Dhabi, United Arab Emirates.

Telephone: (2) 725800; *Fax:* (2) 728890; *Internet:* www.opec.org; *e-mail:* opadfdmn@emirates.net.ac.

ARAB AUTHORITY FOR AGRICULTURAL INVESTMENT AND DEVELOPMENT (AAAID)

Established in November 1976 by 15 Arab states; aims to improve food security in Arab countries.

Activities: Works to develop agricultural resources in OPEC member states by funding all forms of agricultural production and related activities, including: land reclamation; plant, animal and fish production; pastures; forestry; the transportation, storage, marketing, processing and exporting of agricultural produce; and all inputs necessary for agricultural production.

Geographical Area of Activity: OPEC countries in Africa, Asia, Central and South America, and the Middle East.

Contact: Board of Directors: Chair. and Pres. Abdul Kareem Mohammed Al-Amri.

Address: POB 2102, Khartoum, Sudan.

Telephone: (11) 773752; *Fax:* (11) 772600; *Internet:* www.opec.org.

ARAB BANK FOR ECONOMIC DEVELOPMENT IN AFRICA (BADEA)

Established in November 1973, began operations in March 1975; seeks to promote economic, financial and technical co-operation between African and Arab countries.

230

Activities: Operates through financing economic development in African countries, stimulating the contribution of Arab capital to African development, and providing technical assistance.

Geographical Area of Activity: Africa.

Financial Information: Funded by Arab governments.

Contact: Dir-Gen. Medhat S. Lotfy.

Address: Abdel Rahman El-Mahdi St, POB 2640, Khartoum 11111, Sudan.

Telephone: (11) 773646; *Fax:* (11) 770498; *Internet:* www.badea.org; *e-mail:* badea@badea.org.

ARAB FUND FOR ECONOMIC AND SOCIAL DEVELOPMENT (AFESD)

Established in December 1971, the Fund began operating in 1974. Also provides secretariat services for the Co-ordination Secretariat of Arab National and Regional Development Institutions, which meets periodically to discuss ongoing and planned development projects with the intention of streamlining operational procedures among the member institutions. Members of the co-ordination group are the Abu Dhabi Fund for Development, the Arab Bank for Economic Development in Africa, the AFESD itself, the Islamic Development Bank, the Kuwait Fund for Arab Economic Development, the OPEC Fund for International Development, and the Saudi Fund for Development.

Activities: The Fund finances projects for economic and social development in Arab countries, extending concessional loans to governments, and public and private organizations. Preference is given to projects that are of vital importance to the Arab world and to joint ventures involving Arab co-operation, and aiming to strengthen development efforts in beneficiary countries. Also allocates technical assistance grants to its member states, to enhance the efficiency of government institutions and to support training programmes and social development projects, as well as preserving their national heritage and developing information systems. Also operates a fellowship programme, aimed at Arab PhD holders to conduct research or lecture in the world's leading universities. The programme also aims to build bridges between Arab and foreign universities. The fellowships are open to Arab nationals who are currently working in a university in a member country.

Geographical Area of Activity: All 21 members of the League of Arab States: Algeria, Bahrain, Djibouti, Egypt, Iraq, Jordan, Kuwait, Lebanon, Libya, Mauritania, Morocco, Oman, Palestinian Autonomous Areas, Qatar, Saudi Arabia, Somalia, Sudan, Syria, Tunisia, United Arab Emirates and Yemen.

Contact: Chair. and Dir-Gen. Abdlatif Yousef Al-Hamad.

Address: POB 21923, Safat 13080, Kuwait, Kuwait.

Telephone: 1811500; *Fax:* 4815750; *Internet:* www.arabfund.org; *e-mail:* admn@ afesd.qualitynet.net.

ARAB GULF PROGRAMME FOR UNITED NATIONS DEVELOPMENT ORGANIZATIONS (AGFUND)

Established in April 1981 by the governments of Bahrain, Iraq, Kuwait, Oman, Qatar, Saudi Arabia and the United Arab Emirates to support humanitarian projects.

Activities: Provides grant assistance to UN agencies and Arab NGOs in support of humanitarian projects, funding projects in the fields of health, nutrition, water and sanitation, education, disability and environment. The main beneficiaries are mothers and children, particularly in the areas of health awareness, primary health, and environmental health. Also maintains an office in Bahrain.

Geographical Area of Activity: Developing Arab countries.

Financial Information: Funded by the governments of Bahrain, Iraq, Kuwait, Oman, Qatar, Saudi Arabia and the United Arab Emirates.

Contact: Pres. Prince Talal Bin Abdul Aziz Al-Saud.

Address: POB 18371, Riyadh 11415, Saudi Arabia.

Telephone: (1) 441-4168; *Fax:* (1) 441-2963; *Internet:* www.agfund.org/; *e-mail:* projects@agfund.org.

Banks for the Poor

An initiative of the Arab Gulf Programme for United Nations Development Organizations, aiming to promote the principle of micro-credit for the poorest of the poor in developing Arab countries.

Activities: Aims to provide a mechanism through which the poorest people, whether individuals or organizations, who cannot borrow money from commercial banks because of the guarantees required, are granted the skills and money to allow them to initiate a project that has the potential to generate income and contribute to societal change and development. The first Bank for the Poor was established in Yemen, with follow-ups under development in Jordan, Lebanon, Libya, Mauritania, Morocco, Sudan and Syria.

Geographical Area of Activity: Developing Arab countries.

Address: POB 18371, Riyadh 11415, Saudi Arabia.

Telephone: (1) 441-8888; *Fax:* (1) 441-2962; *Internet:* www.agfund.org; *e-mail:* prmedia@agfund.org.

Communications Department: AGFUND International Prize

The Prize is awarded by the Arab Gulf Programme for United Nations Development Organizations (AGFUND), a regional development-oriented institution established in 1980 upon the initiative of HRH Prince Talal Bin Abdul Aziz, and with the support of the leaders of the Arab Gulf States that constitute its membership and contribute to its budget. AGFUND supports sustainable human development efforts, targeting the most deserving groups in developing countries, particularly women and children, in co-operation with organizations and institutions active in this field.

Activities: The AGFUND International Prize is an annual prize of US $300,000, which aims to support distinguished efforts aimed at developing and promoting the concepts and dimensions of sustainable human development; promoting developmental action on scientific bases that could help it achieve its objectives; and highlighting and enhancing pioneering efforts in developing countries, which aim at establishing distinguished NGOs that work towards a better future, in which social security, justice and equality prevail. In 2003 support categories were: rehabilitation and employment of refugees and displaced people, protection of children against abuse and negligence, and innovative initiatives in the field of poverty alleviation.

Geographical Area of Activity: Developing countries.

How to Apply: Nominations for the Prize can be made by filling in the Nomination Form on AGFUND's website. Bodies eligible to nominate include the UN, international and regional organizations, as well as universities, research centres, NGOs and country federations of NGOs.

Financial Information: Annual prize of US $300,000.

Address: POB 18371, Riyadh 11415, Saudi Arabia.

Telephone: (1) 441-8888; *Fax:* (1) 441-2962; *Internet:* www.agfund.org; *e-mail:* prize@agfund.org or.

IRAQI FUND FOR EXTERNAL DEVELOPMENT

Started operations in January 1977; established as an independent agency to promote economic and social development in Arab and other developing countries.

Activities: Promotes economic and social development in Arab and other developing countries, through the provision of concessional loans and technical assistance. Also invests in joint projects involving Arab economic integration, and oversees management of those investments.

Geographical Area of Activity: Arab and developing countries.

Contact: Pres. Dr Faik Ali Abdul Rasool.

Address: POB 5111, Baghdad, Iraq.

Telephone: (1) 8888237.

ISLAMIC DEVELOPMENT BANK (IDB)

Established in April 1975; aims to foster economic development and social progress in member countries and in Muslim communities in accordance with the principles of Islamic Shari'ah.

Activities: IDB's membership consists of 54 countries which are also members of the Organization of the Islamic Conference. IDB has the authority to extend financing and raise funds in many ways to establish special funds for specific purposes and to establish contacts with NGOs.

Geographical Area of Activity: Arab states.

Contact: Pres. and Chair. Board of Exec. Dirs Dr Ahmad Mohamed Ali.

Address: POB 5925, Jeddah 21432, Saudi Arabia.

Telephone: (2) 636-1400; *Fax:* (2) 636-6871; *Internet:* www.isdb.org; *e-mail:* archives@isdb.org.

IDB Merit Scholarship Programme

Aims to develop technically qualified human resources in the Islamic Development Bank (IDB) member countries by providing scholarships to promising and/or outstanding scholars and researchers to undertake advanced studies and/or research in the fields of applied science and technology needed for the development of the member countries.

Activities: Awards scholarships for three-year PhD study and one-year post-doctoral research to be carried out at a number of selected institutions within the fields of: laser and fibre optics; conductors/semi-conductors; polymer science; genetic engineering/biotechnology; nuclear science/engineering; electronics/micro-electronics/telecommunications; computer science; renewable energy/fuel technology; hydrology/water resources; metallurgy; chemical engineering/material sciences; medicine/pharmacy; agriculture/food technology; system engineering; space science/technology; and environmental preservation technology.

Geographical Area of Activity: IDB member countries.

Restrictions: Applicants for one-year post-doctoral research who have had a post-doctoral experience outside their countries within the past two years are not eligible.

How to Apply: Applications must be submitted through the nominating institutions which, in turn, seek endorsement from the offices of the IDB Governors for the country; application forms are available on the website.

Contact: Pres. and Chair., Board of Exec. Dirs Dr Ahmad Mohamed Ali.

Address: POB 5925, Jeddah 21432, Saudi Arabia.

Telephone: (2) 646-6832; *Fax:* (2) 646-6871; *Internet:* www.isdb.org; *e-mail:* archives@isdb.org.

Islamic Research and Training Institute: IDB Prize in Islamic Economics

Recognizes research and outstanding work in the area of Islamic economics.

Activities: Makes an annual award of approximately US $40,000 in recognition of outstanding academic or practical contributions in the field of Islamic economics, including published research.

Geographical Area of Activity: Islamic countries: members of the Islamic Development Bank.

Restrictions: Works which have already won another international prize are not considered.

Financial Information: Annual award of approx. US $40,000.

Address: POB 9201, Jeddah 21413, Saudi Arabia.

Telephone: (2) 646-6129; *Fax:* (2) 637-8927; *Internet:* www.irti.org.sa; *e-mail:* idb-prize@isdb.org.sa.

MSc Scholarship Programme in Science and Technology for IDB Least-Developed Countries

The Programme was established to assist the least-developed member countries of the Islamic Development Bank (IDB) in the development of their human resources, especially in science and technology, that are both relevant and necessary for their development.

Activities: The Programme aims to: increase the number of MSc graduates available for effective technology development, transfer and maintenance; increase access for students to the educational opportunities available under the IDB initiatives in human resource development for member countries by creating a special programme suited to their circumstances and needs; and enhance the ability of students to participate in the existing IDB programmes in science and technology, such as the IDB Merit Scholarship Programme for High Technology.

Geographical Area of Activity: Least-developed member countries of the IDB: Afghanistan, Benin, Burkina Faso, Chad, Comoros, Djibouti, Gambia, Guinea, Guinea-Bissau, Maldives, Mali, Mauritania, Mozambique, Niger, Sierra Leone, Somalia, Uganda and Yemen.

How to Apply: Application form available on the website.

Contact: Pres. and Chair. Board of Exec. Dirs Dr Ahmad Mohamed Ali.

Address: POB 5925, Jeddah 21432, Saudi Arabia.

Telephone: (2) 646-6832; *Fax:* (2) 646-6871; *Internet:* www.isdb.org; *e-mail:* archives@isdb.org.

Office of the Scholarship Programme: Scholarship Programme for Muslim Communities in Non-Member Countries

Operates as a scholarship programme and development programme, supporting both students and their communities.

Activities: Scholarships are given as interest-free loans to the students, who then pay back the loan to a trust fund set up by the Islamic Development Bank (IDB) in each non-member country benefiting from the Programme. Students are also required to take part in the development of their communities, through their respective professions. The repaid fund is then used to provide scholarships for other deserving students from the same community.

Geographical Area of Activity: Muslim countries which are not members of IDB.

Contact: Pres. and Chair. Board of Exec. Dirs Dr Ahmad Mohamed Ali.

Address: POB 5925, Jeddah 21432, Saudi Arabia.

Telephone: (2) 646-6832; *Fax:* (2) 636-6871; *e-mail:* scholar@isdb.org.sa.

Science and Technology Department: Young Researchers Support Programme

The Programme aims to help talented young researchers in their home countries through providing them with the means to pursue their research work in a more favourable environment.

Activities: The Programme's support activities aim to create an Islamic science and technology indigenous capability and contribute to the reduction, and ultimately reverse, a brain-drain damaging to the region. In its first pilot phase,

15 research projects received grants of up to US $15,000; a research grant may be renewed up to two times according to the individual merit of the corresponding research project. The research fields of specialty are agriculture, energy, information technologies, biomedical technologies, textile technologies, pharmaceuticals, biotechnology and genetic engineering, and environmental sciences.

Geographical Area of Activity: Islamic Development Bank member countries.

How to Apply: All applications must be submitted through the Governor of IDB in the country of citizenship.

Financial Information: Fifteen annual research grants of up to US $15,000.

Address: POB 5925, Jeddah 21432, Saudi Arabia.

Fax: (2) 636-6871; *Internet:* www.isdb.org/english_docs/idb_home/yrp_e.htm.

Special Assistance Office (SAO): Special Assistance Programme

The Special Assistance Office of the Islamic Development Bank was established in 1980; aims to promote the development of Muslim communities in non-member countries in the areas of education and health and to alleviate the suffering of those communities afflicted by natural disasters or war in both member as well as non-member countries.

Activities: The Programme operates through: providing assistance to Muslim communities for education and health projects, including setting up schools, vocational training centres, student hostels and health centres; distributing relief in the form of appropriate goods and services to member countries and Islamic communities afflicted by natural disasters and calamities, such as floods, earthquakes and wars; and giving financial assistance for the promotion and furtherance of Islamic causes, including supporting Islamic universities, research centres and cultural organizations.

Geographical Area of Activity: Islamic Development Bank member countries.

Financial Information: Total expenditure US $497,410,000 (1980–2000).

Contact: Pres. and Chair. Board of Exec. Dirs Dr Ahmad Mohamed Ali.

Address: POB 5925, Jeddah 21432, Saudi Arabia.

Telephone: (2) 636-1400; *Fax:* (2) 636-6871; *Internet:* www.isdb.org; *e-mail:* archives@isdb.org.

KUWAIT FUND FOR ARAB ECONOMIC DEVELOPMENT

Started operations in March 1962; the first of the development finance institutions created by OPEC member countries.

Activities: The Fund extends development assistance to developing countries, through the provision of loans, guarantees and grants; technical assistance services; participation in the capital of other development institutions; and representation of the State of Kuwait in regional and international organizations.

Geographical Area of Activity: Developing countries.

Contact: Dir-Gen. Bader Mishari Al-Humaidhi.

Address: POB 2921, 13030 Safat, Kuwait.

Telephone: 2468800; *Internet:* www.kuwait-fund.org; *e-mail:* info@kuwait-fund.org.

OPEC FUND FOR INTERNATIONAL DEVELOPMENT

A multilateral development finance institution, established in January 1976 by the member countries of the Organization of the Petroleum Exporting Countries (OPEC) following a decision taken in March 1975 by the Sovereigns and Heads of State of OPEC members, meeting in Algiers. The Fund aims to promote co-operation between OPEC member countries and other developing countries as an expression of South–South solidarity, and help particularly the poorer, low-income countries in pursuit of their social and economic advancement.

Activities: Promotes South–South co-operation and socio-economic development through providing grants in support of technical assistance, food aid, research and similar activities, and humanitarian emergency relief, and by contributing to the resources of other development institutions whose work benefits developing countries, with the exception of OPEC member states. Also extends concessionary loans for development projects and programmes and for balance-of-payments support, serves OPEC member countries as an agent in the international financial arena whenever collective action is deemed appropriate, and finances private-sector activities in developing countries.

Geographical Area of Activity: Developing countries, with the exception of OPEC member countries.

Financial Information: At end of December 2002 total pledges US $3,439,400,000; by the end of 2003 total grants US $314,200,000. Funding provided by voluntary contributions made by OPEC member countries.

Publications: Annual Report; Newsletter.

Contact: Sec.-Gen. Y. Seyyid Abdulai.

Address: POB 995, 1011 Vienna, Austria.

Telephone: (1) 515-64-0; *Fax:* (1) 513-92-38; *Internet:* www.opecfund.org; *e-mail:* info@opecfund.org.

ORGANIZATION FOR INVESTMENT, ECONOMIC AND TECHNICAL ASSISTANCE OF IRAN

Established in June 1975.

Activities: Supports the centralization, regulation and conduct of loans, grants and credits, and economic and technical assistance provided by Iran to governments and national institutions.

Geographical Area of Activity: Developing countries.

Contact: Pres. Dr Parviz Davoodi.

Address: Ministry of Economic Affairs and Finance, Nasser Khosrow Ave, POB 11365/9618, Tehran, Iran.

Telephone: (21) 3115118; *Fax:* (21) 3901033; *Internet:* www.opec.org.

SAUDI FUND FOR DEVELOPMENT

Established in September 1974 to establish financial co-operation links with other developing countries.

Activities: Operates mainly through extending concessional loans for financing projects that contribute to the social and economic well-being of beneficiary countries. Although all developing nations are eligible for assistance from the Saudi Fund, activities concentrate primarily on the least-developed countries.

Geographical Area of Activity: Developing countries.

Contact: Vice-Chair. and Man. Dir Sheikh Mohammed A. Al-Sugair.

Address: POB 50483, Riyadh 11523, Saudi Arabia.

Telephone: (1) 4640292; *Fax:* (1) 4647450; *Internet:* www.sfd.gov.sa/; *e-mail:* info@sfd.gov.sa.

Organization for the Prohibition of Chemical Weapons (OPCW)

INTERNATIONAL CO-OPERATION AND ASSISTANCE DIVISION

Support for Research Projects in Areas Relevant to the Chemical Weapons Convention

A research grant initiative administered by OPCW's International Co-operation and Assistance (ICA) Division, as part of its programme for capacity building for peaceful applications of chemistry. OPCW was established in 1997 by the countries that have joined the Chemical Weapons Convention (CWC) to make sure that the Convention works effectively and achieves its purpose.

Activities: Supports research projects carried out by research institutions or other organizations for the development and promotion of scientific and technical knowledge in the field of chemistry for industrial, agricultural, research, medical, pharmaceutical or other peaceful purposes, including research on: technologies for the destruction of toxic chemicals in a safe and environmentally sound manner; management, with respect to the handling and use of toxic chemicals; development of analytical methods and validation techniques for toxic chemicals; verification techniques and methods relevant to the Chemical Weapons Convention; medical treatment and prophylactics for exposure to toxic chemicals; alternatives to scheduled chemicals for purposes not prohibited under the Convention; and risk assessment with respect to toxic chemicals. The project should contribute to the strengthening of sustainable research programmes, with preference given to research projects submitted by developing countries. Funding is also provided for training, organization of conferences, seminars and workshops, assistance to laboratories, and the transfer of laboratory equipment between member countries.

Geographical Area of Activity: International; preference for developing countries.

How to Apply: Application forms are available on the website.

Contact: Dir-Gen. Rogelio Pfirter.

Address: Johan de Wittlaan 32, 2517 JR, The Hague, Netherlands.

Telephone: (70) 416-33-00; *Internet:* www.opcw.org/html/db/icprot_frameset.html; *e-mail:* inquiries@opcw.org.

Organization for Security and Co-operation in Europe (OSCE)

One of the world's largest regional security organizations encompassing 55 participating states from Europe, Central Asia and North America. It is active in early warning, conflict prevention, crisis management and post-conflict rehabilitation.

Activities: The Secretariat's mandate involves: support of OSCE field activities; maintaining contacts with international and non-governmental organizations; co-ordinating OSCE economic, environmental and politico-military activities; administrative, financial and personnel services; conference and language services; and information technology and press and public information. Programmes with NGOs include a small grants programme promoting the development of pluralistic, independent and professional media in Bosnia and Herzegovina, as well as the advancement of freedom of expression and journalists' rights.

Geographical Area of Activity: Central Asia, Europe and North America.

Contact: Sec.-Gen. Jan Kubis.

Address: Kärntner Ring 5-7, 4th Floor, 1010 Vienna, Austria.

Telephone: (1) 514-36-18-0; *Fax:* (1) 514-36-10-5; *Internet:* www.osce.org; *e-mail:* info@osce.org.

OFFICE FOR DEMOCRATIC INSTITUTIONS AND HUMAN RIGHTS (ODIHR)

ODIHR is the principal institution of the Organization for Security and Co-operation in Europe (OSCE) responsible for the human dimension; aims to help OSCE participating states ensure full respect for human rights and fundamental freedoms, the rule of law, and respect for democracy, in accordance with the 1992 Helsinki Summit Declaration.

Activities: ODIHR's principal activities involve the promotion of democratic elections through providing observers of national elections; assisting projects aimed at strengthening democracy and good governance; practical support for the consolidation of democratic institutions and the strengthening of civil society and the rule of law through targeted projects on religious freedom and tolerance, fostering dialogue between governments and civil society, reviewing legislation, building functioning democratic institutions, and training members of the judiciary and law enforcement. Also serves as the OCSE contact point for Roma and Sinti issues.

Geographical Area of Activity: Central and Eastern Europe.

Contact: OIDHR Dir Christian Strohal.

Address: Al. Ujazdowskie 19, 00-557 Warsaw, Poland.

Telephone: (22) 5200600; *Fax:* (22) 5200605; *Internet:* www.osce.org/odihr; *e-mail:* office@odihr.pl.

Anti-Trafficking Unit: Anti-Trafficking Project Fund

A grant programme of the Anti-Trafficking Unit of the Office for Democratic Institutions and Human Rights (ODIHR), an institution of the Organization for Security and Co-operation in Europe (OSCE). The programme was launched in January 2003.

Activities: Through grants to NGOs and civil society organizations, the Fund aims to encourage the development and implementation of regional and national initiatives to prevent and to address trafficking in human beings, as well as to empower OSCE field operations and the ODIHR to respond in a timely and flexible manner to ensure protection and direct assistance to victims of trafficking, and to enhance co-operation between the ODIHR, OSCE field missions and other local actors in the fight against trafficking. The Fund targets the entire OSCE region, which covers Central Asia, the Caucasus, Eastern and South-Eastern Europe, Western Europe and North America. Related initiatives include support for the production and broadcast of a series of television programmes aimed at raising human rights awareness among the Armenian public, and draft anti-trafficking legislation drawn up by legal experts and human rights workers in the OSCE Mission in Kosovo and colleagues from the UN and the International Organization for Migration.

Geographical Area of Activity: All 55 OSCE countries.

Contact: Officer on Anti-Trafficking Issues, Anti-Trafficking Unit Gabriele Reiter.

Address: Al. Ujazdowskie 19, 00-557 Warsaw, Poland.

Telephone: (22) 5200600 ext: 4152; *Internet:* www.osce.org/osceprojects /show_project.php?id=370; *e-mail:* gabriele@odihr.pl.

Civic Dialogue Project

A grant programme of the NGO Unit of the Office for Democratic Institutions and Human Rights (ODIHR, q.v.), an institution of the Organization for Security and Co-operation in Europe (OSCE).

Activities: The Project aims to establish a dialogue between government officials and representatives of civil society in Kazakhstan, Kyrgyzstan, Tajikistan and Uzbekistan on human dimension issues.

Geographical Area of Activity: Kazakhstan, Kyrgyzstan, Tajikistan and Uzbekistan.

Contact: Head of NGO Unit Childerik Schaapveld.

Address: Al. Ujazdowskie 19, 00-557 Warsaw, Poland.

Telephone: (22) 5200600 ext: 4160; *Internet:* www.osce.org/odihr/projects/project .php?id=355; *e-mail:* cschaapveld@odihr.pl.

Rule of Law Unit: ODIHR Anti-Torture Programme

A grant programme of the Rule of Law Unit of the Office for Democratic Institutions and Human Rights (ODIHR), an institution of the Organization for Security and Co-operation in Europe (OSCE). The Programme was launched in January 2003.

Activities: The Programme works through funding projects by governmental organizations and NGOs which work towards the eradication of torture and other forms of degrading and inhuman treatment or punishment in the OSCE region, which covers Central Asia, the Caucasus, Eastern and South-Eastern Europe, Western Europe and North America.

Geographical Area of Activity: All 55 OSCE countries.

Contact: Research Asst., Human Rights Section Rachael Kondak.

Address: Al. Ujazdowskie 19, 00-557 Warsaw, Poland.

Telephone: (22) 5200600 ext: 4153; *Fax:* (22) 5200605; *Internet:* www.osce.org /osceprojects/show_project.php?id=374; *e-mail:* rachael.kondak@odihr.pl.

Rule of Law Unit: Technical Assistance for National Human Rights Institutions

A technical assistance grant programme of the Rule of Law Unit of the Office for Democratic Institutions and Human Rights (ODIHR), an institution of the Organization for Security and Co-operation in Europe (OSCE).

Activities: Provides ongoing assistance to the governments of Armenia, Azerbaijan and Georgia in establishing human rights institutions; provides technical assistance for maintaining and upgrading operational functioning of the Ombudsperson Office in Georgia; and provides support to the authorities of the Caucasus countries in facilitating an open dialogue with civil society organizations.

Geographical Area of Activity: Armenia, Azerbaijan and Georgia.

Contact: Head of Rule of Law Unit Cynthia Alkon.

Address: Al. Ujazdowskie 19, 00-557 Warsaw, Poland.

Telephone: (22) 5200600 ext: 4131; *Internet:* www.osce.org/odihr/projects/project .php?id=346; *e-mail:* calkon@odihr.pl.

Pacific Islands Forum (PIF)

Regional Natural Disaster Relief Fund

Established by the Pacific Islands Forum to provide member countries with readily available assistance for immediate relief in the wake of natural disasters.

Geographical Area of Activity: Member countries: Cook Islands, Federated States of Micronesia, Fiji, Kiribati, Nauru, Niue, Palau, Papua New Guinea, Marshall Islands, Samoa, Solomon Islands, Tonga, Tuvalu and Vanuatu.

How to Apply: Organizations submit a formal request for assistance through official contacts (Ministries of Foreign Affairs/External Affairs, Prime Minister's Offices). Detailed information on the disaster and relief requested is required.

Financial Information: Maximum payment per disaster is F $20,000.

Address: Private Mail Bag, Suva, Fiji.

Telephone: 3312600; *Internet:* www.forumsec.org.fj/Home.htm; *e-mail:* info@forumsec.org.fj.

Small Island States Development Fund

Established by the Pacific Islands Forum to support the socio-economic development of the Small Island States (SIS).

Activities: Provides funds for financing critical components of development programmes or projects which aim to improve the social and economic well-being of people in SIS member countries: Cook Islands, Kiribati, Nauru, Niue and Tuvalu. Funding is also available to engage short-term consultants to assist with development, planning, aid co-ordination and project delivery.

Geographical Area of Activity: SIS member countries: Cook Islands, Kiribati, Nauru, Niue and Tuvalu.

How to Apply: Requests should be submitted by SIS member countries through their official channels.

Address: Private Mail Bag, Suva, Fiji.

Internet: www.forumsec.org.fj; *e-mail:* info@forumsec.org.fj.

DEVELOPMENT AND ECONOMIC POLICY DIVISION

Taiwan/ROC—Pacific Islands Forum Scholarships

Established by the Pacific Islands Forum (PIF) in 2003.

Activities: The programme provides scholarships for full-time studies at undergraduate and postgraduate level to students from one of the PIF member countries: Cook Islands, Federated States of Micronesia, Fiji, Kiribati, Marshall Islands, Nauru, Niue, Palau, Papua New Guinea, Samoa, Solomon Islands,

Tonga, Tuvalu and Vanuatu. The study must take place at one of a number of eligible educational institutions in annually chosen priority fields, which vary from country to country.

Geographical Area of Activity: PIF member countries: Cook Islands, Federated States of Micronesia, Fiji, Kiribati, Marshall Islands, Nauru, Niue, Palau, Papua New Guinea, Samoa, Solomon Islands, Tonga, Tuvalu and Vanuatu.

How to Apply: An application form is available on the website.

Contact: Programme Implementation Officer.

Address: Forum Secretariat, Private Mail Bag, Suva, Fiji.

Telephone: 3312600; *Fax:* 3305880; *Internet:* www.forumsec.org.fj; *e-mail:* toakaser@forumsec.org.fj.

Pan American Health Organization (PAHO)

PAHO/World Health Organization (WHO) Fellowships

A fellowship scheme administered by PAHO; aims to fulfil specific learning objectives in the field of health.

Activities: Awards fellowships for specially tailored training activities for individuals or groups with the purpose of fulfilling specific learning objectives in the field of health. It may be of short or long duration, and takes place in a training institution or in the field inside or outside of the Fellow's country. It is awarded in response to nationally approved health or health-related priorities in the context of the Health for All initiative and is consistent with national human resources policies and plans.

Geographical Area of Activity: Africa, North, Central and South America, Eastern Mediterranean, Europe, South-East Asia and the Western Pacific.

Restrictions: No direct applications accepted from individuals.

How to Apply: Each of the six regional WHO offices shares responsibility for management and administration of the Fellowship programme within its region and in direct consultation with the sending or receiving country. Candidates must be nominated by their government, their applications must have the written endorsement of their government, and the applications must be forwarded to the WHO Country Representative by their government's national health administration.

Address: 525 23rd St, NW, Washington, DC 20037, USA.

Telephone: (202) 974-3399; *Fax:* (202) 775-4578; *Internet:* www.paho.org/English /hsp/hsr/fellowships.htm.

HUMAN RESOURCES DEVELOPMENT UNIT

Training Programme in International Health

Created in 1985 to strengthen the capacity of health institutions of the region and the member states.

Activities: Aims to develop the capacity of health institutions to analyze the international and transnational factors that affect their health situation; design innovative policies and strategies of action, using the experiences of the international community and mobilizing its political, financial, and technical resources; relate actively and effectively with organizations within the international system and participate in the definition of their action agenda; and develop co-operative relations, projects, and networks among professionals and institutions in the region. Provides annual training to health professionals living in the Americas, who demonstrate leadership and interest in delving more deeply into the international dimensions of health.

Geographical Area of Activity: PAHO member states.

Address: Office of the Director of Programme Management, 525 23rd St, NW, Washington, DC 20037-2895, USA.

Telephone: (202) 974-3592; *Fax:* (202) 974-3612; *Internet:* www.paho.org/English /dpm/shd/hr/pfsiabout.htm.

PAN AMERICAN HEALTH AND EDUCATION FOUNDATION (PAHEF)

Established as a public non-profit foundation based in Washington, DC, dedicated to improving the health of the people of the Americas and advancing the fundamental objectives of the Pan American Health Organization; also aims to reduce the health disparities among and within the countries of the western hemisphere, and to promote philanthropy as a core social value.

Activities: The Foundation promotes health through the provision of grant support for public health projects, the training of physicians and allied health workers, the publication of medical textbooks, pharmacological bulletins and continuing education materials. Priority programmes are blood safety, children's health, intestinal worms and maternal health. Also makes five international, competitive awards to recognize excellence among public health professionals in Central and South America and the Caribbean, aiming to stimulate continuing improvement in public health in the region: the Abraham Horwitz Award for Leadership in Inter-American Health, the Clarence H. Moore Award for Voluntary Service, the Pedro Acha Award for Veterinary Health, the Fred L. Soper Award for Excellence in Health Literature, and the Manuel Velasco-Suarez Award in Bioethics.

Geographical Area of Activity: Central and South America.

Contact: Chair. Gustavo A. Arenas; Vice-Chair. Enrique Figueroa; Treas. Matthew McHugh; Sec. Arnold B. Simonse; Exec. Dir Jess Gersky.

Address: 525 23rd St, NW, Washington, DC 20037, USA.

Telephone: (202) 974-3399; *Fax:* (202) 775-4578; *Internet:* www.paho.org/eng /pahef; *e-mail:* pahef@paho.org.

RESEARCH CO-ORDINATION

Research Grants Program

The Program is a special fund administered by the Research Co-ordination department of the Pan American Health Organization (PAHO), through which it facilitates the process of generating knowledge in diverse fields of public health and collaborates in strengthening the research capacity of Central and South American and Caribbean countries.

Activities: Aims to promote and support the formulation and execution of research projects aiming to solve relevant public health problems and to seek knowledge and solutions to such problems in the Central and South America, and the Caribbean region. Also collaborates in research training and updating the knowledge and skills of researchers and scientists in public health fields, facilitates the dissemination and utilization of research findings in the formulation of policies and in the decision-making process regarding health issues. Operates two main programmes, Graduate Thesis Grants Program in Public Health and Research Training Grants in Public Health, and carries out Multi-centre Studies, involving comparative studies at the regional level that deal with relevant problems in public health in Central and South America in a collaborative effort among several academic and research centres under the auspices and technical co-operation of PAHO, and operates a regional-level initiative calling for research proposals on relevant themes in the public health field in Central and South America and the Caribbean promoting innovation and creativity among researchers in approaching new themes requiring a systematic research effort.

Geographical Area of Activity: Central and South America, and the Caribbean.

How to Apply: The website provides the following guide-lines: guide-lines for writing a research protocol, guide-lines for writing a progress report, guide-lines for writing the final report and abstract, template for summaries containing policy recommendations, and ethical guide-lines for research involving human subjects.

Address: 525 23rd St, NW, Washington, DC 20037, USA.

Telephone: (202) 974-3399; *Fax:* (202) 775-4578; *Internet:* www.paho.org/english /hdp/hdr/rpg/; *e-mail:* rgp@paho.org.

RESEARCH GRANT PROGRAM

Collaborative Research Program on Molecular Biology

The Collaborative Research Program on Molecular Biology with impact on Public Health problems in the Latin American Region, was established by the Pan American Health Organization in 2003. It is co-ordinated by three organizations; the International Centre for Genetic Engineering and Biotechnology (ICGEB), the Organización Panamericana de la Salud (OPS), and the Red Latinoamericana de Ciencias Biológicas (RELAB).

Activities: Supports collaborative research laboratories and research centres in Argentina, Brazil, Chile, Colombia, Costa Rica, Cuba, Mexico, Peru, Uruguay and Venezuela. In 2003 the first call for proposals concerned Molecular Biology of Viral Diseases and was open to projects addressing original scientific questions, particularly those providing practical applications to health problems, focusing on aspects of genomics and molecular biology of viruses and their infection of humans. Particular attention is given to collaboration between the applicant and laboratories at a lower level of development of infrastructure and research capacity.

Geographical Area of Activity: Argentina, Brazil, Chile, Colombia, Costa Rica, Cuba, Mexico, Peru, Uruguay and Venezuela.

Address: 525 23rd St, NW, Washington, DC 20037, USA.

Internet: www.paho.org/english/hdp/hdr/rpg/rgp.

Pan-European Federation for Heritage—Europa Nostra

Founded by a group of heritage NGOs, headed by Italia Nostra, in the Office of the Council of Europe in Paris in 1963; represents its members at European level and increases their visibility.

Activities: Activities include stimulating a large network of members and external partners; lobbying European, international, national and local authorities; organizing periodical public meetings (forums) on important topical themes on the subject of heritage; organizing an annual Awards Scheme (Europa Nostra Awards) which comprises three different elements: European recognition of personalities who distinguish themselves in the field of heritage (Medals of Honour); European recognition of exemplary restoration or enhancement works (Heritage Awards); and financial encouragement for the restoration of privately owned, threatened elements of the heritage (Restoration Fund Grant); developing and circulating position papers on the main initiatives from the European Institutions concerned with heritage, as well as reports on the results of the forums and other important topical heritage themes; organizing study tours for its members and exhibitions; and producing publications. Also administers the European Union Prize for Cultural Heritage (q.v.).

Geographical Area of Activity: Europe.

Financial Information: Funded by the fees and donations of its collective and individual members, the European Commission and other public bodies, and private sponsors.

Publications: Europa Nostra–The Cultural Heritage Review/La revue du patrimoine culturel (annual); *Bulletin Europa Nostra* (annual scientific review); *Nouvelles/News* (two a year); *Europa Nostra Awards Winners* (annual award scheme brochure); Annual Report.

Contact: Sec.-Gen. Sneska Quaedvlieg-Mihailovic.

Address: Lange Voorhout 35, 2514 EC The Hague, Netherlands.

Telephone: (70) 302-40-51; *Fax:* (70) 361-78-65; *Internet:* www.europanostra.org; *e-mail:* office@europanostra.org.

European Union Prize for Cultural Heritage

Launched in 2002 by the European Commission and co-ordinated by Europa Nostra as part of the European Union's (EU) Culture 2000 programme. Aims to promote high standards of conservation practice, stimulate the exchange of knowledge and experience throughout Europe and to encourage further efforts through the power of example.

Activities: The awards consist of six prizes of €10,000 each as well as the distribution of diplomas and medals in the following categories: an outstanding project in the field of architectural heritage, including the restoration or conservation of buildings, adaptation of buildings to new uses, building additions or alterations, or new building projects in conservation areas, cultural landscapes, including the conservation, enhancement, or adaptation to new uses, of historic gardens and parks, urban or town squares, larger areas of designed landscape, or areas of cultural or environmental importance, collections of works of art, including the conservation or enhancement of a collection of works of art of historic importance, which may include interpretive display for cultural or educational purposes, and archaeological sites, including the conservation or enhancement of an archaeological heritage site, which may include interpretive display for cultural or educational purposes; an outstanding study in the field of cultural heritage; and dedicated service to heritage conservation by individuals or groups.

Geographical Area of Activity: EU member states, candidate countries and members of the European Economic Area.

Contact: Co-ordinator Heritage Awards Laurie Neale.

Address: Lange Voorhout 35, 2514 EC The Hague, Netherlands.

Telephone: (70) 302-40-52; *Fax:* (70) 361-78-65; *Internet:* http://europa.eu.int /comm/regional_policy/index_en.htm; *e-mail:* ao@europanostra.org.

Regional Environmental Center for Central and Eastern Europe (REC)

Established in 1990 by the European Commission and the governments of Hungary and the USA to assist in solving environmental problems in Central and Eastern Europe; aims to promote co-operation among NGOs, governments, businesses and other environmental stakeholders, and by supporting the free exchange of information and public participation in environmental decision-making.

Activities: Also maintains country offices and field offices in 15 countries of Central and Eastern Europe.

Geographical Area of Activity: Central and Eastern Europe.

Financial Information: Total income €12,241,781 (2002).

Contact: Chair., Board Dirs Allan Gromov; Exec. Dir Marta Szigeti Bonifert.

Address: Ady Endre út 9-11, 2000 Szentendre, Hungary.

Telephone: (2) 650-4000; *Fax:* (2) 631-1294; *Internet:* www.rec.org; *e-mail:* info@rec .org.

Italian Trust Fund

Established in 2001 as a targeted contribution of the Italian Ministry for the Environment and Territory to the Regional Environmental Center for Central and Eastern Europe (REC, q.v.); operates within the framework of environmental improvement and co-operation in the countries of Central and Eastern Europe.

Activities: The Fund supports institutional capacity building of NGOs in Central and Eastern Europe, through grants to enhance and develop the management capability and leadership skills of NGO members, empower NGO members with an appreciation of environmental theories and concepts, support NGO activists in raising their personal levels of expertise, create and support an electronic communication network between environmental NGOs, and provide NGO members valuable exchange experience with the Italian NGO community. Also provides technical support, develops joint projects, supports workshops, seminars and training initiatives, and funds institutional strengthening activities in support of ministries of environment, and other environmental institutions and agencies.

Geographical Area of Activity: Central and Eastern Europe.

Contact: Trust Fund Co-ordinator Francesco Paolo Rizzo; Project Man. Lucia Brocato.

Address: Ady Endre út 9-11, 2000 Szentendre, Hungary.

Telephone: (2) 650-4011; *Fax:* (2) 631-1281; *Internet:* www.rec.org/rec/programs/itf /; *e-mail:* frizzo@rec.org.

250

Japan Special Fund

Established in 1993 as a mechanism through which the Japanese government supports the Regional Environmental Center for Central and Eastern Europe (REC) in its efforts to solve the environmental problems of the Central and Eastern European (CEE) region.

Activities: The Fund's priority areas in 2003 were support to the Kyoto Protocol, support to regional co-operative programmes, and technical support to countries in the CEE region. Provides support for: capacity building and public awareness-raising activities in CEE countries to encourage implementation of the Kyoto Protocol; regional and sub-regional cross-border projects in order to initiate international debate on waste management practices in the region and for the implementation of priority co-operative projects with a regional and sub-regional dimension; and operates technical support projects within the areas of regional policy-making, access to information, and public awareness raising.

Geographical Area of Activity: Central and Eastern Europe.

Contact: Project Asst Judit Balint.

Address: Ady Endre út 9-11, 2000 Szentendre, Hungary.

Telephone: (2) 650-4000 ext: 706; *Fax:* (2) 631-1294; *Internet:* www.rec.org/rec /programs/jsf/; *e-mail:* jbalint@rec.org.

Regional Environmental Centre for the Caucasus

NGO Support and Grant Programmes

The Centre's mission is to assist in solving environmental problems in the Caucasus region through the promotion of co-operation at national and regional level among NGOs, governments, businesses, local communities, and all other stakeholders, in order to develop a free exchange of information, in line with the principles of the Aarhus Convention; offer assistance to all environmental NGOs and other stakeholders; and increase public participation in the decision-making process, thereby assisting the states of the Caucasus in the further development of a democratic civil society.

Activities: The Centre provides support to environmental NGOs when and where it is needed the most, through regular grants initiatives and special grant rounds within particular themes. Also administers the Trans-boundary Grants Programme, funded by the Swiss Agency for Development and Co-operation, which makes grants to NGOs in the South Caucasus for development and implementation of co-operative projects targeted at solving regional environmental problems and the promotion of constructive co-operation in the field of environmental protection; operates a Small Grants Programme, providing financial assistance to NGOs to implement projects directed at solving specific environmental problems of local and/or national character; and conducts awareness-raising activities and implements specific actions to attract public attention to acute environmental concerns.

Geographical Area of Activity: Caucasus.

Financial Information: Total budget for the Trans-boundary Grants Programme US $250,000 (2002).

Contact: Chair. Board Dirs Samvel Amirkhanyan; Exec. Dir Nato Kirvalidze.

Address: 74 Chavchavadze Ave, Office 901, 0162 Tbilisi, Georgia.

Telephone: (32) 253649; *Fax:* (32) 253648; *Internet:* www.rec-caucasus.org; *e-mail:* armen.martirosyan@rec-caucasus.org.

Regional Environmental Centre for Central Asia (CAREC)

CAREC Grant Programme for Central Asian NGOs

CAREC is one of the institutions incorporated into the network of similar centres (RECs) established in Central and Eastern Europe and the Newly Independent States (Hungary, Russia, Georgia, Ukraine and Moldova). It was established under the decision of the Fourth Pan-European Conference (1998) in Aarhus, Denmark, on the initiative of the Central Asian states and began full operations in 2001. CAREC aims to develop co-operation among NGOs, governments, businesses, donors and other stakeholders for environment and sustainable development, and increase public participation in the environmental decision-making process, thereby assisting in the further development of civil society.

Activities: The Programme makes grants to NGO environmental projects and initiatives and individuals in Central Asia actively involved in the area of environmental protection and sustainable development, carrying out a range of activities, including promoting public participation in environmental protection and sustainable development activities; supporting environmental education and training, publishing activities and other regional information projects; resolving local environmental protection and sustainable development problems; designing and implementing trans-boundary partnership projects; encouraging public initiatives in developing a legal framework and ensuring transparency in managerial decision-making. Projects should improve inter-sector relations and environmental decision-making mechanisms, consolidate public organizations of the region, and affect the actions of the local population in terms of encouraging them to use natural resources in an efficient way. There are three types of grants available: trans-boundary grants allocated for project implementation by several NGOs representing at least two countries of the region; special/area-specific grants aimed at financing pressing regional problems in such areas as water conservation and energy efficiency; and small grants for financing urgent one-off projects, information dissemination, publications, and participation in activities and training projects. The Programme also operates training activities for the environmental community and carries out an annual survey of NGOs to assess their needs and to select prospective areas of activities for the following year.

Geographical Area of Activity: Central Asia.

Financial Information: The Programme is funded by the US Environmental Protection Agency; total grants US $140,702 (2002).

Contact: Exec. Dir Bulat Yessekin.

Address: 40 Orbita-1, 480043 Almaty, Kazakhstan.

Telephone: (3272) 296646; *Fax:* (3272) 705337; *Internet:* www.carec.kz; *e-mail:* carec@carec.kz.

Secretariat of the Pacific Community (SPC)

Cultural Affairs Programme

The Programme seeks to preserve and promote Pacific Island heritage for future generations of Pacific Islanders, including strengthening the Council of Pacific Arts as an institution, and providing assistance with the organization of the Festival of Pacific Arts.

Activities: The Programme works closely with the Council of Pacific Arts to identify priorities and implement activities for the preservation and promotion of cultural heritage in the Pacific region. The current Programme is guided by the Programme's Strategic Plan 2003–06, which is based on cultural priorities identified by the Council of Pacific Arts, favouring a project-based approach to cultural development.

Geographical Area of Activity: American Samoa, Cook Islands, Federated States of Micronesia, Fiji, French Polynesia, Guam, Kiribati, Marshall Islands, Nauru, New Caledonia, Niue, Northern Mariana Islands, Palau, Papua New Guinea, Pitcairn Island, Samoa, Solomon Islands, Tokelau, Tonga, Tuvalu, Vanuatu, and Wallis and Futuna Islands, and five founding countries: Australia, France, New Zealand, UK and USA.

Financial Information: Donors and project partners include the governments of France, Taiwan, New Caledonia and New Zealand, the Pacific Islands Forum Secretariat and UNESCO.

Address: BP D5, 98848, Nouméa Cedex, New Caledonia.

Telephone: 260142; *Fax:* 263818; *Internet:* www.spc.int/culture; *e-mail:* rhondag@spc.int.

HIV/AIDS AND SEXUALLY TRANSMITTED DISEASES (STDs) PROJECT

Small Grants

The overall aim of the HIV/AIDS and STDs Project is to strengthen the capacity of Pacific Island Countries and Territories (PICTs) to minimize the impact of HIV/AIDS and STDs.

Activities: Operates a small grants scheme for NGOs and community-based organizations in order to support innovative HIV/AIDS and STD community development projects.

Geographical Area of Activity: Pacific Island Countries and Territories.

Address: BP D5, 98848, Nouméa Cedex, New Caledonia.

Telephone: 260142; *Fax:* 263818; *Internet:* www.spc.int/aids/.

LIFESTYLE HEALTH SECTION

Small Grants Scheme

The Scheme aims to support the implementation of projects and activities, which can benefit the health and well-being of the local population.

Activities: The Scheme makes grants to governmental organizations and NGOs for projects promoting healthy lifestyles, including projects focusing on the promotion of lifestyle health to prevent non-communicable diseases (in particular, physical activity, good nutrition, less alcohol, and no smoking); community-level projects; projects that focus on community participation, advocacy and empowerment; pilot projects that have identified funding for continuation or expansion following successful completion of the pilot; and for attendance at regional meetings and training directly applicable to work activities.

Geographical Area of Activity: Pacific states.

Restrictions: No funding for equipment, staff salaries (except short-term consultancies), attendance at meetings outside the Secretariat of the Pacific Community (SPC) region (unless evidence can be given that content is directly relevant to work), or for prizes and cash rewards.

How to Apply: Application forms are available by contacting the Lifestyle Health Adviser; applications can be submitted at any time. Proposals must be submitted to the official SPC government contact with a copy of the proposal sent directly to the SPC Lifestyle Health Section for technical review and comments. A letter of support from the relevant ministry must also be submitted.

Financial Information: Maximum grant available approx. US $3,000.

Contact: Lifestyle Health Adviser Jimaima Schultz.

Address: BP D5, 98848, Nouméa Cedex, New Caledonia.

Telephone: 260142; *Fax:* 263818; *Internet:* www.spc.int/Lifestyle/; *e-mail:* jimaimas@spc.int.

PACIFIC YOUTH RESOURCES BUREAU

Small Islands States Fund

The Fund became operational in 1998; forms part of the Pacific Community's Pacific Youth Strategy 2005 (PYS 2005).

Activities: The Fund prioritizes skills training of young people in 12 Small Islands States: American Samoa, Cook Islands, Kiribati, Marshall Islands, Nauru, Niue, Northern Mariana Islands, Palau, Pitcairn Island, Tokelau, Tuvalu and Wallis and Futuna Islands. Supported training is for a variety of activities, including arts and crafts, trades, computers, small businesses, leadership and organizational skills, personal efficiency, and self-improvement skills. Youth Empowerment Funds have been established in each of the 12 participating countries to distribute funding.

Geographical Area of Activity: American Samoa, Cook Islands, Kiribati, Marshall Islands, Nauru, Niue, Northern Mariana Islands, Palau, Pitcairn Island, Tokelau, Tuvalu, and Wallis and Futuna Islands.

Financial Information: Launched with a £100,000 donation from the UK government.
Address: BP D5, 98848, Nouméa Cedex, New Caledonia.
Telephone: 260142; *Fax:* 263818; *Internet:* www.spc.int/youth.

Society for International Development (SID)

Founded in 1957 to promote social justice and foster democratic participation; the Society has 65 local chapters, 55 institutional and 3,000 individual members in 125 countries. The organization is funded by governments, international organizations and NGOs, including the World Health Organization (WHO), the World Food Programme (WFP), the Canadian International Development Agency (CIDA), the Rockefeller Foundation and the governments of Denmark, Finland and Italy.

Activities: Through locally driven international programmes and activities, SID strengthens collective empowerment and facilitates dialogue and knowledge sharing world-wide. In addressing issues from a multi-sectoral perspective, the Society emphasizes systemic and long-term approaches with a central focus on social and institutional transformation, carried out through collaborative initiatives with NGOs and other organizations.

Geographical Area of Activity: International.

Publications: Development (annual journal).

Contact: Man. Dir Stefano Prato.

Address: Via Panisperna 207, 00184 Rome, Italy.

Telephone: (06) 4872172; *Fax:* (06) 4872170; *Internet:* www.sidint.org; *e-mail:* info@sidint.org.

South Asia Co-operative Environment Programme

An intergovernmental organization, established in 1982 by the governments of South Asia to promote and support protection, management and enhancement of the environment in the region. The Articles of Association have been ratified by the governments of Afghanistan, Bangladesh, Bhutan, India, Maldives, Nepal, Pakistan and Sri Lanka.

Activities: The Programme promotes co-operative activities beneficial to member countries in priority areas of mutual interest, facilitates exchange of knowledge and expertise and provides local resources for implementation of priority activities while mobilizing maximum constructive and complementary support from donor countries and agencies. Also runs training courses, develops policy guide-lines and formulates sustainable development strategies, supports capacity building initiatives, and develops legal frameworks relevant to environmental considerations.

Geographical Area of Activity: South Asia.

Address: 10 Anderson Rd, Colombo 5, Sri Lanka.

Telephone: (1) 589787; *Fax:* (1) 589369; *Internet:* www.sacep.org; *e-mail:* info@sacep.org.

South Asian Association for Regional Co-operation (SAARC)

Promotion of People-to-People Linkages and SAARC Professional Associations

Part of SAARC's programme to enrich and supplement intergovernmental regional efforts through the encouragement of interaction across the South Asian region of professional bodies, the private corporate sector, civil society groups and creative artists to promote socio-economic and cultural development in South Asia.

Activities: As part of SAARC's efforts to promote socio-economic and cultural development in South Asia, grants formal recognition to a number of bodies including NGOs and civil society organizations. Organizations are formally recognized under two categories: SAARC Regional Apex Bodies, and SAARC Recognized Bodies.

Geographical Area of Activity: South Asia.

Contact: Sec.-Gen. Q. A. M. A. Rahim.

Address: POB 4222, Kathmandu, Nepal.

Internet: www.saarc-sec.org/.

SAARC–Japan Special Fund

Established pursuant to a Memorandum of Understanding in Kathmandu on 27 September 1993, to promote socio-economic development in the South Asian region.

Activities: The Fund operates through funding selected programmes and activities identified and managed by the member states, as well as financing programmes and activities identified and managed by the government of Japan. Support is provided for seminars, workshops and training programmes covering a variety of projects relating to agriculture and rural development, health-related issues, telecommunications, economic issues, science and technology, education, social issues and the role of the media.

Geographical Area of Activity: South Asia.

Financial Information: Funded by the government of Japan.

Contact: Sec.-Gen. Q. A. M. A. Rahim.

Address: POB 4222, Kathmandu, Nepal.

Internet: www.saarc-sec.org.

SAARC Chairs, Fellowships and Scholarships Scheme

Co-ordinated by the South Asian Association for Regional Co-operation (SAARC); aims to promote education in South Asia.

Activities: Set up to provide increased cross-fertilization of ideas through greater interaction among students, scholars and academics in the SAARC countries; awards fellowships and scholarships and funds chairs.

Geographical Area of Activity: South Asia.

Contact: Sec.-Gen. Q. A. M. A. Rahim.

Address: POB 4222, Kathmandu, Nepal.

Internet: www.saarc-sec.org.

SAARC Youth Awards Scheme (SYAS)

The Scheme was established by the South Asian Association for Regional Co-operation (SAARC) in 1996, to promote youth development in the South Asian region.

Activities: The Scheme aims to provide recognition to outstanding young talent and to encourage the overall development of youth in the South Asian region, through the provision of annual awards to young people who have excelled in their particular fields of activity. The awards are made on the basis of annual themes, including: Outstanding Social Service in Community Welfare, New Inventions and Discoveries, and Creative Photography: South Asian Diversity.

Geographical Area of Activity: South Asia.

Contact: Sec.-Gen. Q. A. M. A. Rahim.

Address: POB 4222, Kathmandu, Nepal.

Internet: www.saarc-sec.org/.

South Asian Development Fund

Established in 1996, through the merger of the SAARC Fund for Regional Projects (SFRP) and the SAARC Regional Fund (SRF); aims to support socio-economic development in the South Asian region.

Activities: Promotes socio-economic development in the South Asian region, through the provision of grants and funding for industrial development, poverty alleviation, protection of the environment, and balance-of-payments support and for the promotion of economic projects. Also supports feasibility studies, prior to full project funding.

Geographical Area of Activity: South Asia.

Financial Information: Capital approx. US $5,800,000.

Contact: Sec.-Gen. Q. A. M. A. Rahim.

Address: POB 4222, Kathmandu, Nepal.

Internet: www.saarc-sec.org.

TECHNICAL COMMITTEE ON AGRICULTURE AND RURAL DEVELOPMENT

SAARC Youth Volunteers Programme (SYVP)

Established by the South Asian Association for Regional Co-operation (SAARC) to promote youth volunteerism. The Programme is implemented by the Technical Committee on Agriculture and Rural Development.

Activities: The Programme aims to harness the idealism of youth for regional co-operation programmes and seeks to encourage young people to work in other countries in the field of agriculture, rural development and forestry extension work.

Geographical Area of Activity: South Asia.

Contact: Sec.-Gen. Q. A. M. A. Rahim.

Address: POB 4222, Kathmandu, Nepal.

Internet: www.saarc-sec.org/.

TECHNICAL COMMITTEE ON ENVIRONMENT, METEOROLOGY AND FORESTRY

SAARC Meteorological Awards

Established by the South Asian Association for Regional Co-operation (SAARC), following a recommendation for instituting an Annual Regional Award for Young Scientists made by the Working Group on Meteorology at its second meeting held in New Delhi in December 1982.

Activities: Promotes the development of young scientists and the encouragement of excellence in research analysis and outstanding publications in the meteorological fields, through awards. In 1997, instigated an Award for Senior Scientists. The award scheme is currently being reviewed by the Technical Committee on Environment, Meteorology and Forestry.

Geographical Area of Activity: South Asia.

Address: POB 4222, Kathmandu, Nepal.

Internet: www.saarc-sec.org/.

South Pacific Regional Environment Programme (SPREP)

A regional organization established by the governments and administrations of the Pacific region to protect the Pacific environment. It grew from a small programme attached to the South Pacific Commission (SPC) in the 1980s into the Pacific region's major intergovernmental organization charged with protecting and managing the environment and natural resources.

Activities: As of 2003, SPREP operates two programmes: Island Ecosystems and Pacific Futures. The Island Ecosystems programme aims to help Pacific Island Countries and territories (PICTs) manage island resources and ocean ecosystems in a sustainable manner and support life and livelihoods, through focusing on sustainably managing and conserving the terrestrial, coastal and marine ecosystems of Pacific islands, conserving priority threatened species and reducing the impact of alien, invasive species and living modified organisms. Under the programme, SPREP provides resource management advice, information and capacity-building advice, to support the development of community-based income generating enterprises based on sustainable resource use, as well as developing partnerships with other multinational organizations, national institutions and government agencies, NGOs, community groups and the private sector. The Pacific Futures programme aims to help PICTs plan and respond to threats and pressures on island and ocean systems, through supporting the formulation of sustainable development policies for improved environmental governance, and improving the understanding and strengthening the capacity of Pacific island countries and territories to respond to climate change, climate variability and sea level rise.

Geographical Area of Activity: South Pacific.

Address: POB 240, Apia, Samoa.

Internet: www.sprep.org.ws; *e-mail:* irc@sprep.org.ws.

UNITED NATIONS DEVELOPMENT PROGRAMME (UNDP)

International Water Partnership (IWP): IWP Pacific Regional Scholarship Scheme

A regional strategic action programme funded by the Global Environment Facility, implemented by the South Pacific Regional Environment Programme and executed by UNDP.

Activities: The IWP funds the development of pilot projects in the participating countries, in the fields of improved waste management, better water quality, sustainable fisheries, and effective marine protected areas. Through the Regional

Scholarship Scheme, awards are made to students in participating countries to fund postgraduate students interested in studying a technical issue related to the pilot project being implemented in their country..

Geographical Area of Activity: Cook Islands, Federated States of Micronesia, Fiji, Kiribati, Marshall Islands, Nauru, Niue, Palau, Papua New Guinea, Samoa, Solomon Islands, Tonga, Tuvalu and Vanuatu.

How to Apply: Application forms are available from IWP National Co-ordinator or can be downloaded from the SPREP website.

Financial Information: Total budget US $273,000.

Address: POB 240, Apia, Samoa.

Telephone: 21929; *Fax:* 24689; *Internet:* www.sprep.org/iwp; *e-mail:* iwp@sprep .org.ws.

Southeast Asian Ministers of Education Organization (SEAMEO)

Research Fellowships

Administered by the SEAMEO Secretariat.

Activities: A programme providing funding for fellowships to support researchers in South-East Asia, studying in specialist fields that best meet the needs of the South-East Asian region at that time. Annual fellowships include the SEAMEO–Jasper Fellowship, awarded for outstanding research conducted by SEAMEO member country nationals, in the area of Children and Youth Participation in Social Development within any of the following sub-themes: Environmental Protection; Preventing Risky Behaviour (Use of Information and Communications Technology); Promotion of Family and Child Development; and Community Development and Good Governance.

Geographical Area of Activity: SEAMO member countries: Brunei, Indonesia, Malaysia, Philippines, Singapore, Thailand and Vietnam.

Financial Information: Funded with a C $250,000 grant from the Canadian government.

Address: Mom Luang Pin Malakul Centenary Bldg, 920 Sukhumvit Rd, Bangkok 10110, Thailand.

Telephone: (2) 391-0144; *Fax:* (2) 381-2587; *Internet:* www.seameo.org/vl/library /dlwelcome/projects/jasper/general/jasper.htm; *e-mail:* secretariat@seameo.org.

Scholarships for Training and Education

Administered on behalf of SEAMEO member countries and the SEAMEO Network.

Activities: SEAMO administers a scholarship scheme providing financial assistance to SEAMEO member country nationals to complete their studies at SEAMEO centres, in a range of fields including tropical biology, educational innovation and technology, mathematics, science, English, higher education, agriculture, open learning and distance education, the arts, tropical medicine, and vocational and technical education. The scholarship may be applied to short-term courses, and for degree programmes leading to a Master's or Doctorate.

Geographical Area of Activity: SEAMO member countries: Brunei, Indonesia, Malaysia, Philippines, Singapore, Thailand and Vietnam.

How to Apply: Member country SEAMEO Affairs Officers are responsible for scholarship nomination.

Address: Mom Luang Pin Malakul Centenary Bldg, 920 Sukhumvit Rd, Bangkok 10110, Thailand.

Telephone: (2) 391-0144; *Fax:* (2) 381-2587; *Internet:* www.seameo.org /programmes/index.htm; *e-mail:* secretariat@seameo.org.

SEAMEO Educational Development Fund

Established to serve as the central repository of gifts for SEAMEO to help address developmental problems in South-East Asia.

Activities: Aims to meet education and training needs in Southeast Asia by funding special projects and programmes at SEAMEO centres, teacher and student exchange programmes and research directly related to regional economic development, Asian solutions to Asian problems, and the effective mobilization and utilization of resources, facilities and expertise in the region.

Geographical Area of Activity: SEAMO member countries: Brunei, Indonesia, Malaysia, Philippines, Singapore, Thailand and Vietnam.

Address: Mom Luang Pin Malakul Centenary Bldg, 920 Sukhumvit Rd, Bangkok 10110, Thailand.

Telephone: (2) 391-0144; *Fax:* (2) 381-2587; *Internet:* www.seameo.org /programmes/index.htm; *e-mail:* secretariat@seameo.org.

Union of the Baltic Cities

COMMISSION ON ENVIRONMENT SECRETARIAT

Baltic Cities Environmental Award

Aims to encourage the Baltic Sea region cities to develop their administration and services in innovative ways for the benefit of entire municipalities and their citizens.

Activities: An award of €5,000 is made every two years to a city or partnership that includes a city, that uses innovative practices to the benefit of its citizens and supports local environmental development. Themes for the award include air quality, biodiversity, energy, environmental health, and information and education.

Geographical Area of Activity: Baltic countries.

How to Apply: Submissions accepted by e-mail; details on how to apply are available on the website.

Financial Information: Award of €5,000 made every two years; funded by Per Aarsleff A/S.

Contact: Project Officer Anna Granberg.

Address: Linnankatu 41, 20100 Turku, Finland.

Telephone: (2) 2623169; *Fax:* (2) 2568613; *Internet:* www.ubc.net/commissions /environment.html; *e-mail:* anna.granberg@turku.fi.

SECRETARIAT OF THE UNION OF THE BALTIC CITIES COMMISSION ON SPORT

The Commission on Sport was established in September 1995 in order to create and promote contacts and relations among young people in the area of sport and physical education as well as to spread information about Union activities.

Activities: Carries out co-operative activities with sports organizations in the Baltic region for projects promoting youth and adult participation in sport, as well as people with disabilities. Also organizes a range of multilateral sporting activities, including international tournaments and competitions, and awards an annual Equal Opportunities Prize, focusing on activities undertaken to achieve equal rights for people with disabilities and support their full integration into society.

Geographical Area of Activity: Baltic states.

Address: Urzad Miasta Gdyni (RWZ), Al. Pilsudskiego 52/54, 81–382 Gdynia, Poland.

Telephone: (58) 6688208; *Fax:* (58) 6218620; *Internet:* www2.ubc.net/commissions /sport.html#projects supported; *e-mail:* ubcsport@gdynia.pl.

United Nations

BETTER WORLD FUND

Better World Campaign

A project of the Better World Fund, which was created with initial support from businessman and philanthropist R. E. Turner as part of his US $1,000,000,000 gift to support UN causes, which also included the establishment of the UN Foundation (q.v.). The Campaign is a bi-partisan, non-profit education and outreach effort dedicated to enhancing awareness of and appreciation for the vital role the UN plays around the world. In particular, the Campaign works to highlight the UN's work to strengthen international security through multilateral co-operation.

Activities: Campaigns to increase understanding of the UN system, how it operates and its significance for ensuring global security through multilateral co-operation initiatives; lobbies the US government on increasing UN involvement, and conducts public education and outreach work.

Geographical Area of Activity: International.

Contact: Exec. Dir Phyllis Cuttino.

Address: 1225 Connecticut Ave, NW, 4th Floor, Washington, DC 20036-1868, USA.

Telephone: (202) 462-4900; *Fax:* (202) 462-2686; *Internet:* www.betterworldfund .org.

DEPARTMENT OF PUBLIC INFORMATION

NGO Section

Serves as the liaison between the Department of Public Information (DPI) and NGOs associated with DPI. These organizations disseminate information about the UN to their constituency, building knowledge of and support for the UN at the grassroots level. In 2003 approximately 1,600 NGOs from all regions of the world were associated with DPI.

Activities: The NGO section of the DPI provides associated NGOs with a number of services: organizes, in collaboration with the NGO/DPI Executive Committee, the Annual DPI/NGO Conference; organizes weekly briefings on UN-related issues; conducts an annual orientation programme for newly accredited NGO representatives; organizes quarterly communications workshops; and maintains the NGO Resource Center which offers access to current UN documents, press releases, DPI and UN system publications, a video lending library with a collection of UN system videos, monthly mailings of UN information materials to associated NGOs, processes UN passes for NGO representatives, and processes NGO applications for associative status with DPI. The section also publishes the Directory of NGOs associated with DPI, which is available on-line.

Geographical Area of Activity: International.

Contact: DPI/NGO Section Head Paul Hoeffel.

Address: Room S-1070L, UN Plaza, New York, NY 10017, USA.

Telephone: (212) 963-6842; *Fax:* (212) 963-6914; *Internet:* www.un.org/dpi/ngosection/; *e-mail:* dpingo@un.org.

DIVISION FOR SOCIAL POLICY AND DEVELOPMENT—DEPARTMENT OF ECONOMIC AND SOCIAL AFFAIRS

UN Enable

The focal point within the UN system on matters relating to disability, as well as for activities connected to global social development in relation to youth, older persons and the family.

Activities: The Division's programme on Disabled Persons deals with promoting, monitoring and evaluating the implementation of the World Programme of Action and the Standard Rules. In addition, it prepares publications and acts as a clearing-house for information on disability issues; promotes national, regional and international programmes and activities; provides funding to governments and NGOs; and gives support to technical co-operation projects and activities. Also organizes or collaborates in international expert meetings on disability matters. Co-ordinates the UN Voluntary Fund on Disability, UN Youth Fund, UN Trust Fund for Family Activities and UN Trust Fund for Ageing (qq.v.).

Geographical Area of Activity: International.

Address: UN Secretariat, 2 UN Plaza, DC2-1372, New York, NY 10017, USA.

Fax: (212) 963-0111; *Internet:* www.un.org/esa/socdev/enable/.

UN Enable: United Nations Trust Fund for Ageing

Established pursuant to guidance received from the UN General Assembly, to further implementation of the development objectives of international instruments in the social field, with attention given to the needs of ageing people.

Activities: The Fund provides seed grants to governments and NGOs to support catalytic and innovative action in the field of ageing at national, regional and global levels, to develop and test activities which are not yet part of an established programme framework or to reinforce the social perspective in mainstream development. Support is given to pilot projects or activities that form part of a larger development initiative that aim at building national capacities and institutional capabilities to improve livelihood and well-being among ageing people in developing countries; communications support and public information activities that aim to build greater awareness and understanding of the situation of ageing people in overall development; applied research, review and assessment of issues and trends, and evaluation of development strategies and policies from the social perspective; and training and advisory services concerned with analysis, formulation and evaluation of integrated strategies, policies and programmes from the social perspective. Special attention is given to requests for assistance submitted by the least-developed and related categories of developing countries for which special assistance measures have been identified by the international community.

Geographical Area of Activity: International.

How to Apply: NGOs wishing to apply to the Fund first need to obtain the concurrence/non-objection of the concerned governmental officials in their country prior to submitting a request for assistance. NGOs can consult with the local office of the United Nations Development Programme (UNDP) about procedures for obtaining an endorsement/non-objection statement of concerned governmental authorities.

Financial Information: Grants range from approx. US $5,000 to US $20,000.

Address: UN Secretariat, 2 UN Plaza, DC2-1372, New York, NY 10017, USA.

Fax: (212) 963-0111; *Internet:* www.un.org/esa/socdev/enable/spdproj.htm.

UN Enable: United Nations Trust Fund for Family Activities

Established pursuant to guidance received from the UN General Assembly, to further implementation of the development objectives of international instruments in the social field, with attention given to the needs of families.

Activities: The Fund provides seed grants to governments and NGOs to support catalytic and innovative action in the field of family activities at national, regional and global levels, to develop and test activities which are not yet part of an established programme framework or to reinforce the social perspective in mainstream development. Support is given to pilot projects or activities that form part of a larger development initiative that aim at building national capacities and institutional capabilities to improve livelihood and well-being among families in developing countries; communications support and public information activities that aim to build greater awareness and understanding of the situation of families in overall development; applied research, reviews and assessment of issues and trends, and evaluation of development strategies and policies from the social perspective; and training and advisory services concerned with analysis, formulation and evaluation of integrated strategies, policies and programmes from the social perspective. Special attention is given to requests for assistance submitted by the least-developed and related categories of developing countries for which special assistance measures have been identified by the international community.

Geographical Area of Activity: International.

How to Apply: NGOs wishing to apply to the Fund first need to obtain the concurrence/non-objection of the concerned governmental officials in their country prior to submitting a request for assistance. NGOs can consult with the local office of the United Nations Development Programme (UNDP) about procedures for obtaining an endorsement/non-objection statement of concerned governmental authorities.

Financial Information: Grants range from approx. US $5,000 to US $20,000.

Address: UN Secretariat, 2 UN Plaza, DC2-1372, New York, NY 10017, USA.

Fax: (212) 963-0111; *Internet:* www.un.org/esa/socdev/enable/spdproj.htm.

UN Enable: United Nations Voluntary Fund on Disability

Established pursuant to General Assembly Resolution 32/133, in connection with preparations for the 1981 International Year of Disabled Persons. The General Assembly decided in its Resolution 40/31 that the Fund would be renamed the Voluntary Fund for the UN Decade of Disabled Persons (1983–92), and that its resources would support catalytic and innovative action to implement further the World Programme of Action concerning Disabled Persons. By its Resolution 47/88, the General Assembly decided that the Fund would continue in the period beyond the Decade as the UN Voluntary Fund on Disability, and that its terms of reference would include support for action to achieve the target of a Society for All by the year 2010, as endorsed by the General Assembly in its Resolution 45/91.

Activities: The Fund operates by providing seed grants to support catalytic and innovative action in the social field, to develop and test activities which are not yet part of an established programme framework or to reinforce the social perspective in mainstream development. Grants from the Fund support activities by governments and NGOs at national, regional and global levels that: promote greater awareness of disability issues and exchanges of knowledge and experience; build national capacities and institutional capabilities for integrated policies and programmes in the disability field and for national disability legislation; improve data collection, applied research and evaluation; facilitate pilot efforts; and promote wide dissemination of appropriate disability technologies.

Geographical Area of Activity: International.

How to Apply: NGOs wishing to apply to the Fund first need to obtain the concurrence/non-objection of the concerned governmental officials in their country prior to submitting a request for assistance. NGOs can consult with the local office of the United Nations Development Programme (UNDP) about procedures for obtaining an endorsement/non-objection statement of concerned governmental authorities.

Financial Information: Grants range from approx. US $5,000 to US $20,000.

Address: UN Secretariat, 2 UN Plaza, DC2-1372, New York, NY 10017, USA.

Fax: (212) 963-0111; *Internet:* www.un.org/esa/socdev/enable/disunvf.htm.

UN Enable: United Nations Youth Fund

Established pursuant to guidance received from the UN General Assembly, to further implementation of the development objectives of international instruments in the field of young people.

Activities: The Fund provides seed grants to governments and NGOs to support catalytic and innovative action in the field of youth at national regional and global levels, to develop and test activities which are not yet part of an established programme framework or to reinforce the social perspective in mainstream development. Support is given to pilot projects or activities that form part of a larger development initiative that aim at building national capacities and institutional capabilities to improve livelihood and well-being among young people in developing countries; communications support and public information activities that aim to build greater awareness and understanding of the situation of young people in overall development; applied research, reviews and assessment of issues and trends, and evaluation of development strategies and policies from the social perspective; and training and advisory services concerned with analysis, formulation and evaluation of integrated strategies, policies and programmes from the social perspective. Special attention is given to requests for assistance submitted by the least-developed and related categories of developing countries for which special assistance measures have been identified by the international community.

Geographical Area of Activity: International.

How to Apply: NGOs wishing to apply to the Fund first need to obtain the concurrence/non-objection of the concerned governmental officials in their country prior to submitting a request for assistance. NGOs can consult with the local office of the United Nations Development Programme about procedures for obtaining an endorsement/non-objection statement of concerned governmental authorities.

Financial Information: Grants range from approx. US $5,000 to US $20,000.

Address: UN Secretariat, 2 UN Plaza, DC2-1372, New York, NY 10017, USA.

Fax: (212) 963-0111; *Internet:* www.un.org/esa/socdev/enable/spdproj.htm.

DIVISION ON SUSTAINABLE DEVELOPMENT

The substantive secretariat responsible for servicing the Commission on Sustainable Development; for follow-up of the implementation of Agenda 21 as well as the Plan of Implementation (POI) of the World Summit on Sustainable Development.

Activities: The Division aims to: provide leadership and an authoritative source of expertise for governments, the UN system, other international organizations and civil society with regard to the promotion of sustainable development and the implementation of the Johannesburg Plan of Implementation and Agenda 21; promote an integrated, cross-sectoral and broadly participatory approach to sustainable development and its implementation at the local, national, regional and global levels; facilitate intergovernmental decision-making through the provision of substantive support to the work of the Commission on Sustainable Development, and other related bodies; provide technical advice and assistance to governments in support of sustainable development; promote inter-agency and inter-organizational strategies; promote and facilitate exchange and sharing of information; and catalyze joint activities with UN agencies, other international organizations and civil society groups in support of sustainable development; and promote an active and continuous dialogue with governments, civil society and other international organizations aimed at building partnerships to solve key issues and problems related to sustainable development.

Geographical Area of Activity: International.

Contact: Dir JoAnne DiSano.

Address: Dept of Economic and Social Affairs, 2 UN Plaza, Room DC2-2220, New York, NY 10017, USA.

Telephone: (212) 963-2803; *Fax:* (212) 963-4260; *Internet:* www.un.org/esa/sustdev /index.html; *e-mail:* dsd@un.org.

ECONOMIC AND SOCIAL COUNCIL (ECOSOC)

Economic and Social Commission for Western Asia (ESCWA)

The Economic Commission for Western Asia (ECWA) was established by Economic and Social Council Resolution 1818 (LV) of 9 August 1973 as the successor to the United Nations Economic and Social Office in Beirut (UNESOB). In 1985 the Commission was redesignated the Economic and Social Commission for Western Asia (ESCWA), in accordance with Economic and Social Council Resolution 1985/69 of 26 July 1985, in order to acknowledge more fully the social aspect of the Commission's activities. One of the five regional commissions which report to ECOSOC; the other regional commissions are: the Economic Commission for Europe (ECE, q.v.), the Economic and Social Commission for Asia and the Pacific (ESCAP), the Economic Commission for Latin America and the Caribbean (ECLAC) and the Economic Commission for Africa (ECA). ESCWA carries out its work at the Western Asia regional level.

Activities: ESCWA's work centres on the preparation of economic and social studies and reports, convening meetings and conducting training workshops, as well as a number of field projects implemented through five divisions: Globalization and Regional Integration Division; Social Development Division; Sustainable Development and Productivity Division; Information and Communications Technology Division; and the Economic Analysis Division.

Geographical Area of Activity: Western Asia.

Contact: Exec. Sec. Mervat Tallawy; Deputy Exec. Sec. Mariam Al-Awadhi; Sec. of Commission Huda Osseiran; Special Asst to the Exec. Sec. Ahmad Nada.

Address: POB 11-8575, Riad el-Solh Sq., Beirut, Lebanon.

Telephone: (1) 981301; *Fax:* (1) 981510; *Internet:* www.escwa.org.lb/about/main.htm; *e-mail:* webmaster-ecswa@un.org.

Economic and Social Commission for Western Asia (ESCWA): Human Development Policies Team: Human Development Policies Work Programme

The Human Development Policies Team aims to review and analyze member countries' social policies and help them formulate, plan and implement integrated policies that coincide with ongoing global developments. The Team also aims to achieve a balance between interrelated thematic issues, such as governance, gender, poverty and unemployment and population dynamics to promote community and human resource development.

Activities: The Team's Work Programme focuses on fostering accountable governance, promoting strategies for participatory development and greater popular involvement in decision-making on social policies. It also takes into consideration the impact of macroeconomic variables and sectoral policies on the social dimension of development, particularly on social welfare. Operates community development projects aimed at building up the participation of all sectors of the community, including women, young people, elderly people and local community leaders, and funds field projects on the capacity building of NGOs and vocational training.

Geographical Area of Activity: Western Asia.

Contact: Team Leader Walid Hilal.

Address: POB 11-8575, Riad es-Solh Sq., Beirut, Lebanon.

Telephone: (1) 981301 ext: 1406; *Fax:* (1) 981510; *Internet:* www.escwa.org.lb /divisions/sdd/human.html; *e-mail:* hilalw@un.org.

Economic and Social Commission for Western Asia (ESCWA): Urban Development and Housing Policies

Aims to enhance urban planning and management practices by taking into consideration the physical and social factors in the development of cities and villages of the region, especially in conflict-stricken areas, and assisting member states to achieve environmentally sustainable and socially inclusive human settlements, and empower youth and people with disabilities. The team addresses good urban governance by emphasizing the participatory approach in housing and urban development, encouraging networking and links between governments, local authorities and civil society institutions, including the private sector. Special emphasis is placed on a field-oriented approach through the implementation of operational projects and activities, especially designing modalities and devising pilot solutions for socially integrating young people and people with disabilities, and for community development in post-conflict areas.

Activities: Operates programmes and supports pilot projects in conjunction with NGOs and other organizations, designed to achieve environmentally sustainable and socially inclusive human settlements, and empower youth and people with disabilities. Activities include: a micro-credit scheme operated in partnership with the Audi Bank and the Association d'Aide au Développement Rural, targeting new entrepreneurs in disadvantaged communities in South Lebanon; the Economic Assistance for South Lebanon programme, a pilot project to promote local community development; and promoting vocational skills training. Also undertaking the Youth NGO Directory–Network in the Arab Region programme, which aims to strengthen the capacity of Arab youth NGOs, through the provision of information on issues relevant to youth NGOs in the region, including education, employment, health, capacity building, youth policies, young women, environment, human rights and juvenile delinquency.

Geographical Area of Activity: Western Asia.

Publications: Reports and brochures.

Contact: Team Leader Riadh Tappuni.

Address: POB 11-8575, Beirut, Lebanon.

Telephone: (1) 981301 ext: 1400; *Fax:* (1) 981510; *Internet:* www.escwa.org.lb /divisions/sdd/urban.html; *e-mail:* tappuni@un.org.

NGO Section (Division for Social Policy and Development—DESA)

The Committee on Non-Governmental Organizations is a standing committee of the Economic and Social Council (ECOSOC), established by Council Resolution 3 (II) on 21 June 1946. The Committee's mandate is set out in ECOSOC Resolution 1996/31. In 2003 approximately 2,300 NGOs had consultative status.

Activities: The Committee's membership consists of 19 countries: five members from African states; four members from Asian states; two members from Eastern

European states; four members from Central and South American and Caribbean states; and four members from Western European and other states. Its main tasks are: the consideration of applications for consultative status and requests for reclassification submitted by NGOs; the consideration of quadrennial reports submitted by NGOs in General and Special categories; the implementation of the provisions of Council Resolution 1996/31 and the monitoring of the consultative relationship; and any other issues which ECOSOC may request the Committee to consider.

Geographical Area of Activity: International.

How to Apply: To begin the process of applying for consultative status, organizations must submit a letter of intent to the NGO Section of DESA, also known as the Secretariat. The letter should be on the organization's letterhead and signed by its secretary-general or president.

Contact: Section Chief Hanifa Mezoui.

Address: 1 UN Plaza, Room DC1-1480, New York, NY 10017, USA.

Telephone: (212) 963-8652; *Fax:* (212) 963-9248; *Internet:* www.un.org/esa /coordination/ngo/; *e-mail:* desangosection@un.org.

FOOD AND AGRICULTURE ORGANIZATION (FAO)

Founded by the UN in 1945 with a mandate to raise levels of nutrition and standards of living, to improve agricultural productivity, and to better the condition of rural populations. It is now one of the largest specialized agencies in the UN system and the lead agency for agriculture, forestry, fisheries and rural development. An intergovernmental organization, FAO has 183 member countries plus one member organization, the European Community.

Activities: Co-operates with the following types of NGO: farmers' and consumers' associations, co-operatives, credit unions, and women's groups world-wide which are involved in humanitarian and advocacy work. FAO works in partnership with organizations to provide direct assistance to countries so that sustainable food production can occur to improve the lives of the poor.

Geographical Area of Activity: World-wide, with particular emphasis on less-developed countries.

Contact: NGO Programme Officer N. McKeon.

Address: Viale delle Terme di Caracalla, 00100 Rome, Italy.

Telephone: (06) 57051; *Fax:* (06) 57053152; *Internet:* www.fao.org.

Popular Coalition to Eradicate Hunger and Poverty

Established in 1995; a UN–NGO initiative which was the outcome of the Conference on Hunger and Poverty convened by the International Fund for Agricultural Development (IFAD) in November 1995 in Brussels. The conference emphasized the urgent need for policies and programmes to address the lack of access by the rural poor to productive resources, their insufficient participation in decisions that affect their daily lives and the need for reforms in macroeconomic policies that adversely affect them. The Coalition is a global consortium of intergovernmental, civil society and bilateral organizations committed to the empowerment of the rural poor by increasing their access to productive assets, especially land, water and common property resources, and by increasing their direct participation in decision-making processes at the local, national, regional and international levels.

Activities: The Coalition operates by testing innovations to strengthen participation, and replicating successful community-based initiatives in order to enhance the impact of national programmes to eradicate hunger and poverty. Seven civil society organizations plus five intergovernmental organizations comprise the 12-member Popular Coalition Steering Committee. The civil society representatives are selected by their regional peers to achieve balance among eastern and southern Africa; western and central Africa; northern Africa and the Near East; southern and south-eastern Asia and the Pacific; Central and South America and the Caribbean; the Organisation for Economic Co-operation and Development (OECD) countries and northern partners. The intergovernmental organizations are the European Commission, the FAO, the International Fund for Agricultural Development (IFAD), the International Bank for Reconstruction and Development (IBRD—World Bank) and the World Food Programme. The programme of work is undertaken by geographical nodes that provide a decentralized means for participation and grassroots operation. In 2003 there were 23 national and eight regional nodes. The Coalition has established a Community Empowerment Facility (CEF) to support capacity-building activities that assist communities in gaining and protecting their access to land and other productive resources. The CEF is demand-driven and provides grants and support to community-based activities related to the following goals and objectives: increasing the ability of the poor, especially women and indigenous peoples, to gain secure access to land, including common property, water and associated resources; protecting existing access to lands being cultivated by landless workers or peasants, and settling tenancy rights; improving community participation in policy dialogue and local governance; strengthening agrarian institutions in such activities as the delineation and protection of user rights, land registration and contracts regulating land sales and leases; improving the capacity of rural people's organizations to access support services, including extension programmes, technology, inputs, credit and marketing; facilitating conflict-resolution processes; and building on traditional organizations and practices, replicating and scaling-up successful experiences, and disseminating best practices and lessons learned. The Coalition has also established the Agrarian Reform Network (ARnet), an agrarian reform knowledge network, and a forum on emerging land tenure markets to analyze the effects of land privatization on poor producers and the shift towards land policies grounded in the market, including land-leasing, sharecropping and contract farming.

Geographical Area of Activity: Developing countries.

Address: Via del Serafico 107, 00142 Rome, Italy.

Telephone: (06) 54591; *Fax:* (06) 5043463; *Internet:* www.ifad.org; *e-mail:* ifad@ifad.org.

Special Programme for Food Security

The FAO Programme aims to help those living in developing countries, in particular the low-income food deficit countries (LIFDCs) to improve their food security through rapid increases in food production and productivity, by reducing year-to-year variability in food production on an economically and environ-mentally sustainable basis and by improving people's access to food, in line with the 1996 World Food Summit Plan of Action.

Activities: The Programme is carried out in two phases: Phase 1, in which farmers and other local personnel are trained and provided with seeds, tools and the equipment that they need to enhance production through water control, intensification of crop production systems, diversification of production systems and constraints analysis and resolution; and Phase 2, which builds on the successes of Phase 1 and seeks to create suitable conditions for large-scale replication of successful approaches, through the development of programmes for food security and agricultural policy reform, an agricultural investment programme and feasibility studies of bankable projects. Also provides experts as part of its South–South Co-operation initiative.

Geographical Area of Activity: Developing countries.

Address: Viale delle Terme di Caracalla, 00100 Rome, Italy.

Internet: www.fao.org/spfs; *e-mail:* spfs@fao.org.

Technical Co-operation Department: Unit for Co-operation with Private Sector and NGOs

The Unit has overall responsibility for FAO's co-operation with NGOs and civil society organizations.

Activities: Works in close co-operation with a network of NGO/CSO focal points in the technical divisions and Regional Offices of FAO to formulate policy and operational guide-lines on co-operation with civil society, following evolutions in civil society co-operation and exchanging information on best practices with other UN agencies; promotes networking and the exchange of information among FAO units at headquarters and in the field; develops information/documentation exchange and dialogue with CSOs; has established a database on CSOs and monitors the implementation of FAO's NGO/CSO strategy; and promotes innovative co-operation activities and the assessment and diffusion of best practices and experiences. Also develops information projects in collaboration with regional or sectoral NGOs and NGO networks.

Geographical Area of Activity: World-wide, with particular emphasis on less-developed countries.

Publications: FAO policy and strategy for co-operation with non-governmental and civil society organizations.

Contact: NGO Programme Officer N. McKeon.

Address: Viale delle Terme di Caracalla, 00100 Rome, Italy.

Telephone: (06) 57051; *Fax:* (06) 57053152; *Internet:* www.fao.org; *e-mail:* tcdn-ngos-csos@fao.org.

Telefood: Food for All

Launched in 1997 by FAO; a campaign of concerts, sporting events and other activities to harness the power of media, celebrities and concerned citizens to help fight hunger.

Activities: Money raised through the scheme is used to fund small-scale sustainable projects that help small farmers produce more food for their families and communities, throughout Africa, Asia and the Pacific, Europe, Central and South America and the Caribbean, Near East, North America, and the South-West Pacific. Supported projects include school gardens, crop production, food processing and production, irrigation, and initiatives focusing on increasing women's access to food and methods of production.

Geographical Area of Activity: Africa, Asia and the Pacific, Europe, Central and South America and the Caribbean, Middle East, North America and the South-West Pacific.

How to Apply: Guide-lines available to download on the website.

Financial Information: Approx. US $10,000,000 raised since 1997.

Address: Viale delle Terme di Caracalla, 00100 Rome, Italy.

Internet: www.fao.org; *e-mail:* telefood@fao.org.

GLOBAL ENVIRONMENT FACILITY (GEF)

The GEF was established to promote international co-operation and finance actions to address six critical threats to the global environment: biodiversity loss, climate change, degradation of international waters, ozone depletion, land degradation, and persistent organic pollutants (POPs). It brings together 175 member governments, working in partnership with the private sector, NGOs, and international institutions to address complex environmental issues while supporting national sustainable development initiatives. The Facility's programmes are implemented by three agencies: the United Nations Development Programme (UNDP), the United Nations Environment Programme (UNEP), and the International Bank for Reconstruction and Development (IBRD—World Bank).

Activities: GEF funds projects in six focal areas: biodiversity, climate change, international waters, ozone, land degradation, and persistent organic pollutants, with a variety of project types, ranging from its Small Grants Programme (q.v.) and project preparation grants to Medium-Sized Projects (MSPs) and Full-Sized Projects (qq.v.), and Enabling Activities.

Geographical Area of Activity: International.

Contact: Chief Exec. and Chair. Len Good.

Address: GEF Secretariat, 1818 H St, NW, Washington, DC 20433, USA.

Telephone: (202) 473-0508; *Fax:* (202) 522-3240; *Internet:* www.gefweb.org; *e-mail:* secretariat@thegef.org.

Full-Sized Projects

One of the funding programmes of the Global Environment Facility (GEF).

Activities: The GEF works with the operational focal point in each recipient country to develop project ideas that are consistent both with the country's national programmes and priorities and with GEF's operational strategy and programmes. Regional or global programmes and projects may be developed in all countries that endorse the proposed activity and grants are attributed accordingly.

Geographical Area of Activity: International.

Address: GEF Secretariat, 1818 H St, NW, Washington, DC 20433, USA.

Telephone: (202) 473-1000; *Fax:* (202) 477-6391; *Internet:* www.worldbank.org/gef.

GEF Small Grants Programme (SGP)

Established in 1992, the year of the Rio Earth Summit, the Global Environment Facility (GEF) SGP is funded by the GEF, implemented by the United Nations Development Programme (UNDP) and executed by the United Nations Office for Project Services (UNOPS). Aims to support community projects in developing countries that conserve and restore the natural world while enhancing well-being and livelihoods, based on the premise that people will be empowered to protect their environment when they are organized to take action, have a measure of control over access to the natural resource base, have the necessary information and knowledge, and believe that their social and economic well-being is dependent on sound long-term resource management.

Activities: The Programme makes grants and provides technical assistance to community organizations and NGOs in Africa, Asia and the Pacific, Europe, the Middle East, and Central and South America and the Caribbean, to projects that: demonstrate community-level strategies and technologies that could reduce threats to the global environment if they are replicated over time; draw lessons from community-level experience, and support the spread of successful community-level strategies and innovations among CBOs and NGOs, host governments, development aid agencies, the GEF, and others working on a larger scale; and build partnerships and networks of local stakeholders to support and strengthen community, CBO, and NGO capacity to address environmental problems and promote sustainable development. The focal areas are community-level action in the fields of biodiversity, climate change, and international waters; projects that address land degradation issues, primarily concerning desertification and deforestation, can be supported if they relate to one or more of these focal areas. The Programme provides community-based assessment and planning grants, typically no more than US $2,000, to support pre-project participatory assessment and planning activities designed to strengthen community participation in project identification and development; supports pilot demonstration activities that test and demonstrate the viability of innovative community-level approaches to global environmental problems; makes capacity development grants, although most demonstration projects include capacity development grants for targeted technical assistance and training activities which focus on developing CBO and NGO capacities in the GEF focal areas; provides funds to intermediary NGOs and research centres, including universities, to support programme monitoring, to help identify, assess, and document best practices, and to prepare case studies of UNDP/GEF/SGP-supported projects; and promotes dissemination, networking, and policy dialogue aimed at promoting a supportive policy environment for community-level action in the GEF focal areas. A total of 63 countries from Africa, Asia and the Pacific, Europe, Middle East, Central and South America, and the Caribbean, currently participate in the Programme, and there are 53 country offices. The Programme also aims to raise public awareness, build partnerships, and promote policy dialogue, to help create a more supportive environment within countries for achieving sustainable development and addressing global environment issues.

Geographical Area of Activity: Africa, Asia and the Pacific, Europe, Middle East, Central and South America and the Caribbean.

How to Apply: Applications are made directly to GEF national co-ordinators or directly to the Head Office in New York. Initially the project proponent contacts the SGP national co-ordinator to receive project application guide-lines and forms; with assistance from the national co-ordinator and using the standard SGP format, the proponent prepares a brief project concept paper and submits this to the co-ordinator; the national co-ordinator reviews and pre-screens the concept paper according to GEF criteria and criteria adopted by the NSC for activities in that country. If the project is judged eligible, the project proponent prepares a project proposal; in some cases, this step may be supported by a planning grant; completed project proposals are then submitted by the national co-ordinator or the NSC; and the NSC reviews the proposal and either accepts it, rejects it, or returns it to the proposer with a request that further work be done on formulating and refining the project data. Approved proposals enter the national UNDP/GEF–SGP work programme. UNDP/GEF–SGP grants are usually paid in three installments: an up-front payment to initiate the project; a mid-term payment upon receipt of a satisfactory progress report; and a final payment on receipt of a satisfactory project completion and final report.

Financial Information: Funded by 600 organizations world-wide, including the UN Foundation, the European Commission and the government of the Netherlands; the Programme is mandated to raise project co-financing that matches GEF funds. Total grants to date: US $183,001,000.

Contact: Global Man. Delfin Ganapin; Deputy Global Man. Carmen Tavera.

Address: 304 East 45th St, FF-1610, New York NY10017, USA.

Telephone: (501) 822-2688; *Fax:* (501) 822-3364; *Internet:* www.undp.org/sgp; *e-mail:* gefsgp@cabtl.net.

Medium-Sized Projects (GEF MSP)

The MSP scheme of the GEF helps developing countries fund projects and programmes that protect the global environment. Established in 1991, the GEF is the designated financial mechanism for international agreements on biodiversity, climate change, and persistent organic pollutants. The GEF also supports projects that combat desertification and protect international waters and the ozone layer.

Activities: Provides grants of up to US $1,000,000 to NGOs, civil society organizations, governments, academic institutions and private-sector organizations who operate in the GEF priority areas of biological diversity, climate change, international waters and depletion of the ozone layer. Project preparation grants of up to US $25,000 are also available for the development of a medium-sized project.

Geographical Area of Activity: International.

How to Apply: Organizations must develop and submit a project concept paper for preliminary review by one of the three implementing agencies (World Bank, United Nations Development Programme—UNDP or United Nations Environment Programme—UNEP); the GEF focal point in each eligible country must endorse the MSP at the time of approval. Information Kit Supplements for MSP Proposers Working with the World Bank, on the GEF website, provide details on application procedures.

Financial Information: Grants for up to US $1,000,000.

Address: GEF Secretariat, 1818 H St, NW, Washington, DC 20433, USA.

Telephone: (202) 473-1000; *Fax:* (202) 477-6391; *Internet:* http://lnweb18 .worldbank.org/essd/envext.nsf/45bydocname/gefgrantsmedium-sizedproject; *e-mail:* geonline@worldbank.org.

Project Preparation Grants

One of the grant programmes of the Global Environment Facility (GEF).

Activities: Grants for project preparation are made in three categories: Block A grants, of up to US $25,000, fund the early stages of project or programme identification, and are approved through GEF's implementing agencies; Block B grants, up to US $350,000, fund information-gathering necessary to complete project proposals and provide necessary supporting documentation, and are approved by the GEF CEO, with attention to the GEF operations committee's recommendations; and Block C grants, up to US $1,000,000, provide additional financing, where required, for larger projects to complete technical design and feasibility work, and are normally made available after a project proposal is approved by the GEF Council.

Geographical Area of Activity: International.

Financial Information: Grants in three categories: Block A grants up to US $25,000; Block B grants, up to US $350,000; and Block C grants, up to US $1,000,000.

Address: GEF Secretariat, 1818 H St, NW, Washington, DC 20433, USA.

Telephone: (202) 473-1000; *Fax:* (202) 477-6391; *Internet:* www.worldbank.org/gef.

INTERNATIONAL ATOMIC ENERGY AGENCY (IAEA)

Department of Technical Co-operation (TC): Technical Co-operation Programme

The TC Programme helps to transfer nuclear and related technologies for peaceful uses to countries throughout the world. The TC Programme disburses more than US $70,000,000 worth of equipment, services, and training per year.

Activities: The Programme aims to provide the necessary skills and equipment to establish sustainable technology in the counterpart country or region, through training courses, expert missions, fellowships, scientific visits, and equipment disbursement. Projects are grouped within the following fields: safety; physical and chemical applications; nuclear science; security of nuclear material; nuclear fuel cycle, material technologies and disposable radioactive waste management technologies; water resources and protection of the marine and terrestrial environments; food and agriculture; human resource development and capacity building; human health; nuclear power; and others. In 2003 the Programme had around 800 ongoing projects.

Geographical Area of Activity: International.

How to Apply: Requests for participation are generally made within the framework of national or regional projects, by filling out specific forms and submitting them through the relevant national authorities to the IAEA.

Financial Information: Annual total distributions of equipment, training and services worth approx. US $70,000,000.

Address: POB 100, Wagramer Str. 5, 1400 Vienna, Austria.

Telephone: (1) 260-00; *Fax:* (1) 260-07; *Internet:* www-tc.iaea.org/; *e-mail:* mail@ iaea.org.

INTERNATIONAL FUND FOR AGRICULTURAL DEVELOPMENT (IFAD)

Belgian Survival Fund Joint Programme

Established by the Belgian government in October 1983, in response to serious public concern in Belgium regarding the magnitude of drought-inflicted mortalities in Ethiopia and sub-Saharan Africa in the early 1980s. Co-ordinated by four UN agencies: the World Health Organization (WHO), United Nations Children's Fund (UNICEF), United Nations Development Programme (UNDP) and IFAD, which is the lead agency implementing the Fund's grant programme which targets household food and nutritional security, poverty alleviation and empowerment of targeted beneficiaries.

Activities: Aims to combat hunger and deprivation in the region. A new strategy for the Fund was approved by the Belgian government in 2000, covering the period 2001–11, with the focus on: improvement of household food security and the nutritional status of the target group, constituting the entry point for an integrated approach to sustainable livelihoods, drawing on synergies between various components; new partnerships with Joint Programme members, namely WHO, the United Nations Population Fund (UNFPA) and the Popular Coalition; development of participatory approaches for design, implementation and evaluation; and an increased emphasis on nutrition, reproductive health and population programmes.

Geographical Area of Activity: Ethiopia and sub-Saharan Africa.

Financial Information: Established with an initial endowment of 10,000,000,000 Belgian francs.

Contact: Annual Report.

Address: Via del Serafico 107, 00142 Rome, Italy.

Telephone: (06) 54591; *Fax:* (06) 5043463; *Internet:* www.ifad.org/special/bsf/index .htm; *e-mail:* ifad@ifad.org.

IFAD/NGO Extended Co-operation Programme (ECP) Grants

A specialized agency of the UN, established in 1977 as an international financial institution and one of the major outcomes of the 1974 World Food Conference. The Conference was organized in response to the food crises of the early 1970s that primarily affected the Sahelian countries of Africa., and it resolved that an International Fund for Agricultural Development should be established immediately to finance agricultural development projects primarily for food production in the developing countries. The Fund aims to mobilize resources on concessional terms for programmes that alleviate rural poverty and improve nutrition. The IFAD/NGO ECP Grants support NGOs in activities related to technology development and institutional innovation.

Activities: Supports capacity building of NGOs, and institutional development to enable the rural poor to improve their livelihoods, focusing on three major areas: identifying, testing and disseminating appropriate/innovative technologies for application to the agro-ecological and socio-economic conditions of IFAD's beneficiaries; identifying and testing appropriate/innovative institutional approaches/mechanisms in various sectors and sub-sectors of interest to IFAD to ascertain their relevance, acceptability and sustainability; and carrying out knowledge-gathering and dissemination activities and training programmes for improved management of resources through, *inter alia*, the creation of more effective systems of organization, based on viable grassroots organizations, such as farmers' groups, water users' associations and other forms of grassroots networks. Between 1998 and 2000 grants were made within the following fields: technology dissemination, rural finance, policy advocacy, micro-enterprise development, institutional support, information systems and agricultural development. In 2002 funded projects were based in Belize, Bolivia, Colombia, Djibouti, India, Jordan, Laos, Madagascar, Mali, Mauritania, Moldova, Mongolia, Nigeria, Panama, Philippines, Tanzania, Togo, Uganda and Zimbabwe for a variety of initiatives, including the establishment of community-managed credit schemes, restoring livelihood opportunities in disaster-affected areas, rural development and vaccine delivery. Also carries out regular IFAD/NGO consultations to enable NGOs and IFAD staff to discuss policy and operational issues, and the formation of country programmes and project strategies.

Geographical Area of Activity: Developing countries.

How to Apply: Project proposals must be written in one of the official languages (Spanish, French, English or Arabic) of IFAD and include, to the maximum degree possible, the following: summary of proposed project; institutional profile of the NGO, addressing the eligibility criteria as specified in the ECP procedures (information should include complete name and address, authorized representative, e.g. director-general, details of registration, institutional capacity, experience, specialization, staffing); rationale and objectives of proposed project and justification for NGO ECP grant; link(s) to IFAD projects, strategy and concerns; project area and target group (if applicable); description of proposed activities and their duration; expected outcomes, benefits and beneficiaries; nature of innovation and learning involved; implementation arrangements (roles and responsibilities and services/functions to be performed by the NGO(s) concerned); monitoring and evaluation arrangements; description of participating institutions (if applicable) and their respective roles and responsibilities; project costs (by activity) and allocation of the grant into cost categories (e.g. consultants, equipment and materials, training, meetings); financing plan (including co-financing arrangements and specification of IFAD coverage and NGO contribution in cash and/or kind to the project); procurement arrangements, if appropriate; disbursements (including specification of tranches); supervision and reporting; accounting and auditing arrangements; appendices, including a list of goods and services to be financed under the project.

Financial Information: Total programme funding US $3,386,500 (2002); total grants since 1977 US $16,500,000.

Contact: Pres. Lennart Båge.

Address: Via del Serafico 107, 00142 Rome, Italy.

Telephone: (06) 54591; *Fax:* (06) 5043463; *Internet:* www.ifad.org/ngo/ecp/ecp.htm; *e-mail:* ifad@ifad.org.

Project Component Grants

Part of the International Fund for Agricultural Development's (IFAD) support for research-for-development programmes, which aim to have an impact on small-scale agriculture throughout the developing world.

Activities: Project Component Grants are given in exceptional cases to co-finance components of investment projects in the absolute poorest, food-deficit countries with the most severe development problems.

Geographical Area of Activity: Developing countries.

Financial Information: Since 1977 IFAD has made 40 project component grants totalling US $32,400,000.

Address: Via del Serafico 107, 00142 Rome, Italy.

Telephone: (06) 54591; *Fax:* (06) 5043463; *Internet:* www.ifad.org/operations /grants/index.htm; *e-mail:* ifad@ifad.org.

Research Grant Programme

The Programme was established to support research-for-development initiatives, which will have an impact on small-scale agriculture throughout the developing world, drawing attention to the priority concerns of the rural poor and furthering understanding of the difficulties they face, living in resource-poor areas and producing traditional crops and commodities under difficult rainfall conditions.

Activities: Research grants are given to regional and international research institutions within and outside of the Consultative Group on International Agricultural Research (CGIAR, q.v.). The strategic objectives of this type of grant relate to: the International Fund for Agricultural Development's (IFAD) target groups and their household food-security strategies, specifically in remote and marginalized agro-ecological areas; technologies that build on traditional knowledge systems, are gender-responsive, and enhance and diversify the productive potential of resource-poor farming systems by improving productivity and addressing production bottlenecks; access to productive assets (land and water, financial services, labour, and technology, including indigenous technology) and sustainable and productive management of such resources; a policy framework that provides the rural poor with an incentive to reach higher levels of productivity, thereby reducing their dependence on transfers; and an institutional framework within which formal and informal, public- and private-sector, local and national institutions provide services to the economically vulnerable, according to their comparative advantage. The current focus of research grants is on improving partnerships in adaptive research programmes to increase developmental impact with a particular emphasis on the development of technology appropriate to small farms and small-scale innovative projects with a strong exploratory element, leading to future larger scale investment decisions. Grants are directed towards projects in the absolute poorest food-deficit countries with the most severe development problems. Current themes are Agro-forestry Systems, Appropriate Agricultural Technologies, Crop Production Systems, Income Generating Activities, Integrated Pest Management, Livestock Health, Livestock Production, and Plant Genetic Resources Conservation and Management.

Geographical Area of Activity: Developing countries.

Financial Information: Since its inception in 1977, IFAD has made 206 research grants totalling US $162,500,000.

Address: Via del Serafico 107, 00142 Rome, Italy.

Telephone: (06) 54591; *Fax:* (06) 5043463; *Internet:* www.ifad.org/operations/grants/index.htm; *e-mail:* ifad@ifad.org.

Supplementary Funds—Consultant Trust Funds–Finland

The Funds form part of the International Fund for Agricultural Development's (IFAD) supplementary fund programme, which includes all resources that are received by IFAD on a voluntary basis to support various programmes and activities and do not form part of donors' contributions to the regular resources of IFAD. An agreement between the donor and IFAD designates the Fund as administrator and defines the terms and conditions for the use of the funds, which are accounted separately from IFAD's own resources, and serve to enhance the Fund's operational strategies and priorities. There are two categories of Supplementary Funds: Consultant Trust Funds and Programmatic Trust Funds.

Activities: The Funds provide support to studies (including environmental impact assessments), surveys, workshops and short-term operational assignments in connection with the development, implementation, supervision and evaluation of programmes and projects financed or to be financed by IFAD; sector and sub-sector policy assessment studies related to rural development and studies related to investment opportunities; and local capacity-building activities in connection with the start-up, development, implementation, supervision and evaluation of programmes and projects financed or to be financed by IFAD, including training of rural people, project/programme and government staff, and support for effective participatory mechanisms. In 2002 activities included funding to the Rural Financial Services Programme in Uganda.

Geographical Area of Activity: Developing countries.

Address: Via del Serafico 107, 00142 Rome, Italy.

Telephone: (06) 54591; *Fax:* (06) 5043463; *Internet:* www.ifad.org/operations/grants/sup/finland.htm.

Supplementary Funds—Consultant Trust Funds–The Netherlands

A Consultant Trust Fund of the International Fund for Agricultural Development (IFAD), with resources from the government of the Netherlands.

Activities: The Fund supports studies, surveys and short-term operational assignments in connection with development, implementation, supervision and evaluation of programmes and projects financed by IFAD; assignments related to the development and implementation of methodologies to assess, enhance and communicate the impact of IFAD operations with respect to the institution's poverty-reduction goals; sector and sub-sector assessment studies and/or investment studies related to rural development; local capacity-building activities in connection with the development, start-up, implementation, supervision and evaluation of projects financed or to be financed by IFAD, including training of rural people, project/programme and government staff and support for effective participatory mechanisms; and support for participation by IFAD and major recipient country stakeholders in poverty-reduction strategy processes and other donor and recipient co-ordination mechanisms.

Geographical Area of Activity: Developing countries.

Address: Via del Serafico 107, 00142 Rome, Italy.

Telephone: (06) 54591; *Fax:* (06) 5043463; *Internet:* www.ifad.org/operations /grants/sup/netherlands.htm.

Supplementary Funds—Programmatic Trust Fund—Japan

A Programmatic Trust Fund of the International Fund for Agricultural Development (IFAD), funded by the Japanese government.

Activities: The Fund provides support to a range of initiatives promoting rural development, health-care and gender equality, including workshops on gender equity and the empowerment of rural women, and a programme to mitigate the effects of HIV/AIDS on poor rural women, young people and foster families. Also provides support to internal initiatives aimed at developing and testing different strategies, entry points and instruments for the economic advancement of poor rural women and sector-specific approaches to gender, and disseminating and sharing information.

Geographical Area of Activity: Developing countries.

Address: Via del Serafico 107, 00142 Rome, Italy.

Telephone: (06) 54591; *Fax:* (06) 5043463; *Internet:* www.ifad.org/operations /grants/sup/japan.htm.

Supplementary Funds—Programmatic Trust Fund—Norway

A Programmatic Trust Fund of the International Fund for Agricultural Development (IFAD), funded by the Norwegian government.

Activities: The Fund co-finances IFAD projects with a gender focus, either new or ongoing, in sub-Saharan Africa, as well as programmes that aim to improve the impact of IFAD projects directly. In 2002 it supported IFAD's development of strategies to mainstream gender in its operations through the East and Central

Africa Regional Gender Programme, supported the West and Central Africa's Research Learning Action Programme targeting rural women, and funded an evaluation of IFAD's projects in Tanzania.

Geographical Area of Activity: Sub-Saharan Africa.

Address: Via del Serafico 107, 00142 Rome, Italy.

Telephone: (06) 54591; *Fax:* (06) 5043463; *Internet:* www.ifad.org/operations /grants/sup/norway.htm; *e-mail:* ifad@ifad.org.

Supplementary Funds—Programmatic Trust Fund—Portugal

A Programmatic Trust Fund of the International Fund for Agricultural Development (IFAD), funded by the Portuguese government.

Activities: The Fund provides financial and implementation support to agricultural and rural development projects in developing countries. In 2002 the Fund helped finance the Angola Northern Region Food Crops Project (PRODECA), and explored co-financing opportunities for implementation by the UN Convention to Combat Desertification (UNCCD) in Central and South America and the Caribbean region.

Geographical Area of Activity: Developing countries.

Address: Via del Serafico 107, 00142 Rome, Italy.

Telephone: (06) 54591; *Fax:* (06) 5043463; *Internet:* www.ifad.org/operations /grants/sup/portugal.htm; *e-mail:* ifad@ifad.org.

Supplementary Funds—Programmatic Trust Fund—Switzerland

A Programmatic Trust Fund of the International Fund for Agricultural Development (IFAD), funded by the Swiss government.

Activities: The Fund's resources in favour of sub-Saharan African countries are mainly to enable IFAD to undertake economic development activities in the region, and to improve the supervision, monitoring and evaluation of IFAD projects and programmes.

Geographical Area of Activity: Sub-Saharan Africa.

Address: Via del Serafico 107, 00142 Rome, Italy.

Telephone: (06) 54591; *Fax:* (06) 5043463; *Internet:* www.ifad.org/operations /grants/sup/switzerland.htm; *e-mail:* ifad@ifad.org.

Supplementary Funds—Programmatic Trust Fund—United Kingdom

A Programmatic Trust Fund of the International Fund for Agricultural Development (IFAD), funded by the UK government.

Activities: The Fund aims to help IFAD improve the performance of loan and grant projects through improving interdisciplinary diagnosis of poverty and vulnerability at all stages of the project cycle. In 2002 the Fund supported training programmes for IFAD country portfolio managers, consultants and co-operating institutions on sustainable livelihoods, carried out an analysis on livelihood systems of poor rural people in Meghalaya, India, carried out poverty analysis in Bangladesh with specific emphasis on the role and potential of livestock development as a tool for poverty alleviation, supported the St Lucia Rural

Enterprise Project and funded a support programme for the capacity building of groundnut producer grassroots organizations under the Senegal Village Organization and Management Project.

Geographical Area of Activity: Developing countries.

Address: Via del Serafico 107, 00142 Rome, Italy.

Telephone: (06) 54591; *Fax:* (06) 5043463; *Internet:* www.ifad.org/operations /grants/sup/uk.htm; *e-mail:* ifad@ifad.org.

Supplementary Funds—Programmatic Trust Fund–Germany

A Programmatic Trust Fund of the International Fund for Agricultural Development (IFAD), funded by the German government.

Activities: In 2002 the Fund allocated funds for two projects: Mitigating the Impact of HIV/AIDS on Rural Populations in Eastern and Southern Africa; and Gender Mainstreaming in Central and Eastern Europe: A Community Driven Approach.

Geographical Area of Activity: Developing countries.

Address: Via del Serafico 107, 00142 Rome, Italy.

Telephone: (06) 54591; *Fax:* (06) 5043463; *Internet:* www.ifad.org/operations /grants/sup/germany.htm.

Supplementary Funds—Programmatic Trust Fund–Ireland

A Programmatic Trust Fund of the International Fund for Agricultural Development (IFAD), financed by the Irish government.

Activities: The Fund is used mainly to co-finance projects and programmes in Eastern and Southern Africa, which are in harmony with improved traditional/indigenous farming systems, have a definite capacity-building dimension and encompass practices that enhance environmentally and socially sustainable development. In 2002 funded projects were based in Ethiopia, Malawi, Tanzania, Uganda and Zambia.

Geographical Area of Activity: Eastern and Southern Africa.

Address: Via del Serafico 107, 00142 Rome, Italy.

Telephone: (06) 54591; *Fax:* (06) 5043463; *Internet:* www.ifad.org/operations /grants/sup/ireland.htm.

Supplementary Funds—Programmatic Trust Fund–Italy

A Programmatic Trust Fund of the International Fund for Agricultural Development (IFAD), funded by the Italian government.

Activities: Provides support across various IFAD programme areas, including post-conflict assistance, poverty reduction, agriculture/irrigation and food security, rural financial services, and environmental protection. Beneficiaries in 2002 included a relief and development project in the West Bank and Gaza, an initiative to develop participatory irrigation management methodologies in North Africa, and the development of a micro-finance programme for vulnerable rural communities in Iran.

Geographical Area of Activity: International.

Address: Via del Serafico 107, 00142 Rome, Italy.

Telephone: (06) 54591; *Fax:* (06) 5043463; *Internet:* www.ifad.org/operations /grants/sup/italy.htm.

Training Grant Programme

Part of the International Fund for Agricultural Development's (IFAD) support for research-for-development programmes, which aim to have an impact on small-scale agriculture throughout the developing world.

Activities: Training grants aim to strengthen capacities to ensure the sustainability of development activities, through supporting management training for poverty alleviation and responding to the specific needs of those working with poor rural populations.

Geographical Area of Activity: Developing countries.

Financial Information: Since 1977 IFAD has made 295 training and other activities grants totalling US $119,600,000.

Address: Via del Serafico 107, 00142 Rome, Italy.

Telephone: (06) 54591; *Fax:* (06) 5043463; *Internet:* www.ifad.org/operations /grants/index.htm; *e-mail:* ifad@ifad.org.

INTERNATIONAL LABOUR ORGANIZATION (ILO)

Founded in 1919, ILO is the UN specialized agency which seeks the promotion of social justice and internationally recognized human and labour rights. It is the only surviving major creation of the Treaty of Versailles which brought the League of Nations into being and it became the first specialized agency of the UN in 1946. It aims to: promote and realize fundamental principles and rights at work; create greater opportunities for women and men to secure decent employment and income; enhance the coverage and effectiveness of social protection for all; and strengthen tripartism and social dialogue.

Activities: ILO operates through the formulation of international policies and programmes to promote basic human rights, improve working and living conditions, and enhance employment opportunities; the creation of international labour standards, backed by a unique system to supervise their application, to serve as guide-lines for national authorities in putting these policies into action; an extensive programme of international technical co-operation formulated and implemented in an active partnership with constituents, to help countries in making these policies effective in practice; and training, education, research, and publishing activities to help advance all these efforts.

Geographical Area of Activity: International.

How to Apply: Information on how to apply for funding from the ILO's Development Co-operation Department (CODEV).

Financial Information: Financed by 177 member states; estimated total budget approx. US $529,600,000 (2004–05).

Publications: World Employment Report; Key Indicators of the Labour Market; Yearbook of Labour Statistics; International Labour Review; Encyclopaedia of Occupational Health and Safety.

Contact: Dir-Gen. Juan Somavia.

Address: 4 route des Morillons, 1211 Geneva 22, Switzerland.

Telephone: (22) 7997309; *Fax:* (22) 7996668; *Internet:* www.ilo.org; *e-mail:* codev@ilo.org.

International Programme on the Elimination of Child Labour (IPEC)

A UN/International Labour Organization (ILO) initiative; works for the progressive elimination of child labour world-wide, emphasizing the eradication of the worst forms as rapidly as possible. It works to achieve this in several ways: through country-based programmes which promote policy reform and put in place concrete measures to end child labour; and through international and national campaigning intended to change social attitudes and promote ratification and effective implementation of ILO child labour conventions.

Activities: IPEC works in collaboration with NGOs focusing on children's rights, women's rights, education and health, as part of IPEC's multisectoral approach to involve governments, employers' and workers' organizations and civil society, in the fight against child labour. Many major IPEC Action Programmes directly involve NGOs or were originated by NGOs themselves. Examples of IPEC–NGO collaboration include support for an NGO in Peru working to develop new working methods for families; provision of educational opportunities for children in Guatemala as an alternative to child labour via Habitat, an international NGO; and supporting a foundation project in southern India which raises awareness of the issue of child labour amongst parents, eases problems of school enrolment and bridges the gap between the home and formal school. Also funds the Global March, a leading advocate for ratification and implementation of ILO Convention No. 182 on the Worst Forms of Child Labour.

Geographical Area of Activity: International.

Address: 4 route des Morillons, 1211 Geneva 22, Switzerland.

Telephone: (22) 7998181; *Fax:* (22) 7998771; *Internet:* www.ilo.org/public/english/standards/ipec/; *e-mail:* ipec@ilo.org.

INTERNATIONAL ORGANIZATION FOR THE ELIMINATION OF ALL FORMS OF RACIAL DISCRIMINATION (EAFORD)

Established to uphold and promote the International Convention on the Elimination of All Forms of Racial Discrimination, which was adopted by the General Assembly of the UN in 1963 and ratified into law in January 1965. Holds consultative status with the United Nations Educational, Scientific and Cultural Organization (UNESCO) and ECOSOC.

Activities: EAFORD operates by organizing seminars and conferences in collaboration with universities and NGOs on racism and racial discrimination in general, and on apartheid, Zionism and the rights and conditions of indigenous peoples; participates in UN conferences, including sessions of the Commission on Human Rights; publishes and distributes books and analytical papers on specific questions of racism and racial discrimination; grants fellowships to graduate students preparing doctoral dissertations on aspects of racism and racial discrimination; presents the annual International Award for the Promotion of Human Understanding; and supports and co-operates with NGOs engaged in combating racism and racial discrimination.

Geographical Area of Activity: International.

Publications: Without Prejudice (journal, 2 a year).

Contact: Pres. Abdalla Sharafeddin; Sec.-Gen. Dr Anis Al-Qasem.

Address: 5 route des Morillons, Bureau No. 475, Case Postale 2100, 1211 Geneva 2, Switzerland.

Telephone: (22) 7916727; *Fax:* (22) 7886233; *Internet:* www.eaford.org; *e-mail:* info@eaford.org.

INTERNATIONAL STRATEGY FOR DISASTER REDUCTION (ISDR)

United Nations Sasakawa Award for Disaster Reduction

Established in 1986 by the Sasakawa Foundation, now known as the Nippon Foundation, with the aim of promoting humanitarian efforts to help vulnerable communities become more resilient to the impact of natural disasters. Together with the other public information tools of the ISDR Secretariat, the Award is one the main vehicles to promote advocacy and raise awareness among affected communities, on disaster-prevention issues.

Activities: The Award recognizes disaster-reduction efforts world-wide, primarily new and innovative strategies and projects. The awards include a Laureate and certificates of distinction which all receive a financial reward, totalling approximately US $50,000. In 2002 the Laureate was the founder and president of the Armenian Association of Seismology and Physics of the Earth's Interior, and in 2003 the Gujarat State Disaster Management Authority, which was given the award in recognition of outstanding work in the field of disaster management and risk reduction.

Geographical Area of Activity: International.

How to Apply: The prize is awarded on the second Wednesday of October each year, within the global framework of World Disaster Reduction Day.

Financial Information: Total annual amount awarded approx. US $50,000.

Contact: Contact Christel Rose.

Address: ISDR Secretariat, Palais des Nations, 8-14 ave de la Paix, 1211 Geneva 10, Switzerland.

Telephone: (22) 9172786; *Fax:* (22) 9170563; *Internet:* www.unisdr.org/unisdr /sasakawa.htm; *e-mail:* rosec@un.org.

OFFICE FOR THE CO-ORDINATION OF HUMANITARIAN AFFAIRS (OCHA)

Established pursuant to the adoption of the UN Secretary-General's programme for reform. In accordance with the provisions of General Assembly Resolution 46/182, the Emergency Relief Co-ordinator's functions are focused in three core areas: policy development and co-ordination functions in support of the Secretary-General, ensuring that all humanitarian issues, including those which fall between gaps in existing mandates of agencies such as protection and assistance for internally displaced persons, are addressed; advocacy of humanitarian issues with political organs, notably the UN Security Council; and co-ordination of humanitarian emergency response, by ensuring that an appropriate response mechanism is established, through Inter-Agency Standing Committee (IASC) consultations, on the ground.

Activities: Operates primarily through the IASC, which is chaired by the Emergency Relief Co-ordinator (ERC), with the participation of all humanitarian partners, including the Red Cross Movement and NGOs. IASC ensures inter-agency decision-making in response to complex emergencies, including needs assessments, consolidated appeals, field co-ordination arrangements and the development of humanitarian policies.

Geographical Area of Activity: International.

Financial Information: Core annual budget US $42,400,000.

Address: UN Plaza, New York, NY 10017, USA.

Telephone: (212) 963-1234; *Fax:* (212) 963-1312; *Internet:* www.reliefweb.int /ocha_ol/; *e-mail:* ochany@un.org.

Trust Fund for Disaster Relief

Established in 1995 to receive dedicated and non-dedicated contributions for emergency relief assistance.

Activities: Aims to finance humanitarian co-ordination and relief activities in countries affected by conflicts and natural disasters and industrial and technological accidents. The Fund is also used to channel contributions for the provision of emergency relief assistance by the Office for the Co-ordination of Humanitarian Affairs (OCHA), other implementing agencies and programmes of the UN system, specialized agencies and NGOs. Funding governments select how their respective contributions are used and by whom.

Geographical Area of Activity: International.

Financial Information: Funders include the governments of Italy, Japan and Norway.

Address: UN Plaza, New York, NY 10017, USA.

Telephone: (212) 963-1234; *Fax:* (212) 963-1312; *Internet:* www.reliefweb.int /ocha_ol/.

OFFICE OF THE HIGH COMMISSIONER FOR HUMAN RIGHTS (OHCHR)

Assisting Communities Together (ACT)

Established by the United Nations High Commissioner for Human Rights, in partnership with the United Nations Development Programme (UNDP, q.v.), to support local initiatives for the promotion and protection of human rights.

Activities: Provides financial support, through micro-grants of up to US $5,000, to grassroots activities in the field of human rights carried out by community-based organizations or by individuals. Support is given for activities that require a relatively small amount of support to be implemented but can have an important impact on the promotion and protection of human rights at the local level. The fund completed its third phase in 2003.

Geographical Area of Activity: Eligible countries for Phase 3: Afghanistan, Belarus, Bosnia and Herzegovina, Burkina Faso, Burundi, Cambodia, Colombia, Comoros, Democratic Republic of Congo, Egypt, Ethiopia, Former Yugoslav Republic of Macedonia, Guinea, Haiti, Liberia, Madagascar, Malawi, Palestinian Autonomous Areas, Philippines, Samoa, Serbia and Montenegro, Sierra Leone, Tanzania, Uganda, Uzbekistan and Venezuela.

How to Apply: Application forms are available on the website and should be completed and returned to the OHCHR field presence or the UNDP Office in the applicant's country.

Financial Information: Grants available up to US $5,000.

Publications: Report on operations.

Address: Palais des Nations, 1211 Geneva 10, Switzerland.

Fax: (22) 9179003; *Internet:* www.unhchr.ch/html/menu2/9/civilsup/actproj.htm; *e-mail:* agirard@ohchr.org.

Indigenous Project Team: Indigenous Fellowship Programme

Established to give indigenous women and men the opportunity to gain knowledge in the field of international human rights in general and on indigenous rights in particular in order to assist their organizations and communities in protecting and promoting the human rights of their people.

Activities: Promotes human rights and indigenous rights through awarding annual fellowships for indigenous people to be based for five months at the offices of the UN High Commissioner for Refugees (UNHCR) in Geneva. The Programme provides fellows with the opportunity to establish contacts with other intergovernmental and non-governmental organizations and to gain practical experience with the Office of the High Commissioner for Human Rights (OHCHR) and its work with human rights through their practical work as part of the Indigenous Project Team. Preference is given to candidates aged between 25 and 35 who are willing to train other indigenous people after the return to their respective communities/organizations.

Geographical Area of Activity: International.

How to Apply: Applications must be faxed or sent by regular post; e-mailed applications will not be considered.

Address: UNOG–OHCHR, 1211 Geneva 10, Switzerland.

Telephone: (22) 9179434; *Fax:* (22) 9179010; *Internet:* www.unhchr.ch/indigenous /fellowship.htm; *e-mail:* fellowship_prog@ohchr.org.

Support to the Implementation of the UN Decade for Human Rights Education—Phases I and II—Global Projects

In 1994, the UN General Assembly designated 1995–2004 as the UN Decade for Human Rights Education and put the High Commissioner for Human Rights in charge of co-ordinating the implementation of a related plan of action, which provides a strategy for strengthening human rights education programmes at the international, regional, national and local levels. The programme for the Decade is guided by the Decade's Plan of Action and relevant resolutions of the General Assembly and the Commission on Human Rights. The general objective is to support national and local capacities for human rights education and training, specifically: enhancing co-ordination and facilitating information-sharing among international, regional and national governmental and NGOs carrying out human rights education activities; ensuring appropriate support through OHCHR's technical co-operation projects; supporting grassroots human rights education initiatives;   developing human rights education and training materials; disseminating the Universal Declaration of Human Rights globally; and ensuring world-wide co-ordination for the Decade.

Activities: The programme involves support for regional and global initiatives, including organizing education and training activities, funding for grassroots human rights educational initiatives and capacity-building projects for Arab NGOs, supporting the Arab Institute for Human Rights (AIHR), funding research and publications, and developing opportunities for states, NGOs and professionals from Arab states to develop novel approaches to integrate economic, social and cultural rights and the right to insert development into programming at country level.

Geographical Area of Activity: International.

Address: 8–14 ave de la Paix, 1211 Geneva 10, Switzerland.

Telephone: (22) 9179000; *Internet:* www.unhchr.ch/html/menu2/glhred.htm.

Technical Co-operation Programme—NGOs and Civil Society

Operational since 1955; aims to assist states, at their request, in the building and strengthening of national structures that have a direct impact on the overall observance of human rights and the maintenance of the rule of law, including the strengthening of civil society. The Programme is funded by the Voluntary Fund for Technical Co-operation in the Field of Human Rights, which became operational in 1988.

Activities: The Programme provides practical assistance for the building of national and regional human rights infrastructures, including strengthening civil society. Support is also given to appropriate projects run by NGOs.

Geographical Area of Activity: International.

Financial Information: Funded from the regular budget of the UN and from the UN Voluntary Fund for Technical Co-operation in the Field of Human Rights.

Address: 8–14 ave de la Paix, 1211 Geneva 10, Switzerland.

Telephone: (22) 9179000; *Internet:* www.unhchr.ch/html/menu2/areas.htm#ngo.

Trust Funds Unit/Support Services Branch: United Nations Voluntary Fund for Indigenous Populations

Established by General Assembly Resolution 40/131 of 13 December 1985, with the purpose of assisting representatives of indigenous communities and organizations to participate in the deliberations of the Working Group on Indigenous Populations of the Sub-Commission on the Promotion and Protection of Human Rights, by providing them with financial assistance, funded by means of voluntary contributions from governments, NGOs and other private or public entities. The General Assembly further expanded the mandate of the Fund in Resolution 56/140 of 19 December 2001, by deciding that the Fund should also be used to assist representatives of indigenous communities and organizations in attending, as observers, the sessions of the Permanent Forum on Indigenous Issues.

Activities: Provides financial assistance to representatives of indigenous communities and organizations considered unable to take part in the Working Group on Indigenous Populations of the Sub-Commission on the Promotion and Protection of Human Rights and the Working Group on the draft UN declaration on the rights of indigenous peoples, through the provision of grants to cover travel and other expenses.

Geographical Area of Activity: International.

How to Apply: Detailed application criteria and application forms are available on the website.

Financial Information: Total grants approx. US $185,000 (2003).

Contact: Board of Trustees: Lars Anders Baer; Nadir Bekirov; Ahmed Mahiou; José Carlos Morales Morales; Victoria Tauli-Corpuz; Contact Eulàlia Ortadó.

Address: PW 2-041, 1211 Geneva 10, Switzerland.

Telephone: (22) 9179145; *Fax:* (22) 9179017; *Internet:* www.unhchr.ch/html /menu2/9/vfindige.htm; *e-mail:* eortado-rosich@ohchr.org.

Trust Funds Unit/Support Services Branch: United Nations Voluntary Fund for Victims of Torture

The Fund was established by General Assembly Resolution 36/151 of 16 December 1981 to receive voluntary contributions from governments, NGOs and individuals for distribution to NGOs providing humanitarian assistance to victims of torture and members of their family.

Activities: Grants are awarded to NGOs for projects that aim to provide medical, psychological, social, economic, legal, humanitarian and other forms of assistance to victims of torture and members of their families. Subject to availability of funds, a limited number of grants are also given for the training of professionals or for the organization of conferences and seminars with a special focus on the treatment of victims of torture.

Geographical Area of Activity: International.

Restrictions: No grants for governments, national liberation movements or political parties, nor for projects aiming at campaigning against torture, preventing torture or providing financial assistance to other projects.

How to Apply: Applications for grants must be submitted by 30 November each year for analysis by the secretariat of the Fund, as well as the narrative and financial report on the use of any previous grant. Admissible applications are then examined by the Board of Trustees at its annual session in May. All applicants are informed of the decisions by mid-July. The grants are paid at the end of July/beginning of August. Beneficiaries must provide satisfactory narrative and financial reports on the use of grants before 30 November.

Financial Information: Total grants approx. US $7,000,000 (2002–03); the total grant cannot exceed one-third of the project's total costs.

Contact: Board of Trustees: Jaap Walkate (Chair.); Ribot Hatano; Elizabeth Odio-Benito; Ivan Tosevski; Amos Wako.

Address: 1211 Geneva 10, Switzerland.

Telephone: (22) 9179315; *Fax:* (22) 9179017; *Internet:* www.unhchr.ch/html /menu2/9/vftortur.htm; *e-mail:* dpremont.hchr@unog.ch.

Trust Funds Unit/Support Services Branch: Voluntary Fund for the International Decade of the World's Indigenous People

Established pursuant to General Assembly Resolutions 48/163 of 21 December 1993, 49/214 of 23 December 1994 and 50/157 of 21 December 1995, relating to the International Decade of the World's Indigenous People. In accordance with Resolution 48/163, the Secretary-General was requested to establish a voluntary fund for the Decade and was authorized to accept and administer voluntary contributions from governments.

Activities: Provides support to indigenous organizations and NGOs, through grants for workshops, seminars, projects and programmes, in the area of international co-operation for the solution of problems faced by indigenous people in such areas as human rights, the environment, development, education, culture and health. The main supported project areas are: the development of indigenous organizational structures and procedures and their strengthening through education, training and institution and capacity building; education and training in human and indigenous rights; information about indigenous peoples and the Decade; communications and exchanges between the UN system and indigenous peoples and between indigenous peoples; and fundraising initiatives promoting the objectives of the Decade. In 2004 the preference for the allocation of funds was to be for project proposals by indigenous communities and organizations.

Geographical Area of Activity: International.

How to Apply: Application forms should be sent to the secretariat of the Fund before 1 October. Completed applications forms must be in English, French or Spanish, dated and signed by the project leader or a member of the executive body of the organization. Applications to the Fund are considered at the annual session of the Advisory Group in April of each year.

Financial Information: Total grants approved US $274,000 (2003); average grant $10,000, up to a maximum of $50,000.

Contact: Advisory Group: Erica-Irene Daes; Michael Dodson; Naomi N. Kipur; José Carlos Morales Morales; Tove Petersen; Victoria Tauli-Corpuz; José Luís Goméz del Prado.

Address: 1211 Geneva 10, Switzerland.

Telephone: (22) 9179164; *Fax:* (22) 9179017; *Internet:* www.unhchr.ch/html /menu2/9/vfinddec.htm; *e-mail:* pdauchamp@ohchr.org.

Trust Funds Unit/Support Services Branch: Voluntary Trust Fund on Contemporary Forms of Slavery

Established by the General Assembly in 1991 with the purpose of assisting NGOs dealing with contemporary forms of slavery to participate in the deliberations of the Working Group on Contemporary Forms of Slavery and to provide, through NGOs, humanitarian, legal and financial aid to individual victims of such violations.

Activities: Applications for grants are accepted from NGOs dealing with issues of contemporary forms of slavery, and individuals whose human rights have been severely violated as a result of contemporary forms of slavery.

Geographical Area of Activity: International.

How to Apply: Application forms are available on the website and must be submitted by 15 September for analysis by the secretariat of the Fund. Admissible applications are examined by the Board of Trustees at its annual session in January/February. The Board adopts recommendations for approval of the High Commissioner for Human Rights on behalf of the Secretary-General, and the grants are paid in March/April. Beneficiaries have to provide satisfactory narrative and financial reports on the use of project grants.

Financial Information: Total grants US $123,415 (2003).

Contact: Board of Trustees: Swami Agnivesh (Chair.); Cheikh Saad-Bouh Kamara; Tatiana Matveeva; José de Souza Martins; Theo van Boven; Contact Eulàlia Ortadó.

Address: PW 2-041, 1211 Geneva 10, Switzerland.

Telephone: (22) 9179145; *Fax:* (22) 917 9017; *Internet:* www.unhchr.ch/html /menu2/9/vfslaver.htm#contacts; *e-mail:* eortado-rosich@ohchr.org.

OFFICE OF THE SPECIAL REPRESENTATIVE OF THE SECRETARY-GENERAL FOR CHILDREN AND ARMED CONFLICT

Trust Fund for Children and Armed Conflict

The Special Representative was appointed by the Secretary-General in September 1997; the role is to act as: an advocate to build awareness of the needs of war-affected children; a catalyst proposing ideas and approaches to enhance the protection of children in war situations; a convener, bringing together all the key actors within and outside the United Nations to promote more concerted and effective responses; and a facilitator, undertaking humanitarian and diplomatic efforts to unblock difficult political situations.

Activities: The Office does not operate projects directly, but, through its Trust Fund, works with UN agencies, including the UN High Commissioner for Refugees (UNHCR) and the United Nations Children's Fund (UNICEF), and NGOs that run programmes in particular countries and conflict areas, as well as a research programme carried out in conjunction with aid and development NGOs. Also carries out specific initiatives, including the Global Peace School programme, an educational initiative executed in collaboration with peace educators and NGOs; and has established the Youth to Youth Network.

Geographical Area of Activity: International.

Financial Information: Funded by member governments and foundations, including the Hewlett Foundation, Starr Foundation, and United Nations Foundation (q.v.).

Contact: Under Secretary-General Olara A. Otunnu.

Address: Room S-3161, New York, NY 10017, USA.

Telephone: (212) 963-3178; *Fax:* (212) 963-0807; *Internet:* www.un.org/special-rep /children-armed-conflict/; *e-mail:* srsgcaac@un.org.

UN COMMISSION ON SUSTAINABLE DEVELOPMENT/US GOVERNMENT

International AIDS Education and Training Programme

A partnership between the US government and the UN Commission on Sustainable Development; aims to develop training and education in HIV/AIDS in seriously affected countries in Africa, Asia and the Caribbean.

Activities: Operates partnerships with institutes and training organizations, including NGOs. Supported projects should improve the care of people living with HIV/AIDS in heavily affected areas by improving the capacity for training HIV/AIDS care providers, including physicians, nurses, clinical administrators and other key personnel. Also funds projects enhancing training capacity in the areas of diagnosis, treatment and prevention of HIV, develops training programmes and provides technical assistance on the planning, design and management of regional or national HIV/AIDS training programmes and care facilities and programmes.

Geographical Area of Activity: Africa, Asia and the Caribbean.

How to Apply: Detailed application procedure available on the website.

Contact: Dir HIV/AIDS Global Programme Raul Romaguera.

Address: HRSA, HIV/AIDS Bureau, 5600 Fishers Lane, Rockville, MD 20857, USA.

Telephone: (301) 443-2027; *Fax:* (301) 443-9645; *Internet:* www.johannesburgsummit.org/html; *e-mail:* rromaguera@hrsa.gov.

UN INDUSTRIAL DEVELOPMENT ORGANIZATION (UNIDO)

Relations with NGOs

UNIDO was set up in 1966 and became a specialized agency of the UN in 1985. As part of the UN common system, UNIDO has responsibility for promoting industrialization throughout the developing world, in co-operation with its 170 member states, and is represented in 35 developing countries. UNIDO helps developing countries and countries with economies in transition in their fight against marginalization, through mobilizing knowledge, skills, information and technology to promote productive employment, a competitive economy and a sound environment.

Activities: UNIDO contains provisions in its Constitution for NGO participation. Consultative status is granted by the Industrial Development Board and permits NGOs to participate in meetings of the Board, the General Conference and other activities.

Geographical Area of Activity: International; developing countries.

Contact: Dir-Gen. Carlos Magariños.

Address: Vienna International Centre, POB 300, 1400 Vienna, Austria.

Telephone: (1) 260-26-0; *Fax:* (1) 269-26-69; *Internet:* www.unido.org; *e-mail:* unido@unido.org.

UN RELIEF AND WORKS AGENCY FOR PALESTINE REFUGEES (UNRWA)

Established following the 1948 Arab–Israeli war, by UN General Assembly Resolution 302 (IV) of 8 December 1949, to carry out direct relief and works programmes for Palestine refugees, beginning operations on 1 May 1950. The General Assembly has repeatedly renewed UNRWA's mandate, which is currently extended until 30 June 2005.

Activities: Provides support for education, health care, social services and emergency aid to over four million refugees living in the Gaza Strip, the West Bank, Jordan, Lebanon and Syria. In the field of health, supports primary health care, nutrition and supplementary feeding, assistance with secondary health care and environmental health initiatives in refugee camps; in the field of education provides support to primary and secondary education initiatives, vocational and technical training, teacher training, and scholarships; in the field of relief and social services provides immediate aid and develops longer-term infrastructure programmes; and in the field of micro-enterprise and micro-finance provides funding for small-scale enterprises, solidarity groups and micro-enterprise credit.

Geographical Area of Activity: Gaza Strip, the West Bank, Jordan, Lebanon and Syria.

How to Apply: Details on submitting a tender for funding are available on the website.

Financial Information: Total expenditure US $293,862,187 (2002); total budget US $315,000,000 (2003).

Contact: Commissioner-Gen. Peter Hansen; Deputy Commissioner-Gen. Karen Koning AbuZayd; Chief Liaison Officer Matthias Burchard.
Address: Headquarters Gaza, POB 140157, Amman 11814, Jordan.
Telephone: (8) 6777333; *Fax:* (8) 6777555; *Internet:* www.un.org/unrwa.

UN SYSTEM CHIEF EXECUTIVES BOARD FOR CO-ORDINATION

Food and Agriculture Organization (FAO): UN System Network on Rural Development and Food Security

Established in 1997 by the UN Administrative Committee on Co-ordination (now the UN System Chief Executives Board for Co-ordination), it brings together key actors for the achievement of the shared goals of food for all and rural poverty reduction. Comprising 20 UN organizations, the UN System Network is an inter-agency mechanism for follow-up to the World Food Summit (1996) and World Food Summit (2002) and supports the Popular Coalition to Eradicate Hunger and Poverty. The Network Secretariat is managed by FAO, in close collaboration with International Fund for Agricultural Development (IFAD), the World Food Programme (WFP) and the International Land Coalition. The Network aims to support efforts by governments and its partners to implement the World Food Summit Plan of Action and rural development and food security programmes; reinforce ties between UN System organizations and other stakeholders, principally NGOs and civil society organizations; foster synergies between Network members; exchange and disseminate information, experiences and best practices.

Activities: Organizes its activities through national Thematic Groups (TGs) working on rural development and food security issues. Each group defines its themes and agenda according to the different needs and priorities at the national level, and groups have been established in 83 countries in Africa, Asia and the Pacific, Europe, Central and South America and the Caribbean and the Near East. The TGs work on a wide range of activities related to rural development and food security, ranging from the development of national food security strategies, country nutrition profiles, participatory needs' assessments and information systems for the design and implementation of rural development programmes. The TGs also act as effective mechanisms for strengthening linkages with UN initiatives, provide input to the development of national Food Insecurity and Vulnerability Information and Mapping Systems (FIVIMS) (from identifying vulnerable areas and populations at risk, to co-ordinating data collection from various country partners and producing reports). National TGs are comprised of representatives from UN organizations, governments, donors, NGOs, civil society and the private sector, with the aim of creating a collaborative framework in which to plan and implement rural development activities; promote new projects; share information, knowledge and expertise; promote discussion on the main development challenges and ensure co-ordinated technical support to national efforts. The Network website periodically reports on the TGs' activities and provides information on world-wide partnerships and multi-stakeholder initiatives for rural development and food security.

Geographical Area of Activity: International.

Address: Network Secretariat, Rural Development Division, Viale delle Terme di Caracalla, 00100 Rome, Italy.
Fax: (06) 57053250; *Internet:* www.rdfs.net; *e-mail:* rdfs-net@fao.org.

UNITED NATIONS CHILDREN'S FUND (UNICEF)

Global Campaign for Education (GCE)

An initiative of aid agencies, non-government organizations, child rights activists and teachers' and public-sector unions operating in 180 countries; campaigns for the implementation of the Education for All goals and strategies agreed by 185 world governments at Dakar in April 2000.

Activities: The Campaign calls on: governments to involve citizens' groups, teachers and communities in developing concrete plans of action for delivering and sustaining free, good quality public education for all; governments to abolish fees and charges for public primary education, and to increase their own spending on basic education, with priority investments in schools and teachers serving the most disadvantaged groups; the World Bank and rich northern countries to increase aid and debt relief for basic education, and establish a mechanism to back national plans with speedy, co-ordinated and predictable delivery of the additional finance needed; and civil society organizations to hold their own governments and international institutions accountable for upholding the right to education, and delivering on the Education for All goals. Actively encourages and supports the formation of national platforms, bringing together community groups, unions, education NGOs, churches, young people, women and other stakeholders to create broad-based citizen pressure for action on the Education for All goals. Activities include the annual Global Action Week.

Geographical Area of Activity: International.

Contact: Admin. Co-ordinator Emanuel A. Fatoma.

Address: c/o Education International, 5 blvd du Roi Albert II, 8th floor, 1210 Brussels, Belgium.

Telephone: (2) 224-06-27; *Fax:* (2) 224-06-11; *Internet:* www.campaignforeducation .org; *e-mail:* anne@campaignforeducation.org.

UNITED NATIONS CONFERENCE ON NGOS (CONGO)

Established in 1948 to serve as a common platform for NGOs with ECOSOC consultative status.

Activities: CONGO is comprised of thematic sub-committees of consultative status NGOs which aim to co-ordinate and improve UN–NGO relations. Also organizes NGO events linked to UN conferences. Works in conjunction with the CONGO Foundation (q.v.).

Geographical Area of Activity: International.

How to Apply: Full membership is by application, open only to NGOs with ECOSOC consultative status; associate members do not need to hold consultative status.

Contact: Pres. Renate Bloem.

Address: Palais des Nations, Bureau E2B, 1211 Geneva 20, Switzerland.

Telephone: (22) 9171881; *Fax:* (22) 9170373; *Internet:* www.ngocongo.org/index2 .html; *e-mail:* congo@ngocongo.org.

CONGO Foundation

Established in the USA in 1996 to support the goals and purposes of the Conference of Non-governmental Organizations in Consultative Relationship with the United Nations (CONGO).

Activities: Carries out activities consistent with the goals and purposes of CONGO which aim: to ensure that NGOs in consultative status enjoy the fullest opportunities and all appropriate facilities for performing their consultative functions; to foster co-operation and dialogue among all NGOs and with groupings of NGOs related to the UN system; to provide a forum for the exchange of views on matters relating to the consultative process and on strengthening the relationship between NGOs and the UN, including the contributions which NGOs can make to promoting the principles, purposes, and effectiveness of the UN and its related agencies and programmes; to mobilize public opinion in support of the aims and principles of the UN, and to promote education about the UN with special emphasis on the contribution which NGOs make to its work; and to convene meetings of NGOs for the exchange of views on matters of common interest.

Geographical Area of Activity: International.

Address: Palais des Nations, Bureau E2B, 1211 Geneva 20, Switzerland.

Telephone: (22) 9171881; *Fax:* (22) 9170373; *Internet:* www.ngocongo.org /ngowhow/foundbl.htm; *e-mail:* congo@ngocongo.org.

UNITED NATIONS CONFERENCE ON TRADE AND DEVELOPMENT (UNCTAD)

Least-Developed Countries

Established in 1964; aims at the development-friendly integration of developing countries into the world economy, with particular attention to the special difficulties of landlocked developing countries and small island developing states.

Activities: Aims to facilitate a more equitable integration of developing countries into the global economy and to enhance their economic growth and development prospects, through developing technical co-operation initiatives that emphasize knowledge-sharing and enhancement, human resources development, productive capacity building, as well as support to trade facilitation and logistics. Operates in co-operation with NGOs and other organizations, and donor countries.

Geographical Area of Activity: Developing countries: Afghanistan, Angola, Bangladesh, Benin, Bhutan, Burkina Faso, Burundi, Cambodia, Cape Verde, Chad, Comoros, Democratic Republic of the Congo, Djibouti, Equatorial Guinea, Eritrea, Ethiopia, Gambia, Guinea, Guinea-Bissau, Haiti, Kiribati, Laos, Lesotho,

Liberia, Madagascar, Malawi, Maldives, Mali, Mauritania, Mozambique, Myanmar, Nepal, Niger, Rwanda, Samoa, Senegal, Sierra Leone, Solomon Islands, Somalia, Sudan, Tanzania, Togo, Tuvalu, Uganda, Vanuatu, Yemen and Zambia.

Address: Palais des Nations, 1211 Geneva 10, Switzerland.

Telephone: (22) 9071234; *Fax:* (22) 9070043; *Internet:* www.unctad.org; *e-mail:* info@unctad.org.

Relations with NGOs

Established in 1964, the United Nations Conference on Trade and Development (UNCTAD) aims at the development-friendly integration of developing countries into the world economy. Acts as the focal point within the UN for the integrated treatment of trade and development and interrelated issues in the areas of finance, technology, investment and sustainable development.

Activities: Works together with member governments and interacts with organizations of the UN system and regional commissions, as well as with governmental institutions, NGOs, the private sector, including trade and industry associations, research institutes and universities world-wide. Maintains relations with NGOs in three categories of status: general, special, and register. These NGOs have observer status at UNCTAD meetings.

Geographical Area of Activity: International.

Contact: Sec.-Gen. Rubens Ricupero.

Address: Palais des Nations, 8–14 ave de la Paix , 1211 Geneva 10, Switzerland.

Telephone: (22) 9071234; *Fax:* (22) 9070043; *Internet:* www.unctad.org; *e-mail:* info@unctad.org.

UNITED NATIONS CONVENTION TO COMBAT DESERTIFICATION (UNCCD)

The Secretariat for the Convention to Combat Desertification (UNCCD) was established by the UN General Assembly to assist the Intergovernmental Negotiating Committee in the negotiation of the Convention and preparing for the sessions of the Conference of the Parties.

Activities: NGOs form part of the official programme of work of the Conference of Parties, through accreditation as part of UNCCD's recognition that civil society in general and NGOs in particular are key co-operating partners, and have shown commitment to the UNCCD throughout the negotiation process, and that their co-operation with UNCCD contributes significantly to the successful implementation of the Convention. It recognizes that one of the many strengths of the non-governmental community is that it is the voice and interface of grassroots communities, and that this Convention aims to improve the livelihoods of marginalized populations, particularly those communities most threatened by drought and desertification. By 2003 more than 650 NGOs had been accredited with observer status to the Conference of the Parties.

Geographical Area of Activity: International.

Contact: NGO Contact Marcos Montoiro.

Address: UNCCD/ERPI, Martin-Luther-King-Str. 8, 53175 Bonn, Germany.

Internet: www.unccd.int/ngo/menu.php; *e-mail:* mmontoiro@unccd.int.

Regional Office—Africa: TPN 1—Integrated management of international river, lake and hydro-geological basins

The Thematic Programme Network (TPN1) was launched at a meeting held in Accra, Ghana, on 29 November–1 December 2000.

Activities: The Programme's priority activities are to: facilitate and co-ordinate the exchange of information, experiences and local know-how among existing institutions involved in water resources management and the implementation of the UNCCD process in Africa; build a strong link with the African Land and Water Management Initiative (ALWMI) supported by the Global Environment Facility (GEF) and its Implementing Agencies; set up integrated information systems, strengthen their use in the existing documentation centres and create data banks on the thematic area concerned for use by the interested actors.

Geographical Area of Activity: Africa.

Contact: Sector Co-ordinator Phera Ramoeli.

Address: SADC Water Sector Co-ordination Unit, Private Bag A440, 23 Mabille Rd, Red Cross Bldg, Maseru 100, Lesotho.

Telephone: 320720; *Fax:* 310465; *Internet:* www.unccd.int/actionprogrammes /africa/regional/tpn1/menu.php; *e-mail:* sadcwscu@lesoff.co.za.

Regional Office—Africa: TPN 2—Promotion of agro-forestry and soil conservation

The Thematic Programme Network (TPN 2) was launched at a meeting held in Lomé, Togo, in June 2001.

Activities: The Programme's priority activities are to: support regional and sub-regional initiatives for the promotion of domestication, processing and marketing of agro-forestry products (plant species) of socio-economic interest for African countries; and support the African Land and Water Management Initiative through promotion of agro-forestry inputs and use of African expertise. Also takes part in international conferences.

Geographical Area of Activity: Africa.

Contact: Contact Idriss O. Alfaroukh.

Address: c/o Institut du Sahel, BP 1530, Bamako, Mali.

Telephone: 234067; *Fax:* 225980; *Internet:* www.insah.org; *e-mail:* idriss@agrosoc .insah.ml.

Regional Office—Africa: TPN 3—Rational use of rangelands and promotion of fodder crops development

The Thematic Programme Network (TPN 3) was launched at a meeting held in Maseru, Lesotho, on 27–29 November 2001; administered by the Interafrican Bureau for Animal Resources.

Activities: The Programme's priority activities are to: promote capacity building in rational use of rangelands and fodder crops development activities that are better implemented at the regional level; strengthen exchange of information and appropriate techniques, technical know-how and relevant experience as it relates to rational use of rangelands and promotion of fodder crops development; co-ordinate and compile activities related to combating desertification from various aspects, undertaken by different stakeholders, in order to prevent duplication and increase efficiency, thus benefiting countries of the regions with minimum expenditure; and to assist the African countries as well as the relevant sub-regional and specialized institutions to carry out their obligations in implementing the Convention to Combat Desertification at regional level.

Geographical Area of Activity: Africa.

Contact: Acting Dir Dr Jotham Musiime.

Address: c/o Interafrican Bureau for Animal Resources, POB 30786, Nairobi, Kenya.

Telephone: (2) 338544; *Fax:* (2) 332 046; *Internet:* www.unccd.int /actionprogrammes/africa/regional/tpn3/menu.php; *e-mail:* jotham.musiime@oau-ibar.org.

Regional Office—Africa: TPN 4—Ecological monitoring, natural resources mapping, remote sensing and early warning systems

Launched at a meeting in Tunis held in October 2002.

Activities: Aims to facilitate information flow and co-ordination of activities related to ecological monitoring, natural resources mapping, remote sensing and early warning systems; disseminate information; link with other networks; promote partnerships; build capacities; and link with other regional initiatives.

Geographical Area of Activity: Africa.

Contact: Contact Muftah Unis.

Address: BP 102 Hussein Dey, 16040 Alger, Algeria.

Telephone: (21) 231-717; *Fax:* (21) 233-339; *Internet:* www.unccd.int /actionprogrammes/africa/regional/tpn4/menu.php; *e-mail:* oact@wissal.dz.

Regional Office—Africa: TPN 5—Promotion of new and renewable energy sources and technologies

The Programme is co-ordinated by the Agence Nationale des Energies Renouvelables in Tunisia and Environnement et Développement du Tiers Monde in Senegal.

Activities: Aims to promote capacity building, and strengthen exchange of information and appropriate techniques, technical know-how and relevant experience through the promotion of new and renewable energy sources and technologies. In general, the Network co-ordinates activities related to combating desertification through promotion of new and renewable energy sources and technologies from the various activities undertaken by different stakeholders, in order to prevent duplication and to increase efficiency.

Geographical Area of Activity: Africa.

Contact: Dir Naceur Hammami.

Address: 3 rue 8,000 Montplaisir, Tunis–Belvedère 1002, Tunisia.

Telephone: (71) 846-241; *Fax:* (71) 784-624; *Internet:* www.unccd.int /actionprogrammes/africa/regional/tpn5/menu.php; *e-mail:* nhammami@aner.nat .tn.

Regional Office—Africa: TPN 6—Promotion of sustainable agricultural farming systems

The Programme is administered by African Union Semi-Arid Food Grain Research and Development (AU/SAFGRAD) in Burkina Faso.

Activities: Aims to promote capacity building, and strengthening of the exchange of information and appropriate techniques, technical know-how and relevant experience in sustainable agricultural farming systems. In general, the Network co-ordinates activities related to combating desertification through promotion of sustainable agricultural farming systems from various efforts undertaken by different stakeholders, including NGOs.

Geographical Area of Activity: Africa.

Contact: International Co-ordinator Bezuneh Taye.

Address: 01 BP 1783, Ouagadougou 03, Burkina Faso.

Telephone: 30-60-71; *Fax:* 31-15-86; *Internet:* www.unccd.int/actionprogrammes /africa/regional/tpn6/menu.php; *e-mail:* oua.safgrad@fasonet.bf.

UNCCD Regional Co-ordination Unit for Africa: Thematic Programme Networks (TPNs)

Thematic Programme Networks (TPNs), in the context of the Regional Action Programme (RAP) to combat desertification in Africa, are networks of institutions and agencies linked together via an institutional focal point. Regional, sub-regional and national focal institutions involve all key actors at regional, sub-regional and national level in the respective affected countries. Network activities are delegated to participating institutions or agencies at various levels, and work is carried out in co-operation with other networks working on related issues. A number of TPNs are already in place, although as of 2003 implementation of activities was still under preparation. The launched TPNs are in the process of establishing and making operational their institutional arrangements, and identifying funding sources.

Activities: The contribution from NGOs to the work of the UN Convention to Combat Desertification (UNCCD) forms part of the official programme of work of the Conference of Parties. By 2003 more than 650 NGOs were accredited with observer status to the Conference of the Parties, and participate in the implementation of the Convention.

Geographical Area of Activity: Africa.

Address: c/o African Development Bank (ADB), POB 1387, Abidjan 01, Ivory Coast.

Internet: www.unccd.int/actionprogrammes/africa/africa.php#subregional.

UNITED NATIONS DEVELOPMENT FUND FOR WOMEN (UNIFEM)

Governance, Peace and Security: Strengthening Women's Leadership

A UNIFEM programme aiming to promote women's leadership in all sectors, with the goal of giving women an equal voice in shaping the policies that affect their lives and choices. The programme aims to increase women's opportunities to influence the direction of society and to remove obstacles to women's access to power.

Activities: Provides support to a range of programmes that aim to build gender awareness and develop gender equality allies among public servants, strengthening co-operation among women's organizations, women parliamentarians, and women's civil society organizations. Support is provided for training, regional exchanges, and constituency building. In Afghanistan the programme involved UNIFEM providing support to local NGOs to raise awareness of the situation of women and their needs, providing support to internally displaced people through the establishment of community centres, and the provision of technical expertise and information to women's groups.

Geographical Area of Activity: International.

Address: 304 East 45th St, 15th Floor, New York, NY 10017, USA.

Telephone: (212) 906-6896; *Fax:* (212) 906-6705; *Internet:* www.unifem.undp.org /governance/; *e-mail:* unifem@undp.org.

Trust Fund in Support of Actions to Eliminate Violence Against Women

Established in 1996 at UNIFEM by the UN General Assembly, in response to the call for action from the UN Fourth World Conference on Women in Beijing in 1995.

Activities: The Fund aims to operate as a grant-making laboratory to explore new, innovative strategies and best practices, with experiences gained then fed into UNIFEM's national, regional and global programmes as part of its longer-term strategy to eliminate violence against women. Funding is provided for a wide range of initiatives, including education and training, research and the use of media and communications to tackle violence against women. In 2001 the Fund launched a regional advocacy campaign to end violence against women in eight countries of the Commonwealth of Independent States (CIS) and Lithuania, building on lessons learned from UNIFEM's 1998–99 campaigns in Central and South America and the Caribbean, Africa and Asia-Pacific.

Geographical Area of Activity: International.

Financial Information: Total grants since 1996 US $5,300,000.

Publications: With an End in Sight: Strategies from the UNIFEM Trust Fund to Eliminate Violence against Women.

Address: 304 East 45th St, 15th Floor, New York, NY 10017, USA.

Telephone: (212) 906-6400; *Fax:* (212) 906-6705; *Internet:* www.unifem.undp.org /trustfund/index.html.

UNIFEM Arab States Regional Office (UNIFEM ASRO)

Established in 1994 as one of 15 regional UNIFEM offices. Its mandate covers 17 Arab countries: Algeria, Bahrain, Egypt, Iraq, Jordan, Kuwait, Lebanon, Libya, Morocco, Oman, Palestinian Autonomous Areas, Qatar, Saudi Arabia, Syria, Tunisia, the United Arab Emirates and Yemen.

Activities: Projects and initiatives focus on the three main areas of: strengthening women's economic rights and empowering women to enjoy secure livelihoods as entrepreneurs, producers and home-based workers, especially in the context of new trade agendas and technologies; engendering governance and peace-building to increase women's participation in decision-making processes that shape their lives; and promoting women's human rights to eliminate all forms of violence against women and transform development into a more peaceful, equitable and sustainable process. Works by strengthening the capacity and leadership of women's networks and organizations; leveraging political and financial support for women; forging new partnerships amongst women's organizations, governments, the UN system and private sector; undertaking and funding pilot projects to test innovative approaches to women's empowerment and gender mainstreaming; and building a knowledge base on effective strategies for engendering mainstream development.

Geographical Area of Activity: Algeria, Bahrain, Egypt, Iraq, Jordan, Kuwait, Lebanon, Libya, Morocco, Oman, Palestinian Autonomous Areas, Qatar, Saudi Arabia, Syria, Tunisia, the United Arab Emirates and Yemen.

Contact: Dir Dr Haifa Abu Ghazaleh.

Address: POB 830896, Amman 11183, Jordan.

Telephone: (6) 5678586; *Fax:* (6) 5678594; *Internet:* www.unifem.org /global_spanner/index.php?f_loc=arab; *e-mail:* ammam@unifem.org.jo.

UNIFEM Arab States Regional Office (UNIFEM ASRO): Economic Security

UNIFEM ASRO's focus on economic security aims to: engender macroeconomic frameworks and build the capacity of countries to manage globalization and economic transition from the perspective of poor women; promote enabling legal, institutional and regulatory environments for women's equal ownership and access to economic resources; strengthen women's economic capacity and rights as entrepreneurs, producers and home-based workers; and bring a gender analysis to economic policies and the distribution of public resources by the use of gender-responsive budget analysis.

Activities: Supports economic empowerment projects in the Arab states in partnership with and through funding governments, NGOs and community organizations. Supported projects include information and communications technologies empowerment initiatives, promotion of economic rights, and the development of support mechanisms to help the development of viable, equitable and innovative women-owned businesses.

Geographical Area of Activity: Algeria, Bahrain, Egypt, Iraq, Jordan, Kuwait, Lebanon, Libya, Morocco, Oman, Palestinian Autonomous Areas, Qatar, Saudi Arabia, Syria, Tunisia, the United Arab Emirates and Yemen.

Contact: Dir Dr Haifa Abu Ghazaleh.

Address: POB 830896, Amman 11183, Jordan.

Telephone: (6) 5678586; *Fax:* (6) 5678594; *Internet:* www.unifem.org /global_spanner/index.php?f_loc=arab; *e-mail:* ammam@unifem.org.jo.

UNIFEM Arab States Regional Office (UNIFEM ASRO): Governance, Peace and Security Programme

The Programme works to support implementation of the Beijing Platform for Action, aimed at enhancing women's empowerment, improving women's health, advancing women's education and training, promoting women's marital and sexual rights, ending gender-based violence and bringing a gender perspective to constitutional, electoral, legislative, judicial and policy process to help strengthen the rule of law and ensure gender justice.

Activities: The Programme's objectives are: to build capacity and develop skills to strengthen women's leadership in order to promote their access to and participation in decision-making structures; support women's organizations to engender national legislation, policies, plans and programmes; facilitate partnerships between women's organizations and governments; work with local, national and regional media to promote a positive image of women and their role in society; and to strengthen the gender focus in prevention and early warning mechanisms, and improve protection and assistance for women affected by conflict. National projects channelling funding to and implemented by NGOs include capacity building for national women's organizations, development of national strategies for women's advancement; and empowerment of women through the development of a media network.

Geographical Area of Activity: Algeria, Bahrain, Egypt, Iraq, Jordan, Kuwait, Lebanon, Libya, Morocco, Oman, Palestinian Autonomous Areas, Qatar, Saudi Arabia, Syria, Tunisia, the United Arab Emirates and Yemen.

Contact: Dir Dr Haifa Abu Ghazaleh.

Address: POB 830896, Amman 11183, Jordan.

Telephone: (6) 5678586; *Fax:* (6) 5678594; *Internet:* www.unifem.org /global_spanner/index.php?f_loc=arab; *e-mail:* ammam@unifem.org.jo.

UNIFEM Arab States Regional Office (UNIFEM ASRO): Governance, Peace and Security Programme—Arab Women Connect

An initiative of the Governance, Peace and Security Programme (q.v.); considered a first step in UNIFEM ASRO's strategy to integrate Arab women in the information technology (IT) sector, both as users and producers.

Activities: Seeks to integrate Arab women in the IT sector, both as users and producers, in Egypt, Jordan, Lebanon, Palestinian Autonomous Areas, Qatar, Syria, United Arab Emirates and Yemen, by encouraging the utilization of information and communications technologies by Arab women's organizations.

Geographical Area of Activity: Egypt, Jordan, Lebanon, Palestinian Autonomous Areas, Qatar, Syria, United Arab Emirates and Yemen.

Financial Information: Funded by the government of the Netherlands.

Contact: Dir Dr Haifa Abu Ghazaleh.

Address: POB 830896, Amman 11183, Jordan.

Telephone: (6) 5678586; *Fax:* (6) 5678594; *Internet:* www.unifem.org /global_spanner/index.php?f_loc=arab; *e-mail:* ammam@unifem.org.jo.

UNIFEM Arab States Regional Office (UNIFEM ASRO): Regional Programme on Engendering Economic Governance in Asia-Pacific and the Arab States

The Programme aims to engender macroeconomic frameworks and economic institutions to increase women's choices and opportunities and to strengthen women's economic capacities, rights and sustainable livelihoods.

Activities: Works to enhance the collation of national gender statistics and their use by governments and NGOs; build the capacity of women's organizations to understand and advocate for women's concerns, initiate and strengthen gender budgeting through regional gender budgeting initiatives; and facilitate cross-regional and regional-global learning within the field of engendering economic governance, including support to women's participation and a gender perspective in regional trade groupings, improving access for women SMEs and micro- and cottage businesses to private-sector and global markets through women's business councils.

Geographical Area of Activity: South Asia, South-East Asia, the Pacific and Arab states.

Contact: Dir Dr Haifa Abu Ghazaleh.

Address: POB 830896, Amman 11183, Jordan.

Telephone: (6) 5678586; *Fax:* (6) 5678594; *Internet:* www.unifem.org /global_spanner/index.php?f_loc=arab; *e-mail:* ammam@unifem.org.jo.

UNIFEM Arab States Regional Office (UNIFEM ASRO): Regional Technical Resource Network for Women's Small and Micro-Enterprises in the Area

Launched in July 2001; an initiative of UNIFEM ASRO's economic security programme aiming to increase women's access to, and control of, economic resources in the Arab region.

Activities: Promotes women's economic empowerment in the Arab region, through upgrading the technical capacity, outreach and gender-sensitivity of support institutions for micro- and support institutions and developing resources. Also plays an advocacy and networking role to promote co-operation and co-ordination amongst NGOs, governments, enterprise development programmes, and financial and non-financial providers to women entrepreneurs.

Geographical Area of Activity: Arab states.

Financial Information: Funding from UNIFEM and the Arab Gulf Programme for the United Nations Development Organizations (AGFUND).

Contact: Dir Dr Haifa Abu Ghazaleh.

Address: POB 830896, Amman 11183, Jordan.

Telephone: (6) 5678586; *Fax:* (6) 5678594; *Internet:* www.unifem.org.j/trn/; *e-mail:* ammam@unifem.org.jo.

UNIFEM Arab States Regional Office (UNIFEM ASRO): Women's Human Rights

Supports projects that focus on women's empowerment through training, advocacy and the promotion of women's human rights, institutional building and support to NGOs.

Activities: Funding is given to women's human rights projects in three areas: eliminating violence against women and girls through investing in prevention, protection and advocacy strategies; assisting the effective implementation of the Convention on the Elimination of All Forms of Discrimination Against Women (CEDAW); and enhancing the understanding of governments, advocates and UN partners of the relationships between human rights, gender and HIV/AIDS to strengthen responses to the epidemic. National projects, involving funding support to NGOs, include projects to empower migrant women workers, capacity building of NGOs, public awareness raising about women's legal rights, and training and research on and prevention of violence against girls with disabilities.

Geographical Area of Activity: Algeria, Bahrain, Egypt, Iraq, Jordan, Kuwait, Lebanon, Libya, Morocco, Oman, Palestinian Autonomous Areas, Qatar, Saudi Arabia, Syria, Tunisia, the United Arab Emirates and Yemen.

Contact: Dir Dr Haifa Abu Ghazaleh.

Address: POB 830896, Amman 11183, Jordan.

Telephone: (6) 5678586; *Fax:* (6) 5678594; *e-mail:* ammam@unifem.org.jo.

UNIFEM South Asia: Economic Security and Rights

Aims to promote women's employment and economic contribution; build women's capacities and improve their access to larger markets and financial products and services; and improve living and working conditions for women migrant workers.

Activities: Programme activities include support to projects empowering women in especially vulnerable situations, including migrant workers and home-based workers, through the development of networks, dissemination of information, improving services, skills training, promoting dialogue, facilitating networking in partnership with civil society organizations and NGOs. Also funds pilot projects and NGO capacity building which deal with providing women workers with access to global markets, developing information and communications technologies managerial skills, promoting entrepreneurial development amongst women and offering training on micro-credit opportunities.

Geographical Area of Activity: South Asia.

Contact: Regional Programme Dir Chandni Joshi.

Address: 223 Jor Bagh, New Delhi 110 003, India.

Telephone: (11) 4698297; *Fax:* (11) 4622136; *Internet:* www.unifem.org.in /Economic%20Security%20and%20Rights%20Programme.html; *e-mail:* chandni .joshi@undp.org.

UNIFEM South Asia: Engendering Governance

The programme aims to: engender governance by strengthening accountability by engendering institutions, systems and processes of governance; engender the leadership of women in politics to play a transformatory role in policy and development planning in South Asia; enable gender responsiveness in institutional bureaucracy; and strengthen the intellectual and conceptual understanding of South Asia networks of organizations and individuals committed to gender-just and sustainable development.

Activities: Links grassroots women's voices and concerns with policy-makers through networking, conferences and supporting the capacity building and training of women leaders, and the strengthening of women's organizations and networks.

Geographical Area of Activity: South Asia.

Contact: Regional Programme Dir Chandni Joshi.

Address: 223 Jor Bagh, New Delhi 110 003, India.

Telephone: (11) 4698297; *Fax:* (11) 4622136; *Internet:* www.unifem.org.in; *e-mail:* chandni.joshi@undp.org.

UNIFEM South Asia: Promoting Human Rights

The programme aims to: facilitate the implementation of human rights instruments and bring laws into conformity with human rights standards; strengthen institutional mechanisms for gender justice; address different forms of violence against women and girls in the home and community and the socio-cultural practices that perpetuate it; develop actions to address women's human rights in the context of conflict and post-conflict; promote well-defined preventive, protective and prosecution strategies in the region to reduce trafficking of women and children; and project the gender dimension of HIV/AIDS into the public discourse on HIV/AIDS, including governments, NGOs, bilateral and UN agencies.

Activities: Programme activities include supporting governments and NGOs in implementing and reporting on the Women's Convention; collaborating with NGOs on anti-trafficking initiatives; developing partnerships to support women victims of violence; raising awareness of gender issues amongst adolescent boys and girls; training for NGOs to act as advocates; and promoting the ability of UNIFEM and its partners to respond effectively to the concerns of women affected by HIV/AIDS.

Geographical Area of Activity: South Asia.

Contact: Regional Programme Dir Chandni Joshi.

Address: 223 Jor Bagh, New Delhi 110 003, India.

Telephone: (11) 4698297; *Fax:* (11) 4622136; *e-mail:* chandni.joshi@undp.org.

UNITED NATIONS DEVELOPMENT PROGRAMME (UNDP)

The global development network of the UN, established in November 1965 through the merger of two programmes, the UN Special Fund and the expanded programme for Technical Assistance. UNDP is the world's largest multilateral organization for grant-based technical co-operation. Works with people and government in over 170 developing countries through a network of 135 offices.

Activities: The six priority areas of UNDP are: democratic governance, poverty reduction, crisis prevention and recovery, energy and environment, information and communications technology, and HIV/AIDS. UNDP works with civil society organizations at all levels, encouraging policy dialogues between governments, civil society and donors, and advocating for legal and regulatory environments that enable civil society to contribute to the development process. Assists in civil society capacity development by connecting them to knowledge, experience and resources from around the world, including the promotion of networking between civil society organizations in other countries and regions.

Geographical Area of Activity: International.

Publications: Human Development Report; Policy Statement on Collaboration with Civil Society (1997).

Contact: Admin. Mark Malloch Brown.

Address: 1 UN Plaza, New York, NY 10017, USA.

Telephone: (212) 906-5558; *Fax:* (212) 906-5364; *Internet:* www.undp.org.

Adopt-A-Minefield

A programme of the UN Association of the USA and the Better World Fund (q.v.), in partnership with the UN, US Department of State, Heather Mills Health Trust, United Nations Association of Great Britain and Northern Ireland, Canadian Landmine Foundation, the International Trust Fund for Demining and Mine Victims Assistance, and the Mines Advisory Group. The programme is managed by the United Nations Development Programme (UNDP).

Activities: Adopt-A-Minefield engages individuals, community groups, and businesses in the UN effort to resolve the global land-mine crisis. The campaign helps save lives by gathering funds for mine clearance and survivor assistance by raising awareness about the land-mine problem. The campaign seeks national and international sponsors to adopt minefields that the UN has identified as being in urgent need of clearance. Sponsors raise funds in their communities to clear their adopted minefields and return land to productive use, and the campaign provides funds for survivor assistance projects. In 2003 programmes operated in Afghanistan, Bosnia and Herzegovina, Cambodia, Croatia, Iraq, Mozambique and Vietnam.

Geographical Area of Activity: International, including Afghanistan, Bosnia and Herzegovina, Cambodia, Croatia, Iraq, Mozambique and Vietnam.

Address: UN Asscn of the USA, 801 Second Ave, New York, NY 10017, USA.

Telephone: (212) 907-1300; *Fax:* (212) 682-9185; *Internet:* www.landmines.org; *e-mail:* info@landmines.org.

Africa 2000 Plus Network (A2+N)

The Network, previously the Africa 2000 Network, was set up by the UN Development Programme in 1989 to provide institutional support to foster environmentally sensitive poverty-reduction policies to improve the livelihoods and resource management of rural communities in Africa.

Activities: The Network aims to: foster innovative community initiatives that sustain livelihoods, protect the environment, and further its development in ecologically sustainable ways; develop local capacity for project management and responsible governance by strengthening indigenous organizations; develop and support communications activities to foster exchange and replication of good practices; and ensure sustainability of the Network beyond the duration of the project. The Network provides technical assistance and grants of up to US $50,000 to grassroots organizations in 13 countries in Africa. Activities receiving funding include natural forest management, erosion control, range and watershed management, food preservation and storage, fish farming, livestock rearing and dairy farming, bee-keeping and management of accounts.

Geographical Area of Activity: Africa.

Financial Information: Grants of up to US $50,000 available.

Address: 1 UN Plaza, New York, NY 10017, USA.

Fax: (212) 906-5313; *Internet:* www.undp.org/cso/areas.html.

Bureau for Crisis Prevention and Recovery—Small Arms and Demobilization Unit: UNDP Trust Fund for Support to Prevention and Reduction of the Proliferation of Small Arms

Established in 1998 to implement activities and programmes in the area of small weapons reduction, to concentrate efforts on the need to reduce the proliferation of small weapons as part of its development work, and to implement its strategy on small weapons.

Activities: Funds the design and implementation of a number of programmes aimed at limiting the demand for small weapons in different conflict or conflict-prone situations in countries and to develop more comprehensive peace-building strategies recognizing that people need jobs, security, and a voice in society. Provides assistance to governments so they can strengthen their own institutions to control the spread of small weapons, conducts awareness-raising campaigns and supports community-based development initiatives.

Geographical Area of Activity: International.

Financial Information: Funding from the governments of Belgium, Canada, the Netherlands, Norway, Switzerland, and the UK.

Address: 1 UN Plaza, New York, NY 10017, USA.

Internet: www.undp.org/erd/smallarms/index.htm; *e-mail:* bcpr@undp.org.

Bureau for Crisis Prevention and Recovery: UNDP Thematic Trust Fund—Crisis Prevention and Recovery

Established in 2000 by the UN Development Programme's (UNDP) Bureau for Crisis Prevention and Recovery.

Activities: Carries out its activities through seven service lines, implementing a range of strategic approaches: seeking out and sharing innovative policy approaches to guide development actions; offering technical advice and operational support for programme implementation and co-ordination; mobilizing and managing financial and human resources; developing institutional and programme capacity among partners through skills development and training; developing strategic partnerships and alliances; and developing capacities through sharing experiences and best practices. The seven service lines through which these approaches are implemented are: conflict prevention and peace building; recovery; security sector reform and transitional justice; small weapons reduction, disarmament and demobilization of ex-combatants; mine action; natural disaster reduction; and special initiatives for countries in transition. NGOs and other organizations are called upon to implement and execute a number of the Fund's projects.

Geographical Area of Activity: International.

How to Apply: Funding requests channelled through UNDP country offices are received as short-format proposals and acted upon on a fast track basis.

Financial Information: The Fund has mobilized over US $180,000,000 in resources since 2000.

Address: 1 UN Plaza, 20th Floor, New York, NY 10017, USA.

Telephone: (212) 906-5194; *Fax:* (212) 906-5379; *Internet:* www.undp.org/bcpr; *e-mail:* bcpr@undp.org.

Bureau for Development Policy: Thematic Trust Fund for Information and Communication Technology (ICT) for Development

Launched by the UN Development Programme (UNDP) in October 2001; one of its thematic trust funds, to promote the use of Information and Communication Technology (ICT).

Activities: The Fund supports global, national and regional programmes on ICT for development in six main areas, including: the design of national e-development strategies; initiatives to put ICT in the service of democratic governance, poverty reduction and other development imperatives; capacity-building and implementation assistance; and promotion of ICT's potential. It also supports the adaptation of such technologies and related systems to meet local conditions and address regional, national and local needs. To complement ICT strategies at the national level, the Fund dedicates resources to support innovative approaches and bottom-up initiatives in partnership with a range of organizations, including NGOs.

Geographical Area of Activity: Less-developed countries and Africa.

How to Apply: Funding requests channelled through UNDP country offices are received as short-format proposals and acted upon on a fast track basis.

Financial Information: Established with a US $5,000,000 donation from the Japanese government; total budget 2001–03 approx. US $30,000,000.

Contact: Admin. Mark Malloch Brown.

Address: 1 UN Plaza, New York, NY 10017, USA.

Telephone: (212) 906-6914; *Fax:* (212) 906-5778; *Internet:* www.undp.org /trustfunds/tif-ecte.pdf.

Bureau for Development Policy: UNDP Thematic Trust Fund—Energy for Sustainable Development

Established in 2001 to operate alongside the existing UN Development Programme (UNDP)–Global Environment Facility (GEF) programme (q.v.), to address a full range of sustainable energy issues, including capacity-building and rural-development initiatives which fall outside the GEF programme areas.

Activities: Operates within four service lines: national policy frameworks; rural energy services; clean energy technologies; and new financing mechanisms. The emphasis is on innovative policy and programme approaches linking energy and poverty reduction efforts to achieve sustainable human development. A limited number of initiatives are also funded at global, inter - and intra-regional levels, including the development of partnerships with NGOs.

Geographical Area of Activity: International.

How to Apply: Funding requests channelled through UNDP country offices are received as short-format proposals and acted upon on a fast track basis.

Financial Information: Total budget approx. US $60,000,000 (2001–03).

Address: 1 UN Plaza, 20th Floor, New York, NY 10017, USA.

Telephone: (212) 906-6085; *Fax:* (212) 906-5148; *Internet:* www.undp.org /trustfunds/Energy-English-Final.pdf.

Capacity 2015

Capacity 2015 was established following the success of Capacity 21 and other similar programmes aimed at developing the capacity of transition and developing countries to reap the benefits of globalization and meet their sustainable development goals under Agenda 21 and the Millennium Development Goals (MDGs) at the local level.

Activities: The programme supports decentralized initiatives based on transparent, participatory and community-driven approaches and are under-pinned by three broad approaches that guided Capacity 21: integration of the principles of environmentally sustainable socio-economic development into development plans; participation of all stakeholders, including community groups and NGOs; and the creation and enhancement of experience and expertise for sustainable development that is of continued material value for all participants. The programme's primary activities are to: design programmes for capacity building and support for local, national and community-level programmes that focus on meeting the challenges of globalization more effectively and attaining the internationally agreed development goals, including those contained in the Millennium Declaration; develop the capacity of civil society, including youth organizations, to participate, as appropriate, in designing, implementing and reviewing sustainable development policies and strategies at all levels; and build and, where appropriate, strengthen national capacities for carrying out effective implementation of Agenda 21.

Geographical Area of Activity: International.

Address: 1 UN Plaza, New York, NY 10017, USA.

Fax: (212) 906-5313; *Internet:* www.undp.org/capacity2015/.

Civil Society Organizations and Participation Programme

The Bureau for Resources and Strategic Partnerships was established in 2000 to co-ordinate and develop working relationships with donor countries, civil society organizations, international and regional development banks and financial institutions, the private sector and the rest of the UN.

Activities: Works with local, national and international organizations in the UN Development Programme's (UNDP) six priority areas, by promoting and fostering an effective environment in which civil society organizations can contribute towards sustainable human development. It encourages policy dialogue between civil society, governments and donors, supports civil society capacity building through providing accurate information and access to appropriate skills, and gives advice and programme support to UNDP country offices in their collaboration with NGOs. In 2003, operated three programmes: Global; Environment and Social Sustainability; and Indigenous Knowledge (qq.v.).

Geographical Area of Activity: International.

Contact: Dir Caitlin Wiesen.

Address: UNDP, 1 UN Plaza, New York, NY 10017, USA.

Telephone: (212) 906-5906; *Fax:* (212) 906-6814; *Internet:* www.undp.org/csopp /CSO/NewFiles/about.html; *e-mail:* caitlin.wiesen@undp.org.

Civil Society Organizations and Participation Programme: Environment and Social Sustainability Programme

Implemented by the Third World Network programme, and supported by the UN Development Programme (UNDP). The Third World Network is a UNDP partner organization, a network of organizations working in development, third world and North–South issues.

Activities: Assists civil society organizations to take part in international organization conferences and meetings in order to strengthen their role in the decision-making process, by helping civil society representatives to prepare for and participate in the decision-making processes of international organizations and meetings. Also funds research on, and national-level and international-level discussions and processes about, the ownership and control, access to and sustainability of genetic and biological resources and their use, and in particular the rights of indigenous peoples, farmers and local communities, in conjunction with a range of NGOs representing indigenous peoples, as well as supporting the capacity building of NGOs. Throughout its programme of activities there is an emphasis on providing funding to grassroots NGOs and community organizations for environmentally sustainable development.

Geographical Area of Activity: International.

Address: 121-S, Jalan Utama, 10450 Penang, Malaysia.

Telephone: (4) 226-6728; *Fax:* (4) 226-4505; *Internet:* www.twnside.org.sg; *e-mail:* twnet@po.jaring.my.

Civil Society Organizations and Participation Programme: Global Programme

The Programme's full name is the Promotion of Civil Society Organizations and Participatory Development; aims to anchor the work of poverty reduction more deeply into the fabric of citizens and provide coherent and satisfying alternatives for social change.

Activities: Aims to promote poverty reduction, and provide alternatives for social change through supporting the empowerment of people and civil society to participate in, and initiate, poverty-reduction activities; and by promoting collaboration between government, the private sector and civil society in the areas of globalization and poverty.

Geographical Area of Activity: International.

Contact: Dir Caitlin Wiesen.

Address: UNDP, 1 UN Plaza, New York, NY 10017, USA.

Telephone: (212) 906-6814; *Fax:* (212) 906-6814; *Internet:* www.undp.org/csopp /CSO/NewFiles/programmesglobal.htm; *e-mail:* caitlin.wiesen@undp.org.

Civil Society Organizations and Participation Programme: Indigenous Knowledge Programme (IKP)

Established by the UN Development Programme (UNDP) in 1994 in collaboration with the Indigenous Peoples Biodiversity Network (IPBN), with support from the International Development Research Centre, the Swiss Agency for Development and Co-operation, the Norwegian government, and the Royal Danish Ministry of Foreign Affairs. Operates as a global framework for the conservation and promotion of indigenous knowledge.

Activities: Operates as a partnership with indigenous peoples aimed at the recognition of traditional knowledge and the protection of indigenous intellectual property as an important component in reducing poverty and promoting environmental conservation for future generations. Support is given to NGOs, community-based organizations and indigenous peoples organizations for projects which: promote and conserve indigenous knowledge through targeted capacity building and for research projects formulated and implemented by indigenous peoples' organizations; to promote active indigenous participation in international processes and conferences of concern to indigenous peoples, such as the annual Conference of the Parties of the Biodiversity Convention; and to reduce poverty through direct grants for indigenous peoples' self-help initiatives, human resource development and organization building at the community level. In 2003 the priority areas for funding were agricultural biodiversity, coastal, marine and forest biodiversity. The Programme is currently being evaluated.

Geographical Area of Activity: International.

Financial Information: Funding provided by UNDP and a number of partners, including the International Development Research Centre, the Swiss Agency for Development and Co-operation, the Norwegian government, and the Royal Danish Ministry of Foreign Affairs.

Contact: Dir CSO Division Caitlin Wiesen.

Address: 1 UN Plaza, New York, NY 10017, USA.

Telephone: (212) 906-5906; *Fax:* (212) 906-5316; *Internet:* www.undp.org/csopp /CSO/NewFiles/programmesikp.htm; *e-mail:* caitlin.wiesen@undp.org.

Energy and Environment Group: Equator Initiative

The Initiative was established as a partnership between the UN, civil society, business, governments and local organizations; aims to reduce poverty through the conservation and sustainable use of biodiversity in the Equatorial belt by fostering, supporting and strengthening community partnerships.

Activities: Carries out research in conjunction with academic institutions, building on the success of the community-led initiatives receiving the Equator Prize (q.v.). Also operates a policy and advocacy programme which is designed to help improve institutional frameworks and the enabling environment for poverty alleviation and biodiversity protection at local, national and international levels, promoting the position of community representatives for influencing policy decisions through the development of multi-stakeholder dialogues with a particular emphasis on community experiences; and operates a Learning Exchange Programme which makes grants to support the spread of successful community and NGO initiatives, build partnerships and networks of local stakeholders to support the capacity of NGOs and community organizations to address biodiversity conservation and sustainable development, and to promote bottom-up holistic learning packages. Also holds regional workshops and seminars, and international conferences.

Geographical Area of Activity: Equatorial belt countries.

Contact: Environment Programme Team Man. and Biodiversity Conservation and Poverty Reduction Adviser Charles McNeill; Man. Sean Southey.

Address: Bureau for Development Policy, 405 Lexington Ave, 4th Floor, New York, NY 10174, USA.

Telephone: (212) 457-1709; *Fax:* (212) 457-1370; *Internet:* www.equatorinitiative .org; *e-mail:* equatorinitiative@undp.org.

Energy and Environment Group: Equator Initiative—Equator Prize

Established by the Equator Initiative as part of its programme of promoting and championing community-level development projects.

Activities: The Initiative awards biennial prizes in recognition of communities in the tropical belt that demonstrate in practical terms successful efforts to simultaneously conserve biodiversity and reduce poverty. Six grassroots organizations each receive prizes of US $30,000 every two years.

Geographical Area of Activity: Countries of the Equatorial belt.

Financial Information: Six awards of US $30,000 every two years.

Contact: Environment Programme Team Man. and Biodiversity Conservation and Poverty Reduction Adviser Charles McNeill; Man. Sean Southey.

Address: Bureau for Development Policy, 405 Lexington Ave, 4th Floor, New York, NY 10174, USA.

Telephone: (212) 457-1709; *Fax:* (212) 457-1370; *Internet:* www.equatorinitiative .org; *e-mail:* equatorinitiative@undp.org.

Human Rights Strengthening Programme (HURIST)

A joint programme of the UN Development Programme (UNDP) and the Office of the High Commissioner on Human Rights (OHCHR), launched in 2002.

Activities: Aims to support the implementation of UNDP policy on human rights as presented in the policy document, Integrating Human Rights with Sustainable Human Development. Its primary purposes are to test guide-lines and methodologies and to identify best practices and learning opportunities in the development of national capacity for the promotion and protection of human rights and in the application of a human rights approach to development programming. A key component of the Programme focuses on partnerships with indigenous peoples and civil society organizations. Three pilot projects were initiated in 2003.

Geographical Area of Activity: International.

Address: 1 UN Plaza, New York, NY 10017, USA.

Fax: (212) 906-5313; *Internet:* www.undp.org/cso/areas.html.

Inter-Agency Learning Group on Participation (IGP)

Created in 1995, under the auspices of the UN, with three objectives: to advance the mainstreaming of participatory development within international development agencies, to provide a forum for exchange of information and analysis on participatory development, and to build an action network for supporting participatory development, particularly at the local level. Representatives from leading multilateral and bilateral donor agencies and northern and southern NGOs participate in IGP's meetings and joint activities.

Activities: Aims to advance the mainstreaming of participatory development at intergovernmental level and build up a network to support popular participation at the local level. The Group comprises the UN Development Programme (UNDP), International Bank for Reconstruction and Development (IBRD—World Bank), United Nations Development Fund for Women (UNIFEM), Global Environment Facility (GEF), United Nations Children's Fund (UNICEF, qq.v.), bilateral donor agencies, private foundations and NGOs.

Geographical Area of Activity: International.

Address: 1 UN Plaza, New York, NY 10017, USA.

Fax: (212) 906 5364; *Internet:* www.undp.org.

LIFE—Local Initiative Facility for Urban Environment

A UN Development Programme (UNDP) global flagship programme to promote local–local dialogue and partnership between NGOs, CBOs, local governments and the private sector for improving the living conditions of the urban poor and influencing policies for participatory local governance.

Activities: LIFE provides small grants, up to US $50,000, directly to NGOs and CBOs, for needs-based participatory community projects in urban poor communities, principally in support of capacity development of local actors and the promotion of advocacy and policy dialogues using the experience of the projects. In 2003 LIFE operated in 12 developing countries where the LIFE national programmes are managed and monitored by multi-stakeholder National Steering Committees. In addition LIFE supports regional and global NGOs and Cities Associations to demonstrate and advocate participatory local governance for sustainable human development.

Geographical Area of Activity: Developing countries.

Financial Information: Grants available up to US $50,000.

Publications: LIFE: Participatory Local Governance Global Strategy; LIFE Global Evaluation Results and Recommendations; Step By Step Guidelines to Implement LIFE; Technical Paper 1: Participatory Local Governance Method and Experiences of LIFE.

Address: 1 UN Plaza, New York, NY 10017, USA.

Fax: (212) 906-5313; *Internet:* www.undp.org/governance/local.html.

NetAid

Formed as a public–private partnership between the United Nations Development Programme and Cisco Systems, with the mission of raising public awareness and action in the fight against extreme poverty.

Activities: Although NetAid no longer distributes grants directly, it does seek to establish partnerships with organizations on campaigns and awareness-raising initiatives, and aims to match funders to community projects. Organizations can also participate through NetAid's Online Volunteering programme which provides opportunities to interested volunteers. Specific initiatives include the World Schoolhouse Project, a network of organizations which aims to get children world-wide into school, and World Class, an educational role-play game for 8–12 year old children designed to build global understanding and engage young people in advocacy efforts.

Geographical Area of Activity: International.

Restrictions: No funding applications currently accepted.

Financial Information: Total assets US $9,775,857 (2002); total revenue US $2,221,690, programme expenditure US $4,907,618 (2002).

Publications: Connections (monthly newsletter).

Contact: Board of Directors: Carol Bellamy; Mark Malloch Brown; Sharon Capeling-Alakija; John T. Chambers; Quincy Jones; Don Listwin; David Morrison; Chief Exec. David Morrison.

Address: 267 Fifth Ave, 11th Floor, New York, NY 10016, USA.

Telephone: (212) 537-0500; *Fax:* (212) 537-0501; *Internet:* www.netaid.org; *e-mail:* info@netaid.org.

The Perez-Guerrero Trust Fund

Established by the UN in accordance with General Assembly Resolution 38/201 of 20 December 1983, which provided for the liquidation of the UN Emergency Operation Trust Fund and the allocation of its remaining balance. The Fund aims to support activities in economic and technical co-operation among developing countries of critical importance to developing countries which are members of the Group of 77—a grouping of developing countries—in order to achieve national or collective self-reliance, according to priorities set by them. It is named after the late Manuel Perez-Guerrero and its funds are channeled through the United Nations Development Programme, following approval by the Group of 77.

Activities: Provides seed money for financing pre-investment/feasibility studies/reports prepared by professional consultancy organizations in developing countries which are members of the Group of 77; and facilitates the implementation of projects within the framework of the Caracas Programme of

Action on economic and technical co-operation in developing countries. Projects can be submitted by governmental and NGOs, sub-regional and regional institutions of developing countries.

Geographical Area of Activity: Group of 77 developing countries.

How to Apply: The deadline for submission of project approvals is the last day of April of each year. Projects submitted are examined by a committee of six experts and if found appropriate are recommended for financing.

Address: 1 UN Plaza, New York, NY 10017, USA.

Internet: www.g77.org/main/pgtf/info.htm.

Poverty Strategies Initiative

The Initiative was launched in 1996, in the aftermath of the 1995 Social Summit, to support countries in their efforts to formulate and implement national anti-poverty strategies. The multi-donor programme assists programme countries in their efforts to comply with the Copenhagen commitments, by supporting the formulation of national strategies and action plans to fight poverty.

Activities: The Initiative provides catalytic support to country anti-poverty efforts by: raising public awareness of the extent, distribution and causes of poverty, and creating political space for a debate on national development priorities; strengthening the capacity of government agencies and civil society to gather, analyze and monitor social indicators and to review public policies, budgets and programmes that impact on people's well-being; defining national goals and targets for the reduction of overall poverty and the elimination of extreme poverty; improving co-ordination among agencies dealing with social and economic policy; and building a consensus among public, private and civil society actors on the most effective means to tackle poverty in their country. Poverty-reduction strategies and national human development reports have been prepared in around 50 countries world-wide. Various activities are supported in different countries.

Geographical Area of Activity: International.

Financial Information: Programme budget approx. US $20,000,000.

Contact: Dir and Senior Poverty Adviser Stephen Browne.

Address: 1 UN Plaza, New York, NY 10017, USA.

Fax: (212) 906-5313; *Internet:* www.undp.org/poverty/initiatives/psi/index.htm; *e-mail:* stephen.browne@undp.org.

PRODERE—Development Programme for Displaced Persons, Refugees and Returnees in Central America

Aims to facilitate the reinsertion of uprooted populations into their country of origin through development of partnerships with civil society organizations.

Activities: Brings together civil society organizations, ranging from human rights and church groups to village-based organizations, to reconstruct society and re-establish relationships shattered by conflict in Central American countries. Also aims to strengthen civil society at the grassroots level through increasing people's participation in municipal and local development committees.

Geographical Area of Activity: Central America.

Financial Information: Launched with a US $115,000,000 donation from the Italian government.

Address: 1 UN Plaza, New York, NY 10017, USA.

Fax: (212) 906-5313; *Internet:* www.undp.org.

Regional Bureau for Asia and the Pacific (RBAP): APGEN—Promoting gender equality in the Asia Pacific–Phase 2

The first phase of the programme was launched in May 1999 with the participation of 11 countries in the region. Running up until 2002, it aimed to promote gender equality with respect to economic opportunities for women and their participation in decision-making, focusing on four areas: integrating paid and unpaid work into national policies; utilizing science and technology for the empowerment of poor women; promoting women's participation in economic and political decision-making; and facilitating the implementation of the Convention to Eliminate All Forms of Discrimination Against Women (CEDAW). The second phase of the programme was to run from 2003–05.

Activities: Phase two of the programme continues within the rights-based framework of CEDAW, addressing women's economic rights and the mainstreaming of gender into macroeconomic policies, focusing specifically on women's access to the formal labour market and entrepreneurship development as well as gender analysis of budgets and alternative budgeting. A second strategic area is women's participation in decision-making, addressing women's enhanced role in parliamentary processes and in the media, and broad-based gender awareness. Specific activities focus on mainstreaming issues of women's access to science and technology in poverty-reduction policies and programmes; and strengthening capacities of women leaders in public and private sectors and civil society in gender-responsive governance and transformative leadership.

Geographical Area of Activity: Asia and the Pacific.

Financial Information: UN Development Programme funding US $2,000,000 (2003–05).

Publications: Guidebook on Integrating Unpaid Work into National Policies; Making Governance Gender Responsive: A Basic Course; Assessment of Resources, Best Practices and Gaps in Gender, Science and Technology in the Asia Pacific.

Contact: Contact Rosanita Serrano.

Address: 7th Floor, NEDA sa Makati Bldg, 106 Amorsolo St, Legaspi Village, 1229 Makati City, Philippines.

Telephone: (2) 892-0611; *Fax:* (2) 893-9598; *Internet:* www.undp.org.ph/apgen /home.htm; *e-mail:* rosanita.serrano@undp.org.

Regional Bureau for Asia and the Pacific (RBAP): ASEAN Facility: Silk Road—Capacity Building for Regional Co-operation and Development

Established to promote regional co-operation in the People's Republic of China, Kazakhstan, Kyrgyzstan, Tajikistan, Turkmenistan and Uzbekistan, which occupy a pivotal position geographically and economically around which the Silk Road has evolved.

Activities: The programme provides technical assistance mainly in the form of institutional and capacity building to organizations in China, Kazakhstan, Kyrgyzstan, Tajikistan, Turkmenistan and Uzbekistan. The focus of the programme is on the medium-term steps necessary to set in motion a process of peaceful co-operation and socio-economic change to help the Silk Road regain its competitive edge as a major international transportation and trade artery as well as a prosperous economic and social corridor.

Geographical Area of Activity: Participating countries: China, Kyrgyzstan, Kazakhstan, Tajikistan, Turkmenistan and Uzbekistan.

Financial Information: Total budget US $1,100,000 (2001–03).

Contact: Chief, Regional Programme Division Subinay Nandy.

Address: 1 UN Plaza, New York, NY 10017, USA.

Telephone: (212) 906-5850; *Internet:* http://rbaprp.apdip.net/globe/silkroad.htm; *e-mail:* subinay.nandy@undp.org.

Regional Bureau for Asia and the Pacific (RBAP): Asia Pacific Development Information Programme (APDIP)

Launched in 1997; aims to promote the development and application of new Information and Communication Technologies (ICT) for poverty alleviation and sustainable human development in the Asia–Pacific region.

Activities: Operates in three core programme areas: policy development and dialogue; access; and content development and knowledge management. Within each area supports activities that involve awareness raising and advocacy, building capacities, promoting ICT policies and dialogue, promoting equitable access to tools and technologies, knowledge sharing, and networking, through the development of strategic public–private sector partnerships and opportunities for technical co-operation among developing countries.

Geographical Area of Activity: Asia and the Pacific: Afghanistan, Bangladesh, Bhutan, Brunei, Cambodia, People's Republic of China, Cook Islands, Democratic People's Republic of Korea, Fiji, Federated States of Micronesia, French Polynesia, India, Indonesia, Iran, Kiribati, Laos, Malaysia, Maldives, Marshall Islands, Mongolia, Myanmar, Nauru, Nepal, New Caledonia, Niue, Pakistan, Palau, Papua New Guinea, Philippines, Republic of Korea, Singapore, Solomon Islands, Sri Lanka, Thailand, Timor-Leste, Tokelau, Tonga, Trust Territories of the Pacific Islands, Tuvalu, Vanuatu and Vietnam.

Contact: Chief Technical Adviser and Programme Co-ordinator Shahid Akhtar.

Address: Wisma UN, Block C, Kompleks Pejabat, Damansara, Jalan Dungun, 50490 Kuala Lumpur, Malaysia.

Telephone: (3) 2095-9122; *Fax:* (3) 2093-9740; *Internet:* www.apdip.net.

Regional Bureau for Asia and the Pacific (RBAP): Asia Pacific Development Information Programme (APDIP): Information and Communication Technologies (ICT) Research and Development Grants Programme for Asia-Pacific

A programme of APDIP, administered by the Asian Media Information and Communication Centre, and operated in conjunction with the International Development Research Centre and the Asia Pacific Network Information Centre.

Activities: Grants under the Programme are made to projects that aim to build institutional research capacity in the developing countries of the Asia-Pacific region, in the area of Internet networking. It is directed at encouraging original and innovative networking solutions to specific development problems. Grants for suitable research and development projects are available to Asia-based organizations on a competitive basis. Preference is given to projects that focus on practical solutions to real problems in Internet policies and technology applications. Supported activities include: research and development into innovative ICT and networking solutions and applications, with a clear focus on practical and replicable approaches and techniques; development of practical solutions based on the application of proven and readily available Internet technologies with a minimum of basic research; research on the outcomes and social impacts of specific ICT policies and interventions and application of Internet technologies; and research on policy matters affecting Internet networking in the Asia Pacific region, especially where linked to areas such as policy impacts, gender equity, social equity, sustainable communities, and technology diffusion/transfer, and benefits to rural areas.

Geographical Area of Activity: Asia and the Pacific.

Restrictions: No applications from unaffiliated individuals, or from teams of such individuals, are accepted.

How to Apply: Application details are available on the website. The ICT Research and Development Grants Programme Committee meets twice a year to review proposals. Responses to submissions will generally be given by the Committee within four weeks of being reviewed. In certain cases this may take longer, depending on the complexity of the proposal and whether further information needs to be sought by the Committee.

Financial Information: Two types of grant available: up to a maximum budget of US $9,000 over a term not exceeding 12 months, and up to a maximum budget of US $30,000 over a term not exceeding 24 months.

Contact: Contact Nanditha Raman.

Address: Jurong Point, POB 360, Singapore 916412, Singapore.

Telephone: 792-7570; *Fax:* 792-7129; *Internet:* www.apdip.net/ictrnd/ictrnd.asp; *e-mail:* research@amic.org.sg.

Regional Bureau for Asia and the Pacific (RBAP): Environmental Governance and Management of Shared River Waters

Part of RBAP's Regional Co-operation Framework (RCF II 2002–06), operating in the field of the environment and sustainable development.

Activities: The programme aims to: promote co-ordinated policy development and management of shared water resources, in order to maximize the resultant economic and social benefits in an equitable manner without compromising the sustainability of vital ecosystems; support the establishment and development of integrated river basin management mechanisms and to build capacities to manage scarce water resources; strengthen policies and capacities for regional co-operation relating to recovery, prevention and vulnerability reduction in the context of water-related disasters; and strengthen environmental governance, with particular respect to policies aimed at promoting sustainable livelihoods and poverty reduction around shared water resources. The focus is on building capacity for managing water resources on a regional basis, though capacity-building activities including training and education, networking, awareness raising and creating support for partnerships among training institutions in developing countries. Initially regional activities are focused on eight countries in South-East Asia and South Asia. The programme also links closely with the Trans-boundary River Basin Initiative (TRIB) of the UN Development Programme's Global Trust Fund, which emphasizes sharing relevant global and regional experiences for South–South co-operation.

Geographical Area of Activity: Asia and the Pacific.

Address: 1 UN Plaza, New York, NY 10017, USA.

Fax: (212) 906-5825; *Internet:* http://rbaprp.apdip.net/progs/egmsrw.htm.

Regional Bureau for Asia and the Pacific (RBAP): Pacific Sustainable Livelihoods Programme

An umbrella programme launched in 2003 aiming to promote sustainable livelihoods in 10 countries of the Pacific region; builds on the successes of four previous UN Development Programme regional programmes: SMILE, Small Enterprise Development, Non-Formal Education and ICARE.

Activities: Integrates four programmes that address private sector and sustainable livelihoods, non-formal education, resources and environment, and sustainable micro-finance and livelihoods, with the main goal of poverty alleviation through an analysis of the root causes and improvement of the enabling environment and capacity for sustainable livelihoods. The Programme advises on policy development, based on data analysis, sharing of information about good practices, and reviews of laws hindering sustainable livelihood options. It also helps build NGO capacity and broad-based partnerships with the private sector. A crucial focus is the integration of environmental and sustainable livelihood issues.

Geographical Area of Activity: Federated States of Micronesia, Fiji, Kiribati, Marshall Islands, Nauru, Palau, Solomon Islands, Tonga, Tuvalu and Vanuatu.

How to Apply: Exploratory requests for assistance can be made directly to the Regional Programme Manager by government agencies, CSOs, CBOs, the private sector and development partners. These are then formalized through the official government channel, as appropriate, in consultation with respective UNDP Offices in Suva, Apia and Port Moresby.

Financial Information: Total budget US $922,349 (2002–04).

Contact: Project Man. Jeff Lieuw.

Address: UN Fiji Office, Tower Level 6, Reserve Bank Bldg, Pratt St, Suva, Fiji.
Telephone: 3312500; *Fax:* 3301718; *Internet:* www.undp.org.fj/pslp/index.html;
e-mail: fji@undp.org.

Regional Bureau for Asia and the Pacific (RBAP): Pacific Sustainable Livelihoods Programme—Strengthening CSO Capacity

A component of the Pacific Sustainable Livelihoods Programme; its primary emphasis is on the capacity building of civil society organizations, with the Pacific Island Associations of NGOs (PIANGO) as the lead agency.

Activities: The Programme's activities include: strengthening of PIANGO's capacity to mobilize long-term funding to cover core operating costs and programmes in its strategic plan; the provision of mentoring/coaching support to the Secretariat team; strengthening of regional/national links and PIANGO's overall effectiveness as a regional network of NGO support organizations; establishment of a mobile team and initiating efforts to strengthen the National Liaison Units; establishment of a regional network of capacity-building facilitators/practitioners with the PIANGO mobile team as the nucleus; securing of long-term funding support and institutionalization of the Pacific NGO Graduate Diploma Programme in NGO Management within Pacific-based training institutions; strengthening of NGO–Government relations at the regional and national level for policy dialogue on issues affecting social and economic equity; provision of technical support to the United Nations Volunteers/Special Voluntary Fund-funded project on strengthening voluntary efforts and CSOs' capacity building in Vanuatu, Fiji and Tonga; and the transfer of responsibilities, over the life of the partnership, to PIANGO and other regional organizations with a strong CSO capacity-building mandate.

Geographical Area of Activity: Federated States of Micronesia, Fiji, Kiribati, Marshall Islands, Nauru, Palau, Solomon Islands, Tonga, Tuvalu and Vanuatu.

Financial Information: Funded by the Canadian International Development Agency (CIDA).

Address: UN Fiji Office, Tower Level 6, Reserve Bank Bldg, Pratt St, Suva, Fiji.
Telephone: 3312500; *Fax:* 3301718; *Internet:* www.undp.org.fj/pslp/index.html.

Regional Bureau for Asia and the Pacific (RBAP): Pacific Sustainable Livelihoods Programme—Sustainable Livelihoods Matching Grant Facility

An initiative of the Pacific Sustainable Livelihoods Programme.

Activities: This facility provides matching cash grants to enable informal sector enterprises, producer groups and resource owners to develop sustainable business relationships with local and overseas private businesses. The criteria for funding assistance are developed in consultation with stakeholders and are announced regionally.

Geographical Area of Activity: Federated States of Micronesia, Fiji, Kiribati, Marshall Islands, Nauru, Palau, Solomon Islands, Tonga, Tuvalu and Vanuatu.

Address: UN Fiji Office, Tower Level 6, Reserve Bank Bldg, Pratt St, Suva, Fiji. *Telephone:* 3312500; *Fax:* 3301718; *Internet:* www.undp.org.fj/pslp/index.html; *e-mail:* fji@undp.org.

Regional Bureau for Asia and the Pacific (RBAP): Poverty Reduction and Access to Justice for All (PRAJA)

Aims to strengthen the capacity of policy-makers to adopt human rights conventions; strengthen the capacity of implementation agencies to promote and provide good human rights practice; strengthen the capacity of the general public to assert their human rights; and strengthen the capacity of the Regional Rights Resource Team, which promotes human rights, to maintain and deliver innovative and cutting edge human rights support and services to its partners.

Activities: The programme targets policy-makers, including parliamentarians, party leaders, senior government officials, human rights commissions and NGO leaders; service delivery organizations, including legal services; and people and organizations with access to and influence on the grassroots socio-cultural framework, including the media, communal chiefs and local religious leaders, and local community groups. The majority of the programme's work is targeted at these latter groups.

Geographical Area of Activity: Primary focus countries: Kiribati, Solomon Islands and Vanuatu.

Financial Information: Funded by the UK government through the Department for International Development (DFID); total budget US $3,300,000.

Address: UN Development Programme Fiji Office, Tower Level 6, Reserve Bank Bldg, Pratt St, Suva, Fiji.

Telephone: 3312500; *Fax:* 3301718; *Internet:* www.undp.org.fj/praja.htm; *e-mail:* fo.fji@undp.org.

Regional Bureau for Asia and the Pacific (RBAP): Regional Co-operation Framework—RCF II 2002–06

The second Regional Co-operation Framework (RCF II) for Asia and the Pacific responds directly to the UN Millennium Declaration target of halving the proportion of people living in extreme poverty by 2015 and other related goals.

Activities: The programme aims to contribute to the regional fight against poverty by enabling analysis of region-wide trends and policies, innovative tools and approaches to emerging development problems, and facilitating exchange of experiences of effective development practice through knowledge networks. Focuses on three main thematic areas, with the overall objective of poverty reduction and sustainable human development: Democratic Governance for Human Development, aimed at enhancing the political, economic and social frameworks for sustainable human development through a rights-based approach; Environment and Sustainable Development, addressing the poverty-environment nexus and trans-boundary externality concerns; and Globalization and Economic Governance, intended to ensure a more equitable system of globalization for human development. The three areas are linked in their focus on expanding choices and equitable opportunities for the poor, minimizing insecurities to their livelihoods, and empowering those who have been marginalized. This overall framework leads to a comprehensive portfolio of stand-alone and cross-cutting programmes, some of which are new, and some which carry over from the previous RCF.

Geographical Area of Activity: Asia and the Pacific.

Contact: UN Development Programme Asst Admin. and Dir, Regional Bureau for Asia and the Pacific Hafiz A. Pasha.

Address: 1 UN Plaza, New York, NY 10017, USA.

Fax: (212) 906-5825; *Internet:* http://rbaprp.apdip.net.

Regional Bureau for Asia and the Pacific (RBAP): Rights-Based Development

Aims to build on the positive trends of democratization and improved governance in Asia and the Pacific region.

Activities: Focuses on several strategic areas, with a central focus on enhancing institutional capacity at national and local levels to formulate public policies that promote equity, accountability, tolerance and the rule of law, as well as improving transparency, accountability and responsiveness of governance institutions, based on the principles of participation, equity and non-discrimination, and ensuring the protection of press freedoms and the free flow of information within and across countries. Within these areas, the key objectives are to: strengthen human rights knowledge and analytical skills through training in governing institutions, media and civil society organizations; integrate rights-based approaches, tools and methodologies into national development strategies and programmes; facilitate situational analyses of human rights for development, and network governance and human rights institutions in the region for cross-country exchange and learning of good practices. Also operates the Participatory Action Research to Advance Governance Options and Networks (PARAGON) Regional Governance Programme for Asia.

Geographical Area of Activity: Asia and the Pacific.

Address: UN Development Programme Pakistan, c/o UNDP, 1 UN Plaza, New York, NY 10017, USA.

Telephone: (51) 822618; *Fax:* (51) 279080; *Internet:* http://rbaprp.apdip.net/demo/rights.htm; *e-mail:* fo.pakistan@undp.org.

Regional Bureau for Asia and the Pacific (RBAP): South Asia Poverty Programme (SAPAP)

The Programme was established as a direct response to the 1993 South Asian Association for Regional Cooperation (SAARC) Summit Declaration on poverty reduction, which indicated national commitment and attention to achieving specific poverty-reduction targets in SAARC member countries.

Activities: Programme activities have focused on advisory support to mainstream social mobilization into national poverty reduction strategies, and the holding of workshops and study tours to facilitate sharing of best practices within the region. To enable local ownership and sustainability of the Programme, also establishes Social Mobilization Experimentation and Learning Centres, with the first two launched in Nepal and India.

Geographical Area of Activity: South Asia: Bangladesh, Bhutan, India, Iran, Nepal, Pakistan and Sri Lanka.

Contact: Programme Co-ordinator, SAPAP.

Address: UN House, POB 107, Kathmandu, Nepal.

Telephone: (1) 5523200; *Fax:* (1) 5523991; *Internet:* http://rbaprp.apdip.net/globe /sapap.htm; *e-mail:* registry.np@undp.org.

Regional Bureau for Asia and the Pacific (RBAP): Strengthening Policy Dialogue on Indigenous and Tribal Peoples' Rights and Development

Aims to implement the UN Development Programme policy of engagement with indigenous peoples in the Asia and Pacific region, based on the lessons learned from the Highland Peoples Programme (HPP 1995–99). The HPP, a previous regional initiative, was developed in response to the International Decade of the World's Indigenous People (1995–2004) and covered four different countries in the Mekong sub-region: Thailand, Cambodia, Laos and Vietnam.

Activities: The programme focuses on strengthening policy dialogue on indigenous peoples' rights and development in the region, through engagement with civil society organizations, addressing three general areas of concern: issues with respect to ownership and use of land and their natural resources, including related issues of environmental management; cultural autonomy, including issues of language, education, and protection of cultural and intellectual property; and participation in formal decision-making processes of the state, particularly with respect to development, which also invokes issues of citizenship. Participating countries in the current project are Bangladesh, Cambodia, Philippines, Thailand and Vietnam.

Geographical Area of Activity: Bangladesh, Cambodia, Philippines, Thailand and Vietnam.

Address: 1 UN Plaza, New York, NY 10017, USA.

Fax: (212) 906-5825; *Internet:* www.undp.org/rbap.

Regional Bureau for Europe and the Commonwealth of Independent States (RBEC)

Administers the UN Development Programme's (UNDP) programmes in Central and Eastern Europe and the Commonwealth of Independent States (CIS), playing an important role in the transition process through empowering people, organizations and governments to promote sustainable human development. Under a mandate issued by the UN Secretary-General, RBEC (formerly the Regional Directorate for Europe and the Commonwealth of Independent States) began establishing offices and programmes in the CIS states in 1992. In 2003, of the 30 programme countries in the RBEC region, there were UNDP country offices in 23 of them: Albania, Armenia, Azerbaijan, Belarus, Bosnia and Herzegovina, Bulgaria, Croatia, Serbia and Montenegro, Georgia, Kazakhstan, Kyrgyzstan, Latvia, Lithuania, the Former Yugoslav Republic of Macedonia, Moldova, Poland, Romania, Russia, Tajikistan, Turkey, Turkmenistan, Ukraine and Uzbekistan.

Activities: Under the Regional Co-operation Framework (RCF) II for 2002–04 (adopted in June 2002), three regional programmes were developed in the democratic, economic, and environmental governance areas. Each has distinct programme priorities based on regional assessments undertaken by RBEC during the RCF preparation process and through analytical work completed under the initial RCF. The second RCF addresses seven issues in an integrated manner across the regional programme: protecting and promoting human rights; ensuring transparency, accountability and anti-corruption policies; decentralizing and deconcentrating power; addressing the complex intersections of conflict prevention and early warning, conflict mitigation, and post-conflict recovery; promoting equity in development; combating HIV/AIDS; and integrating information and communication technologies as an instrument for development. Programmes involving NGOs include: the Regional Programme to Support Gender in Development in Eastern Europe and the CIS; Democracy, Governance and Participation; Regional Poverty Programme; Regional Programme on Environment and Development; and Small and Medium Sized Enterprise Development (qq.v.).

Geographical Area of Activity: Central and Eastern Europe and the CIS.

Contact: Regional Dir Kalman Mitzei.

Address: 1 UN Plaza, 16th Floor, New York, NY 10017, USA.

Telephone: (212) 906-5000; *Fax:* (212) 906-6595; *Internet:* www.undp.org/rbec; *e-mail:* kalman.mitzei@undp.org.

Regional Bureau for Europe and the Commonwealth of Independent States (RBEC): Democracy, Governance and Participation

The programme seeks to help the countries of Eastern and Central Europe and the Commonwealth of Independent States (CIS) in their efforts to make the transition towards democratic institutions and free-market economies. The first Regional Umbrella Programme in this field was launched in 1997 and collaborates with relevant organizational units of the UN system, including the Office of the UN High Commissioner for Human Rights (OHCHR), the Organisation for Economic Co-operation and Development (OECD) and the Organization for Security and Co-operation in Europe (OSCE).

Activities: The programme focuses on the following six specific areas: democratic governance and public-sector reform, through assistance for creating appropriate enabling legislation and providing technical assistance for the democratic transformation of government institutions; decentralization, through assistance for strengthening the institutional capacity of local governments; support to parliaments, through the provision of technical support for enhancing the capacity, effectiveness and efficiency of parliamentarian structures; ombudsman-type institutions, through strengthening the capacity of national institutions that are concerned with basic human rights issues; participation and strengthening of civil society, though promoting grassroots participation in the governance process and strengthening NGOs and community-based organizations; and supreme audit and evaluation capacity, through support to supreme audit institutions and the evaluation capacities of national and local governments to promote transparency, accountability and effective management.

Geographical Area of Activity: Central and Eastern Europe and the CIS.

Address: 1 UN Plaza, 16th Floor, New York, NY 10017, USA.

Telephone: (212) 906-5000; *Fax:* (212) 906-6595; *Internet:* www.undp.org/rbec.

Regional Bureau for Europe and the Commonwealth of Independent States (RBEC): Regional Poverty Programme

Aims to address poverty issues in Central and Eastern Europe and the Commonwealth of Independent States (CIS).

Activities: The Programme aims to: suggest policy options to governments for addressing poverty; develop frameworks for UN Development Programme-supported country-level activities related to poverty; strengthen institutional capacity within the region to formulate appropriate policies in a market economy; build a network of institutions that share information and knowledge concerning interventions to alleviate poverty within the region; and involve civil society institutions in creating awareness of poverty-eradication policy options and the implications of choices made. Organizes conferences, prepares technical papers on poverty issues, and compiles regional poverty reports.

Geographical Area of Activity: Central and Eastern Europe and the CIS.

Address: 1 UN Plaza, 16th Floor, New York, NY 10017, USA.

Telephone: (212) 906-5000; *Fax:* (212) 906-6595; *Internet:* www.undp.org/rbec.

Regional Bureau for Europe and the Commonwealth of Independent States (RBEC): Regional Programme on Environment and Development

The Programme aims to integrate environmental protection with economic and social development; designed as a framework programme in which countries may participate according to their own priorities and stages of environment policy development.

Activities: The Programme, designed to involve a range of different types of organizations, including NGOs, carries out the following activities: assists governments to set environmental objectives and to formulate their National Agenda 21; improves capacity for policy reforms and their incorporation into legislation; develops the capacity of national institutions, including business associations, technology and training centres, and financial institutions, to form a link between policy-making levels and the business community and to perform a range of environmental and technological services; increases public awareness and participation in environmental planning, monitoring and decision-making, principally by strengthening the role of NGOs and community-based organizations; and provides regional support to national projects and mobilizes external assistance and funds.

Geographical Area of Activity: Central and Eastern Europe and the CIS.

Address: 1 UN Plaza, 16th Floor, New York, NY 10017, USA.

Telephone: (212) 906-5000; *Fax:* (212) 906-6595; *Internet:* www.undp.org/rbec.

Regional Bureau for Europe and the Commonwealth of Independent States (RBEC): Regional Programme to Support Gender in Development in Eastern Europe and the CIS

Aims to assist countries in strengthening their institutional capacity to address gender issues; operates in co-operation with the United Nations Development Fund for Women (UNIFEM).

Activities: The Programme's main focus is on: strengthening the capacity of national Gender In Development (GID) units to influence and network with government structures and to provide support to NGOs and analytical institutions; helping NGOs to strengthen their institutional capacity for in-country and between-country networking in order to increase awareness and advance the GID agenda in civil society; and helping research and training institutions working on gender issues to gather, analyze and disseminate gender-sensitive research. Primarily provides assistance on specific issues and programmes; supports training at the national and sub-regional level; and co-ordinates information sharing and networking between GID units and other participants in the programme.

Geographical Area of Activity: Central and Eastern Europe and the CIS.

Address: 1 UN Plaza, 16th Floor, New York, NY 10017, USA.

Telephone: (212) 906-5000; *Fax:* (212) 906-6595; *Internet:* www.undp.org/rbec /programmes.

Regional Bureau for Europe and the Commonwealth of Independent States (RBEC): Small and Medium Sized Enterprise (SME) Development

Aims to strengthen national frameworks for SME projects in Central and Eastern Europe and the Commonwealth of Independent States (CIS).

Activities: Provides support in the areas of: formulation of national SME projects, and preparation of project documents; evaluation of selected SME policies and making recommendations for improving the enabling environment; setting up or strengthening business counselling centres, business incubators, trade or industry associations, or other private-sector institutions supporting SMEs; increasing the participation of women in business, especially as entrepreneurs and business managers; restructuring privatized SME's and developing a pool of national restructuring consultants; and establishing, managing and operating finance schemes, especially micro-credit initiatives.

Geographical Area of Activity: Central and Eastern Europe and the CIS.

Address: 1 UN Plaza, 16th Floor, New York, NY 10017, USA.

Telephone: (212) 906-5000; *Fax:* (212) 906-6595; *Internet:* www.undp.org/rbec.

Thematic Trust Funds

The Thematic Trust Funds were launched in 2001 to help achieve development goals and to enable donors to provide additional contributions for work in the UN Development Programme (UNDP) practice areas. They support a multi-year funding framework, and represent a compact among donors, host governments and UNDP to implement results-oriented programmes at country, regional and global levels.

Activities: There are seven operational Thematic Trust Funds: Democratic Governance; Poverty Reduction; Energy for Sustainable Development (which comes under the Bureau for Development Policy); Environment; Information and Communications Technology (which also comes under the Bureau for Development Policy); HIV/AIDS; Gender; and Crisis Prevention and Recovery

333

(which comes under the Bureau for Crisis Prevention and Recovery, qq.v.). For the first three years of activity (2001–03), the Funds had a collective budget of approx. US $555,000,000.

Geographical Area of Activity: International.

How to Apply: See individual entries.

Financial Information: Total programme budget US $555,000,000 (2001–03).

Address: 1 UN Plaza, 20th Floor, New York, NY 10017, USA.

Fax: (212) 906-5364; *Internet:* www.undp.org/trustfunds/.

UNDP Thematic Trust Fund—Democratic Governance

Set up in 2001 to help ensure quality, consistency and alignment between democratic governance programmes at country, regional and global level, and to allow UN Development Programme (UNDP) to respond more rapidly and efficiently to requests from programme countries.

Activities: The Fund operates through a number of strategic processes: policy advice and technical support; capacity development of institutions, including NGOs, and individuals; advocacy, communication and public information; promoting and brokering dialogue; knowledge networking and sharing of good practices; and strategic partnerships. Funds are distributed through six service lines: legislators; electoral systems and processes; access to justice and human rights; access to information; decentralization and local governance; and public information and civil service reform. A limited number of interventions are also funded at global and regional level.

Geographical Area of Activity: Less-developed countries, countries in transition or recovering from conflict.

How to Apply: Funding requests channelled through UNDP country offices are received as short-format proposals and acted upon on a fast track basis.

Financial Information: Total budget approx. US $100,000,000 (2001–03).

Address: 1 UN Plaza, 20th Floor, New York, NY 10017, USA.

Telephone: (212) 906-6633; *Fax:* (212) 906-6471; *Internet:* www.undp.org /trustfunds/devgovttf.pdf.

UNDP Thematic Trust Fund—Environment

Established in 2001 to increase the UN Development Programme's (UNDP) efforts to help programme countries reduce poverty and promote sustainable development through sound environmental management.

Activities: Operates within three service lines: integrating environment in national development frameworks; strengthening local environmental governance; and addressing global and regional environmental challenges. Works in conjunction with the Bureau for Development Policy: UNDP Thematic Trust Fund—Energy for Sustainable Development (q.v.).

Geographical Area of Activity: Low-income countries, less-developed countries and Africa.

How to Apply: Funding requests channelled through UNDP country offices are received as short-format proposals and acted upon on a fast track basis.

Financial Information: Total budget approx. US $60,000,000 (2001–03).

Address: 1 UN Plaza, 20th Floor, New York, NY 10017, USA.

Telephone: (212) 906-5073; *Fax:* (212) 906-6973; *Internet:* www.undp.org/trustfunds/environment-english-final.pdf.

UNDP Thematic Trust Fund—Gender

Established to increase the UN Development Programme's (UNDP) commitment to gender equality and the empowerment of women.

Activities: Supports programme countries in strengthening their efforts to mainstream gender throughout all of their programmatic work, through a three-pronged strategy: national capacity building within programme countries; advocacy and scaling up of innovative and successful pilot projects; and sharing knowledge and capacity building in country offices. National capacity building is supported through four service lines: engendering policy, engendering legal frameworks, engendering institutions, and engendering indicators and method-ologies. Also supports a limited number of interventions at global and regional level, focusing on building South–South co-operation through networking, disseminating information on innovative and successful pilot projects, and developing regional services on mainstreaming gender.

Geographical Area of Activity: Less-developed countries.

How to Apply: Funding requests channelled through UNDP country offices are received as short-format proposals and acted upon on a fast track basis.

Financial Information: Total budget approx. US $15,000,000 (2001–03).

Address: 1 UN Plaza, 20th Floor, New York, NY 10017, USA.

Telephone: (212) 906-6085; *Fax:* (212) 906-5148; *Internet:* www.undp.org/trustfunds/tifgender091101e.pdf.

UNDP Thematic Trust Fund—HIV/AIDS

Launched in 2001 to mobilize non-core resources for country-level programmes; aims to increase the UN Development Programme's (UNDP) commitment to the fight against AIDS, in accordance with its mandate as co-sponsor of the Joint United Nations Programme on HIV/AIDS (UNAIDS, in the Other Programmes section, q.v.).

Activities: Primarily focuses on interventions and capacity building designed to help countries effectively respond to the AIDS epidemic, through co-operation with a range of organizations including NGOs. Operates within five service lines: advocacy and policy dialogue; capacity building; mainstreaming; human rights; and information and multi-media. The Fund focuses on supporting programmes in low-income countries, less-developed countries and Africa, with priority given to countries with a high prevalence of AIDS.

Geographical Area of Activity: Low-income countries, less-developed countries and Africa.

How to Apply: Funding requests channelled through UNDP country offices are received as short-format proposals and acted upon on a fast track basis.

Financial Information: Total budget approx. US $50,000,000 (2001–03).

Address: 1 UN Plaza, 20th Floor, New York, NY 10017, USA.

Telephone: (212) 906-3688; *Fax:* (212) 906-5023; *Internet:* www.undp.org /trustfunds/hiv2-5.pdf.

UNDP Thematic Trust Fund—Poverty Reduction

Established in 2001 to complement the the UN Development Programme's (UNDP) regular work in the field of poverty reduction.

Activities: Aims to monitor progress at country level towards the development goals and targets of the Millennium Declaration, including providing support to NGOs to evaluate the impact of their poverty-reduction activities; help expand the outreach of centres of excellence to regions and countries beyond their immediate reach; finance pilot and innovation projects; and strengthen learning and knowledge networks for poverty reduction.

Geographical Area of Activity: Developing countries.

How to Apply: Funding requests channelled through UNDP country offices are received as short-format proposals and acted upon on a fast track basis.

Financial Information: Total budget approx. US $60,000,000 (2001–03).

Address: 1 UN Plaza, 20th Floor, New York, NY 10017, USA.

Telephone: (212) 906-6633; *Fax:* (212) 906-6471; *Internet:* www.undp.org /trustfunds/povredttf.pdf.

United Nations Volunteers Programme (UNV)

The volunteer arm of the UN created by the UN General Assembly in 1970 to serve as an operational partner in development co-operation at the request of UN member states. It mobilizes qualified UN Volunteers and encourages people to become active in volunteering in their countries. It is administered by the United Nations Development Programme (UNDP) and works through UNDP's country offices around the world.

Activities: The Programme maintains a roster covering 115 professional categories, with prominent categories covering agriculture, health, education, human rights promotion, information and communication technology, community development, vocational training, industry and population, partnership with governments, UN Agencies, development banks and non-governmental and community-based organizations. The UNV programmes are usually managed by governments, often with technical input and supervision from one of the UN system's specialized agencies, including the Food and Agriculture Organization (FAO), the International Labour Organization (ILO), the World Food Programme (WFP), the United Nations Educational, Scientific and Cultural Organization (UNESCO), the UN High Commissioner for Refugees (UNHCR), the World Health Organization, the United Nations Children's Fund (UNICEF) and the International Bank for Reconstruction and Development (IBRD—World Bank).

Geographical Area of Activity: Africa, Asia and the Pacific, Middle East, Central and Eastern Europe, Central and South America and the Caribbean.

Contact: Exec. Co-ordinator Sharon Capeling-Alakija.

Address: Postfach 260 111, 53153 Bonn, Germany.

Telephone: (228) 8152000; *Fax:* (228) 8152001; *Internet:* www.unv.org.

United Nations Volunteers Programme (UNV): UNITeS—United Nations Information Technology Service

A global volunteer initiative, led by the UN Volunteers Programme (q.v.), that allows volunteers from any country to give their skills and time to extend the opportunities of the digital revolution to developing countries.

Activities: UNITeS three primary goals are to: improve the capacity of individuals and institutions in developing countries to make practical use of ICT in their development processes, through the co-operation of volunteers from all around the world; establish a significant knowledge base/network on applications of information and communication technologies (ICT) to various areas of human development, including support to small and medium-sized enterprises, health, education, governance, gender equity, environment organizations and human-itarian aid; and promote ICT volunteering in development initiatives and organizations, particularly among volunteer-sending agencies (VSAs), resulting in increased participation of volunteers in efforts to bridge the digital divide. Collaborates with a number of different types of organizations, including all development stakeholder groups: governments, NGOs and civil society organizations (CSOs), development and volunteer-sending agencies, academia and the private sector.

Geographical Area of Activity: Developing countries.

How to Apply: Guide-lines for submitting proposals are available on the website.

Address: Postfach 260 111, 53153 Bonn, Germany.

Telephone: (228) 8152000; *Fax:* (228) 8152001; *Internet:* www.unites.org; *e-mail:* info@unites.org.

World Solidarity Fund for Poverty Eradication

Adopted by the UN General Assembly under Resolution A/57/265 but, as of September 2003, still in the formal process of development. Part of an overall vision of human rights which prioritizes the struggle against poverty, it is modeled on the National Solidarity Fund launched by President Ben Ali of Tunisia in 1992 which aims to help the needy in that country. The Fund was to be administered by the UN Development Programme.

Activities: Once fully established, the Fund will support poverty alleviation projects throughout the developing world, carried out by community organ-izations, NGOs and small private-sector organizations.

Geographical Area of Activity: International, particularly developing countries.

Address: 1 UN Plaza, New York, NY 10017, USA.

Internet: www.solidarity-fund.org; *e-mail:* contact@solidarity-fund.org.

UNITED NATIONS DEVELOPMENT PROGRAMME (UNDP) DEVELOPMENT GROUP

United Nations Capital Development Fund (UNCDF)

A partner in the UNDP Development Group established in 1966 as a special purpose fund primarily for small-scale investment in the poorest countries. Works to help eradicate poverty through local development programmes and micro-finance operations.

Activities: Works to help reduce poverty, specifically through investing in the poor, and building the productive capacity and self-reliance of poor communities by increasing their access to essential local infrastructure and services. The Fund also works to strengthen these communities' influence over economic and social investments that directly affect their lives and livelihoods. Through the Fund's Local Governance Unit, support is given for nationally-designed local development programmes, which give newly elected officials the resources to govern and invest as well as opening up local planning processes. Also achieves this through working with NGOs and civil society organizations to develop means to keep local governments accountable. Also operates in the field of micro-finance through its Special Unit for Microfinance (SUM, q.v.). Serves a number of programme countries in the developing world: Bahrain, Bangladesh, Benin, Bhutan, Burkina Faso, Burundi, Cambodia, Cape Verde, Caribbean (Eastern Region), Chad, Comoros, Côte d'Ivoire, Egypt, Eritrea, Ethiopia, Gambia, Ghana, Guatemala, Guinea, Guinea-Bissau, Haiti, Kenya, Laos, Lesotho, Madagascar, Malawi, Mali, Mauritania, Mexico, Mongolia, Morocco, Mozambique, Nepal, Nicaragua, Niger, Nigeria, Pakistan, Philippines, São Tomé and Príncipe, Senegal, Sudan, Tanzania, Togo, Uganda, Vietnam, Yemen and Zambia.

Geographical Area of Activity: Programme countries: Bahrain, Bangladesh, Benin, Bhutan, Burkina Faso, Burundi, Cambodia, Cape Verde, Caribbean (Eastern Region), Chad, Comoros, Côte d'Ivoire, Egypt, Eritrea, Ethiopia, Gambia, Ghana, Guatemala, Guinea, Guinea-Bissau, Haiti, Kenya, Laos, Lesotho, Madagascar, Malawi, Mali, Mauritania, Mexico, Mongolia, Morocco, Mozambique, Nepal, Nicaragua, Niger, Nigeria, Pakistan, Philippines, São Tomé and Príncipe, Senegal, Sudan, Tanzania, Togo, Uganda, Vietnam, Yemen and Zambia.

Address: 2 UN Plaza, 26th Floor, New York, NY 10017, USA.

Fax: (212) 906-6479; *Internet:* www.uncdf.org; *e-mail:* info@uncdf.org.

United Nations Capital Development Fund (UNCDF): Guichet Microfinance pour l'Afrique de l'Ouest

A decentralized pilot unit of the UNCDF Special Unit for Microfinance (SUM, q.v.) that provides financial and institutional support to micro-finance institutions in West Africa.

Activities: The programme aims to contribute to the improvement, in a sustainable manner, of the socio-economic situation of poor people in the rural areas of West Africa, principally in the countries of the Economic Community of West African States (ECOWAS) and in Mauritania. Grants are made to support institutional development, in particular the development of new operations and for capacity building of partner micro-finance institutions. Also provides technical assistance in micro-finance to the UN Development Programme (UNDP) country offices.

Geographical Area of Activity: ECOWAS countries (Benin, Burkina Faso, Cape Verde, Côte d'Ivoire, Gambia, Ghana, Guinea, Guinea-Bissau, Liberia, Mali, Niger, Nigeria, Senegal, Sierra Leone and Togo) and Mauritania.

Address: c/o UNDP Lomé, BP 911, Lomé, Togo.

Telephone: (221) 80-92; *Fax:* (221) 64-02; *Internet:* www.uncdf.org/english /microfinance/sum_programmes.html#1; *e-mail:* gmf@gmf.cafe.tg.

United Nations Capital Development Fund (UNCDF): MicroSave Africa

Initially a joint effort of the UNCDF Special Unit for Microfinance (SUM, q.v.), UN Development Programme (UNDP) Africa and the UK's Department for International Development.

Activities: Operates as a regional centre of excellence on micro-finance in East and Southern Africa providing technical assistance to selected micro-finance institutions (MFIs). Also carried out a research programme in co-operation with selected Action Research Partner MFIs; is involved in curriculum-development activities; co-ordinates training in micro-finance issues including training trainers from selected international micro-finance network organizations; and disseminates information on micro-finance.

Geographical Area of Activity: East and Southern Africa.

Address: Shelter Afrique Bldg, Mamlaka Rd, POB 76436, Nairobi, Kenya.

Telephone: (2) 724801; *Fax:* (2) 720133; *Internet:* www.microsave-africa.com/home .asp; *e-mail:* msa@microsave-africa.com.

United Nations Capital Development Fund (UNCDF): MicroSave West Africa

MicroSave West Africa is the Francophone arm of the MicroSave initiative for West African countries of the UNCDF Special Unit for Microfinance (SUM, q.v.), UN Development Programme (UNDP) Africa and the UK government's Department for International Development.

Activities: Provides technical assistance to selected micro-finance institutions and savings product development.

Geographical Area of Activity: West Africa.

Address: 2 UN Plaza, 26th Floor, New York, NY 10017, USA.

Fax: (212) 906-6479; *Internet:* www.uncdf.org/english/microfinance /sum_programmes.html#1; *e-mail:* sum@uncdf.org.

United Nations Capital Development Fund (UNCDF): MicroStart

Launched by the UNCDF and the UNCDF Special Unit for Microfinance (SUM, q.v.) in February 1997. The programme aims to build a new generation of micro-finance institutions (MFIs) that have transparent track records and solid institutional and financial performance, which enable them to reach poor clients while operating on a sustainable basis.

Activities: The programme operates as a compliment to the SUM Capital Investments programme (q.v.), through providing support to young promising micro-finance operations in developing markets, in the form of technical and micro-capital grants. Funding is available for a range of micro-finance organizations, including NGOs, commercial banks, credit unions and special investment funds. The programme also provides support in the form of technical assistance, promoting training and learning opportunities and helping to establish operational guide-lines. Priority is given to supporting breakthrough organizations, defined as organizations that become major service providers in their geographic area, attaining substantial independence from donors through financial viability and influencing other providers.

Geographical Area of Activity: Developing countries.

How to Apply: MicroStart country programmes are managed by UN Development Programme (UNDP) Country Offices and local advisory boards.

Financial Information: UNDP country programmes are initially financed from UNDP Country Office funds, with additional support from the Citicorp Foundation, UNDP's regional bureaus (UNDP Africa and Arab States), the United Nations Foundation (q.v.), the Netherlands government, the Canadian government, the African Development Bank, the Finnish government, the Australian government, the UNCDF and the host governments where MicroStart operates. Accumulated resources mobilized US $48,515,121 (June 2002).

Publications: MicroStart: A Guide for Planning, Starting and Managing a Microfinance Programme.

Address: 2 UN Plaza, 26th Floor, New York, NY 10017, USA.

Fax: (212) 906-6479; *Internet:* www.uncdf.org/english/microfinance /sum_programmes.html#1; *e-mail:* sum@uncdf.org.

United Nations Capital Development Fund (UNCDF): Special Unit for Microfinance (SUM)—Capital Investments

The principal programme of the SUM, which was initially a joint effort between the UN Development Programme (UNDP) and UNCDF and is now incorporated into UNCDF and acts at the UNDP's lead unit in the field of micro-finance.

Activities: Provides financial support and technical assistance to micro-finance institutions, including grants to fund start-up costs and operational expenses and provision of capital for lending (often transferred as equity at the project's end) to micro-finance institutions. Projects have been initiated in Haiti, Madagascar, Malawi, Mali, Mauritania, Mozambique, Nicaragua and Palestinian Autonomous Areas.

Geographical Area of Activity: International, including Haiti, Madagascar, Malawi, Mali, Mauritania, Mozambique, Nicaragua and Palestinian Autonomous Areas.

Address: 2 UN Plaza, 26th Floor, New York, NY 10017, USA.

Fax: (212) 906-6479; *Internet:* www.uncdf.org/english/microfinance /sum_programmes.html#1; *e-mail:* sum@uncdf.org.

UNITED NATIONS DEVELOPMENT PROGRAMME (UNDP) REGIONAL PROGRAMME FOR SOUTH AND NORTH-EAST ASIA

TUGI Urban Governance Initiative: TUGI–UNDP Awards

The Urban Governance Initiative (TUGI) is a regional project of the UNDP that acts as a hub for promoting good urban governance through institutional capacity building, providing policy advisory services, enabling innovations on tools and methodologies for good urban governance and ensuring wide information dissemination and collaborative networking on all of the above within and between cities in the Asia-Pacific region. The TUGI–UNDP Awards form part of the project.

Activities: The Awards are designed to enable successful pilot projects, implemented by any of the large number of local, national and international organizations working on improving urban governance in the Asia-Pacific region, towards upstreaming the lessons of their initiatives into local and national policy development. They are made within three categories: the Urban Governance Innovations Facility, the Cybercity Award and the Young Leadership for Good Urban Governance Grant (qq.v.).

Geographical Area of Activity: Asia and the Pacific.

Contact: Senior Regional Advisers Anwar Fazal, Erna Witoelar.

Address: POB 12544, 50782 Kuala Lumpur, Malaysia.

Telephone: (3) 2095-9122; *Fax:* (3) 2093-2361; *Internet:* www.tugi.org/awards.php; *e-mail:* tugi@undp.org.

TUGI Urban Governance Initiative: TUGI–UNDP Awards—The CyberCity Award

The Awards are designed to both reward and foster city-based innovations that use new information and communications technologies (ICT) to improve urban governance processes or city service delivery and which incorporate creativity, participation and sustainability, as well as demonstrating a high potential for replication across the region.

Activities: Three awards ranging from US $10,000 to US $25,000 are made to city initiatives using new ICT to improve urban governance. Criteria for evaluation are based on: the project's demonstrable local impact, primarily projects that are carried out in conjunction with at least two other key urban stakeholder groups; projects carried out with at least two other key urban stakeholder groups that demonstrate a high level of innovative thinking and creative use of ICT for good governance or poverty reduction; and the project's transferability. A further 20 selected projects are pooled with the three winning projects to provide a database of information accessible to cities through the TUGI website.

Geographical Area of Activity: Asia and the Pacific.

How to Apply: Application forms can be downloaded on the website.

Financial Information: Three annual awards ranging from US $10,000 to US $25,000.

Address: POB 12544, 50782 Kuala Lumpur, Malaysia.

Telephone: (3) 2095-9122; *Fax:* (3) 2093-2361; *Internet:* www.tugi.org/awards.php; *e-mail:* tugi@undp.org.

TUGI Urban Governance Initiative: TUGI–UNDP Awards—The Urban Governance Innovations Facility

The Award is designed to both reward and foster the up-streaming and contribution to policy development based on successful initiatives that harness local, national or regional innovations to improve urban governance processes or city service delivery.

Activities: Makes five annual awards ranging from US $20,000 to US $50,000 to city projects that have successfully carried out pilot projects illustrating concrete gains in the area of good urban governance, and which demonstrate a level of creativity, participation and sustainability, as well as high potential for replication across the Asia and Pacific region. The Award is to be used to upscale and advance the project and/or to facilitate the transfer of knowledge and experience to one or more cities in the region. The Awards are made according to particular themes in order to highlight specific urban issues, which are selected annually. In 2003 the selected themes were urban and human security, peace and conflict resolution, and post-conflict reconciliation and reconstruction. A further 20 selected projects are pooled with the winning projects to provide a database of information accessible to cities through the TUGI website. Applicants can be from city authorities or associations of local governments, private-sector organizations, civil society groups or training institutions.

Geographical Area of Activity: Asia and the Pacific.

How to Apply: Application forms can be downloaded on the website.

Financial Information: Five annual awards ranging from US $20,000 to US $50,000.

Address: POB 12544, 50782 Kuala Lumpur, Malaysia.

Telephone: (3) 2095-9122; *Fax:* (3) 2093-2361; *Internet:* www.tugi.org/awards.php; *e-mail:* tugi@undp.org.

TUGI Urban Governance Initiative: TUGI–UNDP Awards—The Young Leadership for Good Urban Governance Grant

The Awards are designed to promote trans-boundary learning by linking local and regional institutions in a relationship facilitated by the grant recipient, and aim to create greater awareness of the role of young professionals in contributing to the development of better governance in the Asia-Pacific region.

Activities: Makes 10 annual awards in the region of US $10,000, to individuals working in conjunction with recognized NGOs, community-based organizations, local governmental bodies or central government agencies working on promoting capacities for peace. In 2003 the awards were made to projects that demonstrated significant achievements in the areas of urban human security, peace and conflict resolution, and post-conflict reconciliation and reconstruction, with the intention of enabling city stakeholder organizations to access professional skills and services that can be used for training and capacity development within the organization. At least a further 15 selected applicants are pooled with the 10 Award recipients to provide a database of information accessible to cities through the TUGI website.

Geographical Area of Activity: Asia and the Pacific.

How to Apply: Applications can be downloaded from the website.

Financial Information: Ten annual awards of approx. US $10,000 each.

Address: POB 12544, 50782 Kuala Lumpur, Malaysia.

Telephone: (3) 2095-9122; *Fax:* (3) 2093-2361; *Internet:* www.tugi.org/awards.php; *e-mail:* tugi@undp.org.

UNITED NATIONS DEVELOPMENT PROGRAMME (UNDP) SPECIAL INITIATIVE ON HIV/AIDS

Regional Programme for South and North-East Asia: Regional Empowerment and Action to Contain HIV/AIDS—REACH Beyond Borders

A special initiative of the UNDP formulated in response to the urgent challenges presented by the HIV/AIDS epidemic to the development of the countries in the region. It brings together 13 countries in Asia to share their concerns and experience, learn from each other and benefit from global expertise to build commitment and capacity to contain the HIV/AIDS epidemic and limit its impact on the people of the region. The Programme provides a common platform for countries facing similar issues for the development of effective strategies to reduce the vulnerability of people to HIV/AIDS and to respond to the needs of those who are HIV-positive.

Activities: The Programme supports the aim of containing the spread and impact of HIV/AIDS in the region through integrated responses that promote gender equality, poverty reduction and good governance. The objectives of the programme are to: advocate for supportive policies and build commitment among key stakeholders in the region to address HIV/AIDS as a development issue; strengthen knowledge and capacity for a sustained multi-sectoral response linking livelihoods, gender and HIV issues; and to protect the dignity and human security of people infected and affected by and vulnerable to HIV/AIDS through strengthened governance. Programme activities are designed to: strengthen regional co-operation and focus on trans-border issues; emphasize multi-sectoral and participatory methodologies; give special attention to gender concerns and address the particular vulnerability of women; develop the capacities of people living with HIV/AIDS to participate in response formulation and implementation; and promote networking and partnerships and encourage learning and experience sharing. The Programme operates in conjunction with governments, civil society and multi- and bilateral partners across the region, combating the vulnerability of mobile populations to HIV/AIDS, the prevention of trafficking of women and children, the role of the media in addressing HIV/AIDS and the legal ethical framework of vulnerability. Special attention is given to the reduction of stigma and discrimination of HIV infected and affected people. The Programme's core areas are policy advocacy, communications and outreach; rights and governance; facilitating learning and capacity development; migration; and trafficking.

Geographical Area of Activity: Afghanistan, Bangladesh, Bhutan, People's Republic of China, Democratic People's Republic of Korea, India, Iran, Maldives, Mongolia, Nepal, Pakistan, Republic of Korea and Sri Lanka.

Contact: Regional Programme Co-ordinator Sonam Yangchen Rana.

Address: 55 Lodi Estate, New Delhi 110 003, India.

Telephone: (11) 4632339; *Fax:* (11) 4631647; *Internet:* www.hivandevelopment.org /; *e-mail:* sonam.yangchen.rana@undp.org.

UNITED NATIONS ECONOMIC COMMISSION FOR AFRICA (UNECA)

African Center for Gender and Development

Established in 1975, a division of UNECA; operates as the regional structure that deals with gender issues and the advancement of women within the UN system in Africa, working in conjunction with national, sub-regional and regional structures engaged in the advancement of women and gender equality.

Activities: Aims to influence the content of policies and programmes debated and adopted by decision-makers at national, sub-regional and regional level in sectors of economic as well as social development. Center activities include: analysis of policies and lobbying for the integration of the gender perspective in national development plans; mobilization of policy-makers and the drafting of a consensus on the progress already achieved, best practices and new priorities that have arisen from the process of the implementation of the Beijing Platform for Action; and technical co-operation with government services, intergovernmental organizations, parliamentary organizations or civil society organizations within the areas related to development of national, sub-regional and regional policies.

Geographical Area of Activity: Africa.

Contact: Dir Josephine Ouedraogo; Information Officer Houda Mejri.

Address: POB 3001, Addis Ababa, Ethiopia.

Telephone: (1) 443300; *Fax:* (1) 512785; *Internet:* www.uneca.org/fr/acgd; *e-mail:* h .mejri@uneca.org.

Development Management Division (DMD): African Centre for Civil Society

Launched on 24 October 1997 by the Economic Commission for Africa (ECA). It was established in response to the positive changes sweeping through Africa, including the development of people-centred agendas, to assist African governments and NGOs/CSOs to acquire the analytical, organizational and practical tools they need.

Activities: The Centre works to build the institutional, human, resource-mobilization and advocacy capacities of African NGOs/CSOs, enhance NGO/government dialogue and co-operation for an enabling environment, build civil society's capacity to develop innovative techniques for conflict-prevention and peace-building, strengthen peaceful, pluralistic society and foster the active involvement of NGOs/CSOs in development and governance issues and activities. It also provides a one-stop regional information repository on national and regional NGOs/CSOs and professional organizations, with a database on their activities, best practices, lessons learnt and emerging issues.

Geographical Area of Activity: Africa.

Contact: Dir James Nxumolo.

Address: POB 3001, Addis Ababa, Ethiopia.

Telephone: (1) 511296; *Fax:* (1) 510276; *Internet:* www.uneca.org/eca_programmes /development_management/civil.htm; *e-mail:* ecainfo@uneca.org.

Development Management Division (DMD): Development Policy and Management

The programme aims to strengthen the managerial and institutional capacity of the public, private and the voluntary sectors, and to facilitate improvements in public- and private-sector performance as well as increased participation of civil society in the development process.

Activities: Operates by conducting analysis and preparing syntheses of best practices, emerging trends and approaches to public-sector management, private-sector development, and the participation of civil society in development. Develops partnerships with relevant organizations, builds networks and databanks, conducts study tours, is involved in discussions and interactions to exchange experiences and share information, and supports capacity-building efforts, training and workshops. Also provides technical and advisory services.

Geographical Area of Activity: Africa.

Contact: Division Chief Kempe Ronald Hope.

Address: POB 3001, Addis Ababa, Ethiopia.

Telephone: (1) 515826; *Fax:* (1) 510365; *Internet:* www.uneca.org/eca_programmes /development_management/areas.htm#civil; *e-mail:* ecainfo@uneca.org.

Sustainable Development Division: Fostering Sustainable Development

The Division aims to serve Africa better to achieve food security and sustainable development, and to become a center of excellence for managing the inter-linked issues of the nexus of population, agriculture and environment. Also aims to play a leading role in raising awareness and guiding the decision-making process on nexus issues and science and technology management.

Activities: Aims to assist member states by: raising policy-makers' awareness of the urgency to integrate food, population and environmental concerns (the nexus issues) in development planning; offering member states feasible solutions drawn from best practices within Africa and around the world; encouraging UN Economic Commission for Africa member states to develop and take full advantage of their abilities to foster and utilize science and technology for development; providing policy analysis support and dissemination services through workshops, training, seminars, networks or information exchange; and providing technical advisory services to enhance the understanding and management of the complex interactions between agriculture, population, environment and food security. The programme targets regional, national, and district level policy-makers and planners, researchers, other decision-makers, technical experts, NGOs, intergovernmental organizations and leaders in the private sector in the fields of population, agriculture, environment and science and technology.

Geographical Area of Activity: Africa.

Contact: Division Chief: Josué Dioné.

Address: POB 3001, Addis Ababa, Ethiopia.

Telephone: (1) 510406; *Fax:* (1) 510350; *Internet:* www.uneca.org /programmes_home.htm; *e-mail:* jdione@uneca.org.

UNITED NATIONS ECONOMIC COMMISSION FOR EUROPE (UNECE)

Committee on Housing Settlements

First established in 1947; aims to support member states in the fields of housing, urban development, land administration, national and local objectives and policies.

Activities: Operates in conjunction with the public, NGOs and the private sector in UNECE countries at regional, national and local levels, facilitating dialogue with intergovernmental, governmental and NGOs, local governments, the private sector and academics.

Geographical Area of Activity: UNECE countries.

Address: Palais des Nations, Office 356, 1211 Geneva 10, Switzerland.

Telephone: (22) 9174444; *Fax:* (22) 9170505; *Internet:* www.unece.org; *e-mail:* info .ece@unece.org.

UNITED NATIONS ECONOMIC AND SOCIAL COMMISSION FOR ASIA AND THE PACIFIC (UNESCAP)

Environment and Sustainable Development: Capacity building on integration of energy and rural development planning

Part of UNESCAP's Environment and Sustainable Development programme; aims to promote rural energy development.

Activities: Promotes rural energy development through capacity building on the integration of energy and rural development issues, stakeholder involvement and facilitation of information exchange among stakeholders. The project is developed to enhance national capacities in identifying linkages between energy and rural development to promote long-term, integrated and well co-ordinated rural energy planning.

Geographical Area of Activity: Asia and the Pacific.

Address: UN Bldg, Ratchadamnoen Nok Ave, Bangkok, Thailand.

Telephone: (2) 288-1234; *Fax:* (2) 288-1000; *Internet:* www.unescap.org/esd/main .asp.

Population and Social Integration Section/Social Integration Section: Disability

Operates in support of the Asian and Pacific Decade of the Disabled Person 2003–12.

Activities: Assists governments and self-help organizations to create an inclusive, barrier-free rights-based society for people with different disabilities, by providing technical assistance, organizing workshops and training courses and by disseminating information through various means.

Geographical Area of Activity: Asia and Pacific.

Contact: Chief Exec. Jerrold W. Huguet.

Address: UN Bldg, Ratchadamnoen Nok Ave, Bangkok, Thailand.

Telephone: (2) 288-1917; *Fax:* () 288-1030; *Internet:* www.unescap.org/sps /disability.htm; *e-mail:* escap-esid-psis@un.org.

Poverty and Development: Poverty Reduction Division

Created on 1 January 2003 as part of the UN Economic and Social Commission for Asia and the Pacific's (UNESCAP) restructuring to forge greater synergy between research and operational activities in poverty reduction. Its key objectives are: to strengthen the capacity of UNESCAP members and associate members to identify and analyze opportunities and constraints for poverty eradication and to design and implement policies and programmes to reduce poverty in accordance with the relevant millennium development goals.

Activities: The Division handles operational activities to support poverty reduction in both rural and urban areas, geared towards the documentation, testing and dissemination of good practices in poverty reduction through pilot projects, and the provision of advice and assistance to build the capacity of countries in the region to adapt and replicate these practices. The best practices are focused specifically on income- and employment-generating activities, community development, provision of services to the poor and the role of information and communications technologies in poverty reduction. A special area of concern is rural–urban linkage to gain a better understanding of relationships between urban and rural areas to bring about greater co-ordination in planning and delivery of services. Special focus areas and projects are: provision of basic services to the poor through public–private partnerships; management of water resources for poverty reduction; support to local governments and regional networks in poverty-reduction activities; support to urban poverty-reduction programmes in areas including slum improvement, women in local government and human security; promotion of the participation of the urban poor in environment management; and replication of Saemaul Undong practices in least-developed countries. In all areas, the emphasis is on the promotion of regional co-operation and exchange of experiences through capacity building of national, sub-national and local governments, NGOs and CBOs, research and training institutes as well as regional institutes and networks. A priority concern is women's representation in policy-making bodies.

Geographical Area of Activity: Asia and the Pacific.

Publications: Economic and Social Survey of Asia and the Pacific (annual); *Bulletin on Asia-Pacific Perspectives* (annual); *The Asia-Pacific Development Journal* (2 a year).

Address: UN Bldg, Ratchadamnoen Nok Ave, Bangkok, Thailand.
Telephone: (2) 288-1234; *Fax:* (2) 288-1000; *Internet:* www.unescap.org/pdd/index .asp; *e-mail:* escap-pdd@un.org.

UNITED NATIONS EDUCATIONAL, SCIENTIFIC AND CULTURAL ORGANIZATION (UNESCO)

Africa Department

The Department aims to give impetus to UNESCO's action in Africa so as to reflect in all its programmes the priority that is specially accorded to the Africa region and ensure that these programmes are adapted to the needs and aspirations of African member states. The Department also promotes the continent's participation in the globalization process and strengthens regional and sub-regional co-operation.

Activities: The Department's co-operation with NGOs in Africa is within the priority areas of Education for All, poverty alleviation, new information and communications technologies (NICTs), HIV/AIDS, culture of peace, women, and youth. Also co-operates with other UN agencies, intergovernmental and African organizations, and the private sector. Specific initiatives involving NGOs include the Project on Inclusive Schools and Community Support Programme, which focuses on supporting projects and disseminating information on small-scale innovations at national, provincial and local levels, promoting the inclusion of children with disabilities and learning difficulties in regular schools, through funding teacher training, the creation of structures to provide pedagogical support, the education of parents, pre-primary education, the education of the deaf, adult education and the transition to the world of work. Also operates projects on empowering rural women at the community level, establishing victim-friendly sexual offences courts, pilot projects on poverty reduction, and through its UNESCO–Chairs programme promotes the development of university net-working and other co-operation agreements linking institutions of higher education at the inter-regional, regional and sub-regional levels.

Geographical Area of Activity: Africa.

Contact: NGO Contact R. Raonimahary.

Address: UNESCO House, 7 place de Fontenoy, 75352 Paris 07 SP, France.

Telephone: 1-45-68-04-99; *Internet:* www.unesco.org/africa; *e-mail:* r .raonimahary@unesco.org.

Co-Action Programme

The Programme is administered by a special section of the UN Educational, Scientific and Cultural Organization (UNESCO) Secretariat. Funded by member states, individuals and private-sector organizations, all administrative costs are borne by UNESCO.

Activities: Aims to promote assistance for developing countries at the grassroots level, through providing grants to projects and proposals of local NGOs and community groups. The Programme gives priority to the needs of women, disabled persons, refugees and other particular groups, in most cases the most underprivileged individuals in the least-developed countries. The projects are usually on a smaller scale than technical co-operation projects, concerning essential facilities such as the provision of water supplies, literacy training or basic education, with the common aim of improving the quality of life at the community level and involving the full participation of local groups for their implementation. Approximately 100 projects receive funding each year under the Programme.

Geographical Area of Activity: Developing countries.

Financial Information: Annual budget US $1,000,000.

Address: 7 place de Fontenoy, 75332 Paris 07 SP, France.

Telephone: 1-53-69-37-78; *Fax:* 1-45-67-16-90; *Internet:* www.unesco.org/coaction.

Communication and Information Sector (CI)

The CI was established in 1990; its programmes are rooted in the UN Educational, Scientific and Cultural Organization's (UNESCO) Constitution, which requires the Organization to promote the free flow of ideas by word and image.

Activities: Activities are carried out by the Communication Development Division, the Division for Freedom of Expression, Democracy and Peace, and the Information Society Division. The Sector also provides the secretariats for two intergovernmental programmes: the International Programme for the Development of Communication (IPDC) and the Information for All Programme (IFAP). The three principal strategic objectives of the Sector's programmes are: promoting the free flow of ideas and universal access to information; promoting the expression of pluralism and cultural diversity in the media and world information networks; and promoting access for all to information and communications technologies. In addition to the Regular Programme, the CI Sector implements various inter-regional, regional and national projects with extra-budgetary funding mainly in Africa, the Arab States, Asia, the Pacific, Latin America and the Caribbean, in collaboration with UN agencies, bilateral development agencies, international and regional non-governmental agencies.

Geographical Area of Activity: International.

Contact: Head Abdul Waheed Khan.

Address: UNESCO House, 7 place de Fontenoy, 75352 Paris 07 SP, France.

Internet: http://portal.unesco.org/ci.

Communication and Information Sector (CI): Research

The CI was established in 1990; its programmes are rooted in the UN Educational, Scientific and Cultural Organization's (UNESCO) Constitution, which requires it to promote the free flow of ideas by word and image. CI's headquarters is in Paris, with additional representation in 27 UNESCO field offices.

Activities: Funding is available to support research studies on communication and information issues of relevance to the Sector's mandate, which is primarily to contribute to the advancement of knowledge, norms and standards, awareness and better understanding of emerging issues in the information society. Funding is available for research studies, carried out in partnership with international and regional bodies, networks of communication and information researchers and scholars, and research institutions addressing communications and information issues such as: press freedom, media independence and pluralism; media, terrorism, peace and democracy; social, cultural and political impact of information and communications technologies (ICTs); cultural and linguistic diversity in the media and information networks; media and social participation; community multi-media centres and multi-purpose telecentres; ICTs, distance and media education; public service broadcasting and production of local content; communication and information policies; and access to ICTs and knowledge.

Geographical Area of Activity: International.

Contact: Chief of the Exec. Office Kwame Boafo.

Address: 1 rue Miollis, 75732 Paris Cedex 15, France.

Telephone: 1-45-68-44-95; *Fax:* 1-45-68-55-81; *Internet:* www.unesco.org; *e-mail:* k .boafo@unesco.org.

Communication and Information Sector: International Programme for the Development of Communication (IPDC)

The Programme aims to strengthen the means of mass communication in developing countries, by increasing technical and human resources for the media, developing community media and modernizing news agencies and broadcasting organizations. The work of the Programme is guided by its Intergovernmental Council, whose 39 member states are elected by the General Conference of the UN Educational, Scientific and Cultural Organization (UNESCO).

Activities: Aims to meet the most urgent priorities for increasing communication activities in over 130 developing countries, supporting projects promoting press freedom, media independence and pluralism; creating community media; developing human resources for the media; and modernizing national and regional news agencies and broadcast organizations. Future priority will be given to supporting national, regional and inter-regional projects which: clearly promote freedom of expression and media pluralism; are concerned with the development of community media; concentrate on human resource development (training and capacity building); and promote international partnerships. Also awards the UNESCO–IPDC Prize for Rural Communication (q.v.).

Geographical Area of Activity: Developing countries.

How to Apply: Projects must be proposed by international or NGOs having consultative status with UNESCO to the Bureau of IPDC.

Contact: Pres. Intergovernmental Council Torben Krogh.

Address: UNESCO House, 7 place de Fontenoy, 75352 Paris 07 SP, France.

Internet: http://portal.unesco.org/ci/.

Culture Sector

Aims to help governments adopt effective cultural policies.

Activities: The UN Educational, Scientific and Cultural Organization's (UNESCO) programme work in the field of culture is carried out within specific themes: Cultural Policy Resources; Issues on Culture and Development; From Diversity to Pluralism; Creativity and the Arts; Copyright; Cultural Enterprises and Industries; Tangible Cultural Heritage; Intangible Cultural Heritage; Legal

Protection for Cultural Heritage; World Heritage Centre; Intercultural Dialogue; General and Regional Histories; Culture in Africa; Culture and Youth; and Culture, Women and Gender. Organizes events, workshops and conferences, awards prizes, provides bursaries to artists, produces publications, and carries out research and collaboration with other UN agencies, intergovernmental organizations, governments, NGOs and community groups, and the private sector. UNESCO has established the International Fund for the Promotion of Culture (q.v.).

Geographical Area of Activity: International.

Contact: NGO Contact G. Poussin.

Address: UNESCO House, 7 Place de Fontenoy, 75352 Paris 07 SP, France.

Telephone: 1-45-68-43-75; *Fax:* 1-45-68-55-91; *Internet:* www.unesco.org/culture; *e-mail:* g.poussin@unesco.org.

Education Sector

The department promotes education as a fundamental right, and aims to improve the quality of education, and stimulate experimentation, innovation and policy dialogue. Its work is based on the principles that education is a right, enhances individual freedom and yields important development benefits.

Activities: Work is carried out within specific themes, namely: Associated Schools; Early Childhood/Family; Education for All; Policies and Strategies; Emergency Assistance; Forum on Higher Education; Higher Education Reform; HIV/AIDS; Inclusive Education; Non-Violence; Primary Education; Right to Education; Secondary Education; Science and Technology; Street/Working Children; Studying Abroad; Sustainable Development; and Technical/Vocational; it encompasses numerous initiatives carried out by the UN Educational, Scientific and Cultural Organization in co-operation with governments, UN agencies and intergovernmental organizations, NGOs, local communities and the private sector. Specific general flagship initiatives include Learning Without Frontiers, Sustainable Future, and Youth and Consumption. NGOs partnering with the department include Education International, International Association for Counselling, International Association for Educational Assessment, International Association of Universities, International Baccalaureate Organization, International Federation of University Women, International Literacy Institute, International Reading Association, Summer Institute of Linguistics, World Council of Associations for Technology Education, World Confederation of Teachers, World Organization for Early Childhood Education, and Worlddidac.

Geographical Area of Activity: International.

Publications: Education Today (newsletter).

Contact: NGO Contact M. Yannarakis.

Address: UNESCO House, 7 Place de Fontenoy, 75352 Paris 07 SP, France.

Telephone: 1-45-68-24-64; *Internet:* www.unesco.org/education/index.shtml/; *e-mail:* m.yannarakis@unesco.org.

Intergovernmental Oceanographic Commission (IOC): Training, Education and Mutual Assistance in Marine Science—TEMA

The TEMA programme of the IOC aims to build capacity and turn scientific ability and knowledge into a useful tool that can fulfil society's needs; IOC was founded by the UN Educational, Scientific and Cultural Organization in 1960.

Activities: The TEMA programme provides on-the-job training of individuals; fellowships to individuals for scientific, technical, and engineering training/formal education; funds regional co-operative development projects directed at limited attainable objectives; assistance in securing resources needed for developing/enhancing infrastructure needed for specific activities; funds short-term residential courses/workshops dealing with specialized subjects, which may result in the award of appropriate accreditation or international recognition from an international institution or a research or academic institution; and awareness-raising activities. Grants available include travel grants of up to US $2,000 for marine professionals from developing countries; study/research grants of up to US $8,000 each to support individuals from developing countries for research or studies related to programmes of the IOC; and two annual grants of US $7,500 each to support capacity-building activities by organizations interested in jointly implementing training courses or other capacity-building activities consistent with the programmes of the IOC.

Geographical Area of Activity: International.

Address: 1 rue Miollis, 75732 Paris Cedex 15, France.

Internet: http://ioc.unesco.org/tema/iocGrants.htm; *e-mail:* ioc.secretariat@unesco.org.

International Centre for Integrated Mountain Development (ICIMOD)

Launched in 1981 following recommendations at a regional meeting of the UN Educational, Scientific and Cultural Organization's (UNESCO) MAB Programme in 1975 and endorsed by UNESCO's General Assembly in 1976; aims to promote the development of an economically and environmentally sound ecosystem and to improve the living standards of mountain populations.

Activities: Aims to support the socio-economic development of mountain people, particularly the 140m. inhabitants of the Hindu Kush–Himalayan region, and the Centre works with them directly or through appropriate local bodies or intermediaries. ICIMOD develops contacts with appropriate local government institutions and NGOs to channel the knowledge it has generated or compiled as well as other forms of support to mountain households and solicits feedback on its appropriateness and effectiveness. Collaboration is with four different groups of stakeholders: individual mountain households, natural resource user groups, other services, and community organizations. Runs a number of integrated programmes designed to facilitate regional co-operation for the management of many economic and environmental problems in the development of mountain areas. Programmes include: natural resource management; agricultural and rural income diversification; water, hazards and environmental management; culture, equity, gender and governance; policy and partnership; and information and knowledge management. The Centre also focuses on developing relations with NGOs, responding to special needs, and providing support to ensure the continuity of a project where necessary.

Geographical Area of Activity: Mountain regions, particularly the Hindu Kush–Himalayan region.

Address: POB 3226, Jawalakhel, Kathmandu, Nepal.

Telephone: (1) 5525313; *Fax:* (1) 5524509; *Internet:* www.icimod.org; *e-mail:* icimod@icimod.org.np.

International Federation for Information Processing (IFIP): IFIP Awards

IFIP is a non-governmental, non-profit umbrella organization for national societies working in the field of information processing. It was established in 1960 under the auspices of the UN Educational, Scientific and Cultural Organization (UNESCO) following the first World Computer Congress held in Paris in 1959; aims to encourage and assist in the development, exploitation and application of Information Technology (IT) for the benefit of all people.

Activities: IFIP makes a number of awards, both internally to members of the IFIP community for their service to IFIP, and to others for their accomplishments, and to make the public aware of the role IFIP plays in the international information-processing community. External awards include the biannual Namur Award, presented for an outstanding contribution to the creation of awareness of the social implications of IT. Also administers the IFIP–UNESCO Project to Assist the Participation of IT Professionals from Developing and Central and Eastern European Countries in International ICT Activities.

Geographical Area of Activity: International.

Address: Hofstr. 3, 2361 Laxenburg, Austria.

Telephone: (2) 236-73-61-6; *Fax:* (2) 236-73-61-69; *Internet:* www.ifip.or.at; *e-mail:* ifip@ifip.or.at.

International Fund for the Promotion of Culture

The Fund was created by the General Conference of the UN Educational, Scientific and Cultural Organization (UNESCO) at its 18th session by Resolution 3.322 in November 1974 to support cultural development. It aims to help cultural artists and managers find additional financing for their projects, so that cultural diversity may benefit from globalization to better assert itself instead of being its victim.

Activities: Grants are made to small projects as well as to support more sizeable projects, which are financed in co-operation with other financing bodies pursuing the same objectives in the spirit of UNESCO's ideals. Grants are awarded within the following categories: promotion of diversity in all its forms of contemporary cultural expression, through the promotion of various cultures (the values they embody and the forms of expression, which ensure their authenticity and identity) in accordance with the autonomy and freedom of expression of the artists; improving the efficiency and the correct management of national or regional, cultural and artistic institutions, as well as of any other structure or equipment with a cultural calling, through, among others, the training of specialists in development and cultural action (planners, managers, artistic activity leaders, and technicians); research in the field of contemporary cultural practices

INTERNATIONAL ORGANIZATIONS FUNDING DIRECTORY

(including cultural development, cultural production and circulation); and promotion of culture with new audiences and new publics, namely by the organization of exchanges and of network development.

Geographical Area of Activity: International.

How to Apply: Applications should reach the Secretariat of the Fund and be registered by it on 31 January of each year at the latest. Incomplete files are not registered until the applicant, in accordance with the indications of the Secretariat, completes them. It is, therefore, preferable that applications be transmitted to the Secretariat of the Fund well before the deadline so that, if need be, the files may be completed in due time. Once registered, each complete application is examined by the Secretariat in order to check its admissibility and is then submitted to the Administrative Council during its ordinary session, at the end of the first quarter of every year.

Address: 1 rue Miollis, 75732 Paris Cedex 15, France.

Telephone: 1-45-68-55-95; *Internet:* www.unesco.org/culture/ifpc/; *e-mail:* dir.ifpc@unesco.org.

International Science Prizes: Carlos J. Finlay Prize for Microbiology

Established in 1980 and named after Dr Carlos Juan Finlay, a prominent Cuban scientist dedicated to promoting research and development in microbiology. Awarded to coincide with the year of the General Conference of the UN Educational, Scientific and Cultural Organization.

Activities: The biennial Prize rewards a person or a group of persons working privately or on the staff of an organization for an outstanding contribution to microbiology, including immunology, molecular biology and genetics, and its applications.

Geographical Area of Activity: International.

Restrictions: Each government or organization is entitled to nominate a single candidate; applications from individuals are not accepted.

Financial Information: Funded by the government of Cuba; total prize award US $5,000.

Address: 7 place de Fontenoy, 75332 Paris 07 SP, France.

Telephone: 1-45-68-10-00; *Fax:* 1-45-67-16-90; *Internet:* www.unesco.org/science/unesco_intern_sc_prizes.htm.

International Science Prizes: Great Man-Made River International Prize

Established in 1999, the Great Man-Made River International Prize for Water Resources in Arid and Semi-Arid Areas, is sponsored by the authorities of the Libyan Arab Jamahiriya.

Activities: The Prize, awarded every two years, recognizes the achievements of an individual, a group of individuals or a research institution having made fundamental and substantial contributions to the assessment, development, management and/or use of water resources in arid and semi-arid areas.

Geographical Area of Activity: International.

Financial Information: Prize of US $20,000 awarded every two years.

Address: 7 place de Fontenoy, 75332 Paris 07 SP, France.

Telephone: 1-45-68-10-00; *Fax:* 1-45-67-16-90; *Internet:* www.unesco.org/water /ihp/prizes/great_man/.

International Science Prizes: UNESCO Science Prize

Administered by the Unit for International Partnership in Science (IPS) within the UN Educational, Scientific and Cultural Organization (UNESCO).

Activities: The UNESCO Science Prize, awarded every two years, rewards a person or group of people for an outstanding contribution they have made to the technological development of a developing member state or region through the application of scientific and technological research (particularly in the fields of education, engineering and industrial development). Applications are open to individuals and organizations.

How to Apply: No direct applications to UNESCO; contact the National Commission for UNESCO or an NGO which has consultative status with UNESCO.

Contact: Contact Yoslan Nur.

Address: SC/AP, 1 rue Miollis, 75015 Paris Cedex 15, France.

Telephone: 1-45-68-39-17; *Fax:* 1-45-68-58-27; *Internet:* www.unesco.org/science /unesco_intern_sc_prizes.htm.

Management of Social Transformations (MOST)

A UN Educational, Scientific and Cultural Organization (UNESCO) programme created in 1994 that promotes international, comparative and policy-relevant research on contemporary social transformations and issues of global importance. It aims to: further understanding of social transformations; establish sustainable links between social science researchers and decision-makers; strengthen scientific, professional and institutional capacities, particularly in developing countries; and encourage the design of research-anchored policy.

Activities: MOST projects and activities focus on a range of issues including multi-cultural and multi-ethnic societies, urban development, globalization and governance. Additionally, MOST contributes to the UN system-wide priorities, such as poverty eradication, governance and indigenous peoples. Partners with MOST National Liaison Committees, based in 59 countries, and also has links with NGOs, UN agencies, funds and programmes including the International Bank for Reconstruction and Development (IBRD—World Bank), United Nations Development Programme (UNDP), United Nations Children's Fund (UNICEF), UN International Drug Control Programme (UNDCP) and other inter-governmental organizations.

Geographical Area of Activity: International.

Contact: Exec. Sec. Timothée Ngakoutou; Co-ordinator Paul de Guchteneire.

Address: UNESCO House, 7 place de Fontenoy, 75352 Paris 07 SP, France.

Telephone: 1-45-68-37-99; *Fax:* 1-45-68-57-24; *Internet:* www.unesco.org/most; *e-mail:* ssmost@unesco.org.

Natural Sciences Sector

One of the five specialist activity areas of the UN Educational, Scientific and Cultural Organization (UNESCO).

Activities: The Sector's focal areas are: fresh water, incorporating the International Hydrological Programme, the World Water Assessment Programme, and various water-related events; people and nature, consisting of the Man and the Biosphere (MAB) programme; oceans; food sciences; coastal and small islands; basic and engineering sciences; and science policy. Also administers a range of intergovernmental programmes, including the International Hydrological Programme, the Intergovernmental Oceanographic Commission, the International Geological Correlation Programme, and the Management of Social Transformations (MOST) initiative (q.v.). Collaborates with intergovernmental organizations, national research institutions and international NGOs. Also awards prizes, organizes events and conferences, disseminates information through publications and compilation of on-line databases.

Geographical Area of Activity: International.

Contact: NGO Contact M. Millward.

Address: UNESCO House, 7 place de Fontenoy, 75352 Paris 07 SP, France.

Telephone: 1-45-68-41-44; *Internet:* www.unesco.org; *e-mail:* m.millward@unesco .org.

Participation Programme

The Programme was established to assist member states and international NGOs in support of the UN Educational, Scientific and Cultural Organization's (UNESCO) activities.

Activities: Grants are available to NGOs enjoying formal or operational status with UNESCO and governmental organizations for activities related to UNESCO projects and programmes, in particular major programmes, trans-disciplinary projects, activities on behalf of women, young people, Africa and the least-developed countries, and the activities of the National Commissions for UNESCO. Assistance under the Programme can comprise the provision of the services of specialists and consultants, fellowships and study grants, publications, periodicals and documentation, equipment, conferences, meetings and training, and general grant funding. Also provides emergency assistance in exceptional cases, which fall outside the general funding criteria.

Geographical Area of Activity: International, particularly Africa and developing countries.

How to Apply: Requests should be submitted to the Director-General by the UNESCO member states through the National Commissions for UNESCO, or, where there is no National Commission, through a designated government channel.

Financial Information: Grants to NGOs do not exceed 10% of the annual Programme budget.

Contact: Dir-Gen. Koichiro Matsuura.

Address: 7 place de Fontenoy, 75352 Paris 07 SP; 1 rue Miollis, 75732 Paris Cedex 15, France.

Telephone: 1-45-68-10-00; *Fax:* 1-45-67-16-90; *Internet:* www.unesco.org/general /eng/about/circulars/cl3609.pdf.

Prizes in Communication and Information: Digital Arts Award

The Digital Arts Award was launched by the UN Educational, Scientific and Cultural Organization (UNESCO) in June 2003; organized in collaboration with the Institute of Advanced Media Arts and Sciences (IAMAS) in Japan.

Activities: The prize is organized within the framework of UNESCO's Digi-Arts Portal and the UNESCO Prize for the Promotion of the Arts to encourage the work of young emerging digital artists around the world. In 2003, the prize was awarded under the theme of Digital Pluralism, promoting digital technology and artistic creativity to foster intercultural dialogue. The Award consists of a first prize of US $5,000 plus a six-month period as artist-in-residence at IAMAS. The second and third prizes consist of awards of US $3,000 and US $2,000 respectively.

Geographical Area of Activity: International.

Financial Information: Funded through the Higashiyama Fund, set up and managed by the National Federation of UNESCO Associations in Japan (NFUAJ).

Address: 7 place de Fontenoy, 75332 Paris 07 SP, France.

Telephone: 1-45-68-10-00; *Fax:* 1-45-67-16-90; *Internet:* www.unesco.org/general /eng/about/prizes/index.shtml.

Prizes in Communication and Information: INFOLAC Web Prize for Latin America and Caribbean Youth

Established in collaboration with the library council of the Universidad Nacional Autónoma de México (UNAM) to support the development of educational websites in Central and South America and the Caribbean.

Activities: Supports the development of websites aimed at young people in Central and South America and the Caribbean; sites must have an educational value for youth in the region and should contribute towards fostering indigenous culture in Central and South America and the Caribbean, by promoting content related to education, science and culture and should not merely be designed for the dissemination of commercial, entertainment or related themes.

Geographical Area of Activity: Central and South America and the Caribbean.

How to Apply: The website must be produced by a private or public institution registered in any Central or South American or Caribbean country; several criteria will be taken into account in judging the websites, including originality, content, graphic design, functionality, accessibility and utility for young people.

Address: 7 place de Fontenoy, 75332 Paris 07 SP, France.

Telephone: 1-45-68-10-00; *Fax:* 1-45-67-16-90; *Internet:* http://infolac.ucol.mx.

Prizes in Communication and Information: IPDC-UNESCO Rural Communication Prize Award

The Award was established in 1985 by the Executive Board of the UN Educational, Scientific and Cultural Organization (UNESCO) in pursuance of a decision of the 5th session of the Intergovernmental Council of the International Programme for the Development of Communication (IPDC).

Activities: The Award, which is presented every two years, is intended to recognize a meritorious and innovative activity by either an individual or organization in improving communication in rural communities, primarily in developing countries, and particularly in the areas of local newspapers, radio and television programmes, printing equipment and films in rural communities. The 2001 award was made to rural radio projects in Argentina and Peru.

Geographical Area of Activity: Developing countries.

How to Apply: Nominations are sent to the IPDC Secretariat and should be accompanied by a biographical statement for the candidate or group of candidates, a detailed description of work for which the candidature is put forward, along with supporting documents, and the completed submission form. The documents are then submitted through the Chairperson of the Intergovernmental Council of the IPDC to its Bureau which acts as the Jury for the selection of the prize winner.

Financial Information: Award of US $20,000 every two years.

Address: 7 place de Fontenoy, 75332 Paris 07 SP, France.

Telephone: 1-45-68-10-00; *Fax:* 1-45-67-16-90; *Internet:* http://portal.unesco.org/ci.

Prizes for Culture: IMC–UNESCO International Music Prize

Created in 1975 to recognize musicians or musical institutions whose activities have contributed to the enrichment and development of music and has served peace, understanding between peoples, international co-operation and other purposes proclaimed by the UN Charter and the constitution of the UN Educational, Scientific and Cultural Organization.

Activities: The Music Prize is open to numerous applicants, including composers, for the whole of their creative output; individual performers or ensembles in the fields of popular, traditional, classical music or jazz, for their overall concert activities; musicologists and music critics for the body of their work; members of the teaching profession for their overall educational output; public figures who have played a major role locally or internationally in more than one field of music; and musical institutions or ensembles, for their outstanding services to music.

Geographical Area of Activity: International.

How to Apply: Candidates can only be nominated by Permanent Delegations to UNESCO, National Commissions for UNESCO and International Music Council members.

Address: 7 place de Fontenoy, 75332 Paris 07 SP, France.

Telephone: 1-45-68-10-00; *Fax:* 1-45-67-16-90; *Internet:* www.unesco.org/imc /prizelist.html; *e-mail:* imc@unesco.org.

Prizes for Culture: International Arirang Prize

Activities: The aim of the Prize is to encourage governments, NGOs and local communities to take the lead in identifying, preserving and drawing attention to their oral and intangible heritage. Contributions by individuals, groups and institutions to the systematic preservation of this heritage are also encouraged.

Geographical Area of Activity: International.

Financial Information: Funding provided by the Government of the Republic of Korea.

Address: 7 place de Fontenoy, 75332 Paris 07 SP, France.

Telephone: 1-45-68-10-00; *Fax:* 1-45-67-16-90; *Internet:* www.unesco.org/culture /heritage/intangible/index.shtml.

Prizes for Culture: International Simón Bolívar Prize

Established by UNESCO, in memory of Simón Bolívar.

Activities: The Prize is awarded to honour an activity of outstanding merit which has contributed to the freedom, independence and dignity of peoples and to the strengthening of a new international economic, social and cultural order. Eligible activities include intellectual or artistic creation, a social achievement or the mobilization of public opinion.

Geographical Area of Activity: International.

Contact: Montserrat Martell.

Address: 7 place de Fontenoy, 75332 Paris 07 SP, France.

Telephone: 1-45-68-10-00; *Fax:* 1-45-67-16-90; *Internet:* www.unesco.org/culture /prizes/html_eng/index_en.shtml.

Prizes for Culture: Melina Mercouri International Prize

The Melina Mercouri International Prize for the Safeguarding and Management of Cultural Landscapes (UNESCO/Greece) was established in honour of Melina Mercouri, a former Minister of Culture of Greece.

Activities: The Prize is awarded to outstanding examples of action to safeguard and enhance the world's major cultural landscapes.

Geographical Area of Activity: International.

How to Apply: Nomination details available on the website.

Address: 7 place de Fontenoy, 75332 Paris 07 SP, France.

Telephone: 1-45-68-10-00; *Fax:* 1-45-67-16-90; *Internet:* www.unesco.org/culture /heritage/prize/html_eng/index_en.shtml.

Prizes for Culture: Sharjah Prize for Arab Culture

Established in November 1998 at the 155th session of the UN Educational, Scientific and Cultural Organization (UNESCO), as part of the activities carried out in 1989 for Sharjah, known as the cultural capital of the Arab Region.

Activities: The Prize is awarded every two years, during the General Conference of UNESCO, to honour intellectually distinguished individuals, groups or institutions world-wide for their activities to promote Arab culture. The Prize is open to nationals of both Arab and other countries for their contribution, through their artistic, intellectual or promotional work, to the development and diffusion of Arab culture in the world.

Geographical Area of Activity: Arab countries.

How to Apply: Candidates for the Sharjah Prize for Arab Culture should apply to their country's National Commission for UNESCO.

Financial Information: Funded by the government of the Emirate of Sharjah.

Address: 7 place de Fontenoy, 75332 Paris 07 SP, France.

Telephone: 1-45-68-10-00; *Fax:* 1-45-67-16-90; *Internet:* www.unesco.org/culture /heritage/intangible/sharjah/html_eng/index_en.shtml.

Prizes in Education: International Reading Association Literacy Award

Established in 1979 to distribute an annual award recognizing contributions to the fight for literacy.

Activities: Aims to intensify the fight for literacy in the context of life-long education; to reward the services of institutions, organizations or individuals displaying outstanding merit and achieving effective results for the fight for literacy. Distributes an annual award of US $15,000, with funding from the International Reading Association Literacy Award USA.

Geographical Area of Activity: International.

Address: 7 place de Fontenoy, 75332 Paris 07 SP, France.

Telephone: 1-45-68-10-00; *Fax:* 1-45-67-16-90; *Internet:* www.unesco.org /education/html/prizes.shtml.

Prizes in Education: King Sejong Literacy Prize

Established in 1990 to recognize outstanding and meritorious achievement in contributing to the fight for literacy.

Activities: Aims to promote literacy, with special consideration given to the development and dissemination of mother tongues in developing countries.

Geographical Area of Activity: Developing countries.

Financial Information: Funded by the government of the Republic of Korea; annual award of US $30,000.

Address: 7 place de Fontenoy, 75332 Paris 07 SP, France.

Telephone: 1-45-68-10-00; *Fax:* 1-45-67-16-90; *Internet:* www.unesco.org /education/html/prizes.shtml.

Prizes in Education: Malcolm Adiseshiah International Literacy Prize

Established in 1998 by the UN Educational, Scientific and Cultural Organization (UNESCO).

Activities: The prizes form part of UNESCO's set of measures designed to intensify the fight for literacy in the context of life-long education, aiming to reward the services of institutions, organizations or individuals displaying outstanding merit and achieving particularly effective results in their contributions to the fight for literacy. The awarding of the prizes also aims to secure and maintain public sympathy and support for literacy programmes in progress.

Geographical Area of Activity: International.

How to Apply: Applicant institutions, organizations or individuals must have carried out literacy or post-literacy activities, including direct teaching, organizing literacy programmes at national or local level, promoting support from the public, producing teaching materials or special media for literacy programmes, carrying out research in fields related to literacy, carrying out special surveys of primary importance for literacy planning, offering young people the possibility of taking part in literacy activities, carrying out non-formal education activities of a social, cultural, economic or political nature incorporating literacy and related activities (including radio and television programmes, publications and press).

Financial Information: Annual award US $20,000.

Address: 7 place de Fontenoy, 75332 Paris 07 SP, France.

Telephone: 1-45-68-10-00; *Fax:* 1-45-67-16-90; *Internet:* www.unesco.org /education/html/prizes.shtml.

Prizes in Education: Nessim Habif Prize/UNESCO

Established in 1962 by the UN Educational, Scientific and Cultural Organization.

Activities: Annual award of US $10,000 recognizing distinguished work in the promotion of literacy through the production of instructional materials (good textbooks) in the languages of Africa contributing to educational progress and socio-cultural development.

Geographical Area of Activity: Africa.

Financial Information: Funded through the interest on a donation by Nessim Habif; annual award of US $10,000.

Address: 7 place de Fontenoy, 75332 Paris 07 SP, France.

Telephone: 1-45-68-10-00; *Fax:* 1-45-67-16-90; *Internet:* www.unesco.org /education/html/prizes.shtml.

Prizes in Education: Noma Literacy Prize (for Meritorious Work in Literacy)

Established in 1980 as an annual award aiming to contribute to the fight for literacy in the context of life-long education; to reward the services of institutions, organizations or individuals displaying outstanding merit and achieving effective results for the fight for literacy.

Geographical Area of Activity: International.

Financial Information: Funding provided by Kodanska Ltd Tokyo, Japan; annual award of US $15,000.

Address: 7 place de Fontenoy, 75332 Paris 07 SP, France.

Telephone: 1-45-68-10-00; *Fax:* 1-45-67-16-90; *Internet:* www.unesco.org /education/html/prizes.shtml.

Prizes in Social and Human Sciences: Félix Houphouët-Boigny Peace Prize

Established in 1991 by the UN Educational, Scientific and Cultural Organization (UNESCO) to honour living individuals and active public or private institutions or bodies that have made a significant contribution to promoting, seeking, safeguarding or maintaining peace in conformity with the Charter of the UN and the Constitution of UNESCO.

Activities: Annual prize of €122,000 awarded to individuals and organizations who have developed significant peace initiatives. If several prize-winners are designated, the amount of the Prize is shared out equally among them.

Geographical Area of Activity: International.

Financial Information: Annual prize award of €122,000.

Address: 7 place de Fontenoy, 75332 Paris 07 SP, France.

Telephone: 1-45-68-10-00; *Fax:* 1-45-67-16-90; *Internet:* www.unesco.org/shs/eng /prizes.shtml.

Prizes in Social and Human Sciences: UNESCO–Madanjeet Singh Prize for the Promotion of Tolerance and Non-Violence

Established in 1995 by the UN Educational, Scientific and Cultural Organization to recognize tolerance and non-violence in the field of science, the arts, culture, education or communication. The Prize was created to mark the 125th anniversary of the birth of Mahatma Gandhi.

Activities: The Prize of US $100,000 is awarded to institutions, organizations or persons who, through their activities, have promoted a spirit of tolerance and non-violence in the field of science, the arts, culture, education or communication. Awarded biennially on the International Day of Tolerance.

Geographical Area of Activity: International.

Financial Information: Funds donated by Madanjeet Singh; biennial award of US $100,000.

Contact: Contact S. Lasarev.

Address: 7 place de Fontenoy, 75332 Paris 07 SP, France.

Telephone: 1-45-68-38-31; *Fax:* 1-45-68-57-23; *Internet:* www.unesco.org/tolerance /prize1e.htm.

Prizes in Social and Human Sciences: UNESCO Prize for Human Rights Education

Established in 1978 by the UN Educational, Scientific and Cultural Organization.

Activities: Biennial award of US $10,000 honouring an institution, organization or individual's work in the field of developing human rights.

Geographical Area of Activity: International.

Financial Information: Funding from UNESCO's follow-up to Resolution 3 [XXXIII] of the UN Commission on Human Rights concerning the celebration of the 30th Anniversary of the Universal Declaration of Human Rights; biennial award of US $10,000.

362

Address: 7 place de Fontenoy, 75332 Paris 07 SP, France.

Telephone: 1-45-68-10-00; *Fax:* 1-45-67-16-90; *Internet:* www.unesco.org /human_rights/hrprize.htm.

Prizes in Social and Human Sciences: UNESCO Prize for Peace Education

Established in 1981 by the UN Educational, Scientific and Cultural Organization.

Activities: Aims to promote all forms of action designed to construct the defences of peace in people's minds and to alert public opinion and mobilize the conscience of mankind in the cause of peace. An annual award is distributed of approximately US $60,000.

Geographical Area of Activity: International.

Financial Information: Funds provided by the Japan Shipbuilding Industry Foundation which donated US $1,000,000; annual award of approx. US $60,000.

Address: 7 place de Fontenoy, 75332 Paris 07 SP, France.

Telephone: 1-45-68-10-00; *Fax:* 1-45-67-16-90; *Internet:* www.unesco.org/shs/eng /prize_peace_ed.shtml.

Relations with International Organizations Division: Section of NGOs and Foundations

The Section is responsible for helping to strengthen co-operation with NGOs in accordance with the Directives concerning the UN Educational, Scientific and Cultural Organization's (UNESCO) relations with NGOs, and with foundations and similar institutions in accordance with the Directives concerning UNESCO's relations with foundations and similar institutions. Manages institutional relations with NGOs, and operates in co-operation with the programme sectors, field units and national commissions, as well as NGOs.

Activities: The Section's operations include: admission of NGOs to official relations, including examination of requests for admission and reclassification and preparation of relevant recommendations to be submitted to the Committee on NGOs of the Executive Board, and implementation of the Directives and specific General Conference resolutions; evaluation of co-operation with NGOs, comprising support to the NGO Committee for the drafting of the sexennial report on the contribution of NGOs to UNESCO's activities and preparation of other Executive Board documents relating to the evaluation of co-operation; co-ordination of co-operation with programme sectors (education, science, social and human sciences, culture and communication sectors); communication, including processing of correspondence with NGOs, requests for information, exchanges with NGOs maintaining official relations, invitations to meetings and requests for Secretariat representation; co-ordination of and support to the collective consultation mechanisms, including co-operation with the NGO–UNESCO Liaison Committee on preparations for, the holding and follow-up to the NGO International Conference, collective consultations and joint programme commissions and mobilization of NGOs for the preparation of major international conferences; and centralization and dissemination of data and information concerning co-operation with NGOs, notably maintaining and updating of the NGO database and the NGO website.

Geographical Area of Activity: International.

Address: UNESCO House, 7 place de Fontenoy, 75352 Paris 07 SP, France.

Telephone: 1-45-68-11-78; *Fax:* 1-45-68-56-43; *Internet:* http://erc.unesco.org/ong /en/; *e-mail:* rio-ngo@unesco.org.

Relations with International Organizations Division: Sector for External Relations and Co-operation: NGO–UNESCO Liaison Committee

The Committee's mandate is to: represent the interests of UNESCO-centered NGOs with regard to UNESCO; co-operate with the Director-General; implement the resolutions adopted by the international conference of NGOs; ensure appropriate exchange of information and make preparations for subsequent sessions of the international conference of NGOs; and ensure that the interests and opinions of NGOs taken collectively are reflected in UNESCO programmes.

Activities: From 2001–03 the Committee's members were Education International, Fédération Internationale des Centres d'entraînement aux Méthodes d'Education Active, International Association of Lions Clubs, International Association of Universities, International Council for Engineering and Technology, International Federation of University Women, International Voluntary Service, World Association of Girl Guides and Girl Scouts, World Federation of UNESCO Clubs, Centres and Associations, and the World Federation of Scientific Workers.

Geographical Area of Activity: International.

Publications: Link (newsletter).

Contact: Pres. Liaison Cttee Monique Fouilhoux.

Address: NGO–UNESCO Liaison Committee, UNESCO House, 1 rue Miollis, 75732 Paris Cedex 15, France.

Telephone: 1-45-68-36-68; *Fax:* 1-45-66-03-37; *Internet:* www.unesco.org/ngo /comite; *e-mail:* comite.liaison.ong@unesco.org.

Social and Human Sciences Sector

One of the UN Educational, Scientific and Cultural Organization's five specialized sectors of activity; aims to advance knowledge, standards and intellectual co-operation in order to facilitate social transformations where the values of justice, freedom and human dignity can be fully realized.

Activities: Operates according to three working principles: to determine what should be (ethics and human rights); to anticipate what could be (philosophy and prospective studies); and to study what is (empirical social science research). In the area of social transformation helps social scientists and decision-makers to provide improved responses to societal issues of high complexity, and through its intergovernmental programme, Management of Social Transformations (MOST), promotes the development and use of social science knowledge that contributes to better understanding and management of social transformations, focusing on improving the linkage between research and policy-making, including the formulation, monitoring and evaluation of development actions and processes, the dissemination of research results, best practices and capacity building within three major areas: international migration and multiculturalism, urban development, and democracy and governance. Works closely with advisory committees, NGOs, networks and professional associations, and civil society groups.

Geographical Area of Activity: International.

Publications: International Social Science Journal (ISSJ) (quarterly); *Diogenes* (journal); *SHS Newsletter* (quarterly).

Contact: NGO Contact M. Forst.

Address: UNESCO House, 7 place de Fontenoy, 75352 Paris 07 SP, France.

Telephone: 1-45-68-45-95; *Internet:* http://portal.unesco.org; *e-mail:* m.forst@ unesco.org.

UNESCO/Guillermo World Press Freedom Prize

Created in 1997, on the initiative of the Executive Board of the UN Educational, Scientific and Cultural Organization, in honour of Guillermo Cano Isaza, a Colombian journalist assassinated on 17 December 1986. The Prize is formally conferred by the Director-General of the Organization, on the occasion of World Press Freedom Day, on 3 May.

Activities: The annual Prize honours a person, organization or institution that has made an outstanding contribution to the defence and/or promotion of press freedom anywhere in the world, especially when this has been achieved in the face of danger.

Geographical Area of Activity: International.

How to Apply: The Prize is awarded on the recommendation of an independent jury of 14 news professionals. Names are submitted by regional and international NGOs working for press freedom, and by UNESCO member states.

Financial Information: Annual prize US $25,000.

Address: 1 rue Miollis, 75015 Paris Cedex 15, France.

Telephone: 1-45-68-39-68; *Internet:* http://portal.unesco.org.

World Heritage Centre: World Heritage Fund

Established by the World Heritage Centre of the UN Educational, Scientific and Cultural Organization (UNESCO) to provide support for the conservation and preservation of heritage sites.

Activities: Funding is provided via member states for the conservation and preservation of heritage sites. There are five types of funding support: preparatory assistance, for the preparation of tentative lists of properties suitable for inclusion on the World Heritage List as well as for the preparation of training courses or large-scale technical assistance projects; technical co-operation, including studies concerning the artistic, scientific and technical problems raised by the protection, conservation, presentation and rehabilitation of the cultural and natural heritage; provision of experts, technicians and skilled labour to ensure that the approved work is correctly carried out, and the supply of equipment which the state concerned does not possess or is not in a position to acquire; training, providing assistance for the training of staff and specialists at all levels in the field of identification, protection, conservation, presentation and rehabilitation of the cultural and natural heritage; and emergency assistance, which can be provided for the preparation of urgent nominations, to draw up emergency plans or to take emergency measures for the safeguarding of properties inscribed on or nominated to the World Heritage List. The Fund also provides assistance for educational, information and promotional activities which: help to create a greater awareness of the different issues related to the implementation of the World Heritage Convention to promote more active involvement in its application; can be a means of exchanging experiences; and stimulates joint education, information and promotional programmes and activities, especially when they involve the participation of young people for the benefit of World Heritage conservation.

Geographical Area of Activity: International.

How to Apply: Requests must be submitted in accordance with the forms established for each of the types of international assistance. The World Heritage Centre examines the request and transmits its recommendation to the Chairperson (requests for preparatory assistance; technical co-operation and training up to US $20,000; and emergency assistance up to US $50,000) or the Bureau of the Committee (requests for technical co-operation and training up to US $30,000; and emergency assistance up to US $75,000). Requests for amounts that are above the amounts that can be approved by the Bureau are transmitted, with the Bureau's recommendation, to the Committee itself for approval. The deadlines for the submission of requests for approval by the Bureau or the Committee are 1 May and 1 September of each year.

Financial Information: The mandatory contribution to the World Heritage Fund is calculated at 1% of member countries' contribution to UNESCO. The payment of these contributions is a requirement for country representatives to be able to present themselves for election in the World Heritage Committee and for receiving technical co-operation and preparatory assistance.

Address: 7 place de Fontenoy, 75352 Paris 07 SP, France.

Fax: 1-45-68-55-70; *Internet:* http://whc.unesco.org/ab_fund.htm#debut; *e-mail:* wh-info@unesco.org.

UNITED NATIONS EDUCATIONAL, SCIENTIFIC AND CULTURAL ORGANIZATION (UNESCO) MAN AND THE BIOSPHERE (MAB)

Bureau of the International Co-ordinating Council: Sultan Qaboos Prize for the Environment

The Prize aims to afford recognition to outstanding contributions by individuals, groups of individuals, institutes or organizations in the management or preservation of the environment, consistent with the policies, aims and objectives of UNESCO, and in relation to the Organization's programmes in this field.

Activities: The biannual prize of US $20,000 is available to individuals or organizations in recognition of outstanding environmental and natural resources research, environmental education and training, creation of environmental awareness through the preparation of environmental information materials and activities, and establishing and managing protected areas such as Biosphere Reserves and natural World Heritage sites.

Geographical Area of Activity: International.

How to Apply: Nominations can be proposed to the Director-General of UNESCO by governments of member states, in consultation with their National Commissions, by intergovernmental organizations or by appropriate NGOs which have consultative status with UNESCO.

Financial Information: Funded by His Majesty Sultan Qaboos Bin Said Al-Said, Oman; biannual prize of US $20,000.

Address: 7 place de Fontenoy, 75332 Paris 07 SP, France.

Telephone: 1-45-68-10-00; *Fax:* 1-45-67-16-90; *Internet:* www.unesco.org/science /unesco_intern_sc_prizes.htm.

Division of Ecological Sciences: Man and the Biosphere (MAB) Young Scientists Awards

Set up to encourage young scientists to conduct interdisciplinary research on ecosystems, natural resources and biodiversity, in line with the programme's focus on sustainable people and biosphere interactions.

Activities: Promotes interdisciplinary ecological research by young scientists, particularly those from developing countries: to use MAB research, project sites and biosphere reserves in their research; encourages young scientists who already use such sites to undertake comparative studies in other sites in or outside their own country; and to assist in the exchange of information and experience among a new generation of scientists. Priority is given to research carried out in biosphere reserves on the theme of ecosystems and water.

Geographical Area of Activity: International, particularly developing countries.

Restrictions: Applicants must be no older than 40; no funding for international travel.

How to Apply: Award applications must be made on the MAB Young Scientists Award application form and be endorsed by the applicant's MAB National Committee, which may endorse only three applications per year.

Financial Information: Ten awards up to a maximum of US $5,000 each annually.

Address: MAB Secretariat, 1 rue Miollis, 75732 Paris Cedex 15, France.

Telephone: 1-45-68-58-04; *Internet:* www.unesco.org/mab/capacity/mys/awarmab2 .htm; *e-mail:* mab@unesco.org.

UNITED NATIONS ENVIRONMENT PROGRAMME (UNEP)

Global Ozone Award

Presented by UNEP as part of its programme of environmental awards.

Activities: The Award is presented to individuals and organizations active in the four categories of: science, vital for understanding the causes of ozone depletion and providing a sound basis for international action; technology, the source of viable alternatives to ozone-depleting substances; policy and implementation, which leads to public support and international co-operation; and NGOs, which help to raise awareness and catalyze solutions.

Geographical Area of Activity: International.

Address: POB 30552, Nairobi, Kenya.

Internet: www.unep.org.

UNEP World Conservation Monitoring Centre (UNEP–WCMC)

The world biodiversity information and assessment centre of UNEP. Its roots go back to 1979 when the World Conservation Union (IUCN) established an office to monitor endangered species; in 1988 IUCN, WWF (the World Wide Fund for Nature) and UNEP founded the World Conservation Monitoring Centre, which passed to the sole administration of UNEP in 2000.

Activities: The Centre's activities include assessment and early warning studies in forest, dryland, freshwater and marine ecosystems, and research on endangered species and biodiversity indicators in order to provide policy-makers with vital knowledge on global trends in conservation and sustainable use of wildlife and its habitats. Operates through three divisions: Information Services Division, facilitating access to information on biological diversity; Assessment and Early Warning, assessing the status, value and management of biological diversity; and Conventions and Policy Support, working with conventions and organizations, and providing capacity-building and information management services. Works in collaboration with governmental, intergovernmental and NGO networks.

Geographical Area of Activity: International.

Contact: Dir Mark Collins.

Address: 219 Huntingdon Rd, Cambridge CB3 0DL, UK.

Telephone: (1223) 277314; *Fax:* (1223) 277136; *Internet:* www.unep-wcmc.org; *e-mail:* info@unep-wcmc.org.

United Nations Environment Programme Sasakawa Environment Prize

Initiated at the UN Conference on the Human Environment held in Stockholm in 1972; then known as the Pahlavi Prize, it was first awarded in 1976.

Activities: The Prize of US $200,000 is awarded every year in November to individuals who have made outstanding contributions to the protection and management of the environment, which are consistent with the policies, aims and objectives of the UN Environment Programme. Candidates can be associated with any field of the environment.

Geographical Area of Activity: International.

How to Apply: Nomination forms are available on the website. Those eligible to make nominations include specialists in environmental sciences, academies of science, engineering and research, members of the UN system, governments and intergovernmental organizations, trade unions and NGOs.

Financial Information: In 1982, endowed with US $1,000,000 from the Japan Shipbuilding Industry Foundation; annual award of US $200,000.

Contact: Selection Cttee: Lord Stanley Clinton-Davis (Acting Chair.).

Address: UN Ave, Gigiri, POB 30552, Nairobi, Kenya.

Telephone: (2) 621234; *Fax:* (2) 624489; *Internet:* www.unep.org/sasakawa2 /history.htm; *e-mail:* elisabeth.guilbaud-cox@unep.org.

UNITED NATIONS ENVIRONMENT PROGRAMME (UNEP)/UNITED NATIONS HUMAN SETTLEMENTS PROGRAMME (UN-HABITAT)

Managing Water for African Cities (MAWAC): Water for African Cities Programme

A joint initiative of UNEP and UN-HABITAT. Aims to tackle the urban water crisis in African cities through efficient and effective water demand management, build capacity to mitigate the environmental impact of urbanization on freshwater resources and boost awareness and information exchange on water management and conservation. It also promotes the exchange of best practices in urban water management in support of the implementation of the Habitat Agenda.

Activities: The Programme aims to build capacity in seven demonstration cities in Africa within the water sector, to provide information on the best practices in urban water management, and to link sector professionals working in the field of water management with each other and with other networks, institutions, governments, municipalities, NGOs and the private sector. Activities include awareness building and public information; public communication and outreach; water conservation flyers; seminars and workshops; training of city managers including study visits promoting a demand-side perspective of water management, including water pollution control methods, gender mainstreaming and improvement of water access for the urban poor and peri-urban areas. The seven demonstration cities are: Abidjan (Côte d'Ivoire), Accra (Ghana), Addis Ababa (Ethiopia), Dakar (Senegal), Johannesburg (South Africa), Lusaka (Zambia) and Nairobi (Kenya); there are plans to expand the programme across Africa.

Geographical Area of Activity: Africa.

Financial Information: Funded by the United Nations Foundation (q.v.) and the United Nations Foundation for International Partnerships.

Publications: Numerous publications on the issue of water management.

Address: POB 30030, Nairobi, Kenya.

Telephone: (2) 623039; *Fax:* (2) 623588; *Internet:* www.un-urbanwater.net; *e-mail:* wacmail@unhabitat.org.

UNITED NATIONS FOUNDATION

Established in 1997 alongside its sister foundation, the Better World Fund (q.v.), following a gift of US $1,000,000,000 from R. E. (Ted) Turner; the Foundation seeks to support the goals and objectives of the UN and its Charter in order to promote a more peaceful, prosperous and just world, with emphasis on the work of the UN, especially on behalf of economic, social, environmental and humanitarian causes.

Activities: Invests in UN-sponsored agencies and programmes. Its four current main areas of activity are: peace, security and human rights; women and population; the environment; and children's health. Selective assistance is also provided to humanitarian causes, and to activities strengthening the UN. Projects receiving funding include the United Nations Population Fund (UNFPA) and the United Nations High Commissioner for Refugees (UNHCR), which have received grants to develop and distribute emergency reproductive health information and services to refugees in Asia, Africa and South-Eastern Europe (especially Kosovo). The Foundation also provides grants to the UNAIDS programme to assist in the prevention of the spread of HIV and AIDS in Botswana and Zimbabwe and, in partnership with organizations such as the World Health Organization (WHO), is working to eliminate polio. In conjunction with the Better World Fund, the Foundation sponsors the daily *UN Wire* news summary on UN and global affairs. In 2003, funded the UN Nobel Peace Prize Memorial Fund, created by UN Secretary-General Kofi Annan upon both his and the UN's receipt of the Nobel Peace Prize in 2001, which provides grants for the education of the children of UN employees killed in the line of duty, and launched the Coral Reef Fund in conjunction with the International Coral Reef Action Network.

Geographical Area of Activity: International.

Financial Information: Total assets US $63,148,642 (2002); annual revenue US $111,967,049, expenditure US $101,745,432 (2002).

Contact: Board of Directors: R. E. (Ted) Turner (Chair.); Timothy E. Wirth (Pres.); Ruth Correa Leite Cardoso; Liang Dan; Graça Machel; Hisashi Owada; Emma Rothschild; Dr Nafis Sadik; Andrew Young; Muhammad Yunus; Chief Operating Officer and Exec. Vice-Pres. Jane Holl Lute; Dir, Programs and Operations Thomas J. Leney.

Address: 1225 Connecticut Ave, NW, 4th Floor, Washington, DC 20036, USA.

Telephone: (202) 887-9040; *Fax:* (202) 887-9021; *Internet:* www.unfoundation.org.

UNITED NATIONS FUND FOR INTERNATIONAL PARTNERSHIPS (UNFIP)

Works in partnership with the United Nations Foundation (q.v.) to develop innovative programmes and projects and to develop funding partnerships with foundations and the private sector.

Activities: Serves as the operational arm of the Secretary-General in its partnership with the United Nations Foundation, aiming to: facilitate programme and project development for channelling Foundation funds into the UN system; collaborate with the United Nations Foundation in its fundraising efforts; and to work to build new and additional partnerships. Encourages innovative partnerships between the UN and civil society and provides a route into partnership opportunities within the UN system.

Geographical Area of Activity: International.

How to Apply: The Advisory Board advises the Secretary-General of the UN on projects and activities to be proposed to the Board of Directors of the United Nations Foundation for funding.

Contact: Chair. Louise Fréchette.

Address: 2 UN Plaza, New York, NY 10017, USA.

Internet: www.un.org/unfip/flash/index.html; *e-mail:* info-unfip@un.org.

UNITED NATIONS HIGH COMMISSIONER FOR REFUGEES (UNHCR)

Established on 14 December 1950 by the UN General Assembly. The agency is mandated to lead and co-ordinate international action to protect refugees and resolve refugee problems world-wide. Its primary purpose is to safeguard the rights and well-being of refugees; strives to ensure that everyone can exercise the right to seek asylum and find safe refuge in another state, with the option to return home voluntarily, integrate locally or to resettle in a third country.

Activities: Operates short-term initiatives, ensuring the basic human rights of vulnerable persons and that refugees will not be returned involuntarily to a country where they face persecution, as well as providing at least a minimum of shelter, food, water and medical care in the immediate aftermath of any refugee exodus, through a world-wide field network. Longer term, the organization helps civilians repatriate to their homeland, integrate in countries of asylum or resettle in third countries. Operates in collaboration with numerous partner organizations, including governments, NGOs, the private sector, civil society and refugee communities, with programmes implemented by partner NGOs. Each year UNHCR signs partnership agreements with over 500 NGOs world-wide, and works with more than 400 others on a variety of projects, including resettlement, research, and raising public awareness of the refugee problem; co-ordinated by the Partnership in Action (PARinAC) programme.

Geographical Area of Activity: International.

Financial Information: Annual budget US $881,200,000 (2001); partnership with NGOs worth approx. US $180,000,000 (2001).

Publications: A Practical Guide to Capacity Building as a Feature of UNHCR's Humanitarian Programmes; Protecting Refugees: a Field Guide for NGOs.

Contact: High Commissioner Ruud Lubbers.

Address: Case Postale 2500, 1211 Geneva 2 Dépôt, Switzerland.

Telephone: (22) 7398111; *Internet:* www.unhcr.ch.

UNHCR Scholarship Programme for Refugees

A scholarship programme for refugees operated through the Albert Einstein German Academic Relief Initiative Fund (DAFI), and funded by the German government; aims to contribute to the self-reliance of refugees by providing them with a professional qualification for future employment.

Activities: Under the Programme, scholarships are available to refugees under the age of 29 for study in the country of asylum, with the aim of allowing refugees to return to their home country and contribute to its reconstruction, or to the development of the country of asylum, or to the development of the refugee community as a whole. Preference is given to women applicants, students with special needs, students who had to interrupt their studies due to flight, and students who interrupted a previous DAFI scholarship in an asylum country due to repatriation.

Geographical Area of Activity: Developing countries, mainly in Africa, Asia and Eastern Europe.

Restrictions: Asylum-seekers not yet formally recognized as refugees as well as refugees seeking resettlement in a third country are not normally eligible to apply.

How to Apply: Applications should be made through local UN High Commissioner on Refugees offices and implementing NGO partners; a list of partners is available on the website.

Address: Case Postale 2500, 1211 Geneva 2 Dépôt, Switzerland.

Telephone: (22) 7398111; *Internet:* www.unhcr.ch.

UNITED NATIONS HUMAN SETTLEMENTS PROGRAMME (UN-HABITAT)

Best Practices and Local Leadership Programme (BPLLP)

Established in 1997 in response to the call of the Habitat Agenda to make use of information and networking in support of its implementation. It is a global network of government agencies, local authorities and associations, professional and academic institutions and grassroots organizations dedicated to the identification and exchange of successful solutions for sustainable development.

Activities: Aims to raise the awareness of decision-makers on critical social, economic and environmental issues and to better inform them of the practical means and policy options for improving the living environment. It does so by identifying, disseminating and applying lessons learned from Best Practices to ongoing training, leadership and policy development activities, through an award programme. Every two years up to 10 outstanding initiatives receive the Dubai International Award for Best Practices to Improve the Living Environment, a biennial environmental award established in 1995 by the Municipality of Dubai, United Arab Emirates. Those initiatives meeting the criteria for a Best Practice are included in the Best Practices database, accessible on the website. The lessons learned from selected Best Practices are analyzed in case studies and guides are transferred to other countries, cities or communities.

Geographical Area of Activity: International.

How to Apply: The Award system reviews and assesses best practice submissions through an independent technical committee and jury.

Address: Urban Secretariat, POB 30030, Nairobi, Kenya.

Telephone: (2) 623029; *Fax:* (2) 623080; *Internet:* www.unhabitat.org/programmes /bestpractices/; www.sustainabledevelopment.org/blp; *e-mail:* bestpractices@ unchs.org.

Huairou Commission on Women and Habitat

Created in partnership with the United Nations Development Programme (UNDP); a network of international grassroots women's and partner organizations. Aims to highlight projects that convey the issues faced by women worldwide, as well as the problem-solving strategies and successes they have devised and to make them easily accessible, and to identify, document and disseminate grassroots women's innovations and learning and to enrich the methodology and processes around best practices in a community-based and gender-sensitive way.

Activities: Operates globally through working closely with international colleagues to introduce a grassroots women's dimension to policy-making, and locally through its A New Way of Partnering: Engendering Democracy At the Local Level programme, which is designed to give grassroots women some of the tools they need to become more effective partners in local planning and decision-making. Negotiates partnerships with NGOs, including the Women's Environment and Development Organization (WEDO) and the Women and Cities Network, as well as the UN, local governments, parliamentarians, scholars and researchers. The Co-ordinating Committee comprises grassroots representatives from the following organizations: Asia Women and Shelter (AWAS); GrassRoots Organizations Operating Together in Sisterhood (GROOTS); Habitat International Coalition–Women and Shelter (HIC–WAS); and the International Council of Women (ICW).

Geographical Area of Activity: International.

Financial Information: Supported by UNIFEM and the UN-HABITAT Women and Habitat Programme.

Address: 2 UN Plaza, DC2-0943, New York, NY 10017, USA.

Telephone: (212) 832-6446; *Fax:* (212) 832-9059; *Internet:* www.sustainabledevelopment.org/blp/partners/huairou.html; *e-mail:* huairou@aol.com.

Risk and Disaster Management Unit

Established to deal with the rehabilitation of social and economic conditions after a disaster or conflict which also offers a unique opportunity to rethink past development practices and improve the sustainability of human settlements against future threats and risks.

Activities: Aims to support national governments, local authorities and communities in strengthening their capacity in managing human-made and natural disasters, to create awareness among decision-makers and communities on mitigation and adequate rehabilitation in human settlements, and to bridge the gap between relief and development by combining the technical expertise and on-the-ground know-how of the UN Human Settlements Programme. Operates through providing support to national governments, local authorities and community organizations, including: fielding assessment and technical advisory missions to disaster-prone countries; assessing global and regional demands for support on disaster management and human settlement; designing, implementing and backstopping projects at national, regional and global level in collaboration with other countries and external support agencies; strengthening co-ordination and networking among communities, NGOs, governments and external support organizations in performing disaster-related activities;

developing techniques and tools for the management of disaster prevention, mitigation and rehabilitation; designing and implementing training programmes, as well as supporting training activities executed by other agencies and field projects; and promoting horizontal co-operation by networking institutions, experts and experience on disaster-related activities in human settlements.

Geographical Area of Activity: Developing countries.

Contact: Co-ordinator Daniel Lewis.

Address: POB 30030, Nairobi, Kenya.

Telephone: (2) 623826; *Internet:* www.unchs.org/programmes/rdmu/; *e-mail:* dan .lewis@unhabitat.org.

Training and Capacity Building Branch (TCBB)

Aims to strengthen national competencies to respond to training and other capacity-building needs, to help communities and their local governments to sustainably manage their growth, meet myriad economic, environmental, social and structural challenges and to ensure the implementation of the Millennium Development Goals of Cities without Slums and Good Governance.

Activities: Supports the managerial, and technical and policy-making capacity of local leaders, employees, NGOs/CBOs and communities to help overcome endemic urban problems, including environmental degradation, poverty, homelessness, informal settlements and under-performing municipal services. The work is structured in regional/sub-regional programmes with particular staff members concentrating on specific regions, maintaining a continuous contact with partner/client institutions, and jointly planning, organizing and implementing programme activities. Programmes are closely integrated with complementary programmes implemented by the Shelter and Urban Development Branch, the three Regional Offices and the Global Campaigns for Secure Tenure and on Urban Governance. TCBB is currently implementing a global project: Strengthening National Training Capabilities for Better Local Governance and Urban Development Project (2002–06), funded by the Netherlands government, which aims to enhance the role and contribution of local authorities and their partners in the fight against poverty and in the realization of improved local governance and sustainable human settlements, by strengthening the response capacities of over 30 national Training and Capacity Building (TCB) institutions. Principal partners are local governments and their associations, relevant government agencies, local development NGOs and community-based organizations.

Geographical Area of Activity: International.

Publications: Range of manuals and handbooks, and training assessment manuals.

Address: POB 30030, Nairobi 00100, Kenya.

Fax: (2) 623092; *Internet:* www.unhabitat.org/programmes/tcbb/contacts.asp; *e-mail:* tcbb@unhabitat.org.

UNITED NATIONS NON-GOVERNMENTAL LIAISON SERVICE (NGLS)

An inter-agency programme with offices in Geneva and New York, established in 1975 to strengthen UN–NGO dialogue and co-operation in the fields of development education, information and policy advocacy on global sustainable development issues. Reflecting its UN inter-agency, system-wide character, NGLS reports annually to its Programme and Co-ordination Meeting (in which its 18 sponsoring UN agencies and others participate), to the Joint United Nations Information Committee (JUNIC), its governing body, and through JUNIC to the UN Administrative Committee on Co-ordination (ACC), the highest administrative committee of the UN system, chaired by the Secretary-General.

Activities: NGLS is concerned with the entire UN sustainable development agenda. It works with Secretariat Departments, UN agencies, programmes, funds, Convention Secretariats and other bodies and organizations of the UN system working in the areas of economic and social development, sustainable development, humanitarian emergencies, human rights, including women's rights and related issues such as disarmament and democratization. NGLS also co-operates actively with relevant and competent NGOs from developed and developing countries, from countries with economies in transition and with international NGOs that work on the global issues on the UN agenda. As an interlocutor on the UN system interface with non-governmental organizations, NGLS organizes its work around four basic programme areas: information outreach and communications; integrated follow-up to UN world conferences and summits; strengthening the capacity of the UN system to engage constructively with NGOs and other organizations of global civil society; and strengthening the capacity of NGOs and global civil society to participate constructively in the work of the UN system. Works primarily with development NGOs in industrialized countries, with international NGOs and NGO networks, and with Southern NGOs wishing to participate in, and contribute to, UN system events, processes and activities. NGLS collaborates with the entire UN development system, particularly the organizations and programmes which sponsor its activities. In 1998 these were: United Nations Children's Fund (UNICEF, lead agency), United Nations Conference on Trade and Development (UNCTAD, administering agency), Food and Agriculture Organization of the United Nations (FAO), International Fund for Agricultural Development (IFAD), International Labour Organization (ILO), UN High Commissioner for Refugees (UNHCR), United Nations Human Settlements Programme (UN-HABITAT), United Nations Industrial Development Organization (UNIDO), UN Department for Policy Co-ordination and Sustainable Development (DPCSD), UN Department of Public Information (DPI), UN Development Programme (UNDP), United Nations Educational, Scientific and Cultural Organization (UNESCO), United Nations Environment Programme (UNEP), UN International Drug Control Programme (UNDCP), United Nations Population Fund (UNFPA), the International Bank for Reconstruction and Development (IBRD—World Bank), the World Food Programme (WFP) and the World Health Organization (WHO, qq.v.). Currently, the Service also receives support from a number of governments, including those of Canada, Denmark, Switzerland and the United Kingdom, and from the United Nations Foundation (q.v.). Activities include bringing important development-related issues and activities of the UN system to the attention of NGOs, supports

NGOs and NGO networks active on issues and themes under discussion in the UN system, and facilitates NGO participation in, and activities around, UN conferences, events and processes; supports the UN system in the development of its policies, activities and co-operation with NGOs through improved mutual understanding, enhanced participation and dialogue, and strengthened partnerships; jointly organizes meetings or other special events with NGOs and/or UN system agencies and puts NGOs in touch with organizations sharing similar interests and with appropriate UN system offices; maintains databases on the NGO community and the UN system and regularly publishes directories, publicizes important and interesting UN and NGO development activities and publishes a wide range of information and other materials; and advises NGOs and others, on request, on the design and implementation of programmes of development education, research, information and public-awareness and advocacy campaigns; and monitors and reports upon the changing roles of Northern, Southern and international development NGOs, and other civil society organizations, their relations with governments and multilateral organizations.

Geographical Area of Activity: International.

Restrictions: No funding available.

Publications: Go Between (newsletter); *NGLS Roundup Series* (approx. 12 editions a year); *NGLS Environment and Development File (E&D File) Series* (approx. 4–5 editions per year); *Development Dossier* (annual); *Voices from Africa* (annual); *Guide to the UN System for NGOs; NGLS Handbook.*

Address: Palais des Nations, 1211 Geneva 10, Switzerland.

Telephone: (22) 9172076; *Fax:* (22) 9170432; *Internet:* www.unsystem.org/ngls; *e-mail:* ngls@unctad.org.

UNITED NATIONS OFFICE ON DRUGS AND CRIME (UNODC)

UN International Drug Control Programme (UNDCP)

Established in 1991 by the UNODC.

Activities: UNDCP has worked with international NGOs (INGOs) and NGOs since its inception; INGO/NGOs have participated in UNDCP programmes as project implementers, fundraisers, project formulators, service providers and policy advocates in prevention, treatment and rehabilitation programmes. Also runs training programmes for NGOs and promotes NGO networks. Between 1990–95 UNDCP disbursed US $21,400,000 through NGOs, mainly for project implementation. Also publishes a directory of NGOs working on drug-related issues, and maintains a database of over 1,300 NGOs active in this field.

Geographical Area of Activity: International.

Contact: NGO Contact Smart Eze.

Address: Vienna International Centre, POB 500, 1400 Vienna, Austria.

Telephone: (1) 260-60-0; *Fax:* (1) 260-60-58-66; *Internet:* www.unodc.org; *e-mail:* unodc@unodc.org.

United Nations Vienna Civil Society Award

Established in 1999 to honour individuals and/or organizations who have made outstanding contributions to the fight against drug abuse, crime and terrorism. The Award is sponsored by the United Nations Office on Drugs and Crime (UNODC), the Austrian Federal Government and the City of Vienna.

Activities: Makes annual awards, up to a total of US $100,000, to NGOs and individuals active in the fight against drug abuse in their communities, beneficiaries including volunteers and drug rehabilitation centres.

Geographical Area of Activity: International.

Financial Information: Total funds available US $100,000.

Contact: NGO Contact Smart Eze.

Address: Vienna International Centre, POB 500 1400 Vienna, Austria.

Telephone: (1) 260-60-0; *Fax:* (1) 260-60-58-66; *Internet:* www.unodc.org/unodc /ngos_and_civil_society_award.html; *e-mail:* smart.eze@unodc.org.

UNITED NATIONS OFFICE FOR PROJECT SERVICES (UNOPS)

Bi-Communal Development Programme in Cyprus

Established in 1998; forms part of the UN Development Programme Bi-communal Development Programme (BDP); funded by the United States Agency for International Development (USAID) and the UNDP and executed by UNOPS. The Programme aims to help foster relations between Greek Cypriots and Turkish Cypriots by helping them to conceive and implement projects of common interest.

Activities: Works to promote peace in Cyprus, bringing together Greek and Turkish Cypriots through identifying areas of common interest; encouraging Greek Cypriots and Turkish Cypriots to work together on projects designed to improve these areas of interest; strengthening the technical and financial capacities of professional and NGOs island-wide; demonstrating the benefit of implementing projects and activities that improve conditions island-wide; fostering an atmosphere of co-operation; and providing humanitarian assistance, including a wide range of medical and social assistance, and liaison with inhabitants of enclaves, supporting the activities of the UN Peacekeeping Force in Cyprus.

Geographical Area of Activity: Cyprus.

Financial Information: Total endowment US $60,500,000 (2002).

Address: POB 21642, Nicosia, Cyprus.

Internet: www.unopspmu.org/; *e-mail:* info@unopsmu.org.

UNITED NATIONS RESEARCH INSTITUTE FOR SOCIAL DEVELOPMENT (UNRISD)

Created in 1963 as part of the first UN Development Decade. UNRISD is an autonomous UN agency engaging in multi-disciplinary research on the social dimensions of contemporary problems affecting development; aims to stimulate dialogue and contribute to policy debates on key issues of social development within and outside the UN system.

Activities: Carries out research in collaboration with scholars and activists, primarily in the developing world, whose ideas are not sufficiently reflected in current debates. For the period 2000–05 UNRISD's areas of research are: Civil Society and Social Movements; Democracy, Governance and Human Rights; Identities, Conflict and Cohesion; Social Policy and Development; Special Events; and Technology, Business and Society (qq.v.). In addition to its collaborative research programmes, UNRISD also consults with other UN organizations, governments, NGOs and research institutes for inputs to the research agenda. Organizes workshops and conferences to disseminate research results.

Geographical Area of Activity: International.

Contact: Dir Thandika Mkandawire.

Address: Palais des Nations, 1211 Geneva 10, Switzerland.

Telephone: (22) 9173020; *Fax:* (22) 9170650; *Internet:* www.unrisd.org; *e-mail:* info@unrisd.org.

Civil Society and Social Movements

The research programme aims to improve understanding of the potential for civic action and local self-organization in different kinds of societies and political regimes around the world and to clarify thinking about the concept of civil society. Encourages a critical review of the concept of civil society, based on new research, and attempts to improve understanding of various forms of local self-organization oriented towards defending or improving access to resources, income and services.

Activities: Research within the Civil Society and Social Movements programme is currently carried out within three categories: Civil Society Strategies and Movements for Rural Asset Redistribution and Improved Livelihoods; Evolving Agricultural Structures and Civil Society in Transitional Countries: the Case of Central Asia; and Grassroots Movements and Initiatives for Land Reform.

Geographical Area of Activity: International.

Publications: Trade Unions and NGOs: A Necessary Partnership for Social Development; Civil Society Organizations and Service Provision; Social Movements, Activism and Social Development in the Middle East; Grassroots Movements, Political Activism and Social Development in Latin America: A Comparison of Chile and Brazil; The Women's Movement in Egypt, with Selected References to Turkey; The Agrarian Question, Access to Land, and Peasant Responses in Sub-Saharan Africa (programme papers).

Contact: Dir Thandika Mkandawire.

Address: Palais des Nations, 1211 Geneva 10, Switzerland.

Telephone: (22) 9173020; *Fax:* (22) 9170650; *Internet:* www.unrisd.org; *e-mail:* info@unrisd.org.

Democracy, Governance and Human Rights

The programme explores some of the political and institutional factors affecting the creation of an enabling environment for democracy and human rights in different country settings.

Activities: Research within the programme covers: Ethnic Structure, Inequality and Governance of the Public Sector; Gender Justice, Development and Rights; Public-Sector Reform and Crisis-Ridden States; Technocratic Policy-Making and Democratization; and Urban Governance.

Geographical Area of Activity: International.

Publications: Pay and Employment Reform in Developing and Transition Societies; Fiscal Decentralization in Developing Countries: A Review of Current Concepts and Practice; Efficiency, Accountability and Implementation: Public Sector Reform in East and Southern Africa; Decentralization Policies and Practices under Structural Adjustment and Democratization in Africa; Human Rights and Social Development: Toward Democratization and Social Justice; Gender of Democracy: The Encounter between Feminism and Reformism in Contemporary Iran; Multiculturalism, Universalism and the Claims of Democracy; African Decentralization: Local Actors, Powers and Accountability; A Declining Technocratic Regime: Bureaucracy, Political Parties and Interest Groups in Japan, 1950–2000; Gender Justice, Development and Rights (programme papers).

Contact: Dir Thandika Mkandawire.

Address: Palais des Nations, 1211 Geneva 10, Switzerland.

Telephone: (22) 9173020; *Fax:* (22) 9170650; *Internet:* www.unrisd.org; *e-mail:* info@unrisd.org.

Identities, Conflict and Cohesion

The programme aims to conduct research on problems of identity in a shrinking world.

Activities: The programme includes work on Racism and Public Policy, with a number of other research areas still to be defined, within the fields of the concept of citizenship, the orderly recognition of difference and a setting for debate on the rights and obligations of different groups in society.

Geographical Area of Activity: International.

Contact: Dir Thandika Mkandawire.

Address: Palais des Nations, 1211 Geneva 10, Switzerland.

Telephone: (22) 9173020; *Fax:* (22) 9170650; *Internet:* www.unrisd.org; *e-mail:* info@unrisd.org.

Social Policy and Development

The programme is one of the main research programmes at the UN Research Institute for Social Development; seeks to stimulate interdisciplinary debate on the nexus between social policy and economic development, and to explore the ways in which social policy can be a powerful instrument for democratic progress and economic development while, at the same time, pursuing such intrinsic goals as social protection and justice.

Activities: Research projects in this programme area include Agrarian Change, Gender and Land Rights; Globalization, Export-Oriented Employment and Social Policy; HIV/AIDS and Development; Neoliberalism and Institutional Reform in East Asia; and Social Policy in a Development Context. Research is organized within two strands: thematic comparative research and region-centred comparative research. The thematic comparative research includes the following four projects: Macroeconomics and Social Policy; Democratization and Social Policy; Globalization and Health Policy; and Gender and Social Policy. The region-centred comparative research focuses on late industrializing countries in the following five projects: Social Policy in Late Industrializers: Transforming the Developmental Welfare State in East Asia; Social Policy in Late Industrializers: A Comparative Study of the Latin American Countries; Social Policy in Late Industrializers: Social Policy and Economic Development in the Middle East and North Africa; Social Policy in Late Industrializers: The Nordic Experience; and Social Policy in Late Industrializers: Sub-Saharan Africa and the Challenge of Social Policy.

Geographical Area of Activity: International.

Publications: External Dependency and Internal Transformation: Argentina Confronts the Long Debt Crisis; Social Indicators and Welfare Monitoring; Empirical Inquiries and the Assessment of Social Progress in Western Europe: A Historical Perspective; AIDS in the Context of Development; Les politiques sociales en Afrique de l'Ouest: Quels changements depuis le Sommet de Copenhague?; Breaking the Mould: An Institutionalist Political Economy Alternative to the Neoliberal Theory of the Market and the State; Social Policy in a Development Context; Dynamique de la politique sociale en Côte d'Ivoire; Gender and Education: A Review of Issues for Social Policy; Agrarian Change, Gender and Land Reform: A South African Case Study; Agrarian Reform, Gender and Land Rights in Uzbekistan; Women's Employment and Welfare Regimes: Globalization, Export Orientation and Social Policy in Europe and North America; Reworking Apartheid Legacies: Global Competition, Gender and Social Wages in South Africa, 1980–2000; Agrarian Change, Gender and Land Rights: A Brazilian Case Study (programme papers and case studies).

Contact: Dir Thandika Mkandawire.

Address: Palais des Nations, 1211 Geneva 10, Switzerland.

Telephone: (22) 9173020; *Fax:* (22) 9170650; *Internet:* www.unrisd.org; *e-mail:* info@unrisd.org.

Special Events

The programme supplements the work carried out in the five Programme Areas with a number of activities that allow the UN Research Institute for Social Development to respond to special requests for collaboration, or to take up new challenges to contribute to the development debate.

Activities: In 2003 research carried out within the Special Events programme area included: Ageing, Development and Social Protection; Improving Research and Knowledge on Social Development in International Organizations; Racism and Public Policy; and Rethinking Development Economics.

Geographical Area of Activity: International.

Contact: Dir Thandika Mkandawire.

Address: Palais des Nations, 1211 Geneva 10, Switzerland.

Telephone: (22) 9173020; *Fax:* (22) 9170650; *Internet:* www.unrisd.org; *e-mail:* info@unrisd.org.

Technology, Business and Society

The programme draws on case studies and debates at national and international levels to explore ways of encouraging a more socially responsible use of science and technology in a number of fields, including information technology, biotechnology and genetic engineering. It also draws on broader studies of corporate responsibility, often generated in relation to social and environmental issues.

Activities: Programme research is in two areas: Business Responsibility for Sustainable Development; and Information Technologies and Social Development.

Geographical Area of Activity: International.

Publications: Les technologies de l'information et de la communication et le développement social au Sénégal: Un état des lieux; Corporate Codes of Conduct: Self Regulation in a Global Economy; Corporate Environmental Responsibility in Singapore and Malaysia; The Development Divide in a Digital Age; Regulating Large International Firms; Corporate Social Responsibility in Indonesia: Quixotic Dream or Confident Expectation?; Les émigrés sénégalais et les nouvelles technologies de l'information et de la communication; Enjeux et rôle des nouvelles technologies de l'information et de la communication dans les mutations urbaines: Le cas de Touba (Sénégal); The Riddle of Distance Education: Promise, Problems and Applications for Development (programme papers).

Contact: Dir Thandika Mkandawire.

Address: Palais des Nations, 1211 Geneva 10, Switzerland.

Telephone: (22) 9173020; *Fax:* (22) 9170650; *Internet:* www.unrisd.org; *e-mail:* info@unrisd.org.

WORLD HEALTH ORGANIZATION (WHO)

Awards: Darling Foundation Prize

Administered by WHO since 1948; the Darling Foundation was created in 1929 in memory of Dr S. T. Darling, a malariologist, who died during a study mission of the Malaria Commission of the League of Nations.

Activities: Annual prize awarded for outstanding achievements in the pathology, etiology, epidemiology, therapy, prophylaxis or control of malaria, awarded at a special ceremony during the World Health Assembly.

Geographical Area of Activity: International.

How to Apply: Member states and Associate Members of WHO, and the members of the WHO Expert Advisory Panel who have already served on an Expert Committee on Malaria, are invited to put forward, within six months, the name of any person who, in their opinion, qualifies for the Award. The nomination has to be accompanied by a written justification. The Expert Committee on Malaria evaluates the candidatures received and recommends to the Darling Foundation Committee the name or names of the candidate or candidates to whom the prize, in the opinion of the Committee, should be awarded. The Darling Foundation Committee, after considering the nominations, makes its recommendations to the Executive Board, which designates the recipient of the prize.

Address: 20 ave Appia, 1211 Geneva 27, Switzerland.

Telephone: (22) 7912111; *Fax:* (22) 7913111; *Internet:* www.who.int/governance /awards/darling/en/; *e-mail:* info@who.int.

Awards: Down Syndrome Research Prize in the Eastern Mediterranean Region

Established in 1999 to encourage research on Down Syndrome, a major health problem in the Eastern Mediterranean region; created on the initiative of and with funds provided by Dr Abdul Rahman Abdulla Al-Awadi, president of the Islamic Organization for Medical Sciences.

Activities: Supports research into Down Syndrome in the East Mediterranean region, through a biennial award of US \$2,000. It is presented during a session of the WHO Regional Committee for the Eastern Mediterranean.

Geographical Area of Activity: Eastern Mediterranean region.

How to Apply: Any national health administration of a member state in the WHO Eastern Mediterranean Region, or any former recipient of the prize, may nominate a candidate for the prize. Proposals are made to the Regional Director for the Eastern Mediterranean, who submits them to the Foundation Committee, together with his/her technical comments. The Foundation Committee decides on the recommendation to be made to the WHO Regional Committee for the Eastern Mediterranean, which designates the recipient of the prize. The award is made during the following session of the Regional Committee.

Address: 20 ave Appia, 1211 Geneva 27, Switzerland.

Telephone: (22) 7912111; *Fax:* (22) 7913111; *Internet:* www.who.int/governance /awards/down_syndrome/en/; *e-mail:* info@who.int.

Awards: Dr A. T. Shousha Foundation Prize and Fellowship

Established in 1966 in memory of Dr Aly Tewfik Shousha, first World Health Organization (WHO) Regional Director for the Eastern Mediterranean.

Activities: The annual Prize is awarded to an individual who has made the most significant contribution to improving health in the Eastern Mediterranean region. The Prize is presented during a session of the WHO Regional Committee for the Eastern Mediterranean. In addition, a fellowship is awarded, approximately every six years, to enable health professionals from the WHO Eastern Mediterranean Region to obtain a postgraduate diploma or a master's degree in public health.

Geographical Area of Activity: Eastern Mediterranean countries.

How to Apply: Any national health administration in the WHO Eastern Mediterranean Region and any former recipient of the prize may propose, at the invitation of the Regional Director, the name of a candidate; the nomination must be accompanied by a written justification. A similar procedure applies to the proposal for the fellowship. In this case the proposal must be accompanied by the necessary background information and a statement that the qualifications obtained by the candidate will be used for the benefit of Eastern Mediterranean countries. The Regional Director submits the nominations received to the Foundation Committee, which meets during the sessions of the WHO Regional Committee for the Eastern Mediterranean to consider the candidatures. The Foundation Committee makes its recommendation to the Executive Board, which designates the recipients of the prize and fellowship.

Financial Information: Prize total 2,500 Swiss francs; fellowship award US $15,000.

Address: 20 ave Appia, 1211 Geneva 27, Switzerland.

Telephone: (22) 7912111; *Fax:* (22) 7913111; *Internet:* www.who.int/governance /awards/shousha/en/; *e-mail:* info@who.int.

Awards: Dr Comlan A. A. Quenum Prize for Public Health

Established in 1987 on the initiative of, and with funds provided by, the government of Cameroon to honour the memory of Dr Comlan A. A. Quenum, the first African to hold the post of Regional Director of the World Health Organization (WHO).

Activities: The biennial Prize is awarded to a person considered to have made the most significant contribution to improving health in the geographical area of Africa; awarded every two years and presented during a session of the WHO Regional Committee for Africa.

Geographical Area of Activity: Africa.

How to Apply: Any national health administration, educational and research organization as well as any former recipient of the prize may nominate a candidate for the award. Proposals are made to the Regional Director for Africa, who submits them to the Prize Committee together with his/her technical comments. The Committee meets to decide on the recommendation to be made to the Programme Sub-Committee of the WHO Regional Committee which designates the recipient of the Prize.

Financial Information: Biennial award of US $2,000.

Address: 20 ave Appia 20, 1211 Geneva 27, Switzerland.

Telephone: (22) 7912111; *Fax:* (22) 7913111; *Internet:* www.who.int/governance /awards/comlan/en/; *e-mail:* info@who.int.

Awards: Francesco Pocchiari Fellowship

Established in 1991 with funds provided by the Italian government to honour the memory of Prof. Francesco Pocchiari, former Director-General of the Istituto Superiore di Sanità (Rome).

Activities: Biennially awards one to two travelling fellowships of US $10,000 each to researchers from developing countries to enable them to gain new experience relevant to their research. Candidates must have a keen interest and a strong record in carrying out research on health issues in developing countries. The recipients of the awards are announced at a special ceremony during the World Health Assembly.

Geographical Area of Activity: Developing countries.

How to Apply: Any national health administration may put forward candidatures for the fellowship. Fully documented proposals are submitted to the World Health Organization (WHO) in Geneva either directly or through one of the six WHO Regional Offices. The WHO Executive Board designates recipients of the fellowships on the recommendation of the Fellowship Committee.

Financial Information: One to two awards of US $10,000 each awarded every two years.

Address: 20 ave Appia 20, 1211 Geneva 27, Switzerland.

Telephone: (22) 7912111; *Fax:* (22) 7913111; *Internet:* www.who.int/governance /awards/pocchiari/en/; *e-mail:* info@who.int.

Awards: Ihsan Dogramaci Family Health Foundation Fellowship and Prize

Established in 1980 on the initiative of, and with funds provided by its founder, Prof. Ihsan Dogramaci, a paediatrician and child health specialist, who signed the Constitution of the World Health Organization (WHO) for Turkey at the International Health Conference held in New York in 1946.

Activities: Aims to promote and raise the standard of family health by encouraging research and by acknowledging individuals who have given distinguished service in the field of family health, through the award of a biennial fellowship and prize, both worth US $20,000. The fellowship is awarded to support research in family health, whilst the Prize is awarded to an individual or group of individuals for accomplished service in the field of family health. The Prize is presented at a special ceremony during the World Health Assembly.

Geographical Area of Activity: International.

How to Apply: Any national health administration, the Executive Director of the United Nations Children's Fund (UNICEF) and the International Children's Centre may propose candidates for the Fellowship to the Foundation Selection Panel. Any national health administration, the Executive Director of the United Nations Children's Fund (UNICEF) and the Bureau of the International Children's Centre (Ankara), as well as any former recipient of the Prize, may nominate a person for the Prize. The Executive Board of WHO designates the recipients of the fellowship and Prize on the proposal of the Foundation Selection Panel.

Financial Information: Total fellowship award US $20,000.

Address: 20 ave Appia, 1211 Geneva 27, Switzerland.

Telephone: (22) 7912111; *Fax:* (22) 7913111; *Internet:* www.who.int/governance /awards/dogramaci/en/; *e-mail:* info@who.int.

Awards: Jacques Parisot Foundation Fellowship

Established in 1969 by Mrs J. Parisot in memory of Prof. J. Parisot, who was associated with the World Health Organization (WHO) from its earliest days, having signed the Constitution of the Organization for France at the International Health Conference held in New York in 1946.

Activities: Aims to encourage research in social medicine or public health by granting a fellowship of US $5,000, which is awarded every two years (even years). The recipients receive the award at a special ceremony during the World Health Assembly.

Geographical Area of Activity: International.

How to Apply: Candidates are proposed in turn by each Regional Committee of the WHO.

Address: 20 ave Appia, 1211 Geneva 27, Switzerland.

Telephone: (22) 7912111; *Fax:* (22) 7913111; *Internet:* www.who.int/governance /awards/parisot/en/; *e-mail:* info@who.int.

Awards: Léon Bernard Foundation Prize

Established in 1937 by international subscription in memory of Prof. Léon Bernard, one of the founders of the Health Organization of the League of Nations. The administration of the Léon Bernard Foundation was transferred to the World Health Organization in 1948.

Activities: The Prize is awarded approximately every two years, when funds permit, to an individual who has accomplished outstanding service in the field of social medicine. The Prize is awarded at a special ceremony during the World Health Assembly.

Geographical Area of Activity: International.

How to Apply: Any national health administration and any former recipient of the Prize may propose the name of a candidate who, in their opinion, qualifies for the award; the nomination must be accompanied by a written justification. The Director-General also submits a list of candidates proposed to him/her since the last award to the Foundation Committee. After consideration of the candidatures, the Foundation Committee makes a recommendation to the Executive Board, which designates the recipient of the prize.

Address: 20 ave Appia, 1211 Geneva 27, Switzerland.

Telephone: (22) 7912111; *Fax:* (22) 7913111; *Internet:* www.who.int/governance /awards/bernard/en/; *e-mail:* info@who.int.

Awards: Sasakawa Health Prize

Established in 1984 upon the initiative and with funds provided by Mr Ryoichi, Chairman of the Japan Shipbuilding Industry Foundation and President of the Sasakawa Memorial Health Foundation.

Activities: The annual Prize of US $100,000 is awarded to individuals, groups of individuals, institutions or NGOs which have accomplished outstanding innovative work in health development, in order to encourage the further development of such work. The Prize is awarded at a special ceremony during the World Health Assembly.

Geographical Area of Activity: International.

How to Apply: Any national health administration as well as any former recipient of the Prize may nominate a candidate for the award. Proposals are made to the Director-General of WHO, who submits them to the prize Selection Panel together with his/her technical comments. The Selection Panel meets to decide on the recommendation to be made to the Executive Board, which designates the recipients of the prize.

Financial Information: Annual award of US $100,000.

Contact: Exec. Chair. Dr Kwaku Afriyie.

Address: 20 ave Appia, 1211 Geneva 27, Switzerland.

Telephone: (22) 7912111; *Fax:* (22) 7913111; *Internet:* www.who.int/governance /awards/sasakawa/en/; *e-mail:* info@who.int.

Awards: United Arab Emirates Health Foundation Prize

Administered by the World Health Organization (WHO).

Activities: The Prize, amounting to approximately US $40,000, is awarded to one or more people, institutions or NGOs that have made an outstanding contribution to health development.

Geographical Area of Activity: International.

How to Apply: Any national health administration of a member state of the WHO, or any former recipient of the Prize, may nominate a candidate for the award. Proposals are made to the Director-General, who submits them to the Foundation Selection Panel together with his/her technical comments. The Selection Panel meets to decide on the recommendation to be made to the Executive Board, which designates the recipient (or recipients) of the Prize.

Financial Information: Initial endowment of US $1,000,000; annual award of approx. US $40,000.

Address: 20 ave Appia, 1211 Geneva 27, Switzerland.

Telephone: (22) 7912111; *Fax:* (22) 7913111; *Internet:* www.who.int/governance /awards/arab_emirates/en/; *e-mail:* info@who.int.

Civil Society Initiative (CSI)

The World Health Organization (WHO) established the Civil Society Initiative in June 2001, in recognition of the growing importance of civil society in health issues. Its main objectives are to facilitate more effective collaboration, information exchange and dialogue with non-governmental organizations (NGOs) and civil society organizations (CSOs); to strengthen WHO's support to member states in their work with NGOs/CSOs on global, regional and national health issues; and to broaden dialogue and joint action with all civil society groups that have a legitimate interest in the work and goals of the WHO.

Activities: The Civil Society Initiative's work includes the following aspects: development of a new WHO policy on NGO relations that aims to simplify, encourage and streamline relations with NGOs; creation and maintenance of a publicly accessible NGO database containing basic information on NGOs that have relations with WHO; creation of a knowledge bank on civil society actors and issues and policy analyses that will serve the WHO Secretariat, member states and the public; administration of the WHO system for official relations with NGOs and the anticipated NGO accreditation system; creation and maintenance of a WHO web site on civil society that will serve as a bridge between WHO,

NGOs/CSOs and the public; improved communications and policy dialogue between WHO and civil society; and strengthening WHO's capacity to support and facilitate member states' relations with civil society as it pertains to public health.

Geographical Area of Activity: International.

Address: 20 ave Appia, 1211 Geneva 27, Switzerland.

Telephone: (22) 7914410; *Fax:* (22) 7911380; *Internet:* www.who.int/civilsociety/en /; *e-mail:* civilsociety@who.int.

Department of Reproductive Health and Research: Making Pregnancy Safer

Aims to strengthen health delivery systems alongside efforts to strengthen the role of women, men, families and communities in improving maternal and newborn health.

Activities: The programme recognizes that essential obstetric care is a crucial component of skilled care, as part of the continuum from self-care, through skilled care in the community, to emergency care for those women who need it. The programme operates through supporting research to identify communities' perceptions of maternal and newborn health with a view to improving intercultural and interpersonal care as well as the responsiveness of services to the communities' needs; and funds programmes aiming to help women, men, families and communities to take care of themselves, each other and their babies, including programmes focusing on enabling women to make the most of breastfeeding, to dry newborns and keep them warm and to be aware of any danger signs, so that they will seek help for themselves and their babies when it is needed.

Geographical Area of Activity: International.

Address: 1211 Geneva 27, Switzerland.

Telephone: (22) 7913372; *Fax:* (22) 7914189; *Internet:* www.who.int /reproductive-health/mpr/index.htm; *e-mail:* reproductivehealth@who.int.

Global Alliance for Improved Nutrition (GAIN)

Launched in 2002, GAIN is an international alliance of public, private and civil society organizations committed to saving lives and improving health through the elimination of vitamin and mineral deficiencies.

Activities: By contributing to the reduction of micronutrient deficiencies, GAIN aims to decrease child and maternal morbidity and mortality, lessen health-care costs, improve productivity and promote the ability of populations to achieve their physical and intellectual potential. Through a regular cycle of calls for proposals, GAIN awards grants for food fortification activities, which are complementary to other interventions for micronutrient deficiency control, including the promotion or production of micronutrient-rich foods, provision of supplements for vulnerable groups, and complementary public health interventions. Grants of up to US $3,000,000 are available for up to three years to assist in capital investment, costs of ongoing operations, and expenditures for capacity building in the public, private, and civil society sectors.

Geographical Area of Activity: Developing countries.

How to Apply: Proposals that satisfy the requirements of the guide-lines are reviewed by an independent Proposal Review Panel. The Panel's recommendations are then submitted to the GAIN Board, which makes final decisions on grant awards. Proposals should be presented in English and be submitted to the Secretariat in both hard-copy and electronic formats (using the proposal form which is a WORD document).

Financial Information: Founding donors Bill and Melinda Gates Foundation, CIDA, US Agency for International Development, Netherlands and German governments and the Micronutrient Initiative (q.v.); grants available of up to US $3,000,000.

Contact: Exec. Dir Rolf Carriere.

Address: 52 rue Giuseppe-Motta, Case Postale 55, 1211 Geneva 20, Switzerland.

Telephone: (22) 7491850; *Fax:* (22) 7491851; *Internet:* www.gainhealth.org; *e-mail:* info@gainhealth.org.

Global Polio Eradication Initiative

Launched in 1988, co-ordinated by the World Health Organization (WHO), a public health initiative aiming to eradicate polio world-wide by 2005. A partnership between UN agencies, including the United Nations Children's Fund (UNICEF), Rotary International, the UN Foundation and the Bill and Melinda Gates Foundation, national governments, development banks, humanitarian organizations and corporate partners.

Activities: The partnership aims to have eradicated polio world-wide by 2005, through a US $1,000,000,000 vaccination campaign, which involves vaccinating children in war-affected countries of Asia and sub-Saharan Africa in collaboration with local community organizations and volunteer vaccinators.

Geographical Area of Activity: International, mainly Asia and sub-Saharan Africa.

Address: 20 ave Appia, 1211 Geneva 27, Switzerland.

Telephone: (22) 7912111; *Fax:* (22) 7913111; *Internet:* www-t.who.int/vaccines /polioeradication/; *e-mail:* info@who.int.

WORLD HEALTH ORGANIZATION (WHO)/ INTERNATIONAL BANK FOR RECONSTRUCTION AND DEVELOPMENT (IBRD—WORLD BANK)

Africa Technical Families—Onchocerciasis: African Programme for Onchocerciasis Control (APOC)

Established by the World Bank in 1997 as a 12-year programme. Administered by the World Health Organization (WHO), the Programme aims to provide community-directed treatment for river blindness (onchocerciasis).

Activities: The Programme supports community-directed programmes carried out in partnership with non-governmental development organizations (NGDOs) and Ministries of Health, enabling NGDOs to provide a range of services including technical assistance, human and financial resources at community level. Funds are distributed through the National Onchocerciasis Task Forces (NOTF) of the 19 African countries participating in the Programme, or their NGDO partners.

Geographical Area of Activity: Africa.

How to Apply: Applicants must be members of the APOC NGDO Co-ordination Group, with track records in delivering effective community health services. Proposals must be developed in partnership with the national Ministry of Health.

Publications: Resource materials; training videos.

Address: c/o WHO, Ouagadougou, Burkina Faso.

Internet: www.worldbank.org/gper; www.who.int/ocp/apoc.

OTHER PROGRAMMES

The Global Compact

A network organization comprising the Global Compact Office and five UN agencies: the Office of the High Commissioner on Human Rights (UNHCR), the United Nations Environment Programme (UNEP), the International Labour Organization (ILO), the United Nations Development Programme (UNDP) and the United Nations Industrial Development Organization (UNIDO), as well as involving governments, which defined the principles on which the initiative is based, companies, whose actions it seeks to influence, labour, in whose hands the concrete process of global production takes place, civil society organizations, representing the wider community of stakeholders, and the UN, as an authoritative convener and facilitator. Aims to support nine principles in the areas of human rights, labour and the environment.

Activities: The Compact offers participating organizations the opportunity to: produce practical solutions to contemporary problems related to globalization, sustainable development and corporate responsibility in a multi-stakeholder context; rally around universal principles and responsible corporate citizenship to make the global economy more sustainable and inclusive; leverage the UN's global reach and convening power with governments, business, civil society and other stakeholders; share good practices and learning; and access the UN's broad knowledge of development issues and its practical reach world-wide. Participants also collaborate through participation in global policy dialogues, local networks, and information sharing. The Compact also encourages companies to participate in partnership projects with UN agencies and civil society organizations that are aligned with UN development goals.

Geographical Area of Activity: International.

Address: Room S-1894, UN Plaza, New York, NY 10017, USA.

Internet: www.unglobalcompact.org; *e-mail:* globalcompact@un.org.

Joint United Nations Programme on HIV/AIDS (UNAIDS)

UNAIDS is the main advocate for global action on the HIV/AIDS epidemic. Aims to lead, strengthen and support an expanded response aimed at preventing transmission of HIV, providing care and support, reducing the vulnerability of individuals and communities to HIV/AIDS, and alleviating the impact of the epidemic. It brings together eight co-sponsors from within the UN system: United Nations Development Programmme (UNDP), United Nations Office on Drugs and Crime (UNODC), United Nations Educational, Scientific and Cultural Organization (UNESCO), United Nations Children's Fund (UNICEF), United Nations Population Fund (UNFPA), International Labour Organization (ILO), the World Health Organization (WHO), and the International Bank for Reconstruction and Development (IBRD—World Bank). Established in 1994 by a resolution of the United Nations Economic and Social Council and launched in January 1996, UNAIDS is guided by a Programme Co-ordinating Board with representatives of 22 governments from all geographic regions, the UNAIDS co-sponsors, and five representatives of NGOs, including associations of people living with HIV/AIDS.

Activities: Aims to help mount and support an expanded response to the HIV/AIDS epidemic that engages the efforts of many sectors and partners from government and civil society. Supports a more effective global response to AIDS. UNAIDS activities include: providing leadership and advocacy for effective action; disseminating strategic information to guide efforts against AIDS world-wide; tracking, monitoring and evaluation of the epidemic and of responses to it; promoting civil society engagement and partnership development; and mobilizing resources to support an effective response. Also organizes campaigns and conferences.

Geographical Area of Activity: International.

Publications: A joint response to HIV/AIDS: Joint United Nations Programme on HIV/AIDS; fact sheets.

Address: 20 ave Appia, 1211 Geneva 27, Switzerland.

Telephone: (22) 7913666; *Fax:* (22) 7914187; *Internet:* www.unaids.org; *e-mail:* unaids@unaids.org.

UN Trust Fund for Human Security

The Fund was established in 1999 by the Japanese government and the UN Secretariat to translate the concept of human security into concrete activities, by supporting projects implemented by UN agencies that address, from the viewpoint of human security, various threats to human lives, livelihoods and dignity currently facing the international community, including poverty, environmental degradation, conflicts, land-mines, refugee problems, illicit drugs and infectious diseases such as HIV/AIDS.

Activities: The Fund supports projects that advance human security in the following fields of activity: poverty, including community reconstruction, vocational training, increase of food production, and protection of children; refugees and internally displaced persons, including support for their return to their home country, and improvement of living standards; medical and health care, including reproductive health, infectious disease control such as HIV/AIDS, and improvement of public health; drug control, including the introduction of alternative crops; and trans-national crime, including control of trafficking of women and children.

Geographical Area of Activity: World-wide, with a focus on island countries, landlocked countries and less-developed countries.

How to Apply: Applications to the Fund are reviewed by both the government of Japan and the UN Secretariat, whose concurrent approval is required to provide support for projects.

Financial Information: Funded by the Japanese government; total contributions approx. 18,900,000,000 yen (1999–2001); annual distributions approx. US $10,000,000.

Contact: Co-Chair. Sadako Ogata, Amartya Sen.

Address: UN Headquarters, First Ave at 46th St, New York, NY 10017, USA.

Internet: www.mofa.go.jp/policy/human_secu/t_fund21/what.html.

United States Institute of Peace

Established in 1984, the Institute is an independent, non-partisan federal institution created by the US Congress to promote the prevention, management, and peaceful resolution of international conflicts.

Activities: Operates through awarding grants to US and foreign individuals and organizations, through inviting proposals for projects that will: carry out basic and applied research on causes of war and other international conflicts; develop curricula and texts for high schools through post-graduate study and conduct teacher training workshops and seminars on causes of war and conditions for peace; conduct training symposia and continuing education programmes for policy-makers and the public that will develop skills in international conflict management and war avoidance; undertake public information efforts, including the development of video and radio projects, speaker programmes, communication forums, debates and the creation of comprehensive print or audiovisual materials to enhance public awareness of peacemaking; and increase information on international peace and conflict resolution and enhance access to this information through the strengthening of library resources. Operates solicited and unsolicited grants programmes.

Geographical Area of Activity: World-wide.

Restrictions: No support for dissertation research; generally, grants are not given for institutional support or development.

Contact: Board of Directors: Chester A. Crocker (Chair.); Seymour Martin Lipset (Vice-Chair.); Pres. Richard H. Solomon; Exec. Vice-Pres. Harriet Hentges; Vice-Pres. Charles E. Nelson.

Address: 1200 17th St, NW, Washington, DC 20036, USA.

Telephone: (202) 457-1700; *Internet:* www.usip.org; *e-mail:* usip_requests@usip.org.

World Association for Animal Production (WAAP)

Established in 1965, after the success of the first World Conference on Animal Production in 1963, organized by the European Association for Animal Production (EAAP) under the patronage of the UN Food and Agriculture Organization (FAO). WAAP has held special consultative status with the FAO since 1974.

Activities: Supports and facilitates collaborative activities and exchange between its member societies; aims to encourage closer collaboration between the animal production organizations and to bring together scientists, educators, technicians and administrators with the objective of reviewing development concerns on the five continents. Also distributes annual awards to recognize and stimulate distinguished service to animal production internationally. Nominees should have made a meritorious scientific contribution by way of teaching, research or other service to animal agriculture over a period of five or more years.

Geographical Area of Activity: International.

How to Apply: Application forms for awards are available on the website.

Address: Villa del Ragno, Via Nomentana 134, 00162 Rome, Italy.

Fax: (06) 86329263; *Internet:* www.waap.it; *e-mail:* waap@waap.it.

World Trade Organization (WTO)

SECRETARIAT

Relations with NGOs

Part of the WTO's Integrated Framework, formulated in 2003, in order to contribute to the WTO's agenda of assisting officials from developing countries in their efforts to better understand WTO rules and procedures and how these rules and procedures can benefit developing countries.

Activities: The WTO Secretariat provides regular briefings for NGOs and is in the process of establishing a special NGO Section on the WTO website with specific information for civil society, including announcements of registration deadlines for ministerial meetings and symposia. In addition, a monthly list of NGO position papers received by the Secretariat is compiled and circulated for the information of members. Secretariat staff also meet with NGOs on a regular basis, both individually and as a part of NGO-organized events.

Geographical Area of Activity: International.

Address: Centre William Rappard, 154 rue de Lausanne, 1211 Geneva 21, Switzerland.

Telephone: (22) 7395111; *Fax:* (22) 7314206; *Internet:* www.wto.org; *e-mail:* enquiries@wto.org.

WorldFish Center

Conceived by the Rockefeller Foundation in 1973, became a small programme of the University of Hawaii in 1975. The WorldFish Center (previously known as ICLARM) was incorporated in Manila in March 1977, and it became a member of the Consultative Group on International Agricultural Research (CGIAR) in May 1992. Aims to conduct, stimulate and accelerate research on all aspects of fisheries and other living aquatic resources.

Activities: The WorldFish Center is an autonomous, non-governmental, non-profit-making, international scientific and technical centre established to conduct, stimulate and accelerate research on all aspects of fisheries and other living aquatic resources. Main areas of research are: improving productivity, protecting the environment, improving policies, saving biodiversity and strengthening national programmes. The Centre operates through research, conferences, publications, scholarships and awarding prizes (the Naga Award is given annually to a nominated scientific paper or book by an author from a developing country in any area of fisheries science). Maintains project offices in nine countries (Bangladesh, Cameroon, Caribbean/Eastern Pacific, Egypt, Malawi, New Caledonia, Philippines, the Solomon Islands and Vietnam) and is currently conducting research projects with collaborators in 50 countries and 39 regional and international organizations. Research is carried out and funded covering both marine and fresh waters in important tropical ecosystems, including coastal waters, coral reefs and inland waterbodies. Operates in partnership with intergovernmental organizations, the Asian Development Bank, NGOs and institutes.

Geographical Area of Activity: International.

Address: Jalan Batu Maung, Batu Maung, 11960 Bayan Lepas, Penang; POB 500, 10670 Penang, Malaysia.

Telephone: (4) 626-1606; *Fax:* (4) 626-5530; *Internet:* www.worldfishcenter.org; *e-mail:* worldfishcenter@cgiar.org.

INDEXES

Index of Projects

Abu Dhabi Fund, 230
Acacia Initiative—Communities and the
    Information Society in Africa
    Programme Initiative, 194
Accidental Marine Pollution, 100
ACP Cultural Foundation, 57
Action Plan for Russia, 44
Action Programme to Combat
    Discrimination: Support to European-
    level NGOs, 89
Action Programme Promoting European
    Environmental NGOs, 100
Actions Undertaken by NGOs in Favour of
    Developing Countries, 115
Adopt-A-Minefield, 313
Afghan Refugees in Pakistan Programme,
    146
Africa 2000 Plus Network (A2+N), 313
Africa Department, 348
Africa Technical Families—
    Onchocerciasis: African Programme for
    Onchocerciasis Control (APOC), 388
African Center for Gender and
    Development, 344
African Centre for Civil Society, 344
African Commission on Human and
    Peoples' Rights, 219
African Economic Research Consortium
    (AERC), 195
African Programme for Onchocerciasis
    Control (APOC), 388
AGFUND International Prize, 232
AGIS—Programme on Police and Judicial
    Co-operation in Criminal Matters, 111
Aid After Natural and Ecological
    Disasters, 45
Aid for Population and Healthcare in
    Developing Countries, 116
Aid to Uprooted People in Developing
    Countries, 116
ALBAN, 117
ALFA II, 117
Analysis and Studies on the Social
    Situation, Demography and Family, 90
Anti-Trafficking Project Fund, 241
Anti-Trafficking Unit: Anti-Trafficking
    Project Fund, 241
Antipersonnel Landmines, 118

APGEN—Promoting gender equality in
    the Asia Pacific–Phase 2, 323
Arab Authority for Agricultural
    Investment and Development (AAAID),
    230
Arab Bank for Economic Development in
    Africa (BADEA), 230
Arab Fund, 231
Arab Fund for Economic and Social
    Development (AFESD), 231
Arab Gulf Programme for United Nations
    Development Organizations (AGFUND),
    232
Arab League Educational, Cultural and
    Scientific Organization (ALECSO), 206
ASEAN Energy Facility Programme, 11
ASEAN Facility: Silk Road—Capacity
    Building for Regional Co-operation and
    Development, 323
ASEAN Foundation, 11
ASEAN Regional Center for Biodiversity
    Conservation (ARCBC): Research
    Grants, 15
Asia–Europe Foundation (ASEF), 12
Asia–Europe Foundation (ASEF) Youth
    Connections Grants, 13
Asia Information and Communications
    Technology (ICT), 118
Asia and Latin America (ALA): Asia Pro
    Eco Programme, 119
Asia and Latin America (ALA): Asia Urbs
    Programme, 120
Asia Link Programme, 123
Asia Pacific Development Information
    Programme (APDIP), 324
Asia Pacific Development Information
    Programme (APDIP): Information and
    Communication Technologies (ICT)
    Research and Development Grants
    Programme for Asia-Pacific, 325
Asia Pro Eco Programme, 119
Asia Urbs Programme, 120
Asian Development Bank
    (ADB)–Department for International
    Development Technical Assistance Co-
    operation Fund for India, 5
Assisting Communities Together (ACT),
    293

399

King Baudouin Award, 169
King Sejong Literacy Prize, 360
Kuwait Fund, 236
Kuwait Fund for Arab Economic
Development, 236

Leader+, 62
Least-Developed Countries, 302
Léon Bernard Foundation Prize, 385
Leonardo da Vinci, 82
Leonardo da Vinci–1 Mobility, 82
Leonardo da Vinci–2 Pilot Projects, 66
Leonardo da Vinci–3 Language
Competencies, 67
Leonardo da Vinci–4 Transnational
Networks, 67
LIFE–Environment, 102
LIFE III, 104
LIFE III: LIFE–Environment, 102
LIFE III: LIFE–Third Countries, 103
LIFE—Local Initiative Facility for Urban
Environment, 320
LIFE–Nature, 103
LIFE–Third Countries, 103
LIFE Unit—Unit D1: LIFE III, 104
LIFE Unit—Unit D1: LIFE–Nature, 103
Local Initiatives Awards, 192
Lorenzo Natali Prize for Journalism, 64

Making Pregnancy Safer, 387
Malcolm Adiseshiah International
Literacy Prize, 360
Man and the Biosphere (MAB) Young
Scientists Awards, 367
Management of Social Transformations
(MOST), 355
Managing the Environment Locally in
Sub-Saharan Africa (MELISSA), 172
Managing Water for African Cities
(MAWAC): Water for African Cities
Programme, 369
Manfred Wörner Fellowship, 214
Margaret McNamara Memorial Fund, 176
Media Plus–Pilot Projects, 83
Medici, 111
Mediterranean Technical Assistance
Programme Pilot NGO Small Grants
Facility (METAP SGF), 176
Medium-Sized Projects (GEF MSP), 280
MEDSTAT, 143
Melina Mercouri International Prize, 359
MicroSave Africa, 339
MicroSave West Africa, 339
MicroStart, 339
Middle East Peace Projects, 131
MOSAIC II—Managing an Open and
Strategic Approach in Culture, 47

MSc Scholarship Programme in Science
and Technology for IDB Least-
Developed Countries, 235
Multi-Country HIV/AIDS Programme
(MAP) for Africa, 166

NATO Science Programme, 215
Natural Sciences Sector, 356
Nessim Habif Prize/UNESCO, 361
NetAid, 321
New Transatlantic Agenda (NTA), 106
NGO Affiliation, 10
NGO Section, 268
NGO Section (Division for Social Policy
and Development—DESA), 274
NGO Support and Grant Programmes, 252
NGOs and Civil Society, 218
Noma Literacy Prize (for Meritorious
Work in Literacy), 361
Non-Discrimination Law Programme—
Combating Discrimination, 93
Nordic Cultural Fund, 208
Nordic Development Fund (NDF), 212
Nordic Grant Scheme for Network Co-
operation with the Baltic Countries and
North-West Russia, 208
Nordic Youth Committee (NUK), 210
NORDPLUS, 209
North American Fund for Environmental
Co-operation (NAFEC), 213
North–South Co-operation Against Drug
Abuse, 134

OAPEC Award for Scientific Research, 228
Observation and Analysis: Socrates II—
Observation and Innovation, 67
ODIHR Anti-Torture Programme, 242
Office for the Co-ordination of
Humanitarian Affairs (OCHA), 292
Office for Democratic Institutions and
Human Rights (ODIHR), 240
Office of the Scholarship Programme:
Scholarship Programme for Muslim
Communities in Non-Member
Countries, 235
OPEC Fund for International
Development, 237
Organization of Commonwealth
Associations (OCA), 38
Organization for Investment, Economic
and Technical Assistance of Iran, 237
Organizations Advancing the Idea of
Europe, 145
Outreach and Partner Relations Section:
Co-sponsorship with Partner Countries
on Security-related Issues, 215

Index of Projects: Main Activities

AID TO LESS-DEVELOPED COUNTRIES; DEVELOPMENT STUDIES

Abu Dhabi Fund, 230
Acacia Initiative—Communities and the Information Society in Africa Programme Initiative, 194
Actions Undertaken by NGOs in Favour of Developing Countries, 115
Africa 2000 Plus Network (A2+N), 313
Africa Department, 348
African Centre for Civil Society, 344
African Economic Research Consortium (AERC), 195
AGFUND International Prize, 232
Aid for Population and Healthcare in Developing Countries, 116
Aid to Uprooted People in Developing Countries, 116
Antipersonnel Landmines, 118
APGEN—Promoting gender equality in the Asia Pacific–Phase 2, 323
Arab Authority for Agricultural Investment and Development (AAAID), 230
Arab Bank for Economic Development in Africa (BADEA), 230
Arab Fund, 231
Arab Fund for Economic and Social Development (AFESD), 231
Arab Gulf Programme for United Nations Development Organizations (AGFUND), 232
ASEAN Facility: Silk Road—Capacity Building for Regional Co-operation and Development, 323

ASEAN Foundation, 11
Asia and Latin America (ALA): Asia Urbs Programme, 120
Asia Pacific Development Information Programme (APDIP), 324
Asia Urbs Programme, 120
Asian Development Bank (ADB)–Department for International Development Technical Assistance Co-operation Fund for India, 5

Bank–Netherlands Partnership Programme (BNPP), 166
Banks for the Poor, 232
Belgian Survival Fund Joint Programme, 282
Best Practices and Local Leadership Programme (BPLLP), 372
Bureau for Crisis Prevention and Recovery: UNDP Thematic Trust Fund—Crisis Prevention and Recovery, 314

Capacity 2015, 316
CARDS—Community Assistance for Reconstruction, Development and Stabilization, 120
Caribbean Council for Europe, 22
CGAP/IFAD Rural Pro-Poor Innovation Challenge, 167
Children and Armed Conflict Trust Fund, 297
Cities Alliance, 181
Civil Society Organizations and Participation Programme, 316

ARTS AND HUMANITIES

CONSERVATION AND THE ENVIRONMENT

ECONOMIC AFFAIRS

EDUCATION

INTERNATIONAL AFFAIRS

LAW AND HUMAN RIGHTS

SCIENCE AND TECHNOLOGY

433

Index of Projects: Geographical Area of Activity

ASIA AND THE PACIFIC

EASTERN EUROPE AND THE REPUBLICS OF CENTRAL ASIA

MIDDLE EAST AND NORTH AFRICA

SOUTH AMERICA, CENTRAL AMERICA AND THE CARIBBEAN

USA AND CANADA

UN Enable: United Nations Voluntary Fund on Disability, 271

UN Enable: United Nations Youth Fund, 271

UN International Drug Control Programme (UNDCP), 376

UN System Network on Rural Development and Food Security, 300

UNDP Thematic Trust Fund—Crisis Prevention and Recovery, 314

UNDP Thematic Trust Fund—Democratic Governance, 334

UNDP Thematic Trust Fund—Energy for Sustainable Development, 315

UNDP Trust Fund for Support to Prevention and Reduction of the Proliferation of Small Arms, 314

UNEP World Conservation Monitoring Centre (UNEP–WCMC), 368

UNESCO/Guillermo World Press Freedom Prize, 365

UNESCO–Madanjeet Singh Prize for the Promotion of Tolerance and Non-Violence, 362

UNESCO Prize for Human Rights Education, 362

UNESCO Prize for Peace Education, 363

Unit for Co-operation with Private Sector and NGOs, 277

United Arab Emirates Health Foundation Prize, 386

United Nations Conference on NGOs (CONGO), 301

United Nations Development Programme (UNDP), 312

United Nations Environment Programme Sasakawa Environment Prize, 368

United Nations Foundation, 369

United Nations Fund for International Partnerships (UNFIP), 370

United Nations High Commissioner for Refugees (UNHCR), 371

United Nations Non-Governmental Liaison Service (NGLS), 375

United Nations Research Institute for Social Development (UNRISD), 378

United Nations Sasakawa Award for Disaster Reduction, 291

United Nations Trust Fund for Ageing, 269

United Nations Trust Fund for Family Activities, 270

United Nations Vienna Civil Society Award, 377

United Nations Voluntary Fund on Disability, 271

United Nations Voluntary Fund for Victims of Torture, 295

United Nations Youth Fund, 271

Voluntary Trust Fund on Contemporary Forms of Slavery, 297

Water and Energy Department: Water Supply and Sanitation, 167

Water Supply and Sanitation, 167

World Habitat Awards, 19

World Heritage Centre: World Heritage Fund, 365

World Heritage Fund, 365

World Solidarity Fund for Poverty Eradication, 337

WESTERN EUROPE

Accidental Marine Pollution, 100

Action Plan for Russia, 44

Action Programme to Combat Discrimination: Support to European-level NGOs, 89

Action Programme Promoting European Environmental NGOs, 100

Actions Undertaken by NGOs in Favour of Developing Countries, 115

AGIS—Programme on Police and Judicial Co-operation in Criminal Matters, 111

Aid After Natural and Ecological Disasters, 45

Aid for Population and Healthcare in Developing Countries, 116

Aid to Uprooted People in Developing Countries, 116

ALBAN, 117

ALFA II, 117

Analysis and Studies on the Social Situation, Demography and Family, 90

Anti-Trafficking Project Fund, 241

Anti-Trafficking Unit: Anti-Trafficking Project Fund, 241

Antipersonnel Landmines, 118

ASEAN Energy Facility Programme, 11

Asia–Europe Foundation (ASEF), 12

Asia–Europe Foundation (ASEF) Youth Connections Grants, 13

Asia Information and Communications Technology (ICT), 118

Asia and Latin America (ALA): Asia Pro Eco Programme, 119

Asia and Latin America (ALA): Asia Urbs Programme, 120

Asia Link Programme, 123

Asia Pro Eco Programme, 119

Asia Urbs Programme, 120

Awards: Darling Foundation Prize, 381

Awards: Down Syndrome Research Prize in the Eastern Mediterranean Region, 382